SLANG

BOOKS BY PAUL DICKSON

Think Tanks
The Great American Ice Cream Book
The Future of the Workplace
The Electronic Battlefield
The Mature Person's Guide to Kites, Yo-Yos, Frisbees and Other Childlike Diversions
Out of This World
The Future File
Chow: A Cook's Tour of Military Food
The Official Rules
The Official Explanations
Toasts
Words
There Are Alligators in the Sewers & Other American Credos (with Joseph C. Goulden)
Jokes
Names
On Our Own: A Declaration of Independence for the Self-Employed
The Library in America
Family Words
The Dickson Baseball Dictionary
The New Official Rules
What Do You Call a Person From . . . ?
Slang
Timelines
Baseball's Greatest Quotations
Dickson's Word Treasury
Dickson's Joke Treasury
On This Spot: Pinpointing the Past in Washington, D.C. (with Douglas E. Evelyn)
Baseball: The President's Game (with William B. Mead)
Myth-Informed (with Joseph C. Goulden)
The Congress Dictionary (with Paul Clancy)
War Slang
The Worth Book of Softball
The Volvo Guide to Halls of Fame (with Robert Skole)
The Book of Thanksgiving
The Joy of Keeping Score
The Official Rules at Work
The Official Rules at Home
What's in a Name?
The Official Rules for Lawyers and Politicians
The Official Rules for Golfers
Labels for Locals

SLANG

THE AUTHORITATIVE TOPIC-BY-TOPIC DICTIONARY OF AMERICAN LINGOES FROM ALL WALKS OF LIFE

REVISED, UPDATED AND EXPANDED

PAUL DICKSON

POCKET BOOKS

New York   London   Toronto   Sydney   Tokyo   Singapore

POCKET BOOKS, a division of Simon & Schuster Inc.
1230 Avenue of the Americas, New York, NY 10020

Library of Congress Cataloging-in-Publication Data

Dickson, Paul.
    Slang : the authoritative topic-by-topic dictionary of American
lingoes from all walks of life / Paul Dickson.
        p.   cm.
    Includes index.
    ISBN 0-671-54920-0
    1. English language—United States—Slang—Dictionaries.
2. Americanisms—Dictionaries.   I. Title.
PE2846.D43   1998
427'.973—dc21   97-32543
                                                          CIP

First Pocket Books hardcover printing of this revised edition April 1998

10   9   8   7   6   5   4   3   2   1

Text design by Stanley S. Drate/Folio Graphics Co. Inc.

A people who are prosperous and happy, optimistic and progressive, produce much slang; it is a case of play; they amuse themselves with the language.

—W. Sumner, A. Keller, M. Davie
(sociologists), 1927

Life is our dictionary. Years are well spent in country labors; in town, —in the insight into trades and manufactures; in frank intercourse with many men and women; in science; in art; to the one end of mastering in all their facts a language by which to illustrate and embody our perceptions. I learn immediately from any speaker how much he has already lived, through the poverty or the splendor of his speech. Life lies behind us as the quarry from whence we get tiles and copestones for the masonry of to-day. This is the way to learn grammar. Colleges and books only copy the language which the field and the work-yard made.

—Ralph Waldo Emerson,
The American Scholar

The official language of the state of Illinois shall be known hereafter as the American language, and not as the English language.

—*Acts of Legislature,* State of Illinois,
Chapter 127, Section 178, 1923

CONTENTS

———— ✳ ————

PREFACE

———— ✳ ————

Sometime back I got into a taxicab and found that the elderly driver was a former carnival man. I told him I was fascinated with slang and hoped to put together a collection someday. Rising to the bait, he gave me a fast tutorial in carnival lingo, and I stepped out of the cab with the feeling that a stamp collector must have when he buys a sheet of stamps and finds they contain some spectacular rarity. Most of his were traditional circus and carnival terms, but one was new to me, and I liked it more than any of the others. The term was *hard flash* and is used to describe a carnival prize that is so appealing that a person will spend vast sums trying to win it. As the man put it, hard flash could be anything from an immense stuffed animal to a lamp in the form of a large bronze palomino horse with a clock implanted in its side.

At that moment I became convinced that I should stop talking about writing a book on slang and actually do it. Actually doing it and getting such a book published became my own version of hard flash. About that same time I became convinced there was a potentially popular and useful reference book begging to be created. It would be a topic-by-topic slang dictionary that would stand in contrast to the fine A-through-Z slang dictionaries then on the market. A first version of that work appeared in 1990, at which time I continued to collect examples, with this book—more than twice the size of the original—being the result.

The idea, though not new, has not been done in more than fifty years. The last—and as far as I can tell, only—American topical slang book was Maurice H. Weseen's long-out-of-print *Dictionary of American Slang,* which is a marvelous book but primarily of historic interest today because it was published in 1934. It went into many printings but was never updated and went out of print when the immense amount of new World War II slang made it obsolete. It is a good companion for reading James T. Farrell or John Dos Passos. Weseen's book has twenty topical slang categories (Aviation, Theatre, Food, etc.), which are followed by a general-slang section. The topical sections are still fun to browse because they give a good overall flavor for the topic at hand as it sounded during the Great Depression.

Despite and because of the fact that the idea had not been tried in such a long time, it was an attractive one. One major reason for a topical slang book is, I think, most of us tend to approach slang topically rather than as a huge alphabetical body of words from many realms. If we are trying to decipher teenage slang, we don't want to have to wade through scores of terms used by the police, computer specialists, and GIs.

So here goes, with a tip of the hat to the carnival guy in the cab, Maurice H. Weseen and his original *Dictionary of American Slang,* and all the people who have helped with both editions of this work. After a short introduction on the subject of slang, over two dozen separate chapters follow, each covering a separate area of slang by topic.

Throughout the book, a number of people will be acknowledged for their help, but three people were of such great assistance, I would be remiss in not thanking and acknowledging their contributions here and now. They are researcher the late Charles D. Poe, writer Joseph C. Goulden, and archivist Randy Roberts of the Tamony Collection at the University of Missouri, Columbia. For their suggestions for making this a much better book, I acknowledge Norman Stevens, Roberta Jacobson, Robert L. Chapman, and Tom Dalzell.

—PAUL DICKSON,
Garrett Park, Maryland

INTRODUCTION

---- ✳ ----

IT AIN'T NO BIG THING

Correct English is the slang of prigs who write histories and essays. And the strongest slang of all is the slang of poets.

—George Eliot, 1872

✳ 1. THE QUICK AND DIRTY

People seem fascinated by slang, and it is widely beloved, especially in the abstract by people who cringe when it is actually spoken. If you can accept it, you can't get all bent out of shape—and start yelling, "Double negative"—when someone says that something "ain't no big thing."

Slang is. Period. Whether it is in favor or out of favor does not matter. It is renegade language that thumbs its nose at the very people who study and write about it. It is unruly, unrefined, irreverent, and illogical. It can be brutally frank and direct or deceptively kind and euphemistic. Euphemism is the verbal trick that has been termed the deodorant of language, and slang has given us dozens of terms for drunkenness and insanity that are remarkably gentle.

What else is it? This is what amounts to the current conventional wisdom on the subject, or at least this slang watcher's beliefs about the beast.

• *That slang is as old as language itself, and that American slang started on the* Mayflower. Mario Pei, in *The Story of Language,* points out that the slang use of *crackpot,* a piece of pottery, for the head has counterparts in ancient languages including Latin and Sanskrit. He also points out that Shakespeare used the slang of his time and, by doing so, gave us such words as *hubbub, fretful, fireworks,* and *dwindle.*

• *That it binds and identifies and thrives in groups with a strong sense of novelty and group activity.* Farmers produce little slang, but boxers, science fiction fans, surfers, high school students, and actors produce a lot.

• *That slang is produced by living languages, and the moment it stops being produced, the language in question is dead.* It is also true that slang replenishes standard language. English words as diverse as *snide, hold up, nice* (as in "nice work"), *bogus, strenuous, clumsy,* and *spurious* were regarded as slang not that long ago. Contemporary slang terms such as *sleazy,*

1

hassle, and *gridlock* look like locks on acceptance—as does *lock on* for that matter. Much slang has become so common that when we use it, we forget that it is slang: "Pick up the *phone* and find out what time the *movie* starts."

• *That it is all but impossible to destroy slang, especially with the argument that it is improper, impolite, or politically incorrect.* For most of the twentieth century there has been a battle waged against the word *ain't.* The anti-ain't-ers never had a chance. When, for example, they criticized the late Dizzy Dean for using the A-word on his radio broadcasts, he all but liquidated their argument by pointing out, "Lots of people who don't say *ain't* ain't eatin'."

The phenomena of political correctness and multicultural diversity runs counter to slang. This is underscored by the case of a document still making the rounds that was created during the summer of 1989 by a group of young journalists who met at the University of Missouri as part of the Multicultural Management Program and titled "The Dictionary of Cautionary Words and Phrases." These were terms that were to one degree or another derogatory and that are to be avoided in print. The list includes a number of obvious slurs that anyone living in the last half of the twentieth century knows to be offensive. But how about any or all of these found in the first letters of the alphabet: *airhead, babe, ball and chain, barracuda* (when directed at forceful women), *beefcake, Bible-belt, blue-haired, burly, buxom, Chinatown, codger, coot, cracker, dear* (as in "He was a dear man" or "She is a dear), *dingbat, dirty old man, ditz, dizzy, Don Juan,* and *Dutch treat?* The reasons for the offensiveness of these terms are spelled out: *airhead* is "an objectionable description generally aimed at women," *buxom* is an "offensive reference to a woman's chest," and *Dutch treat* "implies that Dutch people are cheap."

There is much more, but the point is made that even though these terms have been branded as offensive and may be dying out in print, they are still very much with us in spoken American.

• *That America is particularly hospitable to slang, and it tends to be embraced rather than spurned.* American slang has been called one of the "success stories" of English, and one estimate, made in the *Reader's Digest Success with Words,* claims that some thirty-five thousand expressions are, or once were, American slang. There are those, including the author of this book, who suspect that that immense estimate of thirty-five thousand may be on the low side. In terms of the overall language, the number skyrockets when one considers the British, Irish, Scotch, Australian, and Canadian contributions to the pool.

• *That it is not that hard to create slang, but it is hard to sustain a "new slang" without a group that continues to speak it.* This is exactly what happened to the short-lived citizens band radio slang (1975–77) and the Valley Girl slang (1982–83). Each of these received tremendous media attention, but a few months after each had peaked, they seemed to live on mostly in yellowing paperback quickies such as *The Official CB Slanguage Language Dictionary* and *How to Be a Valley Girl.* If there is a high mortality rate with new slang, it is also true that terms making it through infancy tend to be absorbed as part of the standard language.

- *That it often has as much to do with who says something as what they are saying.* A simple word like *hot* has many conventional and slang meanings, depending on whether you are talking to a musician, police officer, electrician, florist, radiologist, cook, or basketball player. If a television talk-show guest talks about the *greenroom,* he's referring to the room in which guests wait to go on camera, regardless of its actual color. On the other hand, to a surfer on a California beach, the *greenroom* is the sought-for realm inside the curl of a wave. By extension, at some West Coast colleges, to be doing exceptionally well is to be in the *greenroom.*

- *Slang is often as much defined by context and position (in the sense that* cowgirl *and* girl cow, OK *and* KO, *and* breaking ball *and* ball breaker, *all differ) as by the expression itself.* The word *say* is not slang unless it is used at the beginning of a sentence, in the sense of "tell me." This is as much true of the contemporary teenager who says "Say, how much did that cost?" as it is in the line "Oh, say, can you see, by the dawn's early light."

- *Ultimately much slang is being invented as we speak.* In a stunning February 7, 1993, article in the *Los Angeles Times* entitled "Beyond the Melting Pot—Gray Boys, Funky Aztecs, Honorary Homegirls," Lynell George tells us about a crucible of new slang: "L.A. has metamorphosed into a crazy incubator, and the children who live on these streets and submit to their rhythm rise up as exquisite hothouse flowers. They beget their own language, style, codes—a shorthand mode of communication and identification. It's more than learning a handy salutation in Tagalog, being conversant in street slang, or sporting hip-hop–inspired styles. This sort of cultural exchange requires active participation and demands that one press past the superficial toward a more meaningful discourse and understanding."

Despite all of this, people still have a tough time defining slang.

✳ 2. DEFINITIONS

Consider these questions:

- "Hey! No bullshit, but what the hell is slang anyhow?"
- "Could you please define *slang?*"
- "Can a suitable set of parameters be developed through which slang can be, first, identified and defined, and second, distinguished from conventional English, jargon, dialect, lingo, and argot?"

These three questions are, of course, the same question posed three separate ways. But their impact is quite different because of how they are stated. The first version of the question is stated in simple street slang. It is both direct and rude. The second version is phrased in standard, or conventional, English. It is at once forthright and polite. The third question approximates what has been called *bureaucratese* but which is spoken beyond the bureaucracy. It is bloated, indirect, and sleep-inducing. For lack of a better term, it is the jargon of a sizable slice of white-collar America.

The three questions only answer themselves to a point. Slang, conventional English, and jargon sound different, and if we speak English, we pretty much know which is which. But exactly how does slang distinguish itself from argot, cant, and jargon?

The answer is not easy. In his monumental *American Language (Supplement Two),* H. L. Mencken grappled with it and, without even mentioning jargon, wrote, "The boundaries separating true slang from cant and argot are not easily defined," adding later, "There is a constant movement of words and phrases from one category to another." Mencken's conclusion was that cant and argot belonged to the speech of small and cohesive groups, with cant having the extra characteristic of deceiving and mystifying outsiders. At another point (*The American Language,* 4th edition) he says, "The essence of slang is that it is of general dispersion, but still stands outside the accepted canon of the language."

Mencken believed that slang was driven by exuberance and word-making energy. He compared slang's relationship to language to that between dancing and music.

What about jargon? The rough distinction that seems to work is that jargon is technical, professional talk that, as often as not, like cant, acts as a barrier to keep outsiders from understanding what is going on. But not always. For instance, medical doctors have a polysyllabic, Latinate jargon as well as a blunt and sometimes cruel slang. It is one thing to say that one has a bilateral orbital hematoma (jargon), but quite another to say that you have a shiner, black eye, or mouse.

But, by the same token, some slang and some jargon are one and the same; for example, the slang and jargon of truck drivers overlap considerably. Perhaps the simplest definition of jargon was the one made by Mario Pei many years ago in the *Story of Language,* in which he termed it "the special terminology in use in any given walk of life."

Finally there is dialect, which appears to be a different manner of speaking the same language with a different but consistent grammar and set of distinct expressions. By this definition the black English that was so widely discussed and debated in the 1970s would qualify as a dialect. By the same token, many of the words used in predominantly black rap music are slang. Rap slang is much more likely to be understood by a nonblack teenager than by a middle-aged black person. One can, in fact, make the case that rap slang and general teenage slang have so much in common, there are only a handful of words and phrases they do not share.

So if we can give slang a place, it occupies a perch between conventional English and the private, in-group cants, jargons, and dialects.

✳ 3. I HEARD IT ON TV—BROADCASTING SLANG

One final point that should be covered here has to do with the state of slang today. How is it faring in these the last days of the twentieth century?

The simple answer is that it appears as dynamic a force in language as it has ever been during a period of peace and stability. Conflict is a catalyst for the creation of new slang, and English is still digesting terms created during World War II. For their part the motion pictures, radio, and advertising have insured a constant supply of new slang.

But another factor is now in place that over time will rival anything else in history as a dispenser of language. Television has become this great dispenser, soaking up words and phrases from one part of the population and repeating them for all of us to hear. Kids who have never been on a sled know what a *luge* is, and people who have never sat in a Catskills hotel and listened to a Brooklyn-born comic speak of *shtick* and *schlock.* For a moment we all knew enough CB talk (ten-four, good buddy) and Valley Girl talk (gag me with a spoon) to fake those slangs. This was not because we all drove eighteen-wheelers or hung out in the shopping malls and video parlors of the San Fernando Valley, but because we *heard* it on television.

This fact has not been missed by the professional linguists and students of television. Frederick Mish, editorial director at Merriam-Webster Inc. in Springfield, Massachusetts, points out that the electronic media has become a major influence on American English, especially when it comes to new words. "It overarches all the other influences and promulgates them. Whether you're talking about a new word or phrase from technology or cookery, it is likely to come to us through television," says Mish. Tom Shales, the *Washington Post* TV critic, has termed television "America's dictionary as well as its mirror."

Perhaps the most dramatic case of electronically transmitted slang occurred in the spring of 1989 after a group of Harlem teenagers entered Central Park and brutally beat and raped a jogger. Within hours of the arrest of the teenagers, the New York police announced that their interrogation had yielded a name for vile rampage and other acts of senseless violence: *wilding.*

Although the police pointed out that they had never heard the term before that night, the word *wilding* had spread into every nook and cranny of the English-speaking world within hours. Television, with assists from radio and the wire services, had put the term and its grotesque connotations into the minds of tens of millions.

Hearing is the key to all of this. So much is said and written about the visual impact of television, we sometimes forget that it is equally auditory. This was particularly true of both Watergate and Iran-contra—what was spoken and "misspoken"—and America's manned ventures into outer space. The launches, the splashdowns, and costly animation were memorable, but so were the voices of the astronauts, the reporters, and even the official NASA spokesmen. For a while we were all saying A-okay and counting backwards ten, nine, eight, seven . . . Television is a linguistic paradise. You can flip to *Oprah* and hear the latest in sensitive psychological talk, dial up the news and hear the latest in boardroom or diplomatic jargon, screen the new sitcoms for the next catchphrase; and catch a few innings of the ball game to listen for the latest nickname for spitballs (referred to of late as wet ones). Most Americans know what they know of police slang from cop shows ranging from

Dragnet to *Hill Street Blues* to the blue talk heard on *NYPD Blue.* TV westerns of the 1950s invented a slang for the Old West with new terms such as *gun-slinger* and *bounty hunter.*

If this sounds a bit too passive, go to the other extreme and think of the quirky little ways TV talk affects us. Kids who dream of being asked to spell *relief* by their teacher so they can reply, "R-O-L-A-I-D-S," or how they will someday try to tell their kids how they sat back and waited for Hans and Franz, the Teutonic body builders of *Saturday Night Live,* to say "Ve're going to pump *you* up." If half the teenagers in America are at this moment imitating Hans and Franz, the other half are imitating the Church Lady saying "Isn't that special." Their kids probably won't understand what was so special about it, just as my kids draw a blank when I try to tell them how I loved the Burns and Allen signature—"Say good night, Gracie." "Good night, Gracie."

Television, in fact, creates its own indigenous slang in the form of rallying cries and catchphrases. A case in point is "Where's the beef?" which is gone now but marked the winter of 1984 linguistically as it was repeated over and over by the late Clara Peller in a series of ads for the Wendy's hamburger chain and then became a rejoinder in the presidential debates on television.

This kind of thing is nothing new, but the Wendy's commercials are an especially dramatic example of how we mark time with catchwords and phrases in the television age. It goes on all the time, and the odds favor a major, new national pet phrase every few years and numbers of minor ones. It will be fresh one moment and a cliché emblazoned across a million T-shirts the next.

Such was the case with the late Gilda Radner's chirpy "Never mind" from *Saturday Night Live* and Steve Martin's "Well, excuuuuuse me." Then John Belushi took the word *no,* extruded it into something that took three seconds to say, and it became his signature.

The most obvious impact has come with signature lines uttered by characters, comedians, and advertisers. If there were a Hall of Fame for such phrases, it would be hard to know where to begin. Just for starters, you'd have to consider: "Would you believe . . . ?" from Don Adams as Maxwell Smart; McGarrett's "Book 'em" from *Hawaii Five-O;* Flo's endearing "Well, kiss my grits" from *Alice;* Jack Paar's "I kid you not"; Mork's "Na nu, na nu"; and the Fonz's "Aaaaaaaay!" There were a bunch from *Laugh-In,* including Arte Johnson's "Verrrrrrry interesting!" and the ubiquitous "Sock it to me!" Then there is "Heeerrrre's Johnny," Tom Smothers's "Mom always loved you best," and Charlie Brown's "Good grief," which appeared first in the comic strips but needed television to make it a household term.

Shows that long ago left network prime time are still having an effect on language through their second life on cable television. *Five-0* was contemporary teenage slang for the police in 1996 and a clear borrowing from the old *Hawaii Five-O* television show.

It can be argued that *yucky* was in use before *Sesame Street,* but that show did for that article of slang what *The A-Team* did for *sucker.* And speaking of *Sesame Street,* it can be argued that this was the instrument by which the term *you guys,* as slang for males and females as opposed to males alone (as in *Guys and Dolls*), became popular. The show *Star Trek* created its own vocabulary and left a noun in its wake, *Trekkies,* for those who follow the show.

This ability to change the way we speak by electronically transmitted buzzwords and catchphrases is not new. Radio had its impact: *the $64 question* is a permanent part of the language, and people over forty shudder nostalgically with a line like "Gotta straighten out that closet one of these days, Molly." But it is television that has really moved the process into high gear and given it "may-jor mo-tion."

If we like them because of the way they are said, we remember them because they are our mental souvenirs, and we hang on to them for the same reason the Smithsonian hangs on to Archie Bunker's chair, the Fonz's jacket, and J.R.'s cowboy hat. Our souvenirs can, in fact, be the least funny element in a show. For all the great, funny lines from *M*A*S*H,* what we will all recall, even after the reruns have stopped, is the chilling phrase "Incoming wounded." And scores of funny lines from *All in the Family* have been forgotten by people, like me, who can only remember that Archie called his son-in-law "meathead" and his wife "dingbat."

The big question is, Where's the magic? Why do so many of these phrases work? It clearly defies full analysis, but it would appear that timing is terribly important. It is doubtful we all would have been running around saying "Where's the beef?" during the Iranian hostage crisis or during the last days of the Vietnam War. It wouldn't have been an appropriate catchphrase at the time or a verbal souvenir to recall a time of crisis.

If you listen carefully, you'll be among the first to catch someone who will have the touch and give us not one hot, new line or phrase, but a whole bunch of them. Looking back, it can be argued that the last great television phrase-maker was Jackie Gleason, a man with as many signatures as a second mortgage. "To the moon, Alice," "How sweet it is," "One of these days," "And away we go," were all his. He even had words for the times, in the person of *The Honeymooners*' Ralph Kramden, when he got too nervous to talk: "Hommina, hommina."

* 4. A WEB OF WORDOS

If television is never at a loss for words, the Internet is awash in them. Potentially, it could be the greatest of all dispensers of slang and new English since the invention of movable type. The reason for this is simple: almost any person, group, or subculture can reveal itself in a public place for the rest of the world to see. Not only can we see their jargon and slang in their sites as they conduct their business, but hundreds—maybe thousands by the time you read this—of glossaries, dictionaries, and lexicons are on-line with more coming on each day. What's more, these dictionaries are commonly updated daily or weekly.

Many of the subgroups posting glossaries are removed from the mainstream and are for the first time widely accessible. Prisoner slang? There is a growing on-line glossary controlled by prison inmates around the country. Cyberpunk glossaries? There are at least five. Name it and there is probably an Internet slang glossary in place or abuilding—X-rated Esperanto, hard-boiled private-eye lingo of the 1930s, American Civil War slang, slang indigenous to Seattle or Boston.

The Internet has been a major ally in the creation of this book. The Net was all but unknown when the first edition of this book was published, which underscores the point that slang is always springing forth. A separate section of the book covers Internet slang as distinguished from computer slang.

1

ADVERTISING AND PUBLIC RELATIONS

Let's Try a Few and See If They Repeat 'Em

> Advertising, for its part, has so prostrated itself on the altar of word worship that it has succeeded in creating a whole language of its own. And while Americans are bilingual in this respect, none can confuse the language of advertising with their own.
>
> —William H. Whyte Jr. and the editors of
> *Fortune,* in *Is Anybody Listening?*
> (Simon & Schuster, 1952)

> Ads for computers, cars, vacations, phone service, and liquor are popping up faster than you can say World Wide Web. All the big Web sites have them—Netscape, Yahoo, Pathfinder, HotWired, CNet, ZDNet, ESPN Sports-Zone, Playboy—and so do many of the smaller ones.
>
> —Michelle V. Rafter on Internet advertising,
> the *Los Angeles Times,* December 17, 1995

In the late 1950s the nation went gaga over the slangy metaphoric hyperbole of Mad Ave. The phrases were dubbed "gray flannelisms" (from the novel *The Man in the Gray Flannel Suit*) by syndicated columnist Walter Winchell, while fellow columnist Dorothy Kilgallen called them "ad agencyisms." They were all convoluted, and most were based on whether or not something—an ad, a campaign, a slogan, etc.—would work. The most famous flannelism was "Let's send it up the flagpole and see if they salute it," but columnists and TV personalities repeated hundreds more with relish. A few of many:

- Let's pull up the periscope and see where we're at.
- I see feathers on it but it's still not flying.
- Let's toss it around and see if it makes salad.
- Let's guinea-pig that one.
- Let's roll some rocks and see what crawls out.
- Well, the oars are in the water and we're headed upstream.
- Let's drop this down the well and see what kind of splash it makes.

Were these real or were they created to get a line in a newspaper column? It would seem that they were more real than hype. No less an observer than

John Crosby of the old *New York Herald Tribune* deemed them "the curiously inventive (and, in some cases, remarkably expressive) language of the advertising industry." This is not to say a few were not created for outside consumption. In late 1957, when the Soviet Union put a dog in earth orbit, the metaphoric handstand that attracted attention was "Let's shoot a satellite into the client's orbit and see if he barks."

That fad has passed (at least the public side of it has) and things are a little less colorful in advertising and public relations, but plenty remains, and something new is on the horizon, the vast potential for advertising on the Internet, for which there is already a nascent slang with such terms as *banner, button, click-through, hit, impression pixels,* and *traffic tracking* being applied to cyberadvertising.

* A

account side. That half of an ad agency that attracts and keeps clients. The other half is the CREATIVE SIDE.

ad. Print advertisement as opposed to a commercial, which appears on radio or television.

advertorial. An advertisement that sells an editorial point of view as opposed to a product or service.

advid. Advertising video.

agency copy. Material printed or broadcast just as it was when it came from an advertising or public relations firm.

art. Anything graphic—photography, typography, illustration—in advertising. It is used to distinguish everything else in an ad or commercial from COPY.

* B

banner. (Internet) The most common type of on-line ad. Banners are usu-ally rectangular or oblong and run at the top or bottom of a page. They carry short messages and act as a live link to promotional material from an advertiser or a World Wide Web site. The first big user of banners was the Coors Brewing Co., which used the Internet to help launch Zima, the clear malt beverage targeted at Generation X drinkers. Coors put Zima banners on HotWired and NSCA in late 1994 and soon had spots everywhere.

beauty shot. A well-staged and -lit view of a product in a commercial.

bleed. An ad, photo, or illustration that extends to the very edge of a page.

boobads. Ads for bras and other female undergarments.

book. A magazine or other periodical. The *front of the book* is the portion of the magazine before the main editorial section, and the *back of the book* follows it.

boutique. Small ad agency, often noted for its creativity.

brandstanding. Sponsoring a race car,

a rock tour, or some other "special event" to promote one's product.

button. (Internet) An on-line ad, smaller than a BANNER.

 C

click-through. (Internet) Also called click rate. The percent of people viewing a Web page who click on an advertiser's banner. Consumers who "click through" an ad banner to the information beyond are coveted because they're the best candidates to buy a company's goods or services, akin to people who respond to direct-mail ads.

clutter. The collective name for the many advertising spots on television.

commish. A commission paid to an agency.

comp. Short for (1) comprehensive, and (2) complimentary.

co-op. A cooperative advertisement, jointly paid for by the manufacturer and the retailer.

copy. Written or typewritten text in an ad or commercial.

CPM. Cost per thousands of readers. Print publications' ad rates are based on CPM, and many on-line publications are following in their footsteps. The *M* in *CPM* is the Roman numeral for thousand.

creative side. That part of an advertising agency that actually creates ads. The other side is the ACCOUNT SIDE.

customer golf. Term for recognizing

that an agency has to go along with and not "beat" the client. It is based on the notion that you don't go out with your best customer and whomp him at golf.

 D

DINFO. Defense Information; public relations office and function of the Pentagon.

dog and pony show. Press conference: any carefully prepared performance.

double truck. A two-page ad.

E

equity. A theme that has worked over time and increases in value.

F

face. A particular alphabet or typeface.

flack/flak. (1) a public relations person. (2) To push a product, service, or story.

frame grabber. Celebrity who is the center of attention at all events.

G

greek. Garbled letters used to indicate text in a dummy ad.

H

hand-holding. Reassuring an advertising or PR client.

SAY WHAT?

The most common nickname for a PR person has an interesting series of possible origins. Does it come from *flak,* meaning antiaircraft fire? Derived and clipped from the German *Fliegerabwehrkanone*—a gun to drive off aircraft. Sometimes given as an abbreviation of *Flugzeugabwehrkanone.* The authors of *Words of the Fighting Forces* (1942) comment: "A burst of fire from an antiaircraft gun or guns." Or, is *flak* from the theater and show business? That the entertainment-industry weekly *Variety,* birthplace of numerous Americanisms, tried to coin the word *flack* as a synonym for *publicity agent.* The word is said to be derived from Gene Flack, a movie publicity agent; one who sends up interference or messages in the hope that some of what he is offering will be heeded. Or is *flak* from another source? Something *Variety* may have overlooked, however, is that a Yiddish word similar in sound means "one who goes around talking about the other fellow's business."

hits. (Internet) The cumulative number of contacts made to a Web page, including graphics files and live links. Counting hits was the first accepted method of measuring a Web site's popularity. It's now considered inaccurate, but some Web publishers still use it.

hotdogger. Publicity seeker.

hymns. Hidden messages.

hype. Deception through inflated promises in advertising and or promotion.

 I

impressions. (Internet) People who have looked at a given page on the Net. Web publishers use impressions as a basis for setting ad rates, and advertisers use them to choose the best Web pages on which to place their ads.

ink. Press coverage; a goal of public relations.

 J

Jaboney. An accessible expert who makes frequent media appearances.

jingle. Short musical refrain used on radio or television commercials.

 K

kickapoo. The customer's product.

kotex. A free newspaper "shopper," which is seldom read but scanned for ads. It is a derogatory allusion to the brand name of a popular sanitary napkin.

L

live tag. Voice at the end of a commercial that gives current or local information, such as the words "Opens Wednesday at the Cineplex 6" at the end of a movie commercial.

loose cannon. Client who talks too much and without restraint and, for this reason, must be kept from the press.

 M

magalog. Blend of *magazine* and *catalog* for a catalog that acts like a magazine in that it carries ads—among its own ads—for other companies and products.

media. Ad space or time one buys. Not to be confused with the media that is the press.

mention. A short item in the press. Publicists like to be able to say, "Did you see this morning's mention in the *Wall Street Journal?*"

 N

nose hair. Client, especially a demanding one, to some folks in advertising.

O

on-line malls. (Internet) Collective name for the Internet as an advertising and marketing medium.

overexposure. What happens to a ce-

lebrity who endorses too many products and thereby becomes ineffective.

 P

PA. Short for *public affairs*. This is what some companies and almost all government agencies call their public relations operations—usually PAOs for Public Affairs Offices—to avoid the PR label, which is seen as manipulative.

peg. That which is newsworthy or notable in a press release or campaign. Also a SLANT or a handle.

pick-up. The use of a press release, photo, etc., by the media; public relations placement.

pixels. (Internet) Short for picture element, the basic element of measurement on a computer screen. On-line ads are measured by the pixel, so, for example, a banner could be 260 pixels long and 80 pixels deep.

place. To use public relations techniques to get a favorable mention or story in the media.

placement. The process by which name-brand products appear in movies for a fee.

plug. A favorable positioning for a product or service in public relations.

pluggery. A PR firm.

PR. Public relations, both as a noun and a verb. To "PR the public" is to put a message across.

praisery. A PR firm.

product PR. Publicity gained for an

item rather than a person or a company. Product publicists work to get their products shown on television or in the movies.

puffery. Exaggerated claim or promise given to a product or service. Calling something the best that money can buy is often regarded as pure puffery.

puff piece. A flattering article in the press about a client or product.

pull. (1) The ability to create sales, which is said of the most effective ads. (2) To remove an ad or kill an advertising campaign.

put on the map. Successfully promote and advertise a relatively unknown product or service.

 R

release. (1) A press release. (2) A written okay to use a person's face, voice, or name commercially.

remnant space. Odd page spots sold at a discount.

 S

sandwich man. A human billboard; a person wearing a huge sign fore and aft, making a human sandwich. Though less common today than they once were, they are used as an image of disparagement: "We'd be better off with a sandwich man."

score. A public relations coup.

shop. An ad agency.

shot. A publicist's attempt at placement.

sizzle. Image. From the advertising maxim that holds that you should sell the sizzle, not the steak.

slant. The attitude or opinion that a publicist is trying to sell. For instance, a PR slant on nuclear power might be that it is essential to America's future.

space. Pages or airtime that has been purchased for a client. Space can also be obtained through public relations.

spin/spin control. In public relations, the ability to present a client in a certain light and with a certain SLANT. It implies control and probably derived from the word *topspin.*

spin doctor/spin master. PR person with the proven ability to put a certain slant or story across.

stink bomb. A high-profile failure in the world of public relations.

stunt. An event staged as news for the purpose of public relations.

suck wind. In PR terminology, an unsuccessful attempt to get publicity for your client or boss.

sweeps. Periods during which television shows are rated and ranked by audience size. The outcome determines the advertising rates for the show in question.

 T

teaser. Ad or announcement that arouses interest without naming the product, as in, "Coming soon, the movie of the year."

thirty. A thirty-second commercial.

throwaway. Handbill or other printed ad that the advertiser assumes will be looked at for a few seconds before being thrown away.

trade out. Goods or services given for ad space or broadcast time; for instance, meals given in exchange for a restaurant ad in a directory.

traffic tracking. (Internet) Statistical analysis of activity on a Web site or page. Companies such as WebTrack and NetCount sell traffic-tracking services, which Web publishers use as the basis for determining advertising rates.

tub-thump. To make an obvious appeal or pitch for a client or product.

up-cut. To edit a television show, usually a rerun, to fit in one or more extra commercials.

USP. Unique selling proposition; that which separates a product or service from its competitors.

video cart. Recently introduced type of grocery-shopping cart with a video screen that plays commercials for the customer while shopping.

virgin. Focus-group first-timer in market research along with *recycled virgins, semi-virgins,* and *retreads.*

VO or voice-over. Narration in a commercial by person not seen.

white-coat rule. Nickname for the Federal Trade Commission prohibition against commercials that claim or imply that the person on the screen is a doctor.

ZOO. Acronym for *zero on originality.* To work for a zoo agency is to work for one lacking innovation.

SOURCES

A good source of "flannelisms" is two articles by John Crosby on Madison Avenuese that appear in B.A. Botkin's *Sidewalks of America* (Bobbs-Merrill, 1954). Material in the Tamony Collection at the University of Missouri was of great help in preparing this glossary. The article by Michelle V. Rafter in the *Los Angeles Times* for December 17, 1995, entitled "World Wide Sell: The Web Is Becoming the Place to Advertise," was most helpful, as was the glossary that appeared with that article, which originally appeared in the *Washington Times.* Janet Kinosian's "Publicist Patois" in the *Los Angeles Times* for April 24, 1994, was useful for Hollywood PR talk.

✳ 2 ✳

AUCTIONESE

What's Your Pleasure?

In New York dealers call the items "cultural antiques," in northern California the favorite word is "collectibles," in Dallas "new antiques." In Memphis and Madison, Wisconsin, they simply call the stuff junk—but they spell it, with verbal pinkie extended, J-U-N-Q-U-E.

—Wayne King, *New York Times,*
August 22, 1970

How does one get a handle on the world of antiques, collectibles, and flea markets? Simple. At the auctions, where the slang of the auctioneer is the most interesting and colorful slang of the trade.

Auctioneers are under a lot of pressure to be clever. Not only do they have to keep their audience entertained, but they have to keep potential bidders interested in what they are selling. This is especially true of country auctioneers, who may have to move an occasional box lot of rusted chains or a 1974 Dodge Dart without an engine. After all, you don't have to be that clever if you are able to offer a Monet, a Bentley, or John F. Kennedy's golf clubs.

To get a handle on the rich slang and pat phrasing of country auctioneers, as well as better understand how auctions work, I began collecting terms from auctioneers at auctions in Maine, New Hampshire, Massachusetts, Tennessee, and Connecticut over a number of summers (1982 through 1996).

I was helped by other auction buffs who tape-recorded or took notes on auctions that I was not able to attend. To be sure, these are regional, but they are authentic country and give a sense of the flavor of the larger whole. Since beginning in New England, I have begun to spread out and have in recent months been to, among others, a country auction in Hendersonville, Tennessee, and a farm auction in downstate Illinois.

Here is a primer.

 A

absentee bid. A bid that is made by a person not attending the auction and executed by someone working for the auctioneer. Some auctioneers do not accept them, while others encourage them. "Absentee bids are welcome and easily done" are the

16

first words in an ad from auctioneer James D. Julia of Fairfield, Maine, in the August 1993 *Antiques and Collectibles.* It continues, "Simply fill out a form from our catalog, following all instructions, and use your fax, Visa, or Mastercard to secure your bid. A 20% deposit (20% of your top offer) is required to process your absentee bid. This will confirm your bidding intentions and will not be charged to you unless you are delinquent in paying for a successful bid."

absentee bidder's table. At some sales, a place at the front where an employee of the auctioneer keeps track of the bids that have been left. "That's $175 at the absentee bidder's table."

accidental bid. A bid that is made when one swats at a fly, waves to a friend, or scratches one's nose. Largely mythological, the notion of executing such a bid puts fear in the minds of novice auction-goers. However, it is another story if one accidentally raises one's bidding paddle and holds it high.

Some auctioneers go out of their way to allay bidders' fear of an accidental buy. "Don't worry, I know a bid," says one Yankee auctioneer. "Feel free to wave to your friends."

additions. Items included in auction that are consigned by owners other than the person or company whose estate is being sold.

age. Some signs of wear and tear on an older piece, as in, "This piece has some age on it."

aggravation. Flaw. "This bottle is

perfect except for a little aggravation in the neck."

agitation. Same as AGGRAVATION. The extent to which this term and *aggravation* can be applied was shown at a 1988 Rangeley, Maine, auction where the glass covering a framed print was held together by several yards of masking tape. The auctioneer noted playfully that the glass had "some agitation." Later in the same auction, a really decrepit child's chair was described as "agitated" with the explanation, "You'd have a lot of agitation if you were that old."

all for one money. The whole lot is sold as one: "Here are five chairs all for one money." One of three ways of selling a lot; the other two are listed under SO MUCH FOR ONE.

all in and all done. Final bid; last call.

all over the house. Too many bids at one price; need a higher bid to sort them out. "I've got $50 all over the house. Somebody give me $60 quick."

ancestral. Seldom-invoked term in auction ads that is only used when *early* and *old* do not convey the proper sense of antiquity. One of its rare appearances was in an ad for a 1985 Robert W. Skinner auction that contained the line "Ancestral property from central and eastern Massachusetts families."

appraisal. An estimate, for a fee, of what real or personal property might bring if sold at auction or, if used for insurance purposes, what it would cost to replace.

Arizona Windsor. Style designation for a funny-looking chair.

as is, where is. No claim is being made for the condition of an item, and it must be removed from the premises by the buyer. A more colorful admonition: "Don't buy it if you haven't helt it, smelt it, and felt it."

auctioneer. The man or woman or team in charge of the event. Ambrose Bierce, in *The Devil's Dictionary*, defined it as such: "The man who proclaims with a hammer that he has picked a pocket with his tongue."

auction fever. The belief on the part of the buyer that everything on the block is a bargain and that one would be foolish to set limits on one's bidding. Auctioneers encourage this malady.

authentic Shaker. More often than not this term is used facetiously to mean "not authentic Shaker." A running gag during the last several decades, as the prices on Shaker-made furniture and household objects have set higher and higher records, is to say that an item has "Authentic Shaker" stamped on the bottom—something that is no less likely than finding a coin dated 60 B.C. In context it usually comes up like this interchange recorded at a September 16, 1995, Rafael Osuna auction on Nantucket as a wooden box was presented:

POTENTIAL BIDDER: Is it Shaker?

AUCTIONEER: It says Shaker on the bottom. I wrote "Authentic Shaker" on the bottom last week.

∗ B

backfield. The back of the hall: "I've got $50 in the backfield." Some buyers like the backfield because it is easy to see who is in front of them making the bids.

believe he stole it. Auctioneer's pat response to a desirable item selling for a seemingly low price.

Bible box. Generic name for tabletop or repository box for valuables.

bidder's paddle. Object on which the bidder's assigned number is written. The number must be recorded after every successful bid. Bidder's paddles can range from rather nice wooden or plastic affairs (which must be returned) to paper plates on which the numbers are written in crayon.

boat anchor. A heavy item with less than universal buyer appeal. Applied, for instance, to a monstrous old calculating machine at a Northport, Maine, auction. "Come on, folks, what am I bid? You can always use it for a boat anchor."

buyer's premium. Fee charged to the buyer for the privilege of spending money, usually 10 percent of the gavel price.

Some make no small point about not charging this fee: "Of course, no buyer's premium is ever charged," trumpets an ad from a Rhode Island auctioneer in *Maine Antiques Digest*. An ad from Mike True in the *Maine Sunday Telegram* avoids the word *premium* for this practice and says "no buyer's penalty."

buy-in. When a reserve has been set by the seller and no bidder reaches that reserve, the auctioneer "buys in" (or "buys" from the auction in a cashless transaction) for the seller. Often the other buyers do not know that a buy-in has taken place until the final list of prices realized is printed and the space next to the buy-in is blank.

 C

can't cut it any closer. Point at which the auctioneer will take no more half or fractional bids. If the bid is for $160 and the auctioneer is asking for $170, he may accept $165 but "can't cut it any closer" so will not take $162.50.

cash or check. Means of payment at most auctions. Few auctioneers will take credit cards, but most make it remarkably easy for the buyer—even from out of state—to write a personal check.

catered. Food will be served.

change your tune. Something fine is coming up. "Change your tune for this one." Auctioneer Dan Andrews, who believes he was the first to use this phrase in this manner, often prefaces it with a loud "Whoa." Same as TIME TO OPEN YOUR EYES.

character. Said of a piece showing signs of wear and tear.

chowder mug. Chamber pot, see THUNDER JUG/THUNDER MUG.

circular. Mailed auction notice and ad as it is traditionally termed in the Northeast.

clean. Unadulterated. It can be embellished, as when, at a Northport, Maine, auction C. W. "Chas" Hare pointed to a Sheraton washstand and declared that it was "clean as a smelt."

clerking. The process of recording

bids and totals and making sure that all bidders have paid for their purchases, or have "closed out."

closing out. Settling one's bill at the point a bidder leaves the auction.

conditions of sale. The legal terms and provisions of an auction sale, which can be announced, posted, or printed in a catalog or on the back of the bidder's paddle. The conditions of sale address such issues as protested bids, sales tax, absentee bids, buyer's premium, reserves, warranties, and the terms of payment.

country auction. "A true country sale," says a man who runs them, "is when the buyer and seller are allowed to make a fast deal without hidden reserves or other forms of protection. It will contain everything from period chests and fine jewelry to pots and pans and the outhouse door."

 D

did you want to buy it or rent it? Auctioneer's response to a low opening. Variations: "He's here to rent it" and "That's not a bid, that's the rental fee."

dings. Dents or scrapes. It is one of the terms used by auctioneers as well as used-car salespeople and it is almost always cast in the negative. "No dings. No nothing. Great shape."

distortion. Flaw or damage. A large L-shaped rip in an oil painting was termed "a little distortion" in a 1987 auction.

don't dwell, sell. Motto used by an

auctioneer trying to get the action going. Alternative line: "Scream, holler, shout: do something."

don't shoot, I'll marry your daughter. Auctioneer's pat response to a loud noise made when a runner drops a large object. There are others: at a Nantucket auction peopled by well-heeled buyers, auctioneer Rafael Osuna has been heard asking, "Who dropped their wallet?" after a large object has been dropped.

dusty. Untouched and not picked over, something still covered with the dust of an attic or barn loft. An ad for a George Morrill auction that appeared in *The Maine Sunday Telegram* (August 2, 1987) was headlined "dusty country auction" and promised "many wonderful dusty primitives and country items in old paint from the barns and attics . . ."

Dutch auction. One in which the prices go down rather than up. In this day and age, this is a technique more likely to be employed by a used-car or stereo dealer than an auctioneer. A handbill for a 1991 Dutch auction from Audio Associates of Fairfax, Virginia, asks, "What is a Dutch auction?" and answers in part:

- Every display model in every store will be on sale!
- All models are on display now for your inspection.
- All prices for each of the four sale day are clearly marked on special "Dutch Auction" sale tags.
- The price on unsold models goes down every day!
- You decide the price that's right for you.

- Remember . . . all models are subject to prior sale.

E

early. Auctionese for "old." Explained in a July 1981 article in *Washingtonian* on auctions and antiques: "An antique should be at least one hundred years old. Presumably, an early one should be even earlier than that. But some alleged antique dealers consider anything before the Eisenhower era 'early.' "

Sometimes an auctioneer will become redundant in an effort to make something seem appealing, such as describing an item as "good, old, early."

See also OLD.

early fire. Said of eager bidding when the lot is first offered.

ended out. Added to. A chair leg that has been ended out has been given fresh wood. Also, *pieced out*.

end of day. Said of an unusual piece to indicate that it may have been made by a worker at the end of the day either to use up material (e.g., all of the molten glass) or as a special personal item.

estimate. An opinion—not an appraisal—of what price a property will bring at auction.

F

fair room and fair warning. Coded reminder that if the bidder bids quickly, he or she can still make a tidy profit between what is paid and what the item can be sold for later. This item was passed along to the author from Paige McHugh of Cambridge, Massachusetts, after he had written an article on the secret language of auctioneers in the June 1990 issue of the late *New England Monthly.*

fair warning. The bidding is nearing a close, but you still have a moment in which to spend your money.

feed. The flow of goods being brought to the front for sale. A good auctioneer will control the feed so that the items are diverse and the best come up when the buyers are most eager to pay top dollar.

feeder. One who feeds goods to the auctioneer. See RUNNER.

finding story. Tale about how the item came to be in the auction. An account of a 1978 James Julia auction in *Maine Antique Digest* tells of a rare political banner that brought $1,150. Samuel Pennington wrote, "There even was a 'finding' story to go with this one, too. According to auctioneer Julia, the banner had been found by a man hired to clean out a Belfast hall. Part of his payment was that he could keep whatever he found in the hall—not a bad keep, this one."

An occasional finding story involves a treasure discovered at the town dump.

flake. Small chip, as in "a perfect Depression glass decanter with a small flake."

flea market kit. Kind name for a large pile of stuff that could never sell individually, say, a nonworking clock, five unwashed canning jars, four un-

related saucers, a padlock without a key, and a long run of clean *Poultryman* magazines. If this lot did not sell, a few other items would be added to make it "an intermediate-level flea market kit."

flow blue. Desirable form of china decorated in blue. It has also been known to flow from one place to another. At a 1987 Franklin County, Maine, estate auction a lot of flow-blue china that had attracted a lot of interest during the inspection period suddenly disappeared as the auction was about to start. A RUNNER found the plates at the bottom of a box of farming magazines just as he was putting it on the block. The magazines brought $5. The runaway china was offered separately and fetched $190.

folky. Describing an item with folk-art qualities, such as "a great folky rug." Not to be confused with the noun *folkie* for a devotee of folk music.

gallery. Building used for auctions and where sale goods are displayed prior to sale. Galleries are often also used to store recycled newsprint and snowplows.

gimmie what? Words of an auctioneer begging for an opening bid.

give 'em away for Christmas. Consumer tip given by auctioneer Clyde Allen when he was unable to move bidders up from $35 on a lot of augers.

going . . . going . . . gone. The auctioneer's sell line—but only in the movies. An auctioneer is quoted in Joe Connolly's *How to Buy at Country Auctions,* "Do you realize how long it takes to say that four hundred times a night?"

gone. (1) Sold. (2) Missing, as in a mug with a "gone handle."

good. One of the most overly used words in auctionese. It seems to be a filler word used when the auctioneer is not sure what else can be said. At a July 1988 auction in the western-Maine mountains, a totally undistinguished painting was described as "a good early painting, quite good." It sold for $35 with its good frame.

good, early ware. Generic description of a whatsit that appears to have come out of the kitchen.

good trade. Words used when a noteworthy sale that favors the buyer has been made.

gowser. An article in the April 1981 issue of *Maine Antique Digest* reported on a Plainfield, New Hampshire, auction conducted by William A. Smith during which an odd-shaped box came on the block. Smith called it a "gowser" and it sold for $45.

✳ H

hairlines. Network of small cracks.

hall. Preferred name for any inside country auction venue, although it often served another function. For instance, the Central Maine Auction hall in Thorndike, Maine, was once a grain mill.

he ain't too drunk, let him bid against himself. Comment aimed at a bidder who has made two bids in a row. Heard at the Fryeburg (Maine) Agricultural Fair on October 6, 1989, by the legendary Raynor I. "Razor" Crossman at one of his last public auctions. Crossman died in early August 1991 at age eighty-seven.

he/she came early. Common comment when a bidder with number 1, 2, or 3 gets a winning bid.

he'll be back. Said of someone who has just gotten a very good deal on something.

hernia special. Said of any item that is so heavy that it causes the RUNNERS holding it up to turn blue in the face.

honest. Not adulterated; pure. Often stated as *honest as can be.*

✳ I

I can't buy 'em for that. Cry of despair that goes up when an auctioneer has paid more for an item than it is about to be sold for.

If you was that old, you'd have a lot more than chips. Said of a flawed item that was not moving.

important. Expensive.

I never would have thought of it. Commonly said when a half bid is made, especially when the bidding is low. "I've got $5, give me $10, give me $10. Okay, $7.50—I never would have thought of it."

infraction. A high-toned chip. "There's been a small infraction here."

It's got some age on it. OLD. Said for emphasis.

It's no —— (fill in the blank), **but it's a good ——** (fill in the blank) **anyhow.** Phrase used to link an item being offered with a hot property, as in "It's no $50,000 decoy, but it's a good bird anyhow."

junque. Blend word of *junk* + an*tique* and a key element in many country auctions.

kippers. In some parts of the country, members of a bidding pool are referred to as kippers. See POOL.

knockdown auction. Informal auction among members of a pool. See POOL.

left bid. Bid left by a prospective buyer who has the auctioneer bid for him up to a certain limit.

let's show a little respect for this one. Something excellent is coming along.

lookers. Derisive term for people who do not bid. "What's the matter, you all just lookers?"

looks like somebody missed the road to the dump. Candid admission of a low-quality lot. Quoted in a *Maine Sunday Telegram* account of a 1971 auction. Variation on this was *throw it in the swamp,* said of end-of-the-auction items attracting no bids or interest at an Earl Hare auction in Northport, Maine, in July 1986.

lot. Any and all auction items are called lots whether they are single items or a box full of kitchen utensils. This term has been used by auctioneers for so long that it is the source of such long-established idioms as "a lot of them," "a lot of time went into this," and "a bad lot."

lots per hour. Measure by which the speed of an auction or auctioneer is judged. In a fast auction items are knocked down at one hundred per hour.

majolica. Gaudy pottery style. Overheard at a Northport, Maine, auction as piece was being offered:

FIRST WOMAN: What's majolica?
SECOND WOMAN: It's Italian for ugly.

married. Said of two incomplete pieces joined to form one—often bizarre—whole.

new blood. A new bidder(s). Also, *new fire.* Typically, two or three bidders work an item to a certain level, then new blood enters the fray.

New Jersey. State on the East Coast beloved of Yankee auctioneers. It is a special place where the ugly looks good ("This would look great back home in New Jersey"), and values climb meteorically ("Just think what you'd have to pay for it in New Jersey," or, in reference to an item stuck at $25, "Come on, folks, you know you could get $350 for this back in Jersey"). It is believed that most people who buy New Jersey items at auction are from Massachusetts or Connecticut.

New Jersey tourist birds. Lesser decoys in the $15–$25 range.

noes. Auction notices commonly contain one or more of these (no children, no pets, no out-of-state checks, etc.). It has been suggested that the greater the number of noes, the tonier the auction.

no excuses to be made on this one. A good lot. Pet phrase of auctioneer James E. Talbot of Turner, Maine. "Here's a Lincoln rocker. No excuses to be made for it. Let's start the bidding at $50."

nominal bid. Small bids that are normally rejected by auctioneers as a matter of policy. This is what is written on the reverse of one auctioneer's bidding card:

> NOMINAL BIDS: Small opening bids or very nominal advances made with the purpose of disparaging an item may be rejected by the Auctioneer. If there is no apparent interest in an item (appreciable opening bid), the item will be passed from the block by the Auctioneer.

no more partying, let's get with it. Said when an important bid was missed by a man who was talking.

no refund. No return. This isn't JCPenney. Caveat line uttered at the beginning of a no-nonsense north-of-Boston country auction.

no-sale fee. A charge paid by the owner of property offered at "auction with reserve" when the property does not sell. Not all auction firms use this fee.

nothing to hide. Without a problem or flaw.

nothing wrong with it but the price. Invitation to bid higher.

nothing wrong with it, it just needs a new home. Invitation to start bidding.

not that well-known in these parts. Said of an unknown painter or artisan who presumably is known elsewhere. Heard at a Turner, Maine, auction of an Arizona desert scene painted by one Sterling Mock.

of the period. Short for *of the colonial period* and describing seventeenth-century goods. It is also used as an inspired bit of vagueness for a piece of indeterminate age. "Here's a sturdy ladder-back chair—could be of the period. What's your pleasure?" Or, "I don't know if this is period, but it sure looks it."

old. Term of emphasis for that which is *really old*.

old ——— (insert name of color) paint, the. Old or original paint. For reasons unclear, the word *the* is almost always attached to the word *old* when talking about paint.

100 percent. Flawless; perfect.

* P

pass. To move on to the next item without selling the lot on the block. Items are usually passed when there is no bid or the bid is too low. One coastal-Maine auctioneer announced at an August 1987 auction that he would pass on any item that was not bid up to 20 percent of its value.

personality. Term used to describe the quality of an auction. On the National Public Radio *Nightly Business Report* for September 1, 1994, in a report from the Continental Auction School in Mankato, Minnesota, an auctioneer described an auction with a bad personality (one prompted by nasty divorce) versus one with a good personality (one for a beloved family).

phantom/phantom bid. A nonexistent bid "acknowledged" by the auctioneer to give an illusion that encourages other bidders to raise their own bids. An improper practice that is illegal in many jurisdictions. See PICKIN' BIDS.

picker. One who finds selected items for resale or auction consignment; a middle person. Pickers bring items to auction but may also be at the auction, where they have consigned goods, looking for bargains.

pickin' bids. Accepting a nonexistent bid to help jimmy up the price of the lot. The term seems to derive from the idea of "pickin' bids out of thin air," "pickin' bids off the wall," etc.

pool. Illegal, informal agreement among dealers not to bid on an item so that another dealer gets the item at a low price. Those who sit on their hands are paid not to bid. For instance, auctioneer Dan Andrews tells of selling a fine china closet for $950 but later learning that the dealer who got it for that had to pay $200 to the pool to get it at that price. Sometimes one dealer will bid for the whole pool with one item going to one dealer and the next going to another. Dividing up a pile of pooled goods is often done at a KNOCKOUT AUCTION near the location of the legitimate auction.

As more collectors and independent dealers enter an auction, the effectiveness of the pool diminishes. Auctioneer Elsie Andrews adds that "really good stuff tends to break up the pool; greed takes over. This is when you see a member of the pool trying to sneak in a bid from the door of the coatroom."

pop it right out of here. Let's move this quickly.

POS. Piece of shit. Said of a lot that is no good and will be passed on. This is an inside joke between some auctioneers and their best customers who know that when the word POS is heard, it does not mean the same thing as *pass* (although a POS is usually passed).

posteds. Specific printed or written ground rules for the sale that are displayed at the auction site. For example, here is one of the rules attached to a tent pole for a Clyde Allen auction in Carthage, Maine, on July 25, 1987: "In the event that two or more persons believe they have the purchasing bid, the item must be resold with only those persons participating."

✳

SAY, WHAT'S ILLEGAL?

WARNING! WARNING!

O ddly, many in the auction world have been hard-pressed to demonstrate that pooling is against the law. Listen to a part of an editorial in the Center Barnstead, New Hampshire, auction tabloid, *Unravel the Gavel,* by Cathy Greer in the August 20, 1996, issue: "Pooling is a Federal offense, punishable by jail time and heavy fines. . . . If you are still not sure what a 'pool' is besides a favorite spot for a cool dip—then you have nothing to worry about. However, if you are approached at an auction and asked not to bid on certain items; if someone attempts to bribe or intimidate you not to bid—or if you are offered money to leave the auction, Do Not accept it. If the auction is in progress, go to one of the auction staff members such as the auction clerk or front desk and report it immediately."

---

prime time. The best time for selling, generally the hour to ninety minutes after the first half hour. This is the time for the best stuff.

probably. Adverb used to link an item to a possible. For instance, almost any old sled that comes to the block in Maine is "probably from South Paris" (a former hotbed of sled creativity).

puffer. Bidder in league with the auctioneer bidding up prices; a SHILL.

puffing. A price-enhancing technique that may originate with a person employed by the seller to raise the price by fictitious bids. Puffing is forbidden by law, and contracts resulting are void or voidable.

pulling teeth time. One auctioneer's term for the first half hour of the auction, which comes before prime time. During this time, says the auc-

tioneer who used the term, "People gawk, sit on their hands, and generally forget that they have wallets." He stopped short of saying that this was a time when junk was offered, but said that he kept his really good stuff away from the first half hour.

pyramiding. An unorthodox ploy that uses false absentee bids and PHANTOM BIDS in succession to raise the bid several jumps between legitimate bids.

✳ Q

quarter. Twenty-five dollars—as in, "Gimme a quarter and we'll start this one going." By extension, $50 is a couple of quarters.

quick knockdown. Method by which an auctioneer can adroitly mumble a few numbers and then award a plum to a friend or a partner. Illegal in most jurisdictions, it is almost impossible to prove in court.

 R

real wood . . . from a tree. Exasperated cry from an auctioneer unable to get an opening bid on a nice table.

real world. The area outside the auction room. "This rug would bring $1,500 in the real world," said Nantucket auctioneer Rafael Osuna in a September 1995 auction. "Let's start the bidding at $1,500."

right. Pure and unadulterated; a piece that you don't have to worry about. Also, *right as rain* for emphasis.

right where we should've started. Said sometimes when the bidding reaches the point from which the auctioneer tried to start the bidding.

ring. Groups of bidders who agree among themselves not to bid against each other, then later divide among themselves the properties they have cooperatively purchased. Same as a POOL and just as much a practice of questionable legality.

runner. The auctioneer's assistant who helps spot bids, brings items to the front of the room, and holds items up for the audience to see.

 S

sameway. To the same person as the bid before. Instead of saying "sold to number 42," the auctioneer may say "sold sameway."

sea captain's chest. Term used to describe the origin of pieces for sale, and to suggest age and quality, especially in New England. Similar terms are in use in other parts of the country; for example, in the West an item may have come "out of a covered wagon."

sell ya one in a minute. Response to this question posed to auctioneer Clyde Allen about five minutes before an auction was to begin: "You wouldn't have an extra chair for me?" (Like so many on-site country auctions, this one required bidders to bring their own chairs.)

send it down the road. To get the bidding going in the sense that an auctioneer might say, "Gimme $25 to send it down the road."

set it in at. Injunction to start the bidding. "Do I have a hundred, do I have a hundred? Okay, let's set it in at $50." Alternatively, "kick it in at" or "fifty and go."

shill. Bidder who is working for the auctioneer to inflate bids.

sick. Term applied to glass that is cloudy, usually because it was used as a vessel for chemicals, or china that is stained or so weak that it lacks the characteristic ring you should get when you flick it with your fingernail.

signed. Said of anything with the maker's name on it ranging from an oil painting to a soup strainer. An item that was not moving at an August 1986 auction at the Blue Goose Dance Hall in Northport, Maine, had the auctioneer making the plaintive cry, "But, folks, it's a signed Archibald."

smalls. Little items that are presumably appealing to out-of-state dealers and collectors without trucks. Smalls are good for the summer trade, and the best of all are listed in the ads as "Shaker smalls" or "Indian smalls."

Smithsonian would pay thousands for this. One of the many bits of overblown nonsense used to get bidders moving. Used in an estate auction at the Blue Goose Auction Place (and Dance Hall) in Northport, Maine, on August 4, 1993, to describe an item that fetched a whopping $170.

sold! Along with "Gone!" this is how country auctioneers conclude a transaction.

so much for one, take 'em all. One way of selling a group of items. In this case you bid on one but are obliged to pay the same for the others. If one of a set of six chairs is sold this way for $20, the buyer has bought $120 worth of chairs.

so much for one; take one, take all. The buyer of the first item can just take that item—$20 in the case of the aforementioned chair—or take the whole lot for $120. Also known as *choice and privilege,* as in you can take your choice or have the privilege of taking them all.

steal of the evening. Good trade. At a good country auction the auctioneer should deem something the steal of the evening about every half hour.

still plenty of money to be made on this one. An attempt to wake up the dealers in the crowd.

* T

tabletops. Same as SMALLS.

ten-and-ten. The scheme by which both the buyer and the seller pay the auctioneer a 10 percent commission on a lot.

thanks for your help. Said when a bidder drops out after helping to get the bidding up to a level that pleases the auctioneer. Alternatively, "Appreciate the help."

this is not a rental, folks. Time-honored way to let the audience know that the bids are too low.

the three D's. Name for the main causes of consignment: death, debt, and divorce. Mrs. Virginia Weschler of the Weschler Auction house in Washington, D.C., says, "People move, get married, divorce, or their kids grow up, but the bedrock is people dying."

throw it in the swamp. Reaction to a lot attracting no interest and no bids.

thunder jug/thunder mug. Chamber pot, from the noises created when they were used. There are auctioneers who will present the most decrepit example or the lid of one just to be able to say *thunder jug* in public. A variation on this is *chowder mug*—"Here's a beautiful chowder mug," says auctioneer Rafael Osuna. "I mean chamber pot."

time to open your eyes. Same as CHANGE YOUR TUNE.

Tips. Everyone has tips for auctiongoers. Here are some that seem to work:

- Read all warranties and conditions of sale.
- Don't be afraid to ask officials for help. They may alert you to an item's ballpark value.
- Start all cars or electrical equipment beforehand. These items are usually sold as-is.
- Know the value beforehand so you don't overpay.
- Don't feel you have to win a bidding war. Be prepared to walk away.
- Check out the competition. Well-dressed bidders are often dealers willing to go higher than those casually attired and just looking for a bargain.

tray and table lots. Means of lotting glass and china that is a step up from a box lot (a box of assorted items of little value) but not good enough to offer individually or as a set. The objects are literally offered generically in this line from a 1993 Richard W. Withington auction in Hillsboro, New Hampshire: "a large lot of Vic. glass and china to be sold in both tray and table lots."

treewood. Unknown wood. "What's it made of?" is the question from the floor. The auctioneer's answer: "Looks like treewood to me."

turnpike cruiser. A bedpan. Also, referred to as a New York tureen.

20-percenter. Auctioneer who does not charge a buyer's premium but rather takes all of the traditional 20 percent commission from the seller. Besides the traditional 20 percent and the new ten-and-ten scheme, there are other variations. A sign noted in Clyde Allen's auction house in New Sharon, Maine, a few years back said, "20% commission—30% on junk and leftover lawn-sale items."

 U

unfortunately, he isn't here. The last line of a story used by an auctioneer to get a piece of antique furniture over the $100 bid then on the floor. "A man was in here the other day and offered me $260 for it. Pleaded with me to let him have it, but I told him that it was advertised as part of the auction. Unfortunately, he isn't here tonight."

use it for packing. Suggestion made by an auctioneer having a hard time selling a homely brown quilt.

 V

vendue/vendue sale. An auction, but more. In E. C. Janes's *I Remember Cape Cod,* there is this explanation: "Several times during the summer the *Cape Cod Item and Bee,* which came out on Thursdays, carried advertisements for 'vendue sales' by which was meant auctions. These were no ordinary affairs by which householders sought to rid themselves of unwanted junk. Most of them represented, rather, the breaking up of long-established homes through the death of their owners. A number of them included the property and effects of seafaring men who had circled the globe in the sperm whale fishery or had sailed great clipper ships in the China tea trade."

Victorian. Having to do with the period 1837 through 1901 when Queen Victoria reigned. In most auction announcements this great period in history is reduced to the abbreviation Vic.

video auction. Mail auction in which buyers view the lots on videotapes. A 1993 flyer for such an auction from Running Rabbit Video Auctions of Nashville offered three hundred lots of antique marbles on a two-hour video. The cost of the auction tape is $15.

W

we're goin' the other way. One way of telling a bidder that he is bidding lower than the amount now on the floor.

what's it say here? Paul Revere. The kind of transparently bogus line used by country auctioneers to get the crowd into the action. The Revere name works well for silver or pewter bowls, as does Stradivarius for an old fiddle.

what's wrong with it? Challenge to the crowd to start bidding.

where's the pleasure? Who will make an opening bid?

whimsy. Something made to occupy one's time, such as a carving made by a sailor on a long voyage. Often an odd or fanciful object; for instance, an intricate carving of a chain made from one piece of wood. The word is currently popular among auctioneers, museum curators, and antique dealers to describe objects of uncertain utility but clear charm.

white goods. Refrigerators, stoves, washing machines, and other large appliances regardless of their color. Some auctioneers will not handle them and will advertise a sale as "good antiques and household items: no white goods."

Lest there be any question, white goods have become a problem in the era of recycling. A headline in the July 20, 1991, *Lewiston Sun-Journal:* "Towns must join to recycle white goods."

Y

you battin' a fly or are you bidding? Query used to determine if a party is actually bidding. Also, "Is that a bid or are you waving at someone?" or "Are you bidding or scratching your nose?" See ACCIDENTAL BID.

you folks on this side are allowed to bid. Line used when only one side of the hall seems to be bidding.

you just can't seem to win. Said to a bidder who keeps dropping out before the next highest bid takes the item. Sometimes embellished by a line like "One more time you might get it."

you'll never see another one like this. Said of a particularly ugly painting at an Elmer Lyons auction in 1986. Confronted with a similarly ugly work that did not attract a single bid at a Nantucket auction, Rafael Osuna told his RUNNER to put it back facedown.

you're the expert. All-purpose disclaimer, usually followed by something on the order of, "You can tell if it's Louis XIV or Louis XV, I can't" or "Could be Shaker, but you're the expert."

yours. Auctioneer's way of saying that you have the high or winning bid.

you wanna stand up so everyone can see you? Used by a disgusted auctioneer after a bidder had asked to have a lot of good china put up early and then bid $25 when the auctioneer was trying to get an opening bid at $100.

you wouldn't want me to sell it for that if it was your mother's. Nantucket auctioneer Rafael Osuna's way of turning down a very low bid on a consigned item. Lines like this are reassuring to bidders who are also potential consigners.

SOURCES

The following have helped me thus far in the collection of auction terms. Auctioneers appear with their license numbers:

Daniel W. Andrews (Me. 0385), Elsie M. Andrews (Me. 0389), Bill and Virginia Cressey, Frank Dingley, Barbara Hardenbrook, Susan Kenney, Patricia McIlvaine, M.D., Joe Reilly, and Norman Stevens.

Additional material came from the "auction" files in the Tamony Collection. The compiler was helped considerably by reading *Maine Antique Digest,* the fine monthly tabloid from Waldoboro, Maine. An early version of this glossary appeared in the April 1990 issue of the late, lamented *New England Monthly.* Thanks go to Richard Todd for his help. A particularly good book on the subject is E. C. Janes *I Remember Cape Cod* (Brattleboro, Vt.: Stephen Greene Press, 1974).

3

AUTOMOTIVE SLANG

How to Speak Car Talk

> Ever since the first car wheel put rubber to the road, cars have evolved a language of their own. Today, although just about everybody owns and drives a car, few know how to talk car-talk.
>
> —From a booklet on Detroitese, published by
> Chrysler in 1959, found in the
> Tamony Collection

If the automotive world always seems to be in constant change, the informal language associated with the internal combustion engine is not. To be sure, new terms are always being coined, but the old terms endure. *Four on the floor* is still the accepted way of describing a four-gear car with stick shift on the floor, and a *ragtop* is a convertible, just as it was when Ike was in the White House. In fact, some of the slang from the late 1940s found in the Tamony Collection remains remarkably current. A 1949 *San Francisco Examiner* article on hot-rodders talks about *skins, jugs,* and *bent eights.*

It is also slang with its own subsets and dialects. Depending on whether you talk to a used-car salesman, race-car driver, hot-rodder, or mechanic, you will hear a different version of automotive slang. Even within auto racing there are distinct differences depending on whether you are talking to a NASCAR or Indy competitor.

Here is a heavy sampling from all of those realms within a realm.

A

A-bone. Model A Ford, especially one that has been converted into a 1950s-style street rod.

alki/alky. Methanol or alcohol as a fuel.

anchors. Brakes.

apron. The portion of a racetrack that separates the racing area from the infield.

arching/arcing. Racing; going all out.

ark. One of many terms for a hulking, older American car; also a *canoe,* BOMB, SLED, *boat,* etc.

arm lot. Small used-car lot where cars are sold for almost nothing down and for which you pay enormous interest charges. They supposedly got this name because of the strong-arm methods of collecting payments.

autojumble. What they call flea markets in the British Isles and increasingly used for swap meets in the United States where sports-car parts are sold and traded.

 B

back end. In car sales, the money to be made in high-interest financing and high-profit "options" such as paint sealants and rust-proofing.

back haul. Return load a trucker hauls from his first destination back to his point of origin.

back light/backlite. Industry term. Rear window.

back off. To throttle down in racing.

badge. Car's make.

badge engineering. A marketing practice of manufacturing one vehicle and selling it under a variety of brand names. On such vehicles, the only differences are in trim and name badges. For example, the Eagle Summit is a badge-engineered Mitsubishi Mirage. Likewise, the Mercury Topaz is a badge-engineered Ford Tempo.

bagel. A poorly maintained car, to a person looking at it for trade-in.

baldies. Drag-racing tires that are supposed to lack tread, as well as badly worn tires.

balloon foot. A slow driver.

bam and scram. Hit-and-run accident to radio traffic reporters and others.

banger. Trucker's term for a diesel engine cylinder. A six-banger is a vehicle with a diesel engine with six cylinders.

banzai. All-out.

bareback. Said of a tractor less its semitrailer in the parlance of truck drivers. See BOBTAIL.

barefoot. Describing a car with worn-out tires.

barefoot pilgrim. Trusting car buyer who questions nothing.

barrel. (1) Engine cylinder. (2) Carburetor throat, alluded to in the term *four-barrel carburetor.* (3) To speed.

base. Dealer's price.

B-back/beback/be-back. Sales term. Derogatory name for a potential customer who says he or she will return but clearly has no intention of doing so. From the time-honored departure line "I'll be back." A sign that occasionally shows up in the office of a used-car dealer reads, "Bebacks never turn into greenbacks."

beach. To stop a truck or coast into a parking spot.

beached whale. Stolen car found stripped and up on blocks.

bear grease. Racing term—mostly NASCAR—for any packing material used to fill cracks and holes in a track's surface.

beater. Unreliable car.

beauty bolts. Exposed, brightly finished bolt heads displayed for looks.

bedsteader. Sleepy truck driver.

beefer. A complaining consumer, in the lingo of the salesroom.

been in service. Used-car/auto-auction term for a former police vehicle.

bent eight. V-8.

big arm. Piston with a long stroke.

big banger. Big engine; one with large displacement.

big hat. State trooper to a trucker.

big three. Chrysler, Ford, and General Motors—the three major U.S. automobile manufacturers.

Bimmer. A BMW. In his "Dream Machines" column in the *Washington Post,* Brock Yates points out that *Beemer* is proper when referring to one of the company's motorcycles, although increasingly some refer to the car as a *Beemer* or *Beamer.*

binders. Brakes, especially those on a truck or race car.

bite. The adhesion of a tire to a road or track; traction.

bite a turn. To cut a corner, especially among truckers.

black box. Device housing electronic components. Many traditional mechanics do not go inside black boxes.

black-flagged. Describing a race car that has been waved off the track (with a black flag) because of a mechanical problem that endangers other drivers.

blindsided. Hit midcar by another driver who seemingly comes out of nowhere.

blow away/blow off. Defeat, pass, or win in the world of auto racing.

blowed. NASCARese for a world-class engine failure.

blower. Supercharger. Sometimes a turbocharger.

blow lunch. Blow an engine.

blown engine. (1) Engine with a supercharger, in racing circles. (2) All-inclusive term for a serious engine breakdown.

blown gasser. Supercharged car that is fueled by gasoline.

blow off/blow off his doors. In racing, to pass a challenger.

blue book. The stated value of a car, such as, "I'll give you a hundred dollars over blue book for your Ford wagon." From the name and color of the guidebook listing standard prices for used cars.

bobtail. Said of a trucker when he drives a tractor without its semitrailer, as in, "He's runnin' bobtail."

boll weevil. Novice truck driver.

bomb. (1) A bad car. (2) A large old car, lovingly addressed, as in, "I had this great old bomb of a Caprice."

bondo/bondoed. Said of a car to which the product Bondo has been applied heavily to cover rusted areas.

boneyard. Junkyard.

boondockin'. Trucker's practice of avoiding all major roads.

boondocks. Off the course, in racing.

boot. A heavy metal contraption, usually orange in color, used to lock a vehicle wheel in place and cause a car to remain in place. It is used to hold scofflaws and other violators so they cannot avoid paying fines.

booth. Where the papers are signed in closing a sale on a new or used car. It can be an office, cubicle, or desk.

boots. (1) Tires. (2) Tire inserts to reinforce the casing at weak points.

boss. Perfection.

Botts' dots. Raised, reflective pavement markers that cause rumbles when run over to alert drivers to tollbooths and other hazards. They are called Botts' dots because they were invented by Dr. Elbert Botts, working for the state of California, in the 1950s. They are also known as IDIOT BUTTONS.

box. Transmission.

bra. Covering used to prevent the front of a car from suffering damage from pebbles and other road debris. See CAR BRA.

brain bag. Briefcase, portfolio, or attaché case in which a truck driver carries trip reports, bills of lading, and the like.

brain bucket. Racing helmet. See also GOURD GUARD.

brain fade. Racer's term for a momentary lack of attention leading to a mistake during a race.

brains blown out. Describing a car with a sunroof.

branch library. Describing a driver reading at the wheel.

brass hat. Sales term. A slightly used car; a demo.

Brickyard. The Indianapolis racetrack.

bucket. Contour seat for one person.

buff. A great-looking car. "That thing is totally buff."

build a fire. To run a rig at near top speed.

bull ring. A short—less than half a mile long—dirt racing track. Bull rings are common to the South.

bumblebee. Small foreign car.

bumper tag. (1) To drive close to another car, as one were to play at tag. (2) Touching other cars' bumpers in a game of tag in which one car is "it." This game is from the same era and state of mind as CHICKEN.

buried. Describing a car owner who owes more on the car than its trade-in value. See UPSIDE DOWN.

burn rubber. To accelerate with smoke and tire squeal.

bushing. Jacking up the price of a car after the buyer has signed an agreement to buy it. The classic bushing occurs when a salesman uses a high trade-in figure to estimate the final cost to the buyer, only to have the sales manager disallow the figure after the contract to buy has been signed.

busted lung. Spark plug that is not firing.

* C

cackle crate. Truck hauling live poultry.

California stop. Rolling stop, not a full stop—from the common belief that Californians are avid but bad drivers.

cam. Camshaft.

cancer. Rust or corrosion.

car bra. Close-fitting cover to protect the front end of a car from flying debris. Also known as a FRONT END BRA, also BRA.

carcass. An old tire.

cat. Short for Caterpillar engine in a truck.

cement mixer. Vehicle that makes loud noises.

channel. To lower the floor by lowering the chassis.

charger. Aggressive car racer; one who gets to the front and stays there.

cherry. Older car in excellent condition; a nice vehicle.

Chevrolet BB. Any tiny four-cylinder foreign car.

chicken. Hot-rod game in which two cars drive toward each other on a head-on collision course, with the first driver to turn away being the chicken. This game, more talked about than actually played, was part of the outlaw image of the fifties hot-rod culture, but it is still used as a metaphor for unreasonable automotive risk.

chizzler. A Chrysler engine, to a hot-rodder.

chop. To cut the top of a car down; to edit. Custom cars are sometimes chopped and channeled (cut down and lowered).

chop shop. Place where stolen cars are cut up for their parts, which are sold separately.

Christmas tree. (1) Electronic device using lights to ready and start drag races. (2) An array of flashing lights atop a police car, tow truck, fire engine, or ambulance. (3) Car loaded with gadgets and gizmos.

chute. A racetrack straightaway.

clamshell. Large, hinged rooftop luggage carrier that is easily installed and removed and accepts luggage as if it were being ingested by a giant clam.

clean deal. Car sale that does not involve a trade-in.

clunker. A worn-out vehicle or machine, especially a car. The term has been in use since the 1940s. See IRON.

coffin box. Sleeper added to a conventional truck cab, aka *suicide box.*

cold car/cold one. In the used-car business a make, model, or year of car that is not popular and is hard to sell. A car can be cold for no apparent reason.

come in. The sudden rush of power around 30 mph in some turbocharged cars when the turbocharger comes into play.

commuter hooter. Broadcast traffic reporter.

cooler. Air conditioner.

cop caller. Truck with squealing brakes.

cop stop. A roadblock.

corn binder. Any tractor made by International Harvester.

corner. A curve in auto racing.

cowpath. Trucker's term for any inferior (i.e., narrow) two-lane blacktop road.

crank. (1) The crankshaft. (2) To start a car; to crank her up.

crash cage. The confines of a stock car used in racing. It consists of tubular steel formed into a cage that protects the driver when the car crashes.

crate. An unreliable car in poor repair.

cream puff. A used car in fine, clean condition that has customer appeal.

creeper. Board on wheels, on which a mechanic lies to slide under a car.

crunch. A crash in racing.

Cruise, the. Organized gathering of specialty-car owners in which cars are displayed in roped-off areas. Described by the *Washington Post* on June 22, 1993: "The phenomenon is called the Cruise and it's the rage among mostly middle-aged men who gather in local parking lots to show off the dream cars they could never afford in their youth."

cruising. (1) Driving slowly up and down a particular stretch of town or city street, or through a particular area of town. (2) Moving along at a good clip—such as "cruising down the highway."

cube. Short for *cubic feet.*

curb lizard. Used-car-dealer term for one who simply goes slowly past the car lot, but never seems inclined to stop.

curbstoner. Used-car dealer who operates with a few cars, a telephone, and splashy ads.

 D

dagoed. Dropped front axle on a custom street car, giving it the classic high-in-the-back and low-in-the-front look. It is pronounced "day-goed" and derives from the ethnic slur for Italian.

Darlington stripe. The distinctive right-side scrape on the side of a stock car; every NASCAR driver eventually acquires this on turn three at Darlington International Speedway in South Carolina.

dash. dashboard.

day cab. Trucker's term for a tractor without a sleeping compartment.

deadhead. Trucker's term meaning to run empty.

dead man. Racing crew member

who controls the flow of fuel into the tank of a racer, so called because if there is a fire or other problem, he can bring the flow of fuel to a dead stop.

dead sled. Nonworking or abandoned car.

deathtrap. Car that has rusted through, is banged up, and probably has bad brakes and/or faulty steering.

deathwish. A motorcycle, especially to a truck driver.

deck lid. Lid of a trunk.

demo. Sales term for a demonstrator.

detailing. Sales term. The art of touching up a car to hide minor damage and imperfections. It is commonly performed in getting a used car ready for resale. See DOCTORED and DOPING.

Detroit. American, as in, car air-conditioning was a Detroit idea.

deuce. As always, a 1932 Ford coupe. Both the car and term have been given a long lease on life through the Beach Boys' hit "Little Deuce Coupe." The deuce alludes to the two in 1932.

diapers. Winter covering for the front end of a vehicle to keep the engine and radiator warm; a trucker's term.

dimple. Dent.

dirt tracking. A controlled slide in auto racing. See DRIFT.

dirty air. Racer's term for turbulent air, caused by fast-moving cars,

that can cause others to lose control.

doctored. Said of a used car with defects hidden with cosmetics.

dog. Lousy car; one that nobody wants, usually because it needs a lot of work; junker.

donuts. Tires.

doping. Any method used to hide the flaws in a car being prepared for resale. Some of these are legal, some are not.

double-nickel. The 55 mph speed limit.

down/downstroke. Down payment.

downsizing. Reducing the size and weight of a vehicle to achieve better fuel economy. The term came into prominence in 1977, when Detroit began talking like this: "I think when the downsizing gets going, we're going to push them right out to the shores." (Henry Ford II, on foreign competition.)

DP. Down payment; deposit.

drafting. Driving or racing close to the tail of another car to take advantage of the vacuum created, to literally be "pulled" by the lead car. It gives the drafted car extra power without using extra fuel.

drift. To make a controlled slide in racing. See DIRT TRACKING.

drink. To consume fuel, as in, "That car drinks too much."

drop in. Placing a brand-new engine in a car.

drop the hammer. To pop the clutch in drag racing.

dusting. Trucker's term for driving with one wheel off the side of the road to throw up a cloud of dust, done to discourage tailgating motorist or traffic cop.

* E

eatin' concrete. To drive a truck down a highway.

edgy car. Car that needs bodywork, interior work, etc. Automotive equivalent of the "handyman's special" in real estate.

emerjensen. Trucker's term for the emergency brake.

eskimo. Trucker's term for a driver who drives with the windows open in the winter.

ET. Elapsed time in car racing.

everybody rides. Sales term for a van.

executive. Sales term. A car that has been used by the dealership; a fancy name for a demo. On occasion it has been implied that an executive car was driven by a Detroit executive of the company.

exotics. Unusual—usually foreign— cars; for example, when a rental-car company offers a Porsche or Rolls, they are said to be offering "exotics."

eye trouble. Truck drivers' term for the inability to stay awake.

* F

facelift. In the used-car trade, rolling back the odometer.

factory. Manufacturer, or as manufactured. In racing, a factory team is one sponsored and supported by a manufacturer. In NASCAR racing the term refers to one of the big three auto manufacturers.

factory days. Reference to the 1950s and 1960s when the big three car makers actively sponsored race teams.

fender bender. Accident.

fifty-fifty warranty. No warranty. It is a reference to the old gag that goes: "If it breaks in half, we will warranty that you own both halves."

flat-out. As fast as possible.

flea. Car buyer out to get a tremendous bargain.

flypaper. A speed trap, so called because so many people get trapped.

forked-eight. V-8 engine.

four-banger. Four-cylinder engine.

455 air-conditioning. Cooling obtained while driving with four windows open at 55 mph.

4WD or **4×4.** Four-wheel drive.

four-wheeler. A car to a driver of an eighteen-wheeler.

front-end bra. Nylon-wire or plastic-mesh cover fitted to the front of a car to protect it from flying gravel and other minor road hazards.

frozen. Locked up or jammed.

fueler. Short for TOP FUELER.

full dresser. Motorcycle configured

to turn heads—plenty of chrome, gold-plating, etc.

full house. Car or engine loaded with all the accessories and performance gimmicks.

funny car. A vehicle used for drag races only but sporting a chassis that replicates a street car.

 G

gas guzzler. Car that drinks fuel. Also simply known as a GUZZLER.

Gasoline Alley. The garage/pit area at the Indianapolis Motor Speedway.

Georgia credit card. Siphon for stealing gas from other people's tanks. Texan Joseph C. Goulden notes, "In Texas we call them Okie credit cards; in southern California, they are Tijuana credit cards."

getting stale. Vehicle that has not been sold for forty-five or more days in the jargon of used-car sales.

glass. Fiberglass.

glazed donut. A recapped tire.

gobble. To drive fast; to "gobble" up the road.

goin' down. Trucker talk for a run from north to south.

goin' up. Trucker talk for a run from south to north.

goodyear. To run over and kill an animal; from the tire brand name.

gourd guard. Crash helmet.

greasy side up. Trucker talk for a

car or truck that has flipped over on its back.

green pea. Auto sales slang for an inexperienced buyer.

grenade. To blow an engine.

grid. The alignment of cars for the start of a race.

gridlock. Initially a name for a mythical moment at which all the cars and trucks in Manhattan would stop, thereby turning the city into a mammoth used-car lot. The term is on its way to becoming a conventional term for any severe traffic jam.

grind. (1) Car buyer who is able to negotiate a low price on a new car. (2) To work a price down, "to grind the salesman." (3) Also to "grind" gears.

groove. The best route around a track.

ground effect. Items that make a car standing still look as if it is in motion. SPOILERS (air dams) and the like create the illusion.

gumball machine. The lights on top of a police cruiser.

gut. To remove upholstery and other items.

guts. The interior of a car.

guzzler. Car that consumes a lot of gasoline.

 H

hairy. Describing racetrack traffic that is thick and fast.

hand-grenaded. Racer's term for a major-league engine failure.

hand job. Trucker term for a load that must be unloaded by hand.

hang. Turn. Once considered a teenage or hot-rodder term, "hanging a left" has become general slang.

happy man. Traditional term for finance companies or loan officers among car dealers.

hat. (1) Crash helmet. (2) Vinyl roof on a car.

hauler. Car that is really fast; one that hauls ass.

header. An exhaust manifold that is designed for the free flow of exhaust gases.

heap. An unreliable car, usually dented; a crate.

hell driver. Auto stuntman who crashed cars for a living at fairs and carnivals. Hell driver "Lucky" Lee Lott destroyed 17,981 cars plying his trade.

hides. Tires.

high ball. In sales, an estimate that is too high. For instance, a salesman may suggest a higher price for a trade-in than the customer will get after it has been "reappraised." See also BUSHING.

honking. (1) At top speed in racing: "Boy was I honking." (2) To haul ass.

hot car. (1) Stolen car. (2) Used car in great demand because of such factors as condition (a CREAM PUFF), mileage, make, model, and/or year.

house. A car dealership.

house-broken. Used-car-dealer slang for a car that does not leak water, oil, or any other fluid.

HOV. High-occupancy vehicle, usually one with three or more people inside. The term is used on interstate highways to indicate preferential lanes for rush-hour cars with more than one or two occupants. Since it is really a reference to car pools, HOV has been said to stand for "highly obtuse verbiage."

huffers and puffers. Turbochargers and superchargers.

hundred-mile coffee. Strong coffee to truckers. A cup of this stuff presumably has the ability to keep a tired driver awake for another hundred miles.

hungry boards. Side boards on a dump trailer, gravel truck, or the like enabling it to carry more cargo. They are so named because a trucker using them must be hungry for money.

idiot button. Same as BOTTS' DOTS.

idiot lights. Red lights on the instrument panel that flash on to warn the driver of an engine, brake, or electrical problem. They are stand-ins for formerly standard gauges with needles and presumably take less intelligence to understand. It also alludes to the fact that these lights have been known to go on when nothing is wrong.

igniter. Short for *ignition distributor.*

Indy. Of or relating to the Indianapolis 500 and the cars that race in it, which are Indy cars.

iron. (1) Dog of a car; a CLUNKER. (2) Tire chains. (3) Any old truck.

iron orchard. Used-car lot.

it's been muddy. Sales/auto auction term for a vehicle that has been water or flood damaged.

* J

Jack. Showroom nickname for a looker with no intention of buying.

jackknife. To fold like a blade closing in a pocketknife or jackknife. Usually used to describe a tractor-trailer truck gone out of control, with its trailer folded around or broken loose from the cab.

jack-off bar. Emergency-brake handle to truck drivers.

Jack the Bear. According to a 1994 "Winston Cup Glossary": "When someone says his car is running like 'Jack the Bear,' it is moving at optimum efficiency."

jam jar. Car, adoption from cockney rhyming slang.

jug. Carburetor.

June bug. Derisive term used by stock-car racers for the Indianapolis racing car. Sometimes called a WATER BUG.

junker. Car that is in bad shape; one that is almost ready for the junk heap.

* K

Kennie. A Kenworth truck to those who like them.

Kenworthless. A Kenworth truck to those who dislike them.

kidney buster. A hard-driving truck.

kissed by the Santa Fe. A car that was wrecked and then repaired, according to an article on auto-showroom slang in *Newsweek* (August 7, 1989). The reference is not to the city of Santa Fe but to the Santa Fe Railroad.

knee deep in rubber. Sales term for a used vehicle with ample tread left on the tires.

knock-off. Quickly removable wheel lug.

* L

LAHA. Acronym for Life, Accident, and HeAlth insurance, pronounced "La-ha."

land yacht. Large, elaborately styled U.S. car of the 1960s or 1970s.

lay. Leave, as in "lay rubber," meaning to accelerate so fast as to leave black rubber tire marks on the pavement.

laydown. A potential buyer of a new or used car who does not think or ask questions. "Give me twenty laydowns and I can sell twenty cars," says one dealer.

leadfoot. Person who drives fast; one who keeps a heavy foot on the accelerator.

Le Mans start. A racing start in which drivers run across the track, jump in their cars, and start up. It is named for the famous French race where this start originated.

lemon. A bad car; specifically, a new one with mechanical problems, although the term can be used to describe a used car. The word has been in use since at least 1905, when the percentage of cars that were lemons was a lot higher than today.

lemon law. Legislation allowing the buyer of a lemon some legal recourse.

Liddy light. The additional back-window brake light that has become standard equipment on all new cars. It was championed by Ronald Reagan's secretary of transportation, Elizabeth Dole, and took its name from her childhood nickname, Liddy. While her husband, Bob Dole, was running for president in 1996 she attempted to suppress the use of the nickname Liddy.

light the rug/light the tires. To make the tires smoke.

lipstick. Cosmetic changes made to a new model car to give the illusion of a new version of it.

loaded. Describing a car with many extras and options.

lollipop man. Racing crew member who holds a pole and sign (lollipop) over the pit wall to show a driver pit location and stopping point.

long block. To a mechanic, this is a complete engine minus the oil pump and oil pan.

loop. To spin out in auto racing.

loose stuff. Debris on the apron and near the outside wall of a track.

lot lizard. Truck stop prostitute.

low ball. (1) To offer a car at a low price to make a buyer interested. When the deal is about to be consummated, the seller will jack the price up. (2) To offer a car at an outrageously low price for a trade-in or sale to a used-car dealer.

low brakes. Condition in which the brake pedal must be pushed closer to the floor than normal to get the car to stop.

low-rider. A car with springs and suspension adjusted so that it rides only a few inches above the pavement.

lump. The engine.

lunch. To blow an engine, especially in drag racing—"He just lunched his second engine this month." See BLOW LUNCH.

lunch money. A down payment on a car.

✳ M

mag. (1) Short for *magneto*. (2) Wheel cast from magnesium; a mag wheel.

main. Street where cars cruise; not necessarily Main Street.

make. Manufacturer.

mall assault vehicles. Sport utility

vehicles that despite their rugged good looks and toughness are used for hauling kids and shopping.

marbles. Racer's term for track debris—pebbles, tire fragments, etc.

mashed potato drive. Automatic transmission.

maypops. Cheap tires used by low-end used-car dealers who know that they look fine but "may pop."

Mexican overdrive. Coasting downhill.

Mild Ones. Older bikers, who, according to an article in *USA Today* in June 1996, "go grey not crazy." The term is a play on the movie titled *The Wild Ones,* about a motorcycle gang invading a small town.

mill. An engine.

moth-eaten. Describing a car from a harsh-weather state where snow, ice, and road salt have caused corrosion.

mountain climbing job. Moving-truck term for a job in which furniture must be carried up one or more flights of stairs.

mouse house. Dealership in which customers (mice) are fed through an assembly-line sales operation—from salespeople to contract writers or closers.

mudding. Participating in a mud race.

mud doggin'. Driving a four-wheel-drive vehicle off the road for pleasure.

mud flaps. Large flaps behind the back tires of a truck to protect it and those behind it from flying debris, mud, and snow.

muscle. Power in a car, as opposed to the illusion of power given by styling, names, racing stripes, etc.

muscle car. Car of the 1960s made to look and perform like a race car but designed for regular roads. Some later cars fit the category, such as the '90 Mustang GT 25th Anniversary car.

nerdmobile. Any dull full-sized car: family car.

nerf. To nudge another vehicle with your vehicle.

nerf bars. Special bumpers used for pushing other vehicles.

no-parker. Any large car.

ocean fenders. Rippled or dented fenders—that is, those with waves in them.

on the floor. Describing a gearshift on the floor at the driver's right hand, as opposed to the mechanism on the steering post. Depending on the number of forward gears, a car may be said to have three, four, or five on the floor. An automatic floor gear post can be said to be "automatic on the floor."

on the hook. In tow; at the rear of a tow truck.

open the tap. Open the throttle.

outlaw. Race-car driver who runs in a nonsanctioned event.

out of the chute/gate/hole. The start of a drag race.

 P

pacer. (1) Driver who drives a racetrack at a predetermined speed before the green flag is dropped. (2) Car that sets the pace for a race.

packing. Adding extra charges to the base price of a car—dealer prep, document prep, finance fees, etc.

parking lot. Traffic backup to truckers and other users of CB radio.

piece. Car that is a piece of junk; piece of shit.

pimpmobile. A large and showy car with lots of chrome, as would be used by a pimp.

pipes. Dual exhaust system.

pit. Service area; place where one makes a "pit stop."

popcorn eater. Person who wanders through a lot or showroom with no focus on buying.

pop the clutch. To engage the clutch suddenly.

post. The steering column.

pot. Carburetor.

power. Sales term for electrically operated windows, brakes, and seats.

preacher's car. Car without expensive options.

puke. Blow an engine. See LUNCH.

pull. To remove, especially in auto repairs, where components are always pulled—never lifted—from under the hood.

pull system. The factory builds only cars ordered by customers at dealerships.

pump the chump. To push option packages, rustproofing, and other high-profit options in new-car sales.

 R

ragged edge. Racing term for the limit; to run on the ragged edge is to push oneself to the point where it is difficult to maintain control.

ragjob/ragtop. Convertible.

rags. Bad tires to a truck driver.

rail job. Dragster built on bare frame rails, or one that has been created by stripping a car down to its frame.

rails. Frame for a dragster.

raked. Describing a car with a lowered front end—a classic hot-rod look.

R and R. In auto mechanics, to remove and repair, or remove and replace.

rap. Motor knock.

rat. Car that performs poorly.

reefer. Refrigerated cargo trailer.

repro. A repossessed car. One who

does the work of repossession is called a repro man.

rest cure. Practice of sending a car to the repair shop and having it returned to the customer without anything being done to it.

rice burner. Japanese motorcycle or car.

ride. Car.

ride the rails. Racing technique that calls for taking the outside course on the flats and the high part of the banked curves.

roach. (1) Car buyer without credit or with bad credit. (2) Term used by automobile auctioneers to describe dealers who write bad checks.

road pizza. Mature roadkill to truckers and other users of CB radio.

road tar. Truck-stop coffee.

roller. (1) Rolls-Royce. (2) A car in stock; one that a buyer can come into a dealership and see, buy, and drive home in.

roller skate. Subcompact.

rubber. Tires.

rubberneck. To slow down and turn one's head around, as if attached to one's body with a rubber neck, to look at an accident or other roadside event, usually into the lane of oncoming traffic.

rumble strips. Roughened areas in a road designed to make a high-pitched rumbling noise to warn drivers to slow down.

runnin' hot. Trucker term for run-

ning a truck without the right permits, overweight, or otherwise outside the law.

runnin' legal. The opposite of RUN-NIN' HOT.

rust bucket. A car that is rusted through.

S

saddle. Driver's seat to a trucker.

sailboat fuel. Trucker talk for the cargo in an empty trailer.

say hello. To give a competing race car a tap on the rear bumper to let the driver know that you intend to drive through his space—a means of telling him to move over.

scuff. Racing term for a tire that has been used at least once and is held for a future race.

shade-tree mechanic. One who works out of his house or barn rather than at a dealership, service station, or garage.

shaky side. Trucker CB term for the West Coast, so called because of its proclivity for earthquakes.

shaved. A car stripped of ornaments.

shillelagh. Chevy engine, especially an old V-8.

sissy bar. Backrest on a motorcycle that a rider can use to keep from falling off.

six-banger/six-holer. Six-cylinder engine.

skating. In auto sales, moving in

quickly to take another's prospects, e.g., grabbing the next person through the door when the person who is supposed to get that customer is getting a cup of coffee.

skeeching. Holding on to the bumper of a slow-moving car on a snowy or icy street and getting pulled along. Also known as *shagging*.

skid lid. Motorcycle helmet.

skins. Tires.

sled. (1) Big car; also a TANK, boat, etc. (2) To drive in snowy conditions; to drive in winter. (3) In the world of automobile auctions a sled is a vehicle badly in need of repair.

slicks. Wide, smooth-tread racing tires.

slide-ruler. Person coming onto the used car lot or into the showroom with a strong interest in such things as miles per gallon, displacement, and EPA ratings and who often carries a calculator. Not beloved. Worse still is the *pipe-smoking slide-ruler*.

slingshot. (1) A racing maneuver in which a car following in the draft of another breaks out of the vacuum and gets a sudden burst of speed. See DRAFTING. (2) Dragster in which the driver sits behind the rear wheels, like a rock in a slingshot.

slippery. Streamlined.

slipstreaming. Driving or racing close to the tail of another car to take advantage of the reduced air resistance. Also DRAFTING.

slow motion. Prospective car buyer who tends to think things over.

slug. (1) Piston. (2) Used car in need of major repairs.

slush/slush box. Automatic transmission.

sneakers. Tires.

snooze patrol. Cruise control.

snowballs. Traditional big, showy whitewall tires; the kind you'd put on a restored Packard.

souped up. Customized for greater power and speed.

spaghetti. Excess chrome or trim on a car.

special. One of several terms used in car sales for a vehicle that has been advertised or promoted but not necessarily reduced in price— such as cars offered in "sell-athons."

speed bumps. Raised areas in a road to make drivers slow down and observe low speed limits.

spinner. One who illegally sets back the true mileage on used cars to get them ready for market.

spoilers. Metal strips used to control drag, downforce, and airflow. Primarily found on race cars, they appear under the front end and atop the back end (where the trunk would be on a sedan).

sprinkle a load. To make quick stop-offs to partially unload a tractor-trailer.

sputes. Sport utility vehicles.

squint. Tinted windshield glass.

squirrelly. Racing term describing a

car that is given to sliding. It is said to come out of turns "loose in the rear."

squirt. Windshield spray-cleaning solution.

stacking. In sales, lining up more prospects than you can handle; for example, sending a prospect to the back lot to look around while grabbing a second prospect.

stagger. Practice of racing with different-size tires on oval tracks, with slightly larger tires on the outside of the oval giving the car the natural tendency to turn left.

'stang. Ford Mustang.

stick. (1) Describing a manual, as opposed to automatic, transmission. (2) To a race-car driver, tire traction.

sticker. (1) A new tire; from the fact that the manufacturer's label has to be pulled off a new tire. (2) Short for sticker (undiscounted) price, so called because an itemized price list is stuck to one of the car's windows with glue.

sticks. Furniture, in the context of collateral for a car loan.

stock. From the factory; to take from the normal stock.

stove bolt. Chevrolet six-cylinder engine.

straw hat. Convertible.

stroked. Souped or hopped up; specifically, an engine in which the piston stroke length has been increased.

stroker. (1) The opposite of a CHARGER; a driver who never tries to set the pace and is simply content to win. (2) A racer who cannot afford to replace a blown engine, but gets money and a chance to race the following week if he finishes. To finish he "strokes along."

stroking. Describing race-car driver who "lays back" in a race so as not to severely punish his car before the end of the event.

submarine. Car that has been damaged by flooding. The term came into prominence in late 1965 when, according to the March 1968 *Esquire,* some thirty thousand cars were waterlogged by Hurricane Betsy and "many were reconditioned to hide water damage [and then] shipped out of state."

sugar scoop. An indented surface leading to an air scoop.

summertime truck. One that is hard to start in cold weather.

SUV. Sport utility vehicle.

swinging load. Carcass meat to a truck driver.

∗ T

tank. Big car.

T-bone. (1) Model T Ford. (2) To take an accidental right-angle shot at the doorside of another car.

T-bucket. Souped-up Model T Ford.

Texas rat. Used car originally owned by a long-distance driver.

throw under a bus. Sales talk for selling someone a car or van with all the extras and options at full sticker price or better.

ticket. (1) A summons or citation. (2) Driver's license.

ticket-taker. A driver with many traffic tickets.

Tin Lizzie. Ford Model T.

tired iron/tired rat. A beat-up car.

tool. To drive.

toothpick run. Trucker slang for a load of lumber.

top eliminator. Overall winner at a drag race, so called because he has eliminated all other drivers.

top fueler. State-of-the-art dragster.

tossing a rod. Blowing an engine; throwing a rod.

tourists. People who come to look at cars they cannot afford.

tranny. Transmission.

trans. Transportation—i.e., a vehicle of any sort, as in, "I'm dying for a pizza, who's got trans?"

tub. The chassis of an Indy car into which the driver fits.

turbo lag. The split second between slamming the accelerator to the floor and experiencing the takeoff of a turbocharged car.

turn. To generate or achieve a speed; "to turn eighty in the curve," for example.

turtle shell. Trunk or trunk lid of a car.

tweak. (1) Small engine modification made to improve performance. (2) Modification made by a manu-

facturer prior to a model's introduction. Quoting from *USA Today* for December 13, 1994: "Chrysler says it has 'tweaked' the design of its all new minivan, slated to make its debut next year."

200-mile tape. Duct tape so strong it can be used to hold a banged-up racer together to finish a race; racer's tape.

unblown. Without a blower or supercharger.

unglued. Blown, as in a BLOWN ENGINE.

unhorsing. Getting a customer to give up his/her car for a long appraisal period so that the time can be used to sell the customer.

unloading. Losing part of a car, such as a dragster unloading a tire.

up. The next person through the door, as in, "This is your up." For a sales rep to take another person's walk-in is to be "snaking an up."

upside down. Same as BURIED.

ute. Utility vehicle.

vanity plate. License plate customized for the owner of the car. Usually, initials, nickname, spouse's name, etc.

ventilate the block. To throw a rod through the engine; to wreck the engine.

✳

SAY WHIR?

"Vehicle Sounds" is a section in the Ford Motor Company's Customer Diagnostic Evaluation workbook, provided by Ford dealers to customers who bring in a car for service. According to a press release issued by Ford, "the intent of the Customer Diagnostic Evaluation process is to convey customer descriptions directly to the service technician." The company adds that "like the conductor of an orchestra, a service technician has an ear for even minor annoyances that might diminish a vehicle's performance." Here is the quotation from the workbook:

As you drive your vehicle, be aware of normal sounds from the engine, transmission, driveline, exhaust system, and tires. Excessively loud or abnormal sounds fall into the category of "noises." They can be very helpful to service technicians when diagnosing the cause of a problem. The following definitions of common noises are provided to assist you in completing the diagnostic work booklet.

Noise Definitions

boom. Rhythmic sound, like a drumroll or distant thunder. May cause pressure on the eardrum.

chirp. High-pitched, rapidly repeating sound, like chirping birds.

chuckle. Rapid noise that sounds like a stick against the spokes of a spinning bicycle wheel.

click. Light sound, like a ballpoint pen being clicked.

clunk/thunk. Heavy metal-on-metal sound, like a hammer striking steel.

grind. Abrasive sound, like a grinding wheel or sandpaper rubbing against wood.

groan/moan. Continuous, low-pitched humming sound.

growl/howl. Low, guttural sound, like an angry dog.

hiss. Continuous sound like air escaping from a balloon.

roar. Deep, prolonged sound, like an animal, or winds and ocean waves.

squeal. Continuous, high-pitched sound, like running fingernails across a chalkboard.

whir/whine. High-pitched buzzing sound, like an electric motor or drill.

whistle. Sharp, shrill sound, like wind passing through a small opening.

'vette. Corvette.

volcano. Car that burns a lot of oil.

vulture. Trucker term for spotter plane looking for speeders.

 W

wagon. Station wagon.

waif. Inexperienced buyer in car sales.

wail. To run fast and free.

water bug. Same as JUNE BUG.

water dog. Trucker term for a truck with leaky water lines requiring frequent refilling.

waterslide. Wet highway, especially to a trucker.

wayback. The area behind the backseat in a station wagon or van.

wheel. To operate a car.

wheel kicker. A would-be buyer who is actually only interested in looking.

wheels. A car.

whiner. Car making unpleasant noise.

whiskey rash. Disease afflicting cars belonging to habitual drunks. It is used in the used-car trade for a late-model car with numerous scrapes and dents acquired at different times.

windmill. Radiator fan.

winter-beater. Cheap, old car with dependable engine and heater used during the worst of the winter while one's regular car is in storage.

wiped. To be beaten or overtaken in a race.

wires. Wire wheels.

without shots. Out of warranty; car sold with no guarantees, alluding to inoculations and injections (shots) against disease.

working for Exxon. Said of a truck that gets particularly bad mileage.

wrecker. A tow truck.

wrench. Mechanic, especially a racing mechanic.

wrinkle-rod. The crankshaft.

Y

yardstick. Mile marker along highway.

yell bell. Theft alarm.

yellowtail. A rookie driver who may be required to race with a yellow back bumper to alert others to his inexperience.

Z

z. To reinforce and lower the frame of your car, as in "that car's been z'd."

zephyr haul. Trucker term for a light load.

SOURCES

Important help for this chapter has come from Joseph C. (Stroker) Goulden, John Rush, Norman Stevens, Tom Dalzell, Roberta B. Jacobson, James W. Darling, the Tamony Collection, and Gary B. Van Voorhis of the Daytona International Speedway. The "Winston Cup Glossary" published in October 1994 was very helpful as was Montie Tak's *Truck Talk* (Chilton, 1971).

4

AVIATION AND SPACE

Words From the Wild Blue Yonder

During World War II there was so much aviation slang that the newspapers had to run occasional articles to point out that bombs were *eggs*, antiaircraft balloons were *pigs*, planes were *kites* or *crates*, student pilots were *kiwis*, a routine flight was a *milk run*, and the cockpit was a *pulpit*.

This basic slang obtained until the 1950s, when jets, missiles, and satellites came into the picture and to a large degree slang gave way to technical terminology. But this is not to say that there aren't ripe, colorful terms flying about. Here are examples from commercial, general, and military aviation as well as space exploration.

* A

ace face. (military aviation) Red lines on a pilot's face left by a tight-fitting oxygen mask.

air boss. (Navy aviation) Head of the Air Department on board a carrier; he rules the flight deck.

aluminum cloud. (military aviation) The F-14 is so large that it is sometimes referred to by this term.

angels. (military aviation) Altitude, measured in thousands of feet ("angels fifteen" means fifteen thousand feet above sea level). Also, a term lovingly ascribed to the rescue helicopter by any aviator who has experienced an ejection and subsequent helicopter rescue.

A-OK. (space) Fine; the best.

APEX. (commercial aviation) Advance purchase.

arcing around. (Navy aviation) Vigorous but aimless activity.

auntie. (military aviation) *Anti-*, as in antimissile missile.

* B

back of the bus. (commercial aviation) Tourist class.

backout. (space) Reversing a countdown because of a component failure or bad weather.

back to the taxpayers. (military aviation) Where you send a wrecked aircraft.

bag season. (military aviation) Cold weather or water conditions that require the wearing of anti-exposure gear, which is restrictive, uncomfortable, and unpopular.

bandit. (military aviation) Dogfight adversary positively identified as a bad guy. Hostile aircraft.

barbecue mode. (space) An orbiter taking a slow roll in space for thermal conditioning.

barber pole. (commercial aviation) A plane's maximum speed.

barf, beer, and a cigar. (Navy aviation) Fighter pilot's breakfast; also *coke, smoke, and a puke.*

belly landing. Landing without the benefit of wheels.

bent. (military aviation) Damaged or broken.

bingo. (military aviation) Minimum fuel for a comfortable and safe return to base. Aircraft can fly and fight past bingo fuel in combat situations, but at considerable peril.

bird. (1) (space and military aviation) Pilotless objects that fly—satellites, probes, and the like. (2) Helicopter.

birdcage. (commercial aviation) The controlled airspace in the immediate vicinity of an airport.

birdman. (Air Force) Pilot.

birds. (military aviation) Aircraft.

black box. (commercial aviation) Plane's flight-data recorder, which records all of a craft's functions including altitude, speed, and engine data. It also records the cockpit crew's conversations.

blower. (military aviation) Afterburner.

blowoff. (space) The separation of an instrument section or other package from a rocket vehicle by explosive force.

blow show. (commercial aviation) Airsickness; or a flight on which many passengers got sick.

blue letter. (commercial aviation) Letter of complaint about a stewardess.

blue room. (commercial aviation). Lavatory on an airplane.

borex. (Navy aviation) A dull, repetitive exercise (a busy, tense one might be a *sweatex*).

bounce, tap. (military aviation) Unexpected attack on another aircraft.

bubbas. (Navy aviation) Fellow squadron members; anyone who flies the same aircraft as you do.

bucket shop. (commercial aviation) Place offering cheaper fares on major airlines; a consolidator.

bug smashers. (commercial aviation) Small private planes, especially when they are in congested areas.

bumpee. (commercial aviation) One who has been bumped from a scheduled airline flight. A bumpee can be denied a seat because of overbooking or can volunteer to give up a seat for a reward, usually a free ticket.

burnout. (military aviation and space) The moment of final oxidization or combustion of fuel. Burnout velocity is the speed of a rocket or airborne vehicle at the moment it runs out of fuel.

This term, which dates back at least to the early 1950s, was adopted for work in the form of "teacher burnout," "job burnout," etc.

buzz. To fly low over an area, as in, "Let's buzz Toledo."

C

carry-on. (commercial aviation) Luggage carried aboard an airplane by the passenger.

catshot. (Navy aviation) A carrier takeoff assisted by a steam-powered catapult. A *cold cat,* one in which insufficient launch pressure has been set into the device, can place the hapless aircraft in the water. A *hot cat*—too much pressure—is less perilous, but can rip out the nosewheel assembly or the launching bridle. Once a pair of common problems, but practically unheard of today.

cattle class. (commercial aviation) Flying economy or coach.

checking for light leaks. (military aviation) Taking a nap, referring to the eyelids.

cherubs. (military aviation) Altitude under one thousand feet, measured in hundreds of feet

("cherubs two" means two hundred feet).

chicken switch. (space) An abort switch or any other control that stops the mission.

chicks in tow. (military aviation) Fighters lined up for midair refueling.

Chinese landing. Landing with one wing lower than the other. This would appear to be based on the fact that "one wing low" sounds like a Chinese name, rather than being a pure slur.

claw. (commercial aviation) First-time flier.

cod. (naval aviation acronym) Plane that delivers mail and other supplies to an aircraft carrier. It stands for *carrier onboard delivery.*

combat dump. (military aviation) A bowel movement before flying; "sending an admiral to sea."

conk out. Sudden loss of an engine during a flight.

controlled flight into terrain. (commercial aviation) Jargon for a perfectly flyable plane hitting the ground.

counting the rivets. (commercial aviation) When another aircraft comes too close.

crashbait. (commercial aviation) Frequent flier.

crawlerway. (space) Heavily reinforced road built for transporting space vehicles and rockets.

D

dayside. (space) The portion of a planet or moon in daylight.

deadheading. (commercial aviation) For a crew member to fly as a passenger either to return home or to catch a flight to which they are assigned. One is only considered to be deadheading when in uniform, so going on vacation in civvies does not count.

decay. (space) Loss of energy.

deep space. (space) Beyond Pluto.

dogs. (commercial aviation) Passengers.

doolie. (Air Force) Air Force Academy cadet.

double ugly. (military aviation) Fond nickname for the enormously capable but less than beautiful F-4 Phantom. See also RHINO.

drift factor. (military aviation) If you have a high one, you aren't reliable.

driver. (Navy aviation) Pilot.

drone. (military aviation) Unmanned aircraft.

dry run. (military aviation and space) A practice or rehearsal.

* E

elephant. (Navy aviation) Big-shot, flag-level officer.

empty kitchen. (commercial aviation) Name given to female pilots by males—presumably from the fact that the woman is in the cockpit of a plane rather than in her house.

envelope. (military aviation) The maximum performance parameters of an aircraft; flying at the edge of the envelope can be both exciting and dangerous.

equipment. (commercial aviation) The plane. If you are told there has been a slight delay in the arrival of the equipment, it means your plane is late.

exotic. Fuel that delivers a great deal of power for its weight and volume; but which is expensive.

* F

fangs out. (military aviation) When a pilot is really hot for a dogfight.

fangs sunk in floorboard. (military aviation) When a fighter pilot boresights on a kill but ends up getting shot himself.

fat Albert. (Air Force) Jumbo jet that is wide-bodied.

feet wet/dry. (Navy aviation) The former means "over water," the latter "over land."

flat-hatting. (Navy aviation) Unauthorized low-level flying and stunting; thrilling, sometimes fatal, usually career-ending if caught.

fly-by-wire. (military aviation and space) To fly by autopilot.

flying coffin. Dilapidated aircraft.

footprint. (space) The space taken up by a spacecraft after it has landed.

furball. (military aviation) A confused aerial engagement with many combatants. Several aircraft in tight air combat maneuvers.

✳ G

gas burner. (Navy aviation) Unproductive, long-winded officer.

geese. (1) (commercial aviation) Passengers pejoratively. (2) (military aviation) Bombers in formation in the slang of World War II.

gizmo. (military aviation) Piece of technical gear (also *doodad, thingamabob,* or *hoo-ha*).

go juice. (military aviation) Jet fuel.

goo. (military aviation) Bad weather that makes it impossible to see; in the clouds.

go-no-go. (space) The decision to launch or not launch; the point of no return.

good up. (military aviation) Screwup.

grav field. (space) Gravitational field.

green apple. (military aviation) The control knob for the cockpit's emergency oxygen supply.

greenie board. (Navy aviation) Prominently displayed squadron scoreboard where the landing signal officers rate the pilots' carrier landings (any color other than green is bad); also called the weenie board.

✳ H

hangar queen. (military aviation) An aircraft that suffers chronic "downs"; hangar queens are often pirated for spares for the squadron's other aircraft, so when the aircraft leave the carrier at the end of the cruise, the maintenance officer normally flies the hangar queen because he knows which parts have been taken (the queen's ejection seats are especially well preflighted).

hawk. (commercial aviation) Passenger who causes trouble. Sometimes called a VULTURE.

high warble. (Navy aviation) Unduly agitated.

hit the silk. (military aviation) to bail out.

holding hands. (military aviation) Flying in close formation.

hummer. (military aviation) Any ingenious machine—plane, car, or weapon—whose actual name can't be recalled. Also *puppy, bad boy.* The E-2 Hawkeye early-warning aircraft is also nicknamed Hummer, in reference to the sound of its turboprop engines.

✳ I

icing. (all) The phenomenon of ice accumulating on aircraft.

Indian night noises. (Navy aviation) The ominous creaks, pops, and shudders of an aircraft in flight.

Indians. (commercial aviation) Small private planes. Same as BUG SMASHERS.

in the drink. (military aviation) Down at sea.

✳ J

judy. (Navy aviation) Radio call signaling that your quarry is in sight and you are taking control of the intercept.

jump-seat sniffer. (commercial aviation) Derogatory "stew talk" for a passenger who chases stewardesses. Stewardesses sit in the plane's jump seats. This term was first given wide circulation in Jay David's *Sex and the Single Stewardess* (Playboy Press, 1976). Also LOBBY LOCUST.

✳ K

kick the tires and light the fires. (military aviation) Formerly, to bypass or severely shorten the required routine of physically inspecting the aircraft prior to flight. Currently meaning "let's get this aircraft preflighted and outta here, pronto."

KOPS. (space) Short for one thousand (K) operations per second. The speed and quantities required for space exploration call for much use of the letter *K*, as in *K-gal*, which is short for a thousand gallons.

✳ L

LAX. (commercial aviation) Los Angeles and/or Los Angeles International Airport. LAX, suggestive of laid-back, is the three-letter baggage-ticket code for that destination. Others that have been adopted for conversation are ORD for O'Hare Airport in Chicago and MIA for Miami.

layover. (commercial aviation) Time spent by a member of a flight crew in a city other than that person's home base.

leapex. (Navy aviation) A jump-through-your-ass project, exercise, or drill. Something silly that needs to be done *now!*

leather or feather. (commercial aviation) "The choice between filet mignon and chicken cordon bleu that pilots are offered on board," according to *Newsweek,* July 3, 1989.

lobby locust. (commercial aviation) Term used by stewardesses for a man who hangs around hotel lobbies trying to pick up stewardesses. See JUMP-SEAT SNIFFER.

lost the bubble. (military aviation) Got confused or forgot what was happening.

lox. (military aviation and space) Liquid oxygen.

loxing. (military aviation and space) The job of loading liquid oxygen into the fuel tanks of a missile or space vehicle.

✳ M

mark one eyeball. (all) Human sight. This term came into play during the moon landings, which were helped considerably by the mark one eyeball.

Marsdoggle. (space) Wasteful and

highly expensive mission to Mars. It is a blend of *Mars* and *boondoggle*.

Martin-Baker Fan Club. (Navy aviation) If you eject, you're a member (a reference to the Martin-Baker company, manufacturer of ejection seats). An official list of members is maintained.

metsat. (space) Meteorological satellite, for short.

milk run. (Military aviation) Routine mission flown repeatedly.

my fun meter is pegged. (military aviation) Sarcastic comment for, "I am not enjoying this."

near space. Near the earth.

no joy. (military aviation) No other aircraft in sight.

no load. (military aviation) An underachiever.

no-op. A plane that will not operate; one that has been canceled.

nose-picking speed. (Navy aviation) Pointlessly slow.

no-show. (commercial aviation) A passenger who does not appear for a flight on which he or she holds reservations.

NRSA. (commercial aviation) Nonrevenue space available: a free ride, boarded only after paid seats have been filled.

nugget. (military aviation) A first-tour aviator.

nylon letdown. (military aviation) Ejection and subsequent parachute ride.

off-line. (commercial aviation) Travel on a carrier other than the one that sold the passenger the ticket.

open jaw. (commercial aviation) Describing a trip—and the ticket for that trip—in which one flies to one destination and returns from another.

opportunity to excel. (military aviation) A disagreeable job one hasn't the time or resources to properly complete.

padlocked. (military aviation) To have a bandit firmly in your sights.

passing gas. (military aviation) What an aerial tanker does, literally passing gasoline in midair.

PAX. (commercial aviation) A passenger, from the ticket code for passenger.

penalty box. (commercial aviation) An inactive runway where an incoming aircraft waits until a gate becomes available.

pinkie. (Navy aviation) A landing made at twilight between the official time of sunset (or sunrise) and "real" darkness; it officially counts as a night landing, but is cheating; preferred type of "night" landing by senior officers.

pit. (commercial aviation) The belly of the plane where baggage is stored.

plumber. (military aviation) An inept pilot.

pod. Detachable compartment of a spacecraft.

power puke or **power barf.** (military aviation) Projectile vomiting, a symptom of airsickness.

puke. (military aviation) Someone who flies a different kind of aircraft than you, as in "fighter puke" or "attack puke."

punch out. (military aviation) To eject.

the push. (commercial aviation) Time of maximum use at the airport—for example, the late-afternoon rush hour at the beginning of the Thanksgiving weekend.

 Q

quiet sun. (all) Condition of the sun when it is relatively free of sunspots and other factors that interfere with radio transmission.

 R

red-eye. (commercial aviation) A late-night flight, commonly a midnight flight from the West to the East Coast, as in, "I came in on the red-eye from L.A."

retros. (space) Braking rockets or retro-rockets.

rhino. (military aviation) Nickname for the F-4 Phantom. Also DOUBLE UGLY.

roach coach. (commercial aviation) Flight to the tropics.

* S

sardine class. (commercial aviation) Coach or tourist class.

scramble. (military aviation) To take off in a hurry.

scrub. (all) To cancel or to back out of a countdown.

seat-pitch. (commercial aviation) Jargon for legroom.

sending an admiral to sea. (Navy aviation) A bowel movement before flying. See COMBAT DUMP.

Sierra Hotel. (Navy aviation) Phonetic abbreviation for *shit hot,* high praise; the pilot's favorite and all-purpose expression of approval.

slam dunk. (commercial aviation) Landing technique that allows the plane to stay above traffic until the last minute, at which point it quickly drops to land.

smallsat. (space) Small satellite.

smoking hole. (military aviation) An airplane crash site.

smoking materials. (commercial aviation) Cigarettes, in the strange cant of the public address announcement. Smoking materials are never put out, they are extinguished.

soup. (all) Fog.

space junk. (space) Debris in earth orbit.

spacetug. (space) Utility vehicle for servicing orbiting space stations.

spaghetti suit. (space) The long underwear worn by astronauts, which is composed in part of tubes that carry cool water.

splashdown. (space) The landing of a space vehicle in the ocean.

starship. (space) Interstellar vehicle.

stew. (commercial aviation) Stewardess.

stew zoo. (commercial aviation) An apartment where a lot of stewardesses live, or a hotel where they lay over.

stick shaker. (aviation) An alerting device used to indicate that a stall condition may be in the offing.

stick-throttle interconnect. (military aviation) Mock-tech term for a pilot (also called just a *stick*).

stuff. (all) Clouds or weather to any pilot.

three-pointer. (all) Aircraft landing in which the three sets of wheels all touch down at the same time; a good landing.

tiger. (military aviation) An aggressive pilot.

tinman. (space) Aluminum space suit.

tits machine. (Navy aviation) "A good, righteous airplane. Current airplanes need not apply, this is a nostalgic term referring to birds gone by. By all accounts the F-8 Crusader was a tits machine," according to a collection of military aviation slang on the Internet.

touchdown. Landing of a manned or unmanned spacecraft on the surface of the moon, a planet, or on its return to earth.

trick-or-treat. (military aviation) If you don't make this pass, you have to fail.

turnaround/turnaround flight. (commercial aviation) Flight that returns a crew or crew member to their home base on the day of departure.

unobtanium. (space) A substance or piece of hardware that is desired but not obtainable.

upgrade. (commercial aviation) To move from tourist to first class.

vomit comet. Any flight or mission that induces nausea. The ultimate vomit comet may have been the KC-135 used to film the movie *Apollo 13,* in which weightlessness was simulated and filmed by going into a steep dive from a steep climb at high altitude.

vulture. (commercial aviation) A troublesome passenger. Also known as a HAWK.

✳ W

WAG. (military aviation) Wild-ass-guess flying.

warthog. (military aviation) Universal nickname for the A-10 Thunderbolt II close-air-support aircraft.

water walker. (Navy aviation) High-performer.

white knuckler. (1) Short-haul commuter-airline flight. (2) Any flight on which there is turbulence or a close call.

window. (space) Period during which a space mission is possible and/or most economical.

wrong side of the curtain. (commercial aviation) Describing tourist or economy class.

 X

XTAL. (space) NASA-ese for crystal. Over time the National Aeronautics and Space Administration has developed thousands of acronyms and abbreviations. For reasons unclear, a bunch of these shorten words using the letter *X*. Others include XFER for transfer, XFD for cross-feed, XPNDR for transponder, and XMT for transmit.

 Z

zero-dark-thirty. (military aviation) Technically a half hour after midnight, but commonly used to describe any event that is scheduled to take place after midnight and before sunrise.

zero g. (military aviation and space) The state of weightlessness, when there is no—or zero—gravity.

zip fuel. (military aviation and space) High-energy jet fuel.

zoombag. (military aviation) Flight suit.

SOURCES

A remarkable collection of NASA acronyms and terms appears in NASA Reference Publication 1059, *Space Transportation System and Associated Payloads: Glossary, Acronyms and Abbreviations.* A good source of commercial aviation slang shows up as a glossary to Jay David's *Sex and the Single Stewardess* (Playboy Press, 1976). A small but important collection of commercial aviation slang appears in the July 3, 1989, *Newsweek.* A large collection of aviation and aerospace glossaries in the Tamony Collection proved invaluable, as did suggestions from Ralph Hamil, Dave Matheny, and Tom Dalzell, who found a first-rate collection of aviator slang on the Internet.

—— * 5 * ——

BUREAUCRATESE

The Talk of the White-Collar Bailiwick

The language used is bureaucratic gobbledygook, jargon, double-talk, a form of officialese, federalese and insurancese, and doublespeak. It does not qualify as English.
> —Federal judge Jack B. Weinstein, ordering
> the government to remove gobbledygook from
> Medicare forms, July 11, 1984

WASHINGTON—This is the only town in Christendom where corrupting the English language is a community project.
> —Lead to an unsigned Scripps-Howard
> dispatch, December 28, 1959

Most people think of it in terms of the federal government, but it is spoken and written, with variations, in many other places. It seems to be used anywhere that people are sorted into departments and divisions and communicate with each other through memos.

It is the linguistic fuel of state and local government, think tanks and consulting firms, educational administration, nonprofit organizations, and much of corporate America. It is, in short and increasingly, the lingo of white-collar America. Subdivisions of this lingo have been created to serve education *(educanto)*, planning *(plannish,* or *urbabble* in the case of urban planning), the government *(bureaucratese* or *governmentese* or *officialese* or, as the late, ever-provocative San Francisco columnist Herb Caen put it, *bureaucrapese),* and specific agencies of government *(statese* for the State Department, for example).

Lest there be any question, it is proliferating, seeming to grow and reinforce itself with each new leap in communications technology. Its breeding grounds are telephone lines and computer screens and increasingly the Internet, and it reproduces through copy and fax machines. Even television plays a role in the proliferation as it covers events such as Watergate and the Iran-contra hearings, in which many of the key roles were played by people who spoke it fluently.

Some points should be made about it.

1. This slang does not always sound like a slang, but rather, a bloated version of standard English. It is, however, slang in the classic sense of a language particular to a certain group that is *not* used by others and is

meant for widespread dispersal. It also fits the definition of jargon, so it can be called a hybrid.

2. It dotes on extra syllables (*utilize* over *use*, *orientate* over *orient*) and loves to turn nouns into verbs—for instance, to assign a job to a person is to "task" that person. It hates simple words like *money* and *cash* (preferring *resources, funds, allocations, appropriations,* etc.) and dotes on what one critic termed "reductive prefaces" (*debrief, dicensus, disadvantaged, disequilibrium, disincentive*).

3. The slang is accompanied by extended metaphors and colorful clichés. If one tries to save a doomed project, that person is accused of "trying to rearrange the deck chairs on the *Titanic,*" and if one tries to get hold of the elusive, you are said to be "trying to nail jelly to the wall."

4. It has a penchant for the passive voice, the collective *we/us,* and acronyms.

5. It is much maligned and criticized and has been since it first began to grow during World War II. A number of people, including Jimmy Carter, have tried to control it. Despite this, it chugs along in true bureaucratic style and seems to get the job done—that is to say, "it has displayed and demonstrated an ongoing efficacy when confined to certain logical parameters." The latest in a long line of contributors are those bureaucrats and policy wonks who came into power with Bill Clinton who taught us to think in terms of "lifelong learning occupational development," which means training for a new job.

✳ A

acceptable. Possibly acceptable. When used in terms like "acceptable level of unemployment," it means acceptable to those using the term (that is, those who have a job).

activate. Start.

alarmist. Anyone who rocks the boat or questions an important decision.

apologist. One who takes a position on an issue or industry that you don't like.

apples and oranges. That which defies comparison.

appropriate judgmental standards. Good rules.

at this point in time. Now. This phrase came into its own during the Watergate hearings, when one suspected that witnesses used it to give themselves extra time to think.

✳ B

back burner. Metaphor of delay or dismissal—"Let's put that one on the back burner and get back to it later." The back burner amounts to bureaucratic limbo.

backdoor spending. Spending that is provided for outside the normal channels of appropriations.

backgrounder. Session in which a ranking official gives information on the proviso that it is not quoted directly or attributed to an individual.

bailiwick. Realm or area of responsibility, commonly phrased as something that is "not my bailiwick."

ball of wax. The entire situation; the whole enchilada.

ballpark figure. Estimate.

basically. In short.

Beltway. The name for the interstate highway that rings the city of Washington, running through the inner suburbs of Virginia and Maryland. More than the actual road, it refers to a state of mind—an idea may make perfect sense inside the Beltway but not outside the Beltway. In this case "outside the Beltway" refers to the rest of the nation. The term was coined in 1951 to describe what to that point had been known as a "circumferential highway." With the advent of the Washington beltway, the term was capitalized and used as a reference to this particular road.

Beltway bandit. A consultant working out of one of the many think tanks and consulting firms in the Washington, D.C., area. It is more jocular than hostile, and some of the ilk will actually identify themselves as such.

big picture. Larger considerations.

bird-dog. To put something aside; to make no decision. In other quarters, this means to sniff something out; but not here, where one can bird-dog a project that is going nowhere.

boondoggle. A project or program that wastes the taxpayer's money. This is an interesting term in that it was created about 1930 by an American scoutmaster, Robert H. Link, to describe a handmade object of leather, wicker, pipe cleaners, or whatever. From this it became a word for that which is trivial or wasteful.

brainstorm. A collective attempt to be creative and find new ideas or solutions. As a verb, *brainstorm* describes group rather than individual thought.

broad-brush. Crude; rough.

buy. To approve, in the sense of "I'll buy that." This term is never used with money—that kind of buying is *procuring*.

✳ C

can of worms. A mess, problems.

causal factors. Reasons.

charged. Ordered to; told to.

clearance mechanisms. What it takes to get an okay.

coequal. Equal.

cognitive skills. Book learning.

COLA. Acronym for *cost of living adjustment,* it occurs in debates and hearings on Social Security, the Civil Service, and congressional pay. William Safire has noted that in a legislative context a "COLA freeze" is not a way to serve a soft drink.

community. Group of people *not* linked geographically; for example, handicapped community, gay community, etc.

copy. To send a copy; "Copy me on that memo." It replaces the pre-photocopy-era verb *to carbon.*

counterfactual. Untrue, as in a counterfactual proposition, or a lie.

counterintuitive. Surprising; not what you'd expect (unless you thought about it).

CYA. Cover your ass. An almost universal trait in government and politics to make sure that one's decisions are authorized, in writing, or cannot be traced at all.

 D

data. Anything in writing (numbers, figures, facts, graphs, etc.). A precise term that has lost its precision through overuse.

day one. The beginning; the first day. "I could have told you from day one that this would not work."

debrief. To get information from. This term emerged from the Pentagon and spread into other monolithic buildings along with PRE-BRIEF.

destabilize. Overthrow or destroy.

detention center. Jail.

developing nation. A nation that may be developing economically and technologically, standing still, or mired in decay. Formerly underdeveloped or underdeveloped nations.

dialogue. Conversation.

dicensus. Lack of consensus.

disadvantaged. Poor. In 1965 a Jules Feiffer cartoon character tells how he went from being poor to being poor but needy. Then they told him that it was self-defeating to think of himself as needy, so he became deprived. Then they told him that he was underprivileged, and finally he was disadvantaged. The character summed it up, "I still don't have a dime, but I have a great vocabulary."

discipline. Occupational specialty. To be asked "What is your discipline?" is the bureaucratic equivalent of the singles bar question "What's your sign?"

disequilibrium. Out of whack; not in balance.

disincentive. Anything that tends to reduce motivation.

doable. Workable.

domicile. Home.

double-dipper. Person who takes dual compensation from the government, typically, but not always a military retiree who then takes a government job while receiving a military pension.

dysfunctional. Not working.

 E

end result. Result.

end user. Recipient.

etched in sand. Flexible.

etched in stone. Cannot be changed, but often stated in the negative: "This plan is not exactly etched in stone."

ethically disoriented. Describing a cheater in educanto.

excessive resource use. Waste.

exercise. Take or make, such as exercising an option or exercising one's opinion.

expertise. Experience. This term has come to encompass all things and has become totally divorced from the idea of a true expert.

F

facilitate. To ease.

facility. Thing; place.

fallback position. Bureaucratese for a defeat.

feedback. Reaction to; as in reporting, "I'd like some feedback on Friday's meeting."

fig leaf. The expression, stemming from the sculptural artifice for covering the genitals of a nude, applies to flimsy, unsubstantial solutions. Sen. Jim Sasser, D-Tennessee, during February 1992 debates over the economy, called President Bush's proposal a "fig-leaf economic growth plan."

finalize. End.

fine-tune. To work out the details.

FOI. Short for *freedom of information,* a statute and state of mind

that requires much federal information to be disclosed to reporters and citizens.

freeze. To stop or hold in place—from a nuclear freeze to a COLA (cost of living adjustment) freeze.

full-court press. All-out pressure applied by a member of Congress on a government agency.

functional. Working.

functional utilization. Actually being used.

fund. Pay for.

funding. Money. Funding is almost always spoken of in terms of increased or decreased funding.

fungible. Interchangeable, as in, "All shopping centers are fungible."

fuzz. To blur on purpose; to make less direct.

FY. Abbreviation for *fiscal year.*

G

gag rule. Description of a debate-limiting rule by its opponents.

God Squad. Top federal officials who decide which endangered species will be protected. The God Squad is formally known as the Endangered Species Committee and gets its nickname in part from the fact that it alone has the authority to override the Endangered Species Act, thereby "playing God." Membership on the committee is reserved for specific "hats" including the secretary of agriculture, the secretary of the army, the administrator of the Environmental Protection Agency, and the chairman of the president's Council of Economic Advisors. The God Squad meets infrequently and only for the most serious of issues. When it began meeting at the end of 1991 to consider the case of the northern spotted owl, it was the first time it had convened in thirteen years.

good. Fair to poor, as in "good try, but let's try to do it right this time."

goo-goos/googoos. Forces of and for *good* *government*.

green fees. Taxes on gas-guzzling cars, coal-burning power plants, and the like, which are intended to keep the planet green.

H

hands-off. Not involved; as in, "President Reagan had a hands-off management style."

hands-on. Involved; participating.

heretofore. Before.

human resources. People at work. This used to be known as the workforce.

hurry-up spending. The practice by federal agencies to "use it or lose it," exhausting their budgets in the final days of the fiscal year, "practically shipping the money out of the Treasury in wheelbarrows," as Sen. William Cohen, R-Maine, put it.

I

I can live with. Said of something that is mediocre or arrived at through compromise; a lukewarm okay.

impact. Effect, such as a school impacted by dwindling population.

implement. Do.

implementation. Doing.

incent. The people brought in by Bill Clinton use this as a verb, as in "incenting companies to create new jobs."

indicated. Said. "You indicated that you would empty the garbage."

information processing center. Typing pool.

infrastructure. Bridges, sewers, roads, originally; now it is used to describe anything that can be used to increase productivity.

inoperative. Broken; not working.

inside the Beltway. Popular metaphor for the parochialism and political intensity of Washington. A reference to the highway that rings the city (see BELTWAY), the phrase was coined in the 1970s by *Washington Post* columnist Mike Causey. In contrast, the *Washington Post* has defined *Outside the Beltway* this way: "The so-called Real World, as perceived by those unfortunate souls doomed to live east of Seat Pleasant [a suburb in Prince George's County, Maryland] and west of the moon."

interconnect. Connect.

interdependent. Dependent.

interdisciplinary. Describing anything involving people with different backgrounds.

interpersonal. Between humans.

intervention. Interference.

in the loop. Part of what is going on; in the know.

in view of. Since.

irrespective. Regardless.

is of the opinion that. Believes.

 K

K–12. Educanto for the period from kindergarten through the twelfth grade, the last year of high school. It is stated as "K through twelve."

 L

laundry list. List of things to accomplish.

let's discuss. Memo notation from a superior that tells a junior to come down to his office.

low profile. Describing that which is being kept out of the limelight.

 M

maximize. Make the most of.

media center. Library.

methodology. method.

Mickey Mouse. Term for something requiring substantial effort for meager results; petty stuff.

micromanagement. To manage down to the last detail and leave little or nothing unsupervised.

mobile response unit. Police car, ambulance, or fire truck.

motivationally deficient. Lazy.

multidisciplinary. Diverse. A committee with people from various departments or interests is invariably described as a multidisciplinary task force.

 N

needless to say. Needs to be said (if it were actually "needless to say," it would not be said).

neonatal unit. Nursery.

 O

off-load. Unload.

one would think. I think.

on the fence. Bureaucratic code term describing a person with a job who is doing virtually nothing. (See box on page 70.)

OTE. Overtaken by events. Said of a program, report, or concern that has been rendered obsolete by time.

outreach. Reaching the consumer.

overcrowded. Crowded.

oversight. A mistake; a screwup.

 P

paper pusher. Self-deprecating term for one in a bureaucracy. The term

---

✳

SAY WHAT?

A June 20, 1996, article in the *Washington Post* described a federal worker on the fence: "Public Health Service physician James D. Felsen starts each day at the office with a cup of coffee. After coffee he reads a newspaper, checks his mail, and telephones friends. Felsen saves his styrofoam coffee cups because they help him keep track of how many days he has gone to his office in the huge federal Parklawn Building in Rockville [Maryland].

"He has constructed an arch out of the used cups in his office. The first row stretches from the floor on one wall up to the ceiling and down to the floor on the opposite side. He is halfway through the second row."

The article goes on to point out that Felsen had been doing this for three years at a salary of $117,000—including a $15,000 bonus reserved for valued employees.

---

is sometimes useful when things go wrong: "Don't ask me, I'm just a paper pusher."

paper trail. Evidence left by a bureaucrat to prove that he or she acted in a particular way.

past history. History.

pencil in. To tentatively schedule something. It is based on the fact that pencil can be erased. "Pencil in lunch for Wednesday."

phase in. Start; implement.

phase out. Stop; dismantle.

phase zero. The beginning of something.

plum. A political appointment; a job given out by the president.

policy. Predetermined response.

prebrief. Brief in advance of a meeting or event.

preplanning. Planning.

prioritize. To decide what is most important; to assign priorities to things.

the private sector. Business; anything that is not part of the government, which is the public sector.

proactive. Advance planning.

procedural safeguards. Defined by Don Ethan Miller in his *Book of Jargon* as "red tape."

process. Work or activity, as in the "planning process" or the "information process."

procurement. Buying; getting hold of.

program. Almost anything. In 1962 Sen. Stephen M. Young of Ohio defined it as "any assignment or task that cannot be completed in one phone call."

programitis. The thought that for

every problem there is a government project that will solve it.

project. See PROGRAM.

promulgate. Announce; issue an order; start something.

prune. A political appointee with experience; an appointee who has held the job for a while. It is a play on the term PLUM in that a prune is a plum with time on the job.

public sector. The government—federal, state, and local—itself.

qualitative. Having to do with quality and things that cannot be measured.

quantification. Putting a number on something.

quantitative. Having to do with numbers.

quick fix. That which does not exist. In a bureaucracy it is common to state that there is "no quick fix" when a problem cannot be solved by money.

R&D/R and D. Research and development.

redundancy of human resources. Too many employees.

reinventing the wheel. To study something that has already been studied; usually stated negatively,

by those opposed to reinventing the wheel.

reskilling. Retraining. This term may have been invented by Maine governor John R. McKernan, who in 1967 said to a reporter, "That tells you right off the bat that we need serious reskilling of our workforce."

revenue shortfall. One of several clever ways of saying that there is a deficit without saying the word. If the word *deficit* is used, it is never "our deficit," but rather, "the deficit."

revise to reflect. Revise.

revolving door. Metaphoric team used to describe the movement between public service and private employment. It is often mentioned in discussing the lack of tenure among high government officials, who tend to take jobs in the private sector after, say, two years as a "deputy undersecretary" or whatever.

RFP. Initialism for *request for proposals,* which is a notice to bid for a government job or contract.

RFQ. Request for quotations.

Rif/riff. Derived from the acronym for *reduction in force,* it stands for a cutback in staff, or a layoff. It applies to the federal workforce, including the military, and comes up as agency budgets are trimmed and riffing becomes rife.

riffed. To have lost one's job.

root cause. Cause.

* S

scenario. Hypothetical case; a prediction.

seed money. Money used to start something.

selected out. Fired.

shortfall. Not enough. A budgetary shortfall is a shortage of money.

signage. Signs.

significant contribution. Contribution.

silver bullet. A tax break or loophole that benefits a particular interest group, such as, say, a silver bullet for the oil industry.

sleaze factor. That component of an administration, political party, etc., that is corrupt, unethical, controversial, scandal-ridden, or otherwise under a cloud.

sound of the city. An inside-Washington reference to paper shuffling, as in, "Listen carefully and you'll hear the sound of the city."

state-of-the-art. Not out-of-date; current.

subject matter. Subject.

substandard housing. Slum.

sunset law. Legislation that specifies the periodic review of, or stated date of demise for, a program or agency.

sunshine rule. Rule that opens a previously closed proceeding to public scrutiny.

surviving spouse. A widow or widower.

* T

take a fix/take a reading. To try to figure out; to attempt an answer.

target. (1) To aim or earmark. (2) Goal.

task. (1) Job. (2) To assign work.

tasker. Memo or other device used to assign a task.

task force. A temporary committee.

thrust. Direction.

time frame. When; a period of time.

trickle-down. To benefit from a law or a program after it has benefited and been filtered through its prime target.

turkey farm. Bureaucratic equivalent of Siberia: a desk with no duties.

* U

underutilized. Not used often.

unsubstantiated rumor. Rumor.

up to speed. Current.

utilization. Use.

utilize. Use.

* V

verbalize. Say.

viable. Workable. This term came into its own when bureaucratese was criticized for its dependence on the word *feasible.*

visualize. See.

W

watchdog. Term used to describe the OVERSIGHT function of commissions, committees, and certain agencies, notably the General Accounting Office, the investigatory arm of Congress.

when deemed appropriate. When okay.

whistle-blower. One who reveals corruption or mismanagement in an organization.

wiggle room. Quality of a public statement that sounds authoritative but is really so vague that the speaker can later change positions and still use the same words. Writing about such statements in the *Washington Post,* Susan Trausch reported, "The phrase 'cautious optimism' has about a mile of wiggle room on either side. So does 'tentative acceptance' and 'he is leaning in that direction.'"

window. Opportunity.

wired. Describing a grant, contract, or job whose winner is predetermined: "They said it was open to new bidders, but we thought it was wired from the beginning."

within the framework of. Within.

Y

your court. Your problem now, from the tennis metaphor of "the ball is now in your court."

Z

zero fund. To not pay for.

zero-sum game. Conflict in which there will be a winner and a loser, but usually initiated by one who will be able to say, "My gain is your loss."

SOURCES

The author has spent the last twenty years inside and just outside the Beltway and is by now fluent in this lingo. The sizable file on bureaucratese in the Tamony Collection was most helpful, as were the suggestions from Chris Keller and Norman Stevens.

---— ✳ 6 ✳ ———

BUSINESS AND FINANCE

Buzzwords for Big Shots

That guy is no lamb at this game, and right now he's a bull on a lot of cats and dogs I'd never suggest you own. He doesn't get hung up in many pups, though, and some of his hot issues in recent years have been real yo-yos.

—Sylvia Porter, recalling the gist of a conversation she had with a broker a few days earlier, her "Your Money's Worth" column of September 17, 1964

I t has long been argued that slang thrives in informal environments. The point is well taken, but it does not explain why the highly structured, formal realm of money management is as slangy as any baseball dugout or high school locker room. After all, this is a realm in which the gray institutions of fiscal responsibility are known as Fannie Mae, Ginnie Mae, Freddy Mac, and the Fed.

✳ A

Acapulco spread. Transaction with multiple commissions that is so complicated and exhausting that, in the words of the *Wall Street Journal,* it will "send the broker winging off to a Mexican vacation."

accordion management. Quickly increasing and decreasing the size of a workforce by using temporary workers.

air-pocket stock. A security whose value has dropped sharply, like an airplane does when it hits an air pocket.

alligator spread. A transaction in which the commissions eat up the profit.

arbs. Arbitrageurs, or those who speculate in the stock of companies with announced or rumored deals.

asset-stripping. Buy a company, sell the assets, dump the employees.

at the market. The current price of a security.

audits from hell. Excruciatingly detailed random tax audits staged to

74

determine patterns of taxpayer compliance with the law.

 B

Baby Bells. The regional telephone companies created as a result of the breakup of Ma Bell—the American Telephone and Telegraph Company.

baby bond. Bond sold in denominations of less than $1 million.

back-end load. A sales charge paid when selling a mutual fund.

back off. Sudden sinking of stock price after a rise.

bag job. Describing a security bought on a rumor that turns out to be false.

bang for the buck. Value or excitement for the money spent.

bar. One million.

basis point. One hundredth of 1 percent.

bazillion. Indefinite enormous number.

bean-counter. An accountant; a statistician.

beard. To act as a front for another.

bear hug. The embrace that a large company puts on another (not always smaller company), one that it is taking over. The term is apt. *Forbes* magazine explained a bear hug this way: "Big companies buy little companies and usually end up destroying the very thing they coveted the small company for."

bear market. One that is going down; a market driven by uncertainty and/or pessimism.

bear raid. Heavy selling of a stock to force its price down so that large quantities can be purchased at the depressed price.

bed and breakfast. Selling a security and buying it back quickly to minimize capital gains taxes.

bedbug letter. Letter from the Securities and Exchange Commission informing a company of the problems or bugs in its registration statement.

belly-up. Out of business; bankrupt. See WENT TOES.

beta. A measure of the volatility of a fund as measured against a known index such as Standard and Poor's 500. A value of over 1.0 means the fund is aggressive and risky, while a value under 1.0 indicates a more stable or conservative fund.

Big Blue. IBM.

big board. The New York Stock Exchange.

Big D. Economic depression, as in this *Newsweek* headline of January 21, 1991: "Is This Just a Recession—or the 'Big D'?"

biggie. Something or someone important.

BIMBO. Short for *buy-in/management buyout.*

birdseed. Insignificant amount of money.

black book. (1) A preplanned defense against a takeover. (2) A database, such as a brokerage firm's black book on junk bonds.

black hole. The discrepancy in the global balance of payments.

black knight. Predator who mounts a hostile takeover bid.

Black Monday. October 19, 1987, when the stock market crashed.

blackout. A provision of an intended merger banning both parties from negotiating with others.

blind pool. A war chest that a company can tap in the event of hostile takeover bids or any other purpose. It is blind because investors commit to it before they know how the money will be used.

blow back. To sell a new issue quickly. This is usually not popular with the underwriter who brought it.

blowout bid. An offer to buy out a company that far exceeds the real value of the company as measured by its outstanding stock. A blowout bid is meant to scare off rival buyers—to avoid the hassle of a bidding war.

blue chip. Common stock in a major corporation with a long-standing ability to generate profits and dividends.

blue-sky laws. State laws created to protect the public from securities fraud. Supposedly the phrase was coined when a judge likened the value of a stock to the value of a piece of blue sky.

bo dereks. Bonds maturing in the year 2010, from Bo Derek's role as the perfect woman in the movie *10.*

boiler room. Room in which fast-talking salespeople, for outrageous commissions or markups, use the phone to sell securities or commodities that are usually over-priced and have poor investment characteristics.

boot. Cash thrown in with stock in an acquisition; a cash sweetener.

box. One's own holdings. To sell short against one's own portfolio is known as "selling short against the box." (See SHORT.)

brass ring. Wall Street partnership.

breakup value. The value of a company after a takeover, as it is broken up for the value of its component parts.

bucketing. Broker arranging a trade for a customer at a higher price than a market open to all bidders would produce.

bucket shop. Dishonest brokerage house that gambles with its clients' stocks, bonds, and other holdings without permission.

Buck Rogers. Securities that enjoy a sudden rise in a short time.

bull market. One that is going up.

burbed-out. Looking very middle class, suburban.

burn someone down. To hand out a worthless stock tip.

* C

cafeteria plan. Benefit plan that allows an employee some alternative choices, as if that employee were selecting dishes in a cafeteria.

callable. Describing some bonds and preferred stocks that can be redeemed—or called—by the issuer before maturity.

candy-store problem. Situation involving a great variety of good choices.

car. A future contract, a legal commitment to receive a commodity at some point in the future. According to *Lamont's Glossary,* prepared by Lamont and Partners of London, this is "a throwback from the days when commodities were transported in railway cars."

cascade. To send information through a company.

cash cow. Enterprise that creates a lot of surplus cash flow, as opposed to paper profits. For instance, in the newspaper business, the newest cash cow is personal want-ad columns. Widely used, the term is being milked to death.

category killers. Huge retailers in specialized consumer areas who, because of their buying power, can offer lower prices than other retailers—Home Depot and Circuit City are two examples.

CATS. Certificates of accrual on Treasury securities. One of several financial "felines," including *TIGRs* (Treasury investment growth receipts) and *LYONs* (liquid yield

option notes). These are house names for zero-coupon (i.e., those that pay interest on maturity), "stripped" Treasury bonds. They are said to be *stripped* because the interest is separated from the principal and sold separately.

cats and dogs. Stocks of unproven value that, among other things, cannot be used as collateral.

CBOE. Chicago Board of Exchange.

CEO. Chief executive officer; the boss. As William Safire has pointed out, in olden times the boss was called the president or chairman.

chainsaw. To disrupt or destroy a business deal.

Chinese Wall. Term characterizing the procedural barriers that prevent information known to people in one part of the business from becoming known to those in another part.

churning. Churning is an illegal practice, by a broker or financial adviser, of frequently buying and selling stocks, bonds, and mutual funds of a client simply to generate commissions.

closed fund. A mutual fund that no longer lets in new investors. This usually happens when the fund has grown so large that it can no longer reach its objectives.

COLAs. Cost of living adjustments.

cold call. A call made to a stranger, often at night, to get the stranger to buy a security or securities.

comfort letter. Letter from an accountant saying that no false or misleading information is in a financial statement.

contrarian. Person who thinks that the market will move in the opposite direction, up or down, from where the majority believes it is moving.

corner. To take control of the price of a security or commodity by obtaining a major interest in it. See SQUEEZE.

Crazy Mary. Community Psychiatric Centers, whose stock market symbol is CMY.

creeping takeover. Gradual accumulation of large amounts of the shares in a company through purchases on the open market.

cut a melon. For a company to declare a large stock dividend.

 D

damager. Manager.

dawn raid. Quick buy of substantial amounts of a company's stock on the market before the market becomes aware that something is going on.

day order. An order given to a broker that is only good for one day.

dead-cat bounce. Small increase in the market averages after a substantial drop.

deduck. A tax deduction.

deep pockets. A reliable source of money.

diddly-squat. Nothing; a big zero.

dividend-capture. Investment strategy in which stocks are bought just before they declare dividends and sold immediately thereafter.

dog. Enterprise that costs more to operate than it produces in income. The opposite of a CASH COW.

downsize. Euphemistic term used to describe layoffs, perhaps one of the most reviled bits of nineties' jargon.

DRIP. Acronym for *dividend reinvestment plan*, which automati-

SAY WHAT?

One of the places where corporate names are most revealing is on the ticker tapes of the major stock exchanges, where the symbols are often models of clarity.

Anheuser-Busch is BUD, Dr Pepper Co. is DOC, Magic Marker Industries is PEN, After Six Inc. is TUX, Nutrition World Inc. (a health food chain) is NUTS, Seagram Co. Ltd. is VO, a restaurant chain featuring potatoes, called 1 Potato 2 Inc., shows on the tape as SPUD, the Boston Beer Co. is SAM (it makes Sam Adams beer), and the Cheesecake Factory is CAKE.

cally reinvests cash dividends from stock into the purchase of new shares of that same stock.

drop-dead fee. Money paid to those who have backed a raider if the raid fails; a kill fee.

ducats. Money.

duck. Any deduction from one's paycheck.

dummy. A member of a board of directors who has no direct interest in the company but represents someone who does; a human proxy.

dump. To unload goods in a foreign country at a low price to prevent a domestic oversupply.

* E

equities. Ownership interest possessed by stockholders in a corporation. Basically, equities are stocks.

ERISA. Employee Retirement Income Security Act.

ESOP. Employee Stock Ownership Plan.

ex-dividend. Without dividend—a stock sold after the dividend has been credited to the previous owner is sold "ex-dividend."

* F

face card. A business leader.

Fannie Mae. The Federal National Mortgage Association.

fast track. Describing the path of quick ascent to the top of the heap.

Fed, the. The Board of Governors of the Federal Reserve System, and the Federal Reserve Bank; constituting the "system."

Fed time. The half hour between eleven-thirty and noon, eastern standard time, when Federal Reserve Banks are, by tradition, most likely to buy and sell securities.

FIFO. Acronym for *first in, first out,* an accounting term used in areas ranging from computing interest to computing inventory value. LIFO stands for *last in, first out.*

fill or kill. The stock-trading equivalent of speak or forever hold your peace.

FILO. Acronym for *first in, last out.*

fixed-income investment. A term that includes bonds, certificates of deposit, and other instruments that pay a fixed rate of interest—as opposed to stocks, where payments vary with a company's profits.

floor. The huge trading area of the New York Stock Exchange.

footsie. The British FT-SE 100, an index of share prices of the one hundred largest UK companies.

friendly takeover. Purchase of a company that is welcomed or unopposed.

front-end load. A sales charge paid when buying a mutual fund.

front run. For a broker to load up

friends and favorite customers on a stock, hype it, then sell it to later customers at a higher price. Illegal.

* G

garbitrageur. Derogatory blend of *garbage* and *arbitrageur,* for those who manipulate rather than simply speculate in stock of companies with announced or rumored deals.

get face. To gain respect.

get off the dime. To get a business deal moving.

get someone's motor running. To sell one's business ideas to another.

get the gate. To be layed off.

GIC. A guaranteed investment contract. An investment product issued by an insurance company where a rate of return is guaranteed for one to seven years, as long as the insurance company has the financial ability to make the payments.

gilt edge. Term used to describe the highest-quality stocks and bonds. The term originated in the British government-securities market.

glass ceiling. The invisible but real limit on women's ascendance in most business hierarchies.

go blooey. A company or stock about to go under.

golden handcuffs. Packaged perks and forms of delayed compensation that keep executives locked into their jobs. To qualify for these benefits, which include annuities and stock purchase plans, the executive must stay in place for a defined time.

golden parachutes. Compensation packages, usually a combination of money and benefits, for executives, providing them with substantial benefits to allay their fears in the event that the company is being taken over or they are fired.

go naked. To sell an option without owning the security to which it is linked or a stock one does not own.

goose job. Forcing up the value of a stock by strategic purchases.

go public. To sell the shares of a private company to the public.

grave-dancer. Someone who profits from another person's business misfortune.

gray knight. An opportunistic bidder intervening in a hostile takeover—less noble than a WHITE KNIGHT.

gray market. Retail operation that falls into the "gray" area between the legitimate and the illegal (or black market).

grease. Extraordinary amount of commission on the sale of a stock because the stock the firm acquired for sale to customers was cheap. This is usually legal.

greenmail. Money paid by a takeover target to a raider to avert a takeover; blackmail of a different sort and color. It is usually paid in terms of a highly inflated stock price.

greenmailer. One who stages a raid so as to be paid to call it off.

GRIT. Grantor-retained investment trust.

GTC order. Order to buy or sell a stock that is "good till canceled."

 H

haircut. The percentage by which specific categories of securities and assets must be reduced—cut back neatly—for the purpose of computing a registered broker-dealer's net capital.

halo effect. The blessing bestowed on a particular stock once it has been purchased by an important player.

hickey. Broker's loss from a customer's failure to deliver a check on a purchase (usually because the price went down by the payment date) or to deliver stock on a sale (for the opposite reason).

Hokey. Nickname for bonds of the Home Owners Loan Corp.

home run. Large capital gain in a stock in a short time.

hoovering. Acquiring stocks as if one were sucking them up with a vacuum cleaner.

hot new issue. A new stock or bond that is met with heavy demand, driving up the market price when it is first offered publicly.

hung up. Unable to sell a security without taking a large loss.

hushmail. Unethical situation in which stock is bought from the director of a company by a raider at a substantial premium in return for the silence of that director.

hype. Excessively exaggerated news on a stock.

 I

iced. A business deal settled once and for all.

ink slinger. The person who signs his/her name to the contract; the person ultimately responsible.

insiders. Top executives, directors, and large stockholders associated with a given stock. The buying and selling of insiders is carefully watched as a judge of the health of a stock.

IPO. Initial public offering.

 J

james bond. A security due in the year 2007, a nickname inspired by the code number of the famous fictional spy.

January effect. Uncanny tendency for small-cap stocks to take off during the first month of the year.

junk bond. Bonds that offer higher yields at the cost of higher risks. They have gained added notoriety because they have fueled takeover bids by providing financing.

* K

killer bees. Firms and outside individuals used to help fight off a takeover. Killer bees include law firms, PR firms, and proxy solicitors.

killer technology. An invention or new technology that renders another invention or technology obsolete.

knockout. Share or shares of Coca-Cola stock whose New York Stock Exchange symbol is KO.

* L

lamb. Inexperienced investor; one given to buying and selling on rumor and questionable tips.

leads. A list of prospects from which a broker works, making cold calls. Brokers sometimes pay for leads or obtain them from some business or industry related to the stocks they're selling.

lemons and plums. Bad deals and good in the lingo of those involved in corporate buyouts. All deals begin as plums.

lettered stock. Restricted stock that cannot be sold unless registered with the SEC.

liar's poker. A game played by bond traders using the serial numbers on dollar bills instead of cards; made popular by the best-selling book of the same name.

LIBOR/LIBID. Acronyms for City of London interbank offer rate or London interbank bid rate.

LIFO. Last in, first out. See FIFO.

LILO. Last in, last out. See FIFO.

Load. The fee, or commission, an investor pays to buy an investment, such as a mutual fund. A front-end load is charged when you buy the product; a back-end load is charged to investors who take their money out before a specified time. "No-load" funds don't charge either fee, and some mutual funds with loads waive them for IRAs and Keoghs.

lollipop. An offer by a company to buy shares from stockholders at a premium, thus avoiding a hostile takeover. Also known as a sugar pill, the opposite of a POISON PILL, but accomplishes the same thing.

London fix. Price given twice each business day by London bullion dealers to set the value of an ounce of gold.

long. A bullish position in which one holds securities in anticipation that they will go up in price. By extension, anything that one has possession of: "This company is long on goodwill and short on cash."

loonie. The Canadian dollar because of the loon on the $1 coin.

LYON. Liquid yield option note. See CATS.

* M

Ma Bell. The American Telephone and Telegraph Company.

Mad Dog. McDonnell Douglas, a nickname that plays off its stock symbol, MD.

magic bullet. Specific, fail-safe solution to a business problem.

melon. Large stock or cash dividend. See CUT A MELON.

meltdown. The October 1987 market crash.

mentor. Senior executive who takes on a younger protégé.

mil/millie. One million.

milk. To pull as much money as possible out of a company or security.

mommy track. Path of a mother and career woman, often seen as "Female career path that is interrupted and slowed by having children."

mortgage-backed. A security whose value is based on a pool of home mortgages.

motors. Shares of General Motors stock.

mouse-milking. Term for an effort that seems too great for the results it generates; for instance, a broker spending a lot of time on a small account.

mullets. Broker's derogatory term for customers.

munchkin. A person of low status in a corporation.

new-issue whore. Brokerage client who wants to get the hot new issues to make a quick profit. See WHORE.

noise. Stock market movement caused by phenomena not reflective of general sentiment. Programmed trading—i.e., that triggered by computer programs—is a prime source of noise.

no-load. Investment that carries no fee for investment but may penalize you with a declining charge over a five-year period, if you redeem. Usually applied to mutual funds.

no-load fund. A mutual fund that sells its shares at net asset value without a sales charge. They're the most popular type among people who do their own investing.

odd lot. (1) A lot of less than a hundred shares, or a bond with less than $100,000 in principal value. (2) Used to describe anything out of the ordinary.

odor lucri. Latin for the smell of money; expectation of gain.

Pac-Man defense. Named after the popular video game, it describes a move in which a target company turns around and tries to swallow the company that is trying to acquire it. Sometimes it works simply because it is an audacious move that scares away the pursuer. It is so named because a key element in Pac-Man is the ability of the pursued to turn on its pursuer.

PALs. Passive activity losses. Tax shelters that use debt and depreciation to create a loss that is deducted against income. See PIGS.

paper profit. An unrealized profit on a security that is still being held.

pard. Business partner.

pencil whipping. Falsifying records, in the parlance of the white-collar criminal.

penny stock. An inexpensive security, usually under five dollars a share, but many in this class sell for under a dollar and are priced in terms of pennies.

PIGs. Passive income generators. Syndicated investments whose earnings are designed to be sheltered by PALS.

pink sheets. Listing of over-the-counter (OTC) stocks that are not always listed in the newspapers. They list all traded OTC stocks.

pip. The smallest unit of any given currency: cents, pfennig, etc.

pit. Where commodities are traded, as opposed to a floor where stocks and bonds exchange hands.

plastic. Credit card(s).

plateauing. Moving sideways in a corporation.

plunge. Reckless speculation.

point. In terms of stocks, equal to a dollar.

poison pill. Making a takeover so unattractive, by diluting a com-

pany's stock, that someone attempting a hostile takeover passes it up. See LOLLIPOP.

porcupine provisions. Legal provisos made to deter takeovers.

privatize. The opposite of going public—that is, converting a publicly owned company into a private one.

product. Goods. "Anyone can talk about computers, but can he move product?"

prudent-man rule. Common-law standard of care by which a trustee or other fiduciary must act to the standard of a man of discretion and intelligence seeking preservation of capital and reasonable profits.

puddle. Item in a company's overall inventory (or pool).

puds. Nickname for bonds of public utility districts.

pups. Cheap, inactive stocks; dogs.

push money. Extra money paid to a salesperson to aggressively sell certain merchandise.

∗ Q

QTIP. Pronounced like the small swab you stick in your ear, it is an acronym for *qualified terminal interest property*—a trust.

quants. Computer technologists working in the financial industry, designing sophisticated investment strategies and computer models; the folks who made "program trading" possible.

quick-and-dirty. A business transaction done rapidly and carelessly.

rag out. To dress in an expensive business suit.

raider. One who swoops down and buys other companies by acquiring large amounts of stock.

ratchet. An incentive arrangement in which managers get a bigger share of equity if the venture performs well.

red herring. Prospectus that cannot be used to confirm the sale of a security because it still lacks clearance from the Securities and Exchange Commission to become the final prospectus, so-called because such documents have a legend so stating, along with two red lines running down the left side and the top of the cover only.

regs. Regulations (written or unwritten) of a company.

REITs. Real estate investment trusts. Pronounced "reets." Mutual funds invested in real estate whose earnings go directly to shareholders and avoid corporate taxation.

rep. Representative, as in "sales rep."

repo. An agreement to sell a government bond for cash together with an agreement to repurchase the bond (on a specified date later) at a higher price reflecting the loan of the cash for a specified period.

resistance level. Dollar level at which a stock or bond seems to stop rising in a rally.

retread. Employee trying out a new career area.

rig. To manipulate a stock.

rightsize. To lay off workers, a term that makes *downsizing* seem downright draconian.

ring the register. Take a profit.

RIPP. Acronym. A reduction-in-personnel plan; a layoff, as in a five-hundred-person RIPP.

roadkill. Company that has been steamrollered by the competition.

rollups. Procedure where limited partnerships are converted into publicly traded entities.

round lot. A hundred shares, or a multiple of a hundred shares, in the case of stock, and for a bond $5,000.

run one's rhymes. To give a sales pitch.

safe harbor. Relief from regulation. Attempts have been made in Congress to allow small companies to have a safe harbor in discussing their future prospects while being relieved from shareholder suits if those prospects do not work out.

Sallie Mae. The National Student Loan Marketing Association.

scenery. A board of directors selected for their status and respectability.

scorched earth. Destructive antitakeover measure by which a company takes steps to make itself less attractive.

screwed, blued, and tattooed. Cheated on a business deal.

seagull model. Term used to describe a consultation in which the consultant flies off, makes a couple of passes over his client, drops a strategy on the client, and returns home.

seat. Membership in a commodities or securities exchange.

securitization. To change any asset into a security, such as loans, credit-card loans, and home mortgages.

shakeout. A period of market activity or crisis that causes small investors to drop out of the market.

shallow river running fast. Describing a stock, stocks, or the whole market moving in response to rumors.

shark. One who attempts a hostile corporate takeover; an avaricious raider.

shark repellent. Any measures that a target company uses to fend off a SHARK; for instance, changing a company's rules to require stockholder approval before a takeover can be accomplished.

short. To sell stocks one does not own, borrowing to make delivery in anticipation of buying the stocks back after a drop in value. In contrast, to be LONG is to actually own stock.

showstopper. Legal move made to thwart a hostile takeover.

skunk works. Backroom corporate think tank convened to foster new ideas.

slam dunk. A stock, usually a new issue, that is supposed to have a quick rise when it opens, so that it can rapidly be sold. A "sure thing."

SLOB. What else but a secured-lease obligation bond?

smidge. Small amount of price: one-eighth of a point (one dollar), for instance.

soft landing. Economic turn of events that avoids recession but achieves a slower period of growth without inflation.

spiff. Extra money paid to a salesperson to aggressively sell certain merchandize.

spot price. In international trade the price of a currency delivered today as opposed to a future, or forward, date.

squeeze. To control the price of a security. See CORNER.

squib. A tiny advertisement; a mention of the company or a product name.

Stalingrad. To snow under with paperwork, or, as Michael M. Thomas explains in *Hard Money*, "Russian winter with subpoenas instead of snowflakes."

Steadman. Term that has become mutual-fund-industry slang for dreadful performance, as in "the fund pulled a Steadman." To get an idea how bad Steadman funds are, consider what Charles A. Jaffe wrote in the *Washington Times* on

September 7, 1995: "If you were to list the ten worst-performing funds the past ten years, all four Steadman funds would be there."

steenth. Short for one-sixteenth of a point in verbal stock and bond reports.

story stock. Stock that is more dependent on a good story than on its balance sheet.

street name. The name of a brokerage house or bank that is put on a stock registration for the benefit of the client who owns it. This makes it easier to buy and sell stock.

stripped. Said of a financial instrument whose interest has been separated from its principal and sold separately. See CATs.

suboptimal. A failure.

sucker rally. Name for a stock rise in the midst of a bear market when sophisticated investors steer clear of the market.

suit. Top businessman or -woman; anyone who is in charge.

swooner. Stock that is particularly sensitive to good or bad news.

System, the. See the FED.

tabbed. Well-dressed.

take away. Measure of success for a business meeting. "I had great take away from our meeting with the sales reps."

take the spear in the chest. To accept full blame for something.

tape watcher. Small investor who monitors his or her investments by watching the transaction tape, whether it be in a brokerage office or on the cable Financial News Network, which runs the tapes continuously.

tapped out. Out of available cash; bankrupt.

target. Object of a takeover bid.

teeny. One-sixteenth of a point.

Texas disease. Epidemic savings-and-loan failure.

thou. One thousand.

thunderbolt thinker. Person with sudden insights that create new business and profits.

TIGRs. Treasury investment growth receipts. See CATS.

tin parachute. Plan guaranteeing employees severance pay—the poor cousin of the GOLDEN PARA-CHUTE.

top tick. To buy a stock at the highest price of the day.

toxic waste. Bonds that go beyond junk bonds.

triple witching hour. One of the four Fridays in each year on which the options and futures contracts expire.

turkey. A lousy deal.

twiggy bond. Thin coverage—from the name of the thin fashion model of the 1970s.

✳ U

ultra. Consumer who demands the best of everything; the upper end of upscale.

up tick. Securities transaction made at a price higher than the last one.

✳ V

velvet. An easy or quick profit.

vulture fund. Pool of investment money used to purchase distressed real estate at cheap prices.

✳ W

walk-in. Brokerage customer who simply walks into the office without an appointment.

war babies. Defense stocks.

wash tub. Bond issued by the Washington Suburban Sanitary District.

went toes. Synonym for BELLY-UP.

whisper stock. Stock in a company that is believed or rumored to be ripe for a major play.

white bread. Dull, unimpressive transaction.

white knight. A friendly suitor who intervenes in a hostile takeover and saves the target company and its assets. An opportunistic second bidder is a GRAY KNIGHT.

white squire. A WHITE KNIGHT who

buys less than a majority interest in the target company.

whore. Customer who wants the hottest new-issue stock coming out so that it can be sold quickly at a profit. Also known as NEW-ISSUE WHORE.

widget. Any unspecified product, commonly used in hypothetical situations: "Say I've got two million widgets and not enough trucks hired to haul them."

wild duck. An innovative employee who has a different perspective.

window dressing. Anything done to make a mutual fund or stock look good just prior to the end of a period, to improve the quarterly or year-end reports sent to stockholders.

with ice. When issued.

wooden ticket. A fictitious trade in an issue that a broker promised to sell, but couldn't get anyone to buy. He will quietly try to cancel the transaction later on.

✳ X

xd. Ex-dividend, pronounced "x.d." It refers to a security after its current dividend has been paid.

✳ Y

Yankee bond. Foreign bond issued in dollars and registered for sale in the United States.

yard. A billion (dollars, yen, units, etc.).

yo-yos/yo-yo stocks. Pricey, volatile

issues that fluctuate wildly in price.

* Z

zero. A zero-coupon bond or one on which interest is not paid until maturity.

zero out. To not pay taxes legally.

zero tick. Describing a security transaction in which the sale price is identical to the previous transaction.

zinger. Paid stock promotion masquerading as an unbiased report.

*

SOURCES

The late Irving Hale and Stephen Brent Wells provided much help in the preparation of this chapter. This glossary was also built from a mammoth pile of clippings from the financial pages, magazines including *Forbes,* and a large collection of financial and business glossaries found in the Tamony Collection. Help was also rendered by *Lamont's Glossary,* prepared by Lamont and Partners of London, a first-rate contemporary guide to the financial terminology used on both sides of the Atlantic. It was helped to some degree by the author's year in a brokerage firm back when Bessie was the nickname for Bethlehem Steel and there was only *one* phone company.

---- ✻ *7* ✻ ----

COMPUTER CYBERSPEAK—
A WEB OF WORDS

Making the Leap From Lurker to Net.personality

The word *Internet* may be the most important new term of the 1990s for the simple reason that it may be the most important development of the 1990s.

Predictably, it is not only spinning off its own rich slang but is becoming a great carrier of American slang. Lexicographer Anne H. Soukhanov, author of the new book *Word Watch: The Stories Behind the Words of Our Lives,* was asked in 1995 what she thought were the most important trends in the English language today. "There are two," she replied. "American English in its everyday form is turning into something equivalent to vulgar Latin. And the slang vocabulary of American English, thanks to the Internet, is expanding all around the world."

On to the cyberslang.

✻ A

AFK. Away from keyboard, one of the many TLAs (three-letter acronyms) common to on-line communications. The Internet is awash in these acronyms and initialisms.

anonymous remailer. A computer that takes E-mail messages, strips the identifying names, and sends them on their way.

AOL. America Online, the leading Internet provider.

aplet. Temporary software applications built into the Internet that allow the user to use such things as elaborate computer animation without owning the software. Aplets have been likened to a park bench that is used by one person after another.

archie. Program that searches archives for particular software titles.

✻ B

backbone. A high-speed line or series of connections that forms a major path within a network.

BAK. (TLA) Back at keyboard.

bandwidth. Originally a technical term referring to the amount of data per unit of time a computer or transmission line can handle. Netters use it as a general description of net traffic, as in, "That was a real waste of bandwidth."

bit-spit. Any form of digital correspondence—text, fax, image— or the act of sending same. "Did you bit-spit that file to Joe?"

bogosity. The quality of being bogus, or something that is bogus—the Internet stand-in for *bullshit.*

bot. Robot program that controls and keeps a channel open.

bozo filter. Program that identifies E-mail from unknown senders and files it in an electronic mailbox. Same as TWIT FILTER.

BRB. (TLA) Be right back.

browser. Generic term for programs that allow a person to navigate and view documents on the Web.

BTW. (TLA) By the way.

Bulletin board system (BBS). A computerized service that connects with your computer by modem and allows you to upload and download files, leave messages (E-mail), and talk to other users. Sometimes called a *host system.*

* C

chat. An area in cyberspace where a group of users can type to each other live—to talk in type. Each message is seen by all the users in a *chat room.*

chat group. A number of Internet users who communicate with each other simultaneously.

client. A client can be a personal computer or one of the class of powerful small computers called work stations.

client-server. Describing many small computers linked together to swap information and work.

community network. A network devoted to local public-interest information and the discussion of local issues.

cybercrime. Internet criminality.

cybercrud. Obfuscatory tech talk.

cyberporn. On-line pornography.

cybersleep. Term created on the spot on August 7, 1996, when America Online crashed, leaving its 6 million subscribers in the lurch.

cyberslut. Woman willing to exchange electronic sexual messages.

cyberspace. The popular word for describing computerized communications. When you enter a bulletin board, you're in cyberspace. The term was coined by novelist William Gibson to describe the area of interaction between a virtual-reality system and a hacker's brain.

cybrarian. Librarians using the Internet in their work.

* D

dialer. Program that automatically dials a telephone number through a modem and connects one machine with another.

domain. The parts of an E-mail address to the right of the @ sign.

dot. The period before the last part of an Internet address, which indicates the type of Internet account. Business accounts are followed by *.com,* government accounts are identified by *.gov,* and military accounts are known as *.mil.* Similarly, bulletin boards—known as newsgroups—have their own identities. Offbeat topics usually begin with *alt.* for *alternative.* Thus, the newsgroups alt.sex.fetish.feet and alt.slick.willy.tax.tax.tax.

Recreational newsgroups begin with *rec.,* followed by the specific topic. For example, rec.kites is for kite-flying enthusiasts.

Subscribers are identified by a series of letters and symbols that look something like this: skip?asu.edu. That's the Internet address for Skip Brand, a graduate student and chief Internet guru at Arizona State University.

downloading. Moving a file via modem from a bulletin board or another computer to your computer.

* E

E-mail. Electronic mail that can be sent and received by your computer via modem. An E-mail message that waits in an electronic mailbox until it's read. The recipient doesn't have to be signed on at the time to receive a piece of E-mail. The Internet allows you to send messages to anyone with an Internet address or an on-line service account.

E-mailbox. The electronic address to which E-mail is sent.

E-mailer. User of E-mail.

emoticon. Punctuation-based symbols used to denote emotion in a message, as in (tilt head to left, then continue reading) :) (smile).

Not everyone is as enamored of the symbols as those who send them; Chet Raymo of the *Boston Globe* for one. Writing in the May 22, 1995, issue, he said, "Then there is the pretentious tendency of E-mailers to use only lowercase type, unconventional punctuation, and those breathlessly silly combinations of punctuation marks called emoticons—typographical smiley faces and frowny faces that are supposed to convey human feeling."

e-zine. Electronic magazine. Different from print magazines. Writing in the *Boston Globe* on June 5, 1996, Michael Saunders said, "The best e-zines offer deep content and take full advantage of the sound and video multimedia gewgaws that print magazines can't reproduce."

* F

FAQ. A frequently-asked-questions list, the document most USENET NEWSGROUPS maintain to keep NEWBIES from wasting BANDWIDTH with stuff everyone else already knows. As the newsletter *Internet News-*

*

SAY WHAT?

Punc Speak

They are called smileys or emoticons and are used as emotional punctuation in on-line correspondence.

Tilt your head slightly to the left to read these punctuation-based symbols.

:) or :-)   Smile, smiley face, or happy face.
D or :D   Big smile; laughing.
:-))   Very happy.
:-))))   Keep smiling.
:-o   Surprised or shocked.
:-}   Ironic smile.
:->   Impish grin.
:/)   Not funny.
:-(or :(Sad.
:(Frowning.
>:->   Angry.
()   Hugging.
((()))   Lots o' huggin'.
[!]   A hug.
:* or :-*   Kiss.
:**:   Returning kiss.
:-J   Tongue in cheek.
:-?   Licking your lips.
8-)   Wearing glasses/sunglasses; or grin with glasses/sunglasses.
B:-)   Wearing glasses/sunglasses on head; or with designer glasses on head.
x->   Laughed so hard my glasses are crooked.
[x,x]   Laughed so hard my contacts broke.
 _/
#-)   Punker in shades.
|-| No way, buster.
0:-)   Angel.
:+>   Blushing sheepishly.
:-$ Biting one's tongue.
:-P or :P   Sticking out her tongue at you.
:-!   Foot in mouth.
:-# or :-Z or :-X or :-x   My lips are sealed; zipping lip.
8(:-)   a propeller head.

L:-) Just graduated.
[:-) Wearing a Walkman.
5:-) Writer is Elvis.
;-) or ;) Winking; winking smile.
:-@ Screaming.
:-0 Shouting.
:-| Strictly neutral.
:-{ Alas, too bad, sorry.
:-Q Nyah, nyah.
:-Q I'm a smoker.
:-] Grim smile.
>:-> devil.
:-& Twisted, wry expression.
:+< Hard night last night.
:-@ Grrr, grrr.
:-o Whispering.
:-0 Put a sock in it.
=(:o+ Mr. T.
:-p Raspberry.
:-3 With handlebar mustache.
:-? Humphrey Bogart, talking out of the side of his mouth with a
     cigarette in place.
:-B Tongue in cheek.
||<| The robot's face.
;^) Woodhead's mark.
Fe) Ironic grin.
:E Vampire.
|:#/ Groucho.
:-u Aside, by the way.
:=| Person with a deviated septum.
:(or :-(Frown.
:-[Severe displeasure.
:-() About to vomit.
>:-o So shocked or surprised that one's hair stands on end.
=):-) Uncle Sam.
=|:-) Abe Lincoln.
:-; Disgusted.
:-B Drooling.
=:) Punker.
(o)(o) Breasts.
:-c or :< Bummed out.
<:-) or <:-(Feeling stupid, or asking a dumb question.

room put it, "Reading the FAQ is a good way to avoid getting FLAMED."

FCOL. For crying out loud.

finger. Internet software term for locating people on other Internet sites.

firewall. Combination of hardware and software separating a local area network (LAN) into two or more parts for security reasons.

flamage. What those newsgroup readers not involved in a FLAME WAR end up wading through.

flame. (1) A hostile response to another user's stupid posting; to make such a response. Those who dare to post a note advertising their vitamin supplements or Amway products on the network risk being "flamed" with sharp messages from other users who resent such commercial intrusions. (2) More recently, *flame* has come to refer to any derogatory comment no matter how witless or crude.

flame bait. A posting intended to trigger a FLAME WAR or flurry of nasty replies.

flame out. To anger someone.

flame war. What you get when one flame begets another. At their worst, flame wars have been known to take over entire newsgroups. They tend to erupt easily, sometimes over very little—mistakes in grammar, for example—burn brightly for a time, then die out. It can be unsettling to be flamed, but it's one way norms are enforced on the Internet.

forum. Electronic subdivision where many users discuss one topic. Forums often contain *rooms,* with even more topics.

FTP. (1) File transfer protocol. Internet procedure that allows you to download text and programs from computers all over the world. Whether you want business software, games, educational programs, or digital photos of *Sports Illustrated* models, FTP lets you transfer the contents of an Internet computer library to your personal computer. (2) *FTP* is also a verb, as in "I'll FTP that new game from Berkeley."

F2F. Face-to-face. One of the rules of NET etiquette is to behave as if you are F2F even if you are a world apart.

F2F world. The world outside the Net.

 ∗ G

g. Grin or giggle. See also SMILEYS.

gate-crashers. Users who barge into a conversation with a bogus message.

gateway. Machine or machines used to relay packages from one network to another.

GMTA. Great minds think alike.

going postal. To send something by SNAILMAIL.

Gopher. Program that searches the Internet for subjects you specify. Instead of wandering around looking for a certain kind of file or program, you send Gopher out to scour the Internet and fetch stuff for you. Gopher tames the Internet for non-computer-junkies. It is being superseded by the WORLD WIDE WEB (www).

 H

hacker. Traditionally an avid user of computers, but in the context of the Internet it refers generally to any traveler on the net.

home page. The first page of a Web site or document, an electronic front door that often includes an index to further information.

 I

icon. A small symbol displayed on the computer screen used to access a program or file.

IMHO. In my humble opinion.

IMHO WIVH. In my humble opinion, which is very humble.

infobahn. Information superhighway, a play on the German "autobahn" highway system.

information superhighway. A Clinton administration buzzword for the convergence of communications technology. It includes not only the Internet but also telephone communications and cable television.

Internaut. User of the Internet.

Internet. A worldwide network linking computers belonging to various individual entities. Strictly speaking, the Internet is for university and research purposes;

its business equivalent is the Alternet, but this term is increasingly rare. Usenet is the recreational end of the Net and is full of specialty newsgroups such as comp.lang.c, rec.arts.comics, and alt.sex.fetish.diapers.

Internet relay chat (IRC). Service that allows you to "chat" in real time with anyone on the Internet. Your comments appear on one side of the screen, the other user's comments on the other. This is the Net's "party room," a forum that allows real-time conversation with a variety of users. This is probably what Mike Doonesbury was logged on to when he was flirting with "Dancer."

Internetter. User of the Internet.

I-way. Short for *information highway.*

 K

kevork. To ban electronically from a site or bulletin board, from the name of Jack Kevorkian, the suicide doctor.

KIBO. Central deity in the parody religion Kibology, created by net prankster James Parry, who goes by the username KIBO. Believed to stem from acronym of *knowledge in, bull out.*

 L

line noise. Electronic transmission interference, resulting in garbage characters.

LMAO. Laughing my ass off.

LOL. Laughing out loud. You use it in "chat" to show that someone has made you chortle.

LSHITIWMP. Laughing so hard I think I wet my pants.

lurker. Someone who reads a forum conversation but doesn't contribute.

lurkerly. Characterized by lurking—the first citation on this term in *American Speech* (winter 1994) is from an Internet message rather than a printed source.

∗ M

mailbomb. (1) To send or urge others to send massive amounts of E-mail to a single system or person, especially with the intent to crash the recipient's system. (2) To fax an endless sheet of black paper to a target thereby using up his paper and ink (toner) supply. (3) Self-multiplying computer notes are also known as mailbombs.

MAM. Middle-aged man/men, describing a male mind-set that is the bane of Internet Help Desks. According to "The Glossary of Internet Terminology and Slang" by Mike Bowen: "For the same reason men cannot stop at service stations and ask directions until their wives threaten to get out of the car and walk, MAM (the age varies from about 19 to just over 106) cannot call the Help Desk and ask for assistance until they are so frustrated and mad, they are ready to bite the heads off chickens."

MEGO. My eyes glaze over.

modem. A device installed in a computer that allows it to connect with other computers or bulletin boards over a telephone line.

Muds. Multi-user dimensions or multi-user dungeons are virtual suites (or cities) where you can "walk" from room to room. MUDs allow dozens of people to hang out in the same place. Most MUDs are used for conference discussions or role-playing fantasy adventure games. They are, for the lack of a better way of putting it, electronic hangouts.

∗ N

navigate. To read and move from place to place on the Net.

net. A network. Usually refers to Internet or USENET.

netiquette. Proper behavior on the Net: on-line etiquette. A basic case in point: all caps are rude. YOU DON'T HAVE TO SHOUT, SO DON'T DO IT. OK?

netizen. Citizen of the Net—newbie and old-timer alike. The term tends to refer to a collective Net consciousness, as in this line from the May 25, 1995, *Computing* magazine: "Netizens are not deterred by the fear, uncertainty, and doubt (FUD) factors related to some alleged snippers or hackers on the highway." Netizen is a blend of the words *Net* and *citizen*.

net.personality. One who posts regularly or extravagantly enough to become famous within a newsgroup or newsgroups.

netrash. Junk sent over the Internet.

netrock. Strident complaint sent over Internet.

netter/nettie. Internet user.

netwriter. One who uses the Internet to send messages.

newbie/newbee. One new to the Net. As in, "Read the FAQ, newbie!"

newsgroup. Any Usenet topic group, usually designated by discussion type (e.g., *comp.* for computer-interest groups, *rec.* for recreational groups, etc.). Among the better-known newsgroups are alt.sex, misc.jobs.offered, and comp.unix.wizards.

NIFOC. Nude in front of computer.

nuts on the Net. Anarchists, plotters, and saboteurs on the Internet. In a *Washington Times* piece, "Internet Becomes Haven for Anarchists," on May 14, 1995, by Arnaud de Borchgrave, the following revelation was made: "Secret Service agents scanning the Internet even before the Oklahoma City bombing had identified what the computer experts considered were eleven credible plots to assassinate President Clinton, according to one of the agency's cybersleuths. Thousands of other threats are simply discounted as the work of 'nuts on the Net,' said the investigator, who spoke on condition his name not be used."

nyetwork. A network when it is acting flaky or is down—from the Russian *nyet* for "no."

OTOH. On the other hand.

phreaking. Using the Net to crack telephone long-distance codes and the like.

PITA. Pain in the ass.

place. A page in hyperspace.

posts. Messages; that which is posted on the net.

PUMG. Puking up my guts—laughing real hard.

quux. An expression of mild disgust.

remailer. Computer that retransmits E-mail messages without identifying the sender.

ROFL. Rolling on the floor laughing—E-mailese for "I find this rather droll."

ROTFLOL. Rolling on the floor laughing out loud; that is, "That was very funny."

*

WHAT'S MOO?

S ome of the topics of discussion in the newsgroup alt.cows.moo. moo.moo:

—> I love cows!
—> Anyone go cow tipping?
—> A cow is a person to another cow
—> Cows are trendy

Some of the topics of discussion in the newsgroup alt.fan.super-big-gulp:

—> I WANT my OPAQUE lids!
—> 7-Eleven in academia
—> More Hollywood appearances

Some of the topics of discussion in the newsgroup rec.arts.bodyart:

—> Typo on tattoos
—> Tongue pierce
—> What to do on job interviews?
—> ITCHING BACKPIECE!!!!

A sample posting from the newsgroup alt.non-sequitur:

—> "Can anyone aspire to wall sockets, or must we resume tropical marsupials first?"

A sample posting from the group rec.humor.funny:

—> "How do you tell an extroverted computer nerd? . . . He looks at your shoes when he's talking to you."

Some of the topics of discussion from the newsgroup alt.animation. warner-bros:

—> Why not Yakko Wakko and Dot?
—> Bugs Bunny versus M. J. Frog
—> Help! Cartoon laws of physics

✻ S

SATAN. Acronym for Security Administrator Tool for Analyzing Networks, it is a tool that has given crypto-anarchists an alarming edge over the intelligence community. This "scout" enables assorted troublemakers on the Internet to find vulnerabilities in seemingly impenetrable electronic "fire walls." In a *Washington Times* piece, "Internet Becomes Haven for Anarchists," on May 14, 1995, by Arnaud de Borchgrave, an unnamed security specialist commented on SATAN: "There is much disinformation on the 'Net specifically designed to overload the circuits of the intelligence and law-enforcement communities and send us scurrying for clues. And yet you never really know what you're dealing with."

search engine. Device enabling user to find things of interest among the hundreds of thousands of Web sites.

send storm. A deluge of private messages received while a user is trying to do something else online.

server. A shared computer on the network that can be as simple as a regular PC set aside to handle print requests to a single laser printer.

site kill file. Name for hypothetical means of blocking messages from a certain computer or part of the network.

smileys. Any facelike illustration made with standard characters used to convey emotion or satirical intent. For example, :) or :-) means "I'm happy" (lean your head to the left, and it looks like a smiley face), while ;) or ;-) means "I'm kidding." Use of noses optional. Also known as EMOTICONS.

snailmail. The U.S. Postal Service to those using E-mail.

spam. To deploy mass postings on the net. Considered in extreme bad taste. According to the February 1996 *Wired* magazine, Spam King Jeff Slaton will flood the net with your message, hitting up to 6 million potential customers, for $425. From the Monty Python song "Spam, spam, spam, spam . . . ," according to computer lore, although there are those who insist it is from the fact that the canned meat Spam splatters messily when hurled. *Spam* is a registered trademark of the Hormel Corporation and is a blending of *spiced* plus *ham.*

spamming. The act of flooding the net, sending the same message to hundreds or thousands of discussion groups.

spider. Software that traverses the Web to find sites of interest to the user.

SPUNK. British slang for semen, it's the largest known "anarcho-computing" directory in Britain. It is one of a number of anarchist sites on the Internet. An anarchist loner with a plan to sabotage a government system can find twenty like-minded people in as many countries—and in as many minutes. The urban guerrilla handbooks of the 1970s have been updated to include electronic sabotage, and the Internet acts as a force multiplier as the latest terrorist how-to course suddenly appears on one or several among the thousands of bulletin boards. Special schools in Europe now teach the techniques of cross-border hacking.

STTNG. *Star Trek: The Next Generation,* a major topic for those on the Net.

surfing. The act of skimming through the Internet, following trains of thought from one network to another.

sysop. System operator; the programmer in charge of a bulletin board.

 T

TAFN. That's all for now.

thread. A series of postings on the same subject to an electronic bulletin board.

TIA. Thanks in advance.

TLA. Three-letter acronym. These are common to on-line communications. See XTLA.

traveler. One navigating the Net.

trolling. Sending a tongue-in-cheek message intended to irritate others.

TTFN. Ta-ta for now! Usually used at the end of a message before signing off.

TTYL. Talk to you later.

twit filter. Computer program that identifies E-mail from unknown senders and files it in an electronic mailbox. Same as BOZO FILTER.

 U

Uploading. Moving a file from your computer to another computer or to a bulletin board via modem.

URL. (pronounced "url") Uniform resource locator, an address on the Web.

Usenet News. Usenet consists of more than 3,500 bulletin boards that span a dizzying topical range . . . current events in Bosnia, Rush Limbaugh, science fiction, philosophy, foot fetishes, you name it. These bulletin boards, called newsgroups, provide a forum for people with common interests to mouth off, argue, and learn from the resulting discourse. "Jeffersonian democracy meets punk anarchy" is how J. C. Herz of Knight-Ridder described it in a 1993 article.

 V

Veronica. Acronym for Very Easy Rodent-Oriented Net-wide Index to Computerized Archives. Database developed at the University of Nevada containing the names of almost every item on thousands of gopher menus.

 W

WB. Welcome back!

Web, the. Also known as the World Wide Web. An information space on the Internet, unified by a common addressing system and distinguished by documents capable of being linked from one computer to another.

Web browser. One who browses the World Wide Web.

webhead. One addicted to searching the Web.

webmaster. Person in charge of a Web site, modeled on the word *postmaster.* Writing on this term in the May 1996 newsletter *The Editorial Eye,* Keith C. Ivey reports, "By the way, *webmaster* seems to be a gender-neutral job title. There are some webmistresses out there, but they are in the minority among women in Web sites."

webmeister. Super web expert; guru of the Net.

WTG. Way to go!

www. Electronic address for the World Wide Web.

XTLA. An eXtended TLA (three-letter acronym).

SOURCES

The Internet Literacy Consultants' "Glossary of Internet Terms," "The Glossary of Internet Terminology and Slang," copyrighted by Mike Bowen, an unsigned "Web Terminology Glossary," and a half dozen additional Internet glossaries were most helpful in the preparation of this chapter.

Some definitions are drawn from *Downsizing Information Systems* (Carmel, Ind.: Sams Publishing, $39.95), one of a trio of valuable reference books written by Steven Guengerich and other experts at BSG Consulting, a systems integration company based in Houston. The winter 1994 issue (vol. 69, no. 4) of *American Speech* contained a major listing of Internet terms in the "Among the New Words" section by John and Adele Algeo.

A number of sources were used in gathering the emoticon collection, including *Newsweek,* March 9, 1992, Mike Stackpole's files, and the August 1995 issue of *Boston Computer Currents.*

* 8 *

COMPUTERESE DOWNLOADED

What Do You Say to a Chiphead?

The Chipheads Are (Sigh) Winning

—Headline in the *San Francisco Examiner,*
January 3, 1983

The personal computer created a revolution. It also created an odd means of expression through which it seemed everything got renamed. The TV screen became a monitor, writing became word processing, and a list of options became a menu. Not enough to call something portable, computers came out as laptops, palmtops, notebooks, and the odd subnotebook.

It also embraced an odd proclivity for misnomer: floppy disks that are hard, hard copy that is floppy, peripherals that are central, and global searches that are intensely localized. As if to tweak the noses of the language purists, the computerists converted large numbers of nouns into transitive verbs—*to format, to access, to array, to input, to output, to interface,* to name but a few.

Many things were given other names, yielding no little confusion among those who don't know a computer mouse from Mickey Mouse, a byte from a bite, and thought that a hard drive is leaving work at rush hour.

Computer slang is, in a word, quirky. Traditionally, this country has created great slang. Whether you were talking about lumberjacks, hoboes, GIs, or short-order cooks, you were talking about people with a rich, colorful slang. But then came the computer revolution, and with it a less than dynamic slang—at least at first. But as computers got smaller and cheaper, all sorts of people got into the act, and soon there was a burgeoning slang that even included terms created by outlaw hackers.

Here is a heavy sampling, including some that no longer sound like slang to those who are at home in the world of bits, bytes, Ks, and modems.

Speaking of modems, this device created a new universe through the Internet. The previous chapter contains this new slang, which is growing at supersonic speed. Computers had been upstaged by the Net, which, seemingly overnight, had its own culture with its own language.

Meanwhile, back to the computer slang, which in the face of the Internet is beginning to have a slightly quaint sound to it.

* A

AAC. Alter all commands, one of the many letter codes used by hackers and programmers. Dozens more are salted through this chapter.

AAR. Alter at random.

AB. Add backwards.

abend. An *ab*normal or *ab*ortive *end.* This is what can happen when a machine is fed bad data or shut down before it completes a routine.

abterm. *ab*normal *term*ination, same as ABEND.

AFFB. A force-five belch, allegedly humorous hacker initialism.

AFVC. Add finagle variable constant.

AIB. Attack innocent bystander, to hackers who speak in initialisms.

algy. *Algorithm* for short.

antidote. Program or programs used to protect computers from a computer virus. These programs tend to have apt names like Vaccine, Flu Shot, and Syringe.

Apple Orchard, the. IBM corporate headquarters in Armonk, New York, a site that was once an apple orchard.

architecture. The selection and interrelationship of components of different kinds of computer systems.

ASCII. American Standard Code for Information Interchange; the 128-character standard used by most computers.

A.T. It originally stood for Advanced Technology, an IBM Corp. PC that uses an 80286 chip. Now any 80286 chip.

AWTT. Assemble with Tinkertoys.

* B

BAB. Bourbon and branch water.

BAC. Branch to Alpha Centauri.

back door. A hole in computer security deliberately left by designers, also known as a TRAP DOOR.

BAF. Blow all fuses.

bagbiter. Something or someone that has created problems.

banana problem. Not knowing when to bring an activity to a close. It comes from the old joke about the child who knew how to spell *banana,* but didn't know when to stop.

bandwidth. The capacity of a circuit or other medium that carries information, such as the "bus" of a computer. The higher the bandwidth, measured in cycles per second, the more information can be processed. "Bill Gates is a high-bandwidth kind of guy."

barf. To fail or malfunction.

baud. Measurement, in bits per second, of the speed by which computers move data from one place to another. Also called BPS.

BDC. Break down and cry.

BDT. Burn data tree.

bead. A small program module.

bells and whistles. Unessential, but often alluring, features. Sometimes the words *and gongs* is added to the phrase for emphasis.

beta. The final stages of development before a product is released to market. "The software is in beta" means it is in advanced development (after alpha, or preliminary development). "Her baby is in beta" means she is expecting soon. In the software industry, beta has been known to last a year or more.

beta test. The first tests of new software outside the company that developed it (where the company did the alpha testing).

big iron. Mainframe computers. This term was in common use at IBM.

bit. The smallest unit of information, represented by an 0 or a 1. It is a compression of the words *bi*nary digi*t*.

black box. Small piece of equipment that will make everything work right.

black-box approach. To accept computed results without questioning the method used to get those results.

blem. Problem, possible blend of *ble*mish plus probl*em*.

blue. An IBM computer, from the Wall Street nickname Big Blue for IBM. A "true-blue shop" is a computer center where all the equipment comes from IBM.

blue collar. Computer working in a factory.

bluespeak. Jargon of those who work for IBM, which is a sizable language unto itself. The tenth edition of the "IBM Jargon and General Computing Dictionary," which was published in 1990 at IBM UK, contained more than 1,400 entries. More than a mere vocabulary, its editor called it "a window on the IBM culture." Some examples were also contained in the September 27, 1993, issue of *Business Week*.

boat anchor. Old computer of dubious utility.

Bogon. A person who is bogus or says bogus things. A Bogon is also a mythical subatomic particle bearing the unit charge of *bogosity*. These related terms were brought to national prominence by *The Hacker's Dictionary*.

bogosity. The degree to which something is bogus. See BOGON.

bomb. To fail or malfunction. Bombing is less than crashing; that is, a program may bomb, but a system crashes.

boot. To start. To restart is to reboot. The term is short for *bootstrapping*, alluding to the bootstrap loader, a small program that when

✳

SAY WHAT?

In 1993 when a new president took over at IBM, he vowed to get rid of some of the language that was particular to that one company. First off the bat, he banished the IBMism *LOB* (line of business). Here are other examples of bluespeak that have escaped from the inside:

all blue. Describing a customer who has bought all of its equipment from IBM.

blue glue. That which binds IBM components together.

boil the ocean. To attempt something too ambitious, as in, "He's really boiling the ocean on that problem."

drink from a fire hose. To be at the receiving end of a flood of information.

eat one's lunch. To consume personal time.

exterior wet conditions. Rain. This term was once used by an IBM division to explain why it had not conducted a fire drill.

flatten. To resolve an issue, as in, "We have to flatten this before tomorrow's meeting."

goat-roping. A gathering of the key players needed to resolve an issue, as in, "We'll have to have a goat-roping on this PC pricing strategy."

hypo. A high-potential employee, generally destined for management.

IBMois. French version of bluespeak.

milk a mouse. To pursue a trivial issue.

nonconcur. To disagree.

open kimono. To go open kimono is to reveal everything to another.

panoota. To guess, to estimate. Originally from the acronym *pull a number out of the air.*

pay for the coffee. To suffer mild pressure.

reswizzle. To improve something, as in, "Frank's boss asked him to reswizzle his foils." Synonym: to tweak.

ROJ. Retired on job, applied to those not pulling their loads.

sheep dip session. Sales seminar.

side sucker. Program that uses an intemperate amount of system resource.

slope shoulders. To refuse to take responsibility for a problem.

tip of the ice cube. Visible part of something small and insignificant.

tired iron. Old data-processing equipment.

uncork. To make an internal problem public.

moved into memory will load the rest of the system.

bootstrap. A small program that gets the computer up and running. Metaphorically, all of this harks back to the image of one pulling himself or herself up by his or her bootstraps.

boudoir. An area containing a coupled processor and memory. An area where the processors and memory elements are separated is called a dance hall.

box. A computer.

bozotic. Absurd, from Bozo the clown.

BPS. Bits per second; see BAUD.

breadboard. A board on which experimental electronic circuits can be laid out.

bridgeware. Hardware or software that serves as a bridge between one kind of system to another.

bug. An error, defect, or problem; cleaning up such a program is called debugging. Navy computer pioneer Grace Hopper has claimed that the term was coined in 1945 by her team, working on the Mark II, the first large-scale American computer. It was created in response to a glitch that occurred when a two-inch moth got stuck in one of the Mark II's relays.

The term had been used before to describe an error or failure, but this was its first application to computers. Hopper taped the original bug to the page of her logbook for the day on which it was dislodged from the machine.

bulletproof. Said of a program that is safe from both hackers and the inept.

burn in. To run a computer or software for a certain time, usually at least twenty-four hours, to ensure it is not faulty.

burst. To tear printer paper along its perforated line, as in, "Print and burst that report please."

bus. The physical and electronic connections that allow data to move where it needs to be in a computer. Sometimes used interchangeably with ARCHITECTURE, as in "AT. bus."

byte. Eight bits. It is the standard unit of computer information. See CHARACTER.

 C

card. (1) Printed circuit. (2) A cybernetic age ago this term referred to the punched computer cardboard card with the timeless admonition, "Do not bend, fold, spindle, or mutilate."

careware. Type of shareware for which part of the registration fee goes to charity.

CBNC. Close but no cigar.

CH. Create havoc.

chad. Specks of paper that drop out of a computer card or paper tape when it is punched. Obsolete today, the term *chad age* is used among old-timers in the computer business to allude to the period prior to 1975 when the data-processing world was awash in chad.

character. A letter, number, symbol, or space. A character is equivalent to one BYTE. *The Hacker's Dictionary,* by Guy L. Steele and others, points out the elaborate hacker vocabulary for the various keyboard symbols. For instance, the number symbol (#) is called a "hash mark, MESH, CRUNCH, [and] pigpen," and the exclamation (!) is variously verbalized as "EXCL, exclam, BANG, SHRIEK, [and] WOW."

chip. An integrated circuit on a wafer slice, usually made from silicon.

chiphead. Computer enthusiast. Listen to Sandy Grady writing on this term in the *San Francisco Examiner* (January 3, 1983): "The human race, you see, is now divided into Chipheads and Squareheads. The Chipheads—and there are millions of them—think computers are changing the world. A Chiphead will rhapsodize endlessly about his Atari or Osborne or IBM. A Chiphead swears computers are the greatest things since food and sex."

chomp. To fail or lose, or, as stated in *The Hacker's Dictionary,* "to chew on something of which more was bitten off than one can."

chrome. Fancy, flashy features.

client. (1) A personal computer. (2) One of the class of powerful small computers called work stations.

clone. (1) *n.* Generally a cheaper computer copy that operates identically to a name-brand (IBM or Apple) unit. There are also software clones. (2) *v.* To make a copy.

closed architecture. Equipment specifically designed to work only with the accessories made by the same company.

CMD. Compare meaningless data.

CML. Compute meaning of life.

CNB. Cause nervous breakdown.

coffee break. Unscheduled failure.

COLB. Crash for operator's lunch break.

cold fault. Any malfunction or fault that is apparent as soon as the machine is turned on.

compuspeak. Jargon of chipheads: cyberbabble.

computer virus. See VIRUS.

connectivity. The ability of computers to talk to each other; generally applied to communication among different computer architectures. (Interestingly, software people usually say "connecTIVity"; hardware people usually say "CONnectivity.") In this regard, the "connector conspiracy" is the tendency of manufacturers to come up with new products that are not compatible with old ones.

core dump. To unload a computer's main memory or—by extension—to get something off your chest. Also *dump.*

CPU. Initialism for *central processing unit;* it is the electronic brain of any computer system.

crack. To gain unauthorized access to a computer; a more correct term than *hack* in this situation because the person is cracking the system in the sense that a safecracker breaks into a strongbox or safe.

cracker. One who is adept at breaking into computer systems: a hacker with a criminal bent.

crash. (1) To stop working; to freeze up. (2) A major malfunction resulting in the loss of information.

CRASH. Continue running after stop or halt.

creeping featurism. The tendency for a complicated program to become more so as new features are added.

crippleware. Software infected with a virus or viruses, as in, "I had better things to do than sort through 650 megs of crippleware looking for the problem."

CRT. Initialism for *cathode-ray tube;* the computer screen.

cruftware. Cruddy software or hardware.

crufty. (1) Bad, poorly built. (2) Yucky, such as ketchup smeared on one's keyboard.

crunch. To process or compute routinely.

CS. Crash system.

CSL. Curse and swear loudly.

cursor. Movable screen character—usually a vertical dash or a small square—that indicates where the next character will be generated.

cuspy. Excellent.

CVG. Convert to garbage.

cybercrud. Cybernetic bullshit; hype.

cyberizing. Bringing someone into the electronic universe.

cyberphobe. One with a fear of a the computer.

cyberpunk. High-technology enthusiast with, as a writer for the *Los Angeles Times* put it, "futuristic ideas and outlaw nature."

* D

daisy wheel. A print wheel on which type is positioned like the petals on a flower. They are used on some printers that rely on the impact of type on paper.

daughterboard. A small circuit board directly attached to the MOTHERBOARD.

DBZ. Divide by zero.

DDC. Dally during calculations.

DDT. A debugging program, from the name of the famous insecticide.

deadlock. Stoppage created when two computer processes wait for the other to do something. In some circles this is referred to as a deadly embrace. See HANG.

debugging. See BUG.

default. A preset value for a variable. For instance, the default in a word-processing program might be to double-space each line of text.

diddle. To work aimlessly; not seriously.

digerati. Digital equivalent of literati, it is a reference to a group of people who are especially knowledgeable about the digital revolution.

digizines. CD-ROM–based periodicals.

disk farm. Massive data-storage facility, such as those maintained by the National Aeronautics and Space Administration.

display. What you look at while working on a computer; the CRT, or monitor.

dithering. The substitution of black-and-white dots for shades of gray in computer graphics. It can be used to make curving patterns less jaggy.

DLN. Don't look now. Along with the next two entries, one of the many three- and four-letter codes used to convey nontechnical comments and insults.

DMPE. Decide to major in phys ed.

DOC. Drive operator crazy.

docs. documentation; the instruction manual.

dogwash. Crisis in hackerspeak, as in, "Is this a real dogwash?"

dongle. Any silly device hanging from or attached to a computer. It comes from a small device—seldom used these days—that attached to one of the ports of the computer to prevent nonauthorized people from pirating programs.

dot matrix. Printing system that uses tiny dots to form characters and images.

down. Said of a system that has crashed; out of order.

downsizing. The process of moving from big computer systems to smaller ones, also called rightsizing. This is the same *downsizing* (see chapter 6) that was applied to firings in the 1990s (and called dumbsizing by those who are suddenly out of work).

downtime. Period during which a computer is out of operation.

DPMI. Declare programmer mentally incompetent. Along with the next two items, part of the nontechnical shorthand of computerdom.

DPR. Destroy program.

DTC. Destroy this command.

DUD. Drive user to drink (free with Windows).

dump. See CORE DUMP.

DW. Destroy world.

DWIM. Do what I meant.

✳ E

EBRS. Emit burned-resistor smell.

ECO. Electrocute computer operator.

EIAO. Execute in any order.

EIL. Execute infinite loop.

electronic bulletin board. Information offered on a computer not attached to a network. Each bulletin board stands alone and has its own phone number.

electronics hobbyist. Term used facetiously and euphemistically for and by those who have gotten into cybernetic mischief, such as illegally breaking into a secure system.

elegant. Describing a solution that is uncluttered and smooth; not clumsy. See KLUDGE.

E-mail. A message written on a computer, sent over a system, and deposited in an electronic mailbox until it's read. The recipient doesn't have to be signed on at the time to receive E-mail.

EMIF. Erase most important file.

encryption. To scramble information with a code or password so that other people can't read it.

end user. The person who buys and/or uses the computer, known as a *user* in other realms.

ENF. Emit noxious fumes.

EPB. Execute program bug.

EPI. Execute programmer immediately.

ethernet. A local area network standard that uses radio frequency signals carried by coaxial cables.

execute. To run a program.

expert system. A program that mimics the intelligence of a human expert in a specific field of knowledge, such as mining or medicine.

* F

face time. Meeting held with an actual person rather than over terminals.

feep. The soft beeping sound that a computer terminal makes when it is booted.

firmware. Elements of a computer system that are neither hardware nor software, usually a program burned into ROM.

FKEY. Keys on a computer keyboard that can be given different interpretations depending on the program one is using. The letter *F* in *FKEY* refers to the word *function.*

flavor. Variety.

FLI. Flash lights impressively.

floor sort. A split-open box of computer cards—now largely obsolete slang.

floppy disk. An encapsulated sheet of plastic that is used to store information. Because of the stiff plastic jacket in which they are locked, they are not the slightest bit floppy. They come in several sizes with the larger five-inch version fast becoming obsolete.

flyback. The time it takes for the cursor to go from the end of one line on a computer monitor to the beginning of the next.

footer. That which consistently appears at the bottom of the page in word processing. See HEADER.

footprint. Floor or desk space taken up by a computer or printer.

freeware. Copyright software available free of charge.

freeway. Public domain software.

friction feed. A method of moving paper by pressing rollers against the page and spinning them.

frobnitz. An unspecified physical object; a widget.

fry. To fail; to become inoperable

The Hacker's Dictionary adds, "Said especially of smoke-producing hardware failures."

FSM. Fold, spindle, and mutilate.

FUD/FUD factor. Initialism for *fear, uncertainty, and doubt,* which is applied to the idea of recommending or buying unknown hardware or software; part of what keeps IBM so profitable.

fuzzification. The process of making fuzzy.

fuzzify. To convert to FUZZY LOGIC. To convert back to crisp nonhuman logic is to *defuzzify.*

fuzzy logic. Logic based on the premise that statements may not all be true or false: the modeling of computer reasoning on the kind of imprecision found in human reasoning.

* G

garbage. Unwanted data. To amass this data in a separate file, disc, or buffer to make room for more is to make a "garbage collection."

gateway. The connecting computer link that translates between two different kinds of computer networks.

GCAR. Get correct answer regardless.

GDP. Grin defiantly at programmer.

gearhead. Programmer.

gig. *Gigabyte* or 1,073,741,824 bytes.

gigabyte. About 1 billion bytes, often abbreviated as GB.

GIGO. Garbage in, garbage out—that is, solutions from bad data will also be bad.

glitch. A flaw. It differs from *bug* in that bugs tend to appear in software while glitches appear in hardware. A loose wire is a glitch. (This is an interesting distinction, given that the first BUG [see] was in hardware.)
   Also, a sudden interruption in electrical service.

global. Describing a search that covers an entire file; for example, looking for all instances of a given name.

gooie. Acronym-based term for *GUI* or *graphical user interface.*

graunch. A devastating error.

gray market. The not quite legal buying and selling of computers through nonauthorized dealers.

gritch. To complain, believed to be a blend of *gripe* plus *bitch.*

grok. To understand. The verb made its terrestrial debut in Robert A. Heinlein's *Stranger in a Strange Land.*

gronk. To clear a machine that has been jammed or WEDGED.

gronked. Inoperative. It can be applied to people when they are sick or exhausted.

gronk out. To stop working.

groupware. Network software.

growzy. Describing a computer that is slow to respond to commands.

Said to be a blend of *grumpy* and *drowsy.*

gubbish. Junk; bad data—a blend of *garbage* and *rubbish.*

GUI. Pronounced "gooie," it is an acronym for *graphical user interface.*

gulp. Multiple bytes, a play on words.

guru. An expert. Implies not only wizard skill but also a history of being a knowledge resource for others.

gweep. User.

∗ H

Hack. A term at the heart of computing slang, with many shades of meaning, including the twelve meanings given in *The Hacker's Dictionary.* The most common verb-form meanings are to work quickly, to work cleverly, to use a computer for pranks or deception, and to work aimlessly (as in hacking around).

hack attack. A period of frenzied programming.

hacker. (1) One who enjoys getting into the details and creative side of computing, as opposed to one who simply uses a computer. For hackers, there are even greetings (such as "How's hacking?") and farewells (such as "Back to hacking"). (2) A genius programmer. (3) One devoted to the computer enterprise to the point of excluding normal social and working life. (4) A malefactor who can range from a fun-loving but irritating prankster to a bona fide cybernetic criminal. It is this definition that infuriates the good hackers. A writer to the British computer magazine *Computer Weekly* protests, "It was hackers who were responsible for the creation of Unix and the Internet, and they are not the people using these systems for illegal purposes."

hair. Difficulty.

handshake. An introductory exchange of electronic signals.

hang. To wait—sometimes interminably, as in a DEADLOCK or *deadly embrace.*

hard copy. Printed version of what appears on the computer screen; printout.

hard disk. Rigid platter used for storing computer data magnetically. The speed and storage capacity of a hard disk is much greater than that of a floppy disk. Unlike a floppy disk, a hard disk is seldom removable.

hardware. (1) Equipment: the computer, disk drivers, monitor, etc. (2) The broader category of physical capital, the physical machinery necessary to computation.

hardwired. A circuit designed to do one specific task—by extension, a person with a narrow and rigid view of his or her job. "Those folks at the Department of Motor Vehicles are really hardwired."

hash. Unwanted or meaningless data.

header. That which consistently

appears at the top of the page in word processing. Its corresponding element at the bottom of the page is called a footer.

heat sink. Piece of metal with small fins that draws heat away from computing chips that get hot.

hedgehog. Person whose abilities are limited to one machine or program.

home. The starting position for the cursor on a screen; usually in the upper left-hand corner.

home page. The main point of entry into a multimedia program, usually with icons representing the largest categories into which the contents have been divided.

host. The controlling unit in some computer networks; usually refers to a MAINFRAME computer, which refers to the huge processors—fewer and fewer these days—set in large frames.

housekeeping. Routine chores—cleaning up files, getting rid of unneeded material, backing up, etc.—that have nothing to do with problem solving per se.

hungus. Large, unmanageable, humongous (from which it appears to derive).

hygiene. Describing steps taken to prevent systems from being infected by a computer virus. A tenet of computer hygiene is not trusting foreign data or other people's machines.

* I

IB. Insert bug.

icon. A command in pictorial form

pioneered by Apple Computer and adopted by Microsoft Windows. Click a mouse on it and the program opens.

IDE. Integrated drive electronics, a type of interface for controlling hard drives.

IFM. Is it a full moon?

incantation. Any particularly arbitrary or obscure command that one must mutter at a system to attain a desired result.

Internet. A global computer network of thousands of smaller networks, linked so they can share information. (NB. A separate glossary for Internet slang and jargon appears in this book as chapter 7, the previous chapter.)

ISC. Insert sarcastic comments.

J

jitter. The brief instability of a signal—not enough to cause a crash.

joystick. An input device, used primarily in computer gaming, that gives the computer directions by tilting a stick. Like its namesake, the aviator's joystick of World War II, it is a reference to the erect male member.

JTZ. Jump to twilight zone.

Juice a Brick. To recharge a big Nicad battery.

* K

K or kilobyte. A thousand BYTES. Often used as a unit to measure how much information a computer can store at one time. It is also used to measure the size of a file or program. One K equals 1,024 letters or characters. *K* is always written in uppercase.

killer app. An applications program that is so compelling that people begin lusting to own PCs. Spreadsheet programs were early killer apps.

KISS. Short for *keep it simple stupid,* a long-established bit of computer dogma and graffiti.

kludge/kluge. (1) A clumsy solution to a problem; a jury-rigged piece of hardware. (2) A clever programming trick intended to solve a particularly nasty case in an expedient, if not clear, manner. Pronounced "klooje," it is the opposite of *elegant,* a term sometimes used to describe a skillful, neat solution.

 L

LAP. Laugh at programmer.

launch. To start an applications program running; commonly used by Macintosh users.

learning curve. The time it takes to learn something in the computer world.

letter-quality. Said of a printer that produces letters that are as good as those produced by an old-fashioned portable typewriter.

liveware. People, especially technicians, users, etc., found around computer systems.

logic board. Apple-speak for MOTH-ERBOARD.

logic bomb. Outlaw term. A computer virus whose effects are triggered and felt when a certain result is specified during routine computation.

LPA. Lead programmer astray.

 M

Macintoy. Macintosh.

macro. A program within a program.

magic. Too complicated to explain, as in, "How does it do that?" Answer: "Magic."

mailbomb. To send or urge others to send massive amounts of E-mail to a single system or person, especially with the intent to crash the recipient's system.

mainframe. A large computer rapidly becoming obsolete with the growing efficiency and power of minicomputers. The name comes from the big bulky frame holding the machine.

masquerading. Assuming the identity of another to get into a system.

master/slave arrangement. When one device (a slave) is controlled by another to which it is connected (a master). Master/slave arrangements are found in disk-drive arrays and other hardware configurations.

MAZ. Multiply answer by zero.

MDE. Mindless data entry.

meatware. The human body.

meg/megabyte. A million bytes, for short.

menu. Listing of options; a table of contents.

Michelangelo. Virus that remained dormant in a computer until March 6, 1992, named after the Italian Renaissance artist. It created great dismay, although it did not live up to its advance billing. So many viruses are out there—a 1995 census identified 2,900 of them—that only those with interesting names and stories make news.

mickey. Unit of displacement for— what else?—a computer mouse.

micro. PC. Generally speaking, a micro—or microcomputer—implies a single user, while a mini has many.

mindshare. To discuss an idea or issue: "Let's mindshare on that one."

mini. A minicomputer; a midrange machine between a PC and a mainframe.

mips. Acronym from *million instructions per second;* a measure of a computer's processing capability.

mnemonic. A way of naming something that helps you remember its purpose, as in *Alt-F-S,* which is a keyboard *file save* command in Windows.

moby. Immense, as in Herman Melville's *Moby Dick.*

mode. State of. For instance, *The Hacker's Dictionary* says that *night mode* is "the state a person is in

when he is working at night and sleeping during the day."

modem. Short for *modulator/ demodulator;* a piece of hardware that allows two computers to "talk" to each other over a phone line.

modem pilot. PC operator who engages another in simulated aerial combat by modem.

monospacing. Uniform and equal spacing between the letters of words.

morph. To undergo transformation from one set of graphic characteristics to another on screen by use of computer technology. The term is a contraction of the word *metamorphosis.*

motherboard. Circuit board to which the main processor chip, memory, and slots for additional cards are attached to form the guts of a computer. See LOGIC BOARD.

mouse. A small electromechanical box with a button or buttons that is attached to a computer by a tail-like cable. As it is moved across a desk, the cursor moves across the computer screen. A button on the mouse is pushed to give commands.

MTBF. Mean time between failures—how long it takes for a chip or other element of hardware to break down.

multitasking. The ability to run several programs at once.

mung. To change irrevocably or to destroy, such as, "I really munged that program." In *The Book of Jar-*

gon, Don Ethan Miller points out that this term began as an acronym of *mushed until no good.*

mutation engine. VIRUS type—deemed by *Newsweek* in its March 16, 1992, issues to be the "scariest new virus."

MW. Malfunction whenever.

MWT. Malfunction without telling.

 N

n. A number, usually a large one.

neat hack. (1) Clever technique or deed. (2) Practical joke.

nerdling. Immature hacker.

nerd pack. Plastic shirt-pocket protector pack in which one keeps pens and pencils.

newbie. A new computer user.

nibble. Half a byte; a four-bit word. Sometimes written *nybble,* presumably to match BYTE.

number crunching. Repetitive, routine numerical calculating. A computer or person employed to do this kind of work is sometimes called a number cruncher.

 O

OBC. Omit backup copies.

off-the-shelf. Standard program or piece of equipment that has not been customized or tailored for a specific group of users, nor needs to be. The military refers to it with the acronym *COTS* for *common off-the-shelf.*

OML. Obey Murphy's Law, which holds that "anything that can go wrong, will." It is used as a reminder that these machines and their operators are disaster prone.

open architecture. Describing an expandable system that allows for the easy replacement and upgrading of circuit boards. It also implies that you can use boards made by third parties.

orphan. (1) Computer system that gets no software support from its parent company. Orphans are usually created because the manufacturer has gone out of business or because the company has abandoned a line of computers. Examples: the Apple Liza and everything with the names Kaypro, Morrow, Sinclair, and too many others to recall. (2) Odd programs and bits of software that are in your computer. An article in the *Montgomery* (Md.) *Journal* on a new program to clean computers of odd files carried the headline "Windows Cleaner-Upper Finds and Kills Orphans."

 P

paste. To insert an item such as text, graphics, or records from a database and numbers from a spreadsheet previously cut or copied from elsewhere.

PC. Personal computer; generally taken to mean one compatible with an IBM PC.

PEHC. Punch extra holes in cards.

peripherals. Anything that connects

to the computer, including disk drives, screens, and printers, or, as defined by John Held in the *Washington Post,* "what you discover you also need if you go to buy a personal computer."

phage. A program that modifies other programs or databases in unauthorized ways.

phreaking. Gaining illegal access to phone lines.

pixels. Tiny dots that comprise the characters on a computer screen. The greater the number of pixels, the better the quality of the image.

pizza box. Low-profile desktop computer, usually with a monitor on top.

planar/planar board. IBM-speak for MOTHERBOARD.

PLOKTA. Acronym for *press lots of keys to abort.* To press random keys in an attempt to get some response from the system. One might plokta when the abort procedure for a program is not known, or if trying to figure out if the system is just sluggish or really in bad shape.

plug-and-play. Term meaning that you add the card or peripheral; the computer automatically figures out how to make it work with your system.

P-mail. Physical mail, as opposed to E-mail. Also, *snailmail.*

pnambic. Relating to a process whose apparent operations are, in part or in whole, false. It is a semi-acronym from a line from the movie the *Wizard of Oz:* "Pay no

attention to the man behind the curtain."

PNRP. Print nasty replies to programmer.

ports. Connectors through which the computer sends and receives data to and from other computers, printers, keyboards, etc.

power user. Someone who may not be as proficient as a hacker but knows how to get the most out of his computer and software and is experienced and adept at problem solving.

prompt. Signal from the computer telling the user that it is ready to take a command. A prompt can take various forms from a blinking cursor to a full question stated in plain English.

propeller heads. Programmers.

put more lipstick on the pig. To make cosmetic changes on a software program to make it more appealing to consumers.

∗ Q

QBE. Query by example. A technique by which a user shows a program how to ask questions of a database to get information.

∗ R

RA. Randomize answer.

RAM. Random-access memory. Chips on which data are stored temporarily as the computer is working. That information is wiped out when the machine is turned off. See ROM.

RCB. Read commands backward.

RDA. Refuse to disclose answer.

reality check. The simplest kind of test of software or hardware; doing the equivalent of asking what 2 + 2 is and seeing if you get 4.

release. A particular version of a piece of software, such as Wordstar 6.0 or Word for Windows 6.

resident. That which exists in memory, generally taken to mean in RAM and therefore not permanent.

rich text format. A type of file format, usually readable by most major word processors.

RLI. Rotate left, indefinitely.

ROD. Roll over and die.

ROM. Read-only memory. Computer chips on which permanent information is stored. Unlike data in RAM, ROM is data installed by the manufacturer and cannot be altered.

RPM. Read programmer's mind.

RRSGWSSNK. Round and round she goes, where she stops, nobody knows.

RTDD. Read the damn documents.

RWDDF. Rewrite disk, destroying fat.

RYFM. Read your fucking manual.

RYT. Rotate your tires. See SYW.

 S

sagan. A large quantity of anything, from astronomer Carl Sagan, who will always be recalled for the uttering of the words "billions and billions" on his television series *The Cosmos*.

SAI. Skip all instructions.

salami attack/salami technique. Outlaw term. Computer crime in which the culprit instructs the computer to do his dirty work a small slice at a time (hence salami). Typically, such an attack is mounted when the malefactor instructs the computer to transfer a few cents from hundreds of accounts and deposits them in his account. For instance, a few seldom-noticed cents might be deducted from every monthly service charge.

SCCA. Short circuit on correct answer.

screen dump. A printout of the image that appears on-screen.

screwdriver shop. Computer retailer who assembles computers on the spot, usually selling at prices below comparable name-brand equipment.

scroll. To move up or down through text on a screen.

scrub. To clean or purge a file of unneeded data.

SCSI. Pronounced "scuzzy," it is an acronym for *small computer system interface;* a method of connecting PERIPHERALS to a computer.

send storm. A deluge of private messages received while a user is trying to do something else online.

serial port. A PORT, or connection,

on the back of a PC that allows data transfer, one bit at a time.

SFH Set flags to half-mast.

SFT. Stall for time.

shareware. A program that is distributed freely under the assumption that anyone who uses it will pay for it (that is, it is not FREE-WARE or public-domain software).

shovelware. Often useless software dumped onto a CD-ROM or computer software bundle to fill space.

Silicon Valley. Area outside San Francisco that has attracted many semiconductor and computer manufacturers. Similarly, there is Silicon Beach in southern California and Silicon Prairie in the Midwest. The area between Detroit and Ann Arbor has been called Automation Alley because of its concentration of robotics firms.

slave. Machine that is under control of another. See MASTER/SLAVE ARRANGEMENT.

smoke test. Test in which one turns on a machine and gives it a passing grade if it does not smoke, spark, or burst into flames.

snarf. To grab, especially to grab a large document or file for use with or without the author's permission.

sneaker net. Human alternative to a local area network in which humans run from one machine to another bearing floppy disks.

social engineering. In the world of computer criminality, this is conning someone with access to a network into divulging a password.

software. (1) Programs that tell the hardware to do useful work: the lengthy, complicated codes of instructions that program the machinery to accomplish tasks. (2) In the larger economic world, software can be anything we think of as being a valuable idea.

SOHO. Small office, home office; describing a large market segment for computers.

SOS. Sign off, stupid.

spaghetti code. Program written without a coherent structure.

spaz. To behave erratically.

spike. A sudden surge of electricity that can create computer havoc. Same as SURGE.

splash. To shoot something down; to cancel, especially a new program.

spoofer. One who fools a system into believing it is being accessed by an approved user.

SQL. Structured query language; a specialized way of getting information from a database; generally, one stored in a larger computer. Sometimes pronounced "sequel."

steel collar. Industrial robot in the sense that *blue collar* stands for industrial worker.

stoned. Computer virus that revealed itself circa 1992 that erases everything on your machine and leaves the screen proclaiming, "Your computer is now stoned. Legalize marijuana."

superprogrammer. A prolific programmer; one who can code exceedingly well and quickly. Not all hackers are superprogrammers, but many are.

surge. A spike or sudden burst in power that can literally fry computer chips.

SYW. Spin your wheels. See RYT.

 T

TARC. Take arithmetic review course.

task bar. A thin strip along the bottom of the computer screen. In Windows 95, the start button is located here.

techie. Technician.

tech-mech. Engineer or techie who "sold out" to the military or a large corporation.

technoslut/technotrash/ technoweenie. Brilliant technician who is a social disaster.

template. A "master" document for a word processor or spreadsheet or other application that is used as the starting point or a rough draft for other documents.

thrashing. Randomly hitting keys in the hope that you will trigger covert possibilities in a computer program.

tiled. On-screen windows that do not overlap.

TILO. Turn indicator lights off.

time bomb. Outlaw term. Instructions built into a program that cause destruction of data at a particular time.

time sink. A project that consumes unbounded amounts of time.

TN. Take a nap.

TPDH. Tell programmer to do it him/herself.

trackball. A ball nested in the computer that takes the place of a conventional mouse. One moves the on-screen cursor by moving the ball.

transparent. A process not obvious to the user.

trapdoor. Outlaw term. A gap in a program, created by accident or deliberately, that allows access to that program by bypassing its security system. It may be designed on purpose by somebody who has legal entry but plans to make an illegal foray later, or who doesn't want to take the time to jump through all the security loops with each entrance to the program. See also BACK DOOR.

Trash 80. Affectionate name for the old Tandy TRS computer.

Trojan horse/Trojan. Outlaw term. Any secret set of illegal instructions built into an existing program. The affected program acts normally until the hidden commands are triggered or a certain date and time are reached (for example, Friday the thirteenth at noon). A mad ingenuity is at work here including one known as no-troj, which according to the *New York Times* of May 19, 1987, "pretends to be a program that guards against Trojans. It's actually a time bomb that will wipe out your hard disk after it is more than 70 percent full.''

TRQ. To read queue.

TSR. Terminate and stay resident. Said of a program that stays in memory (RAM) after it has been executed. By remaining in memory, it is readily available for the user to run again.

TTA. Try, try again.

tweak. To fine-tune; to make a slight adjustment.

tweak freak. A computer techie obsessed with finding the root of all tech problems, regardless of the relevance.

 U

Up. Working or up and running. A machine is often said to be up after it has been down (CRASHED).

UP. Understand program.

upgrade. The new, improved version (usually of something you were told was the new, improved version in the first place).

user. One who works with the computer but does not get into the innards of programs. Not a hacker. See END USER.

user-friendly. Industry jargon for easy to use. User-friendly computers usually have many menus. Especially user-friendly equipment is, according to the "IBM Jargon and General Computing Dictionary," *user-cuddly.*

 V

vactor. Synthetic actor used in computer animation. A blend of—take your pick—video plus *actor* or *virtual* plus *actor.*

vanilla. Ordinary; standard; the usual flavor, such as a piece of equipment with no special features.

vaporware. (1) Software that does yet not exist but that is often announced by a software company and discussed and given coverage in the trade press. It has been termed a realm of hype and illusion where promises and deadlines are sometime things. After Windows 95 missed three target delivery dates after its initial announcement in February 1994, folks were for a time alluding to it as vaporware. (2) Hardware that has yet to materialize on the market but is promoted as if it were about to revolutionize the computer industry.

VAR. Value-added reseller. Generally, a person who puts together computer systems complete with software, hardware, and peripherals.

variable. In software, a data element that can be changed.

virtual. Not physical but behaving as if physical; a simulation.

virus. Outlaw term. Program or instruction created to cause mischief. A virus may clog a system with useless information or erase or alter existing information. Like true biological viruses, they spread and cause the electronic equivalent of epidemics. Individually named viruses include the infamous "Christmas virus" of December 1987, which hid its germ and transmission instructions in a Christmas greeting, or the older "cookie monster," which could only be stopped when the word *cookie* was typed into the machine.

* W

WA(H)G. Wild-assed (hairy) guess.

wallpaper. Lengthy printouts that give more information that will ever be used.

-ware. All-purpose ending for computer goods. In her book *Word Watch,* Anne H. Soukhanov points out that the trademarked program for do-it-yourself divorces called Divorceware shows how far we have come from the simple business of hardware, as in a hardware store. With the advent of computers *hardware* begat *software,* which begat, among others, *vaporware, crippleware, careware, freeware, fontware, liveware, groupware,* and *firmware. Wetware,* in the newest wrinkle of Silicon Valley lingo, refers to those who operate the machinery, and to the combination of knowledge and character that they bring to their tasks.

warm boot. To restart a computer using the [Ctrl]-[Alt]-[Del] key combinations.

wave a dead chicken. To go through the motions even though you are sure that the results will be futile.

wedged. To get stuck.

wetware. (1) The human brain and its DNA code. (2) Humans when using computers. As opposed to software or hardware.

WIBNI. Hacker's initialism for *Wouldn't it be nice if . . . ?*

window. The portion of a text that appears on the computer screen at any given moment; also divided or superimposed screens.

wirehead. Fanatic tinkerer and fixer addicted to computers to the extent that other things in life are neglected.

wizard. Illustrated, detailed, step-by-step instructions on how to accomplish a task—a Windows 95 term.

WOMBAT. Computerese for *waste of money, brains, and time.*

wonky. Broken.

word wrap. The ability of a word-processing program to drop a word to the next line rather than allow a word to be broken at the end of a line. The word is literally wrapped around to the next line and eliminates the need for the carriage return at the end of each line. In Notepad under Windows, for example, the word-wrap function must be turned on, otherwise words will run off the right side of the screen.

work station/workstation. Described by the *Wall Street Journal* as "a souped-up personal computer typically used by engineers and scientists." Increasingly, however, it has come to mean little more than a computer sitting on a desk.

worm. A rogue program that endlessly duplicates itself, thereby causing the infected system to bog down. A worm caused some six thousand computers to malfunction on November 2, 1988. Unlike a virus, a worm does not attach itself to a program; it survives independently.

WSWW. Work in strange and wondrous ways.

WYKIWYL. What you know is what you like. Pronounced "wicky-will."

WYSIWYAG. What you see is what you almost get.

WYSIWYG. What you see is what you get. Pronounced "wizzy-wig." It refers to the alleged ability to view a display and see exactly what will be printed in terms of typography and graphics.

WYSLN. What you see looks natural. Pronounced "wizz-lin."

* X

X.T. IBM's second-generation personal computer. Reputedly standing for *extended technology,* the X.T. offered more memory and slots for new circuit boards.

* Y

yo-yo mode. Condition of a system that is alternately up and down (working and not working).

* Z

zap. To erase.

zipperhead. One with a closed mind.

zorch. To move quickly.

ZSI. Zap space invader.

SOURCES

Richard Danca, writer and computer journalist, Ross Reader, Norman Stevens, and David Broome, the king of hacker acronyms and initialisms, provided invaluable help in the preparation of this collection. Although it is fast becoming dated, the key work on computer slang is the aforementioned book *The Hacker's Dictionary,* which was produced by a team of six professional computer wizards led by Guy L. Steele Jr. and first published by Harper & Row in 1983 with later updates. Alan Freedman's *Computer Glossary* was also useful, along with Webster's *New World Dictionary of Computer Terms.* The tenth edition of the "IBM Jargon and General Computing Dictionary" was also most useful.

9

COUNTERCULTURAL SLANG

The Slang of Yesterday Sounds
a Lot Like Today

> Remember when hippie
> meant big in the hips,
> And a trip involved
> travel in cars, planes,
> and ships?
>
> —From an anonymous poem that appeared
> in *Parade* magazine for November 14, 1971.
> Peter Tamony had a mimeographed copy as
> early as 1968. Tamony's copy was titled
> "Psychedelirium Tremens."

The slang of the 1960s and 1970s is still very much with us. To be sure, few flower children are around, and not many people can say *groovy* with a straight face. But a body of words and expressions—especially having to do with state of mind—are as clearly of the period as teach-ins, underground newspapers, and face-painting.

The approximate period in which this slang came into being and showed strength was between 1965 and 1975. Some was old and borrowed, such as calling a job a gig, which was an old jazz term, but most of it was new, daring, and well-publicized. It was also quickly adopted by the mainstream, a point that was made in *Newsweek* (February 3, 1969): "*Groovy. Beautiful. Out of Sight.* The jargon of the alienated, the oppressed, the discontented, is becoming the idiom of Middle . . . America. Television writers babble like acidheads, newspaper columnists sound like black militants, and advertising copywriters echo the slogans of teenyboppers."

As the 1970s wore on, it was periodically declared that the language of Haight-Ashbury and Woodstock was dying out to be replaced by the banter of post-Watergate teens, who called good-looking guys *hunks* and *studs,* deemed *bad* to be good, and called those who were "out of it" *airheads.*

Oddly, this was not to be. Much of the old slang hung on tenaciously, as those who grew up with it grew older . . . as they got into middle age, if you wish. Today they work hard to keep it together: to be up-front about their hang-ups, to avoid confrontations and rip-offs, and to maintain a hassle-free lifestyle. They strive to keep from getting uptight, strung out, or down on their kids, even if they've trashed their rooms. Heavy.

In the summer of 1996, Karl Vick dedicated a column in the *Washington Post* to the routine use of sixties drug talk in official Washington. He quoted a Coast Guard admiral alluding to an issue that had "a lot of people strung out," an FBI official talking about "a real upper," and a Republican senator talking about people "freaking out."

What follows is a collection of the slang of "then" that is in large part still in use "now." To give this slang a special sense of time and history, 83 of the terms are labeled "POW—Air Force." These were terms the U.S. Air Force compiled and defined in 1973 for the prisoners of war returning from Vietnam. The glossary of 160 terms was called "semi-official" and was based on a poll of POW families, to see which terms were actually in use in their homes. It was published by the Air Force with this comment: "We hesitate whether or not to call the language progress, but facts are facts. This is part of the slang being used by your sons and daughters. The main purpose is to get you and your offspring off to somewhat of an equal start." The original definitions from the Air Force list are contained in quotation marks.

The glossary has also been salted with a collection of slang peculiar to the Vietnam War that stayed with us as well. As Martin F. Nolan write in the *Boston Globe* (July 18, 1982), "The patois of the Vietnam experience infiltrated the American consciousness slowly, for more than a decade, on a Ho Chi Minh trail of the mind." These terms have been marked with the fact that they are from the war. It is noteworthy that many of the terms from Vietnam—especially those having to do with killing and getting killed—live on as part of the American urban nightmare of the 1990s.

* A

acid. (POW—Air Force) "Refers to the hallucinogenic drug lysergic acid diethylamide (LSD)."

acid freak. (POW—Air Force) "Frequent user of LSD."

acid head. One who uses LSD.

acid rock. (POW—Air Force) "Psychedelic music; emphasizes electronic sounds, has a prominent beat and repeated sounds, very loud."

Afro. (POW—Air Force) "Naturally black hairstyle; hair not straightened, but left in its natural curly state and styled. Also prefix denoting black (Afro-American)."

alternative. Nonconforming, as in alternative schooling, alternative press, etc.

Amerika. A bad America; the one that was the stage for the Kent State shootings.

at. (1) Place; where things are happening; where it's "at." (2) One's position; for instance, "This is where I'm at."

* B

babe. Woman, girl, one's *old lady.*

bad news. (POW—Air Force) "A depressing or undesirable person."

bad scene. (POW—Air Force) "Unpleasant experience, place, or event; a disappointment."

bag. (1) (POW—Air Force) "Person's way of life, now generally replaced by the term *trip.* Ex: 'He's into a jazz trip.'" (2) Quantity of marijuana, usually an ounce or less, contained in a sandwich bag.

ball. To copulate.

banana clip. (War in Vietnam) A curved ammunition clip designed to hold thirty rounds.

banji. Marijuana. This is one of thirty-one terms for the substance that appear in Joel Makower's *Boom! Talkin' About Our Generation.* Most of the other terms for marijuana come from Makower's collection.

beautiful. (POW—Air Force) "Expression of approval; usually exclamatory."

be down on. (POW—Air Force) "Dislike or disapprove of something or someone, usually intensely. 'He's down on pollution.'"

be in. (POW—Air Force) "Gathering of people for spontaneous and hopefully creative activities."

Black Panthers. (POW—Air Force). "Militant organization of blacks who are engaged in promoting the welfare of black people. The organization is now downplaying armed confrontation and encouraging community self-help and building popular support in the black community."

blow your cool. (POW—Air Force) "Loss of control of temper or emotions. The term is still used, though far less frequently."

blow your mind. (1) To overwhelm; to make a startling point. (2) To amaze or delight. (3) To lose touch with reality because of drugs.

bogart. To be selfish; to "bogart a joint" is to not share a marijuana cigarette.

boo. Marijuana.

bopper. (POW—Air Force) "Hip, aware young person in tune with the modern scene. Usually short for *teenybopper.*"

bottle baby. Alcoholic.

bread. Money. (Often forgotten is that this term began as a play on the slang *dough* for money.)

brick. A kilogram of marijuana.

brother. (1) (POW—Air Force) "Term mostly used by a black man or woman to identify a black male, and as a term of address. Also being used by Chicanos and American Indians." (2) Term used by hippies to indicate that another individual is "cool": "Don't worry about him, he's a brother."

bud. Marijuana bud. This meaning was probably not forgotten in the Budweiser beer motto "This Bud's for you."

Bumfuck, Egypt. Remote site of

hardship assignments; East Over-shoe.

bummer. (POW—Air Force) "Un-pleasant experience, especially with drugs. It is also an exclama-tion of disgust or sympathy for anyone's bad experience." This term was derived directly from *bum trip.*

burn. (1) (POW—Air Force) "Hurt emotionally, being taken." (2) To cheat, especially in a drug deal.

burned out. (POW—Air Force) "In-capacitated, mentally and/or physi-cally, temporarily or permanently, from drugs."

burp. (War in Vietnam) A marine, especially to an infantryman.

bush. (1) Marijuana. (2) (War in Vietnam) The field or the boonies. (3) Short for *ambush.*

bust, busted. (POW—Air Force) "Arrest, arrested."

C

cactus. Peyote.

cat. (POW—Air Force) "Any male, especially a sharp dresser (*dude* is more common now)." The term long predates the sixties, espe-cially in jazz circles.

catnip. To sell something other than drugs in a drug deal—catnip for marijuana, etc. A line in Wil-liam Burroughs's *Naked Lunch* is "I'll catnip the jerk."

check it out. To pay attention to; to have a look at.

chick. (POW—Air Force) "Young girl." In the sixties, almost every female was a chick. There were genres of chicks: surfer chicks, biker chicks, beatnik chicks. On television, the ultimate chick was Peggy Lipton in *The Mod Squad,* with her long hair and go-go boots.

commune. (POW—Air Force) "Community where nothing is pri-vately owned, usually associated with hippies. Social structures and values vary considerably."

confrontation. Hostile demonstra-tion.

connection. Source, especially for drugs.

contact high. (1) Vicarious experi-ence of being high with someone on a trip. (2) Also, a marijuana high derived from being in a mari-juana-smoke-filled room, but with-out having actually smoked it.

cool. (1) (POW—Air Force) "Self-assured, knowledgeable. One who is aware of the times." (In some circles to be cool was to be a user of drugs.) (2) To be calm, not overly excited or easily rattled.

This term predates the period in question, and along with *cat* and *dig,* goes back much further to Jack Kerouak's *Dharma Bums* and the beats, to Kookie of *77 Sunset Strip,* and the bop school of jazz.

cop. To obtain; for instance, to cop a joint.

cop out. (POW—Air Force) "Refuse to face an issue or responsibility, usually a social one."

cosmic. (1) Important. (2) Relating to anything inexplicable.

SAY WHAT?

"Like it or not, the sixties word *chick* is back on the scene," was the word from Colleen O'Connor of the *Dallas Morning News* in an article published on July 24, 1995. "Other bits of hippie slang—like *stone fox*—may languish in the retro-chic ragbag. But *chick* is chic."

This despite the fact that it was especially vilified and despised by women of the immediate post–Vietnam era. (There was actually a button women wore that read: "No Vietcong ever called me chick.") Evidence submitted by O'Connor:

- Chrissie Hynde of the Pretenders says she likes being called a chick. So do the Dixie Chicks.
- A baby-shower invitation for Mary Matalin of CNBC's *Equal Time* said, "Chicks only."
- Hillary Rodham Clinton laughed when the media called her trip to Asia a "chicks' trip."
- PBS ran an all-female movie-reviewer show called *Chicks on Flicks.*
- And a new summer movie, *A Little Princess,* is now being dubbed a "chick-ette movie" for young girls.

O'Connor reported that some credit Hollywood with resurrecting the dead-and-buried *chick.* "*Chick flick* was used for the first time in *Sleepless in Seattle,*" says Jack Nachbar, professor of popular culture at Bowling Green State University in Ohio.

---

counterculture. (POW—Air Force) "A style of living. Values are different from current society. Usually associated with hippies and communes."

crash. (1) To collapse, or sleep, usually when high. (2) To come down quickly from a drug-induced high.

crash pad. Place to sleep, or to come down from being high.

 D

deal. To sell or deal in; "I don't deal drugs."

devil weed. Marijuana.

dew. Marijuana.

dig. (POW—Air Force) "Enjoy, comprehend to the fullest extent possible."

digger. Hippie social worker; altruist of the counterculture.

dig it. (POW—Air Force) "Exclamatory meaning enjoy it or appreciate it, get into it."

do. Take or participate in, as in, "I don't do acid anymore." This meaning of *do* comes into play in the Hollywood invitation "Let's do lunch."

do a number. (1) To affect or try to influence; to pester. "She tried to do her support-payment number on me again last night." (2) To deliberately mislead; see also MIND-FUCKING. (3) To smoke a marijuana cigarette.

doobie. Marijuana cigarette.

dope. (POW—Air Force) "Any drug; though most frequently in reference to marijuana."

down. (POW—Air Force) "(1) Unhappy, depressed. (2) No longer under the influence of a drug." Also, (3) barbiturate that is an activity suppressant, and (4) to be upset with or feel negative about: "I'm down on school."

downer. (1) A depressant drug, especially a barbiturate, which lessens activity. (2) An unpleasant person or activity.

do your own thing. (POW—Air Force) "Follow your own interest and activities. Usage has decreased in frequency."

drag. (POW—Air Force) "Boring. A tedious experience."

drop. To take LSD.

drop out. To turn away or withdraw from conventional society.

dude. (POW—Air Force) "Any male."

dynamite. Great.

∗ E

earth. (1) The home planet. (2) Of the natural environment, the opposite of plastic; organic: Earth Day, "Spaceship Earth," *The Mother Earth News, The Whole Earth Catalog,* the earth mother, earth tones.

ego trip. (POW—Air Force) "An achievement or success." However, it has a negative connotation, as someone on an ego trip is usually self-obsessed.

establishment. (POW—Air Force) "The power structure of institutions (politicians, police, teachers, etc.)."

∗ F

far-out. (POW—Air Force) "All-purpose expression of approval for an unusual experience. Used as exclamation. Now often used sarcastically to indicate disgust or boredom."

fed. Federal narcotics agent.

flip/flip out. To perform an emotional cartwheel.

flower child. Youngster of the late 1960s who believed that love and beauty could overcome materialism and war.

As a footnote to this dry definition, here is an ALTERNATIVE definition prepared by John O. Clark, who was there when the term was coined and still has no trouble expressing himself in the argot of the Haight:

" 'Flower child': This is pure San Francisco, 1966 or 1967. There was a 'riot' and the National Guard was called—or was it just a whole bunch of cops? I dismember [*sic*]—so a whole bunch of teenyboppers and hippie-dippies, mostly zonked on acid or 'shrooms, went to the park where they gathered flowers. As I remember, daffodils and daisies predominated. Pictures appeared in the dailies of young girls reaching up on tiptoe, their firm, nubile young nipples almost bursting from their tattered, tie-dyed T-shirts . . . and their sweet damps practically embracing the butts of the assault rifles as they put daisies in the gun barrels, while the military formation sweated and wrestled with their hard-ons. . . . I think that the term 'flower child' was birthed in a photo caption of one of the Haight-Ashbury foxes pouting at the soldier with a 'Don't you wish you could but you never will' smile as she stuffed a daf in his bang-bang."

flower power. The hippie notion of the power of natural beauty, and the belief that society could be changed through love and peace.

freak. (1) Drug user; one who has freaked out. (2) Any member of the COUNTERCULTURE circa 1967. (3) An enthusiast: food, freak, rock freak, beach freak, etc.

freak/freak out. (1) To become crazy on drugs; to have a bad or extreme drug experience. (2) To lose control of one's temper. (3) To shock or surprise, as in, freaking somebody out.

freaky. Psychedelic; bizarre.

 G

ganja. Marijuana.

gas, it's a. (POW—Air Force)

"Cool, great. Refers to an event. Ex: A favorite TV program might be referred to as 'it's a gas.'"

gay. (POW—Air Force) "Homosexual. Acceptable term by homosexuals."

get down. (1) To begin; to get down to it. (2) To have a good time: "Hey, let's party; let's really get down."

get into. (POW—Air Force) "Become absorbed or involved in something intensely, usually with a positive attitude."

get it on. To commence; to get going; to GET DOWN.

get it together. (POW—Air Force) "To get organized."

goof on. (1) To laugh at or make fun of. (2) To mislead.

gook. (War in Vietnam) Derogatory term for an Asian, from Korean slang for person.

go straight. (POW—Air Force) "(1) Give up the use of drugs. (2) Return to an approved lifestyle."

granny glasses. Old-style wire-rim glasses with small lenses.

grass. (POW—Air Force) "Marijuana; dope, pot, reefer, weed."

groove. (1) To concentrate on, to meditate with. (2) To like; to enjoy. (3) A fine thing: "What a groove."

groovy. Good, nice, COOL.

groupies. Young women who followed rock musicians with whom they tried to have sex.

guru. Spiritual leader; mentor; not

just Indian gurus or spiritual teachers.

✳ H

hairy. Thorny, worrisome.

hang me up. Keep me waiting; to not show up.

hang up/hang-up. (POW—Air Force) "(1) Dislike, a mental block. (2) Reoccurring problem, source of irritation, or disappointment with no apparent solution." Also, (3) neurosis, quirk, or obsession.

The past participle *hung up* or *hung up on* means to be obsessed or neurotically preoccupied with.

happening. (POW—Air Force) "Event."

hash. Hashish.

hassle. (POW—Air Force) "(1) Problem; troublesome or irritating situation or event, conflict situation. (2) To disagree, argue, or bother."

hay. Marijuana.

head. (1) (POW—Air Force) "Drug user; freak." Also, (2) enthusiast in the sense that "Deadheads" are fans of the Grateful Dead. (3) The mind.

head shop/head store. Place for drug paraphernalia, psychedelic posters, underground comics, etc.

heat. (1) The police. (2) Police pressure.

heavy. (POW—Air Force) "Deep, complicated, meaningful. Bad or disgusting." The term lives on, among other places, in heavy metal.

hemp. Marijuana.

herb. Marijuana.

hip. (1) (POW—Air Force) "Aware. Connotes understanding and familiarity with drug scene and/or the radical view of political activity." (2) To make aware; to inform: "She hipped me to the fact that there was some quick money to be made."

hippie/hippy. (POW—Air Force) "Predominantly middle-class white youth ranging in age from twelve to twenty-five; some drop out of society, do not work, take drugs, have long hair. Anybody with long hair is considered a hippy."

hold. To possess drugs; to "carry."

honky/honkie. (POW—Air Force) "Any white person, connotes racist."

hooch. (1) Marijuana. (2) Hut or shelter to a soldier.

hooked. (1) Addicted to. (2) In love with.

hustle. (POW—Air Force) "Try to interest someone sexually. A way of obtaining money, or drugs, that is usually illegal or deceptive."

✳ I

in. (POW—Air Force) "Socially acceptable within a group, usually a subculture, now used sarcastically to indicate disgust with attention to conforming."

-in. Suffix for an event of mass participation: be-in, sit-in, live-in, teach-in, smoke-in, love-in, etc.

The suffix keeps finding new applications. In 1989, a headline in the *National Farmers Union Newsletter* read, "NFU Legislative Fly-in Is Set for June 17–20."

inner space. One's inner self, which some believed could be affected by drugs.

into. (POW—Air Force) "Involved, interesting, engrossed in, pursuing the study of. Ex: 'She's into astrology.'"

J

Jesus freak. (POW—Air Force) "A young person who openly and publicly finds 'Salvation in God'—will tend to be evangelical."

jive. (1) Nonsense. (2) To joke with.

joint. Marijuana cigarette.

juicehead. One whose drug of choice is alcohol.

K

killer weed. Marijuana, especially high quality.

kilo. A kilogram of drugs, usually marijuana.

L

lid. A quantity of marijuana, usually one ounce.

lifestyle. (POW—Air Force) "A way of living according to some subcultures."

loco weed. Marijuana.

M

man, the. Person or persons in control, often applied to a police officer.

Mary Jane. Marijuana. The name is based on the letters *m* and *j* in *marijuana,* as well as being a play on the pronunciation, a rough translation from the Spanish, "mary-juana."

matchbox. A small quantity of marijuana, originally the amount that would fit inside a matchbox.

maxi. (POW—Air Force) "Meaning larger. Ex: *maxicoat,* a long coat of ankle length."

mike. One microgram—one millionth of a gram—of LSD.

mindfucking. Doing bad things to the mind and spirit, as opposed to *mindblowing,* which is good. Examples of those practicing the former would be Charles Manson and James Jones, while the Grateful Dead and light shows characterized the latter. See DO A NUMBER (2).

movement, the. The general move to the left, and the specific move to stop the Vietnam War.

Ms. (POW—Air Force) "Women's liberation term which is an abbreviation meaning either 'Miss' or 'Mrs.'"

N

narc. Originally short for *narcotics agent* but extended to include any law enforcement person.

nitty-gritty. The heart of the matter; the essence.

no days like that! (War in Vietnam) Not likely to happen.

no way. (POW—Air Force) "Impossible."

 O

off. To kill; to bump off.

old lady/old man. The steady woman/man in a man's/woman's life, even if the old lady/old man in question is only eighteen. This lives on in biker slang.

oregano. Marijuana. This term may be an acknowledgment that oregano was sometimes sold as the real stuff to the uninitiated.

out of it. (POW—Air Force) "To be out of touch with reality when under the influence of a drug, especially hallucinogens. To lack understanding and awareness, especially in a subculture."

out of sight. (POW—Air Force) "Wonderful or terrific."

overkill. Excessive and wasteful. Term borrowed from the Pentagon, where it was used for excessive nuclear capability.

 P

pad. (POW—Air Force) "Place where one lives. Room or residence."

paraphernalia. An assortment of drug-related implements, including rolling (cigarette) papers, ROACH CLIPS, and water pipes.

people, the. Everybody, it seemed, but "white moderates," the police, government bureaucrats, and hard hats.

pig. (1) Derogatory term for a police officer, or any powerful member of the establishment (Presidents Johnson and Nixon were both pigs). (2) The system itself became known as the pig from about 1970 through 1972.

planet, the. The EARTH.

plant your seed. Hippie motto suggesting that the doctrine of love and pacifism be spread by example.

plastic. Insincere, phony, unreal.

pot. Marijuana.

pothead. Marijuana user.

pounds, shillings, and pence. LSD. "There were a bunch of Englishers hanging around the Haight in the sixties," says John O. Clark, who was there, "so it was inevitable: L with a line through, S for shilling, and D for pence spelled LSD."

psychedelic. (POW—Air Force) "Refers to a new social movement, including the change in moral structure, music, dress, and the arts." It originally referred to something that was influenced by hallucinogenic drugs—the intensely colorful and florid "psychedelic art," for example.

pudding. The cosmic oneness; the godhead—the state of one who is into the pudding.

pull yourself together. (POW—Air

Force) "Secure, emotionally clear conception of one's self and relationship to others and life in general. Have everything or something clear in one's mind."

putdown/put down. (1) An insult. (2) To insult.

put-on/put on. (1) A joke or prank. (2) To pull a joke on; to tell a lie or mislead for entertainment (rather than deception).

✳ R

R & R. Rest and relaxation, or rest and recuperation. In Vietnam, R & R was a three-to-seven-day vacation from combat zones. "Rape and ruin" is just one of a number of unofficial interpretations of R & R.

rap. (POW—Air Force) "Conversation, usually about a 'meaningful' subject. A sort of lecture or specific approach to a subject." This term was applied to a form of music in the 1980s.

reefer. (1) Marijuana. Clearly a term from an earlier generation, given a great boost by the reissue of *Reefer Madness,* a campy, shrill antimarijuana movie. (2) (War in Vietnam) Refrigerator or refrigerated vehicle.

REMF. (War in Vietnam) Rear-echelon motherfucker, or base-camp support troop.

retailer. Drug dealer.

right on! (POW—Air Force) "Exclamation of agreement with impor-

tance or truth of a statement. Means the same as *perfect.*"

rip off. (POW—Air Force). "Steal and or cheat. Mislead in order to get the upper hand."

rip-off artist. One who deceives for a living—a slumlord, confidence man, dishonest lawyer, etc.

ripped. High on drugs.

roach. The remains of a marijuana cigarette.

roach clip. Any device used to hold a roach while smoking it, so as not to burn one's fingers.

ruined. High on drugs.

✳ S

scene. (POW—Air Force). "Place of action. An experience."

scuz/scuzz. Marijuana.

shades. (POW—Air Force) "Eyeglasses—usually sunglasses."

shit. Marijuana.

shuck. (1) To deceive. (2) A phony person or thing; that which is bogus.

smashed. High on drugs.

smokables. Marijuana.

smoke. Marijuana.

soul. (POW—Air Force) "An inherent quality black people feel they have and whites rarely do. It implies an awareness and understanding of life and a naturalness of expression." *Newsweek* carried this definition in 1969: "In American Negro parlance, omnibus term for courage, sensitivity, humor, style, arrogance, and grace.''

soul brother. (POW—Air Force) "Black person."

soul sister. (POW—Air Force) "Black female."

spaced/spaced-out/spacey. (1) Dazed and distracted, often from drugs. (2) Goofy.

spliff. Marijuana.

split. (POW—Air Force) "Go. Leave or depart."

stash. (1) A secret supply, usually drugs. (2) To hide drugs.

stoned/stoned out. High on drugs.

straight. (POW—Air Force) "(1) Off drugs either at the time or permanently or (2) not homosexual." Also, (3) outside the realm of freaks and hippies.

strung out. (1) To become ill (physically or mentally) because of drugs. (2) To be excitable, nervous, at wit's end. (3) To be addicted to drugs.

Summer of Love. Summer 1967.

swacked. High on drugs.

 T

tea. Marijuana.

tell it like it is. (POW—Air Force) "To be open and honest. Withholding nothing about what one thinks or believes."

tent peg. (War in Vietnam) Stupid or worthless soldier.

thing. That which compels; that which one concentrates on. "His thing is playing checkers."

together. Balanced; in harmony; calm and content. Some guy who has gotten his mental life in order has "gotten his shit together." This is also the together of the Beatles' "Come Together."

toke. (1) Marijuana. (2) To inhale the smoke of marijuana or hashish.

trash. Damage or destroy.

tribes. Those who were part of the movement, from the Gathering of the Tribes on January 20, 1967, on the Polo Field in Golden Gate Park.

trip. (1) Feelings under the influence of drugs, especially LSD. (2) Attitude or lifestyle—a power trip, for instance, or a guilt trip. (3) Any exceptional experience.

trucking. (POW—Air Force) "Walking—using legs to get somewhere." Used in the motto Keep on Trucking, which was often displayed with a Robert Crumb cartoon featuring Mr. Natural.

tune in. To focus, zero in on, especially to the culture.

turn his/her head around. To change someone's mind; to arouse interest.

turn off. (POW—Air Force) "Disgust or repulse someone." Antonym of TURN ON.

turn on. (POW—Air Force) "(1) Get high on drugs. (2) Arouse sexually." Also, (3) to introduce someone to drugs or something new. (4) Anything that is exhilarating or sexually arousing.

U

underground. (POW—Air Force) "Unsanctioned by prevailing social attitudes; antiestablishment."

up. High, but not necessarily on drugs.

up-front. (1) Honest, uninhibited, open. (2) At the head of a line or demonstration.

uptight. (1) (POW—Air Force) "In a state of tension. Worried, upset, or inhibited." Also, (2) intimate with, close to, as in, tight with or up tight with.

 V

vibes. (POW—Air Force) "Vibrations. Nonverbal expressions of thoughts or feelings."

 W

wacky t'backy. Marijuana.

wacky weed. Marijuana.

wasted. High; under the influence of.

weed. Marijuana.

what's happening? (POW—Air Force) "Salutation meaning 'What is going on?' "

where it's at. (POW—Air Force) "The core of a situation or event."

women's lib. (POW—Air Force) "Women's liberation activist movement to secure equal rights for women."

wrecked. High; under the influence of.

 Y

yippie. (POW—Air Force) "Person associated with the Youth International Party, an eccentric group of hippies." (What is left out of the Air Force definition is that the yippies were intensely political and opposed to mainstream politics.)

 Z

z. An ounce of marijuana; from the abbreviation *oz* for ounce.

zap. (1) (POW—Air Force) "Emphasize in an unforgettable manner." Also, to hit figuratively—for instance, to zap with understanding and love. (2) (War in Vietnam) To kill.

zippo raid. (War in Vietnam) Search-and-destroy mission in which villages are set afire.

zonked. (POW—Air Force) "Extremely high on a drug."

SOURCES

Wordheads and argot freaks who helped in the preparation of this glossary are Joel Makower, president of Tilden Press, whose own books include *Boom!*

Talkin' About Our Generation and *Woodstock: The Oral History,* and John O. Clark of Philo, California, who "majored" in all of this. Material in the Tamony Collection was also most useful.

The Air Force list appeared in a number of newspapers when it was first released, including the *New York Times,* March 8, 1973. One of the few good articles to appear on the subject of sixties slang, "If You Think It's Groovy to Rap, You're Shucking," by Mike Jahn, appeared in the *New York Times Magazine,* June 6, 1971.

— ✳ *10* ✳ —

CRIME, PUNISHMENT, AND THE LAW

Words You Don't Hear on the Outside

The slang—or, as it used to be called, "cant"—of thieves, gypsies, vagabonds, and their fellows has enriched the English language and its literature since Shakespeare's time.

—Geoffrey Nunberg in the *New York Times Book Review*, May 2, 1982

Most of the early works on slang in English were concerned with the cant of criminals. *The Tom and Jerry Flash Dictionary*, published in London in 1825, for instance, contained an elaborate slang that included no less than sixty orders of *coves*—or receivers of foreign goods—including *footpads, rumpadders, twirlers, maces, pab priggers, cadgers, dubsmen,* and *swaddlers.*

Then, as now, this is a rich area for the collector of slang. Today, four sets of slang are associated with crime and punishment. The first is that of the criminal, the second is that of prison, and the third is that of the police. Those three are addressed in this chapter. The fourth, the slang of drugs, is the subject of the next chapter.

Although there are differences in these various slangs, they are interrelated.

✳ A

all day. A life sentence in the lingo of prisoners.

all day and night. A life sentence to prison.

armor. Weapons, to a convict.

✳ B

baby raper. Inmate term for older convict who has committed a sex-ual offense against a minor or whose crime is unknown.

badge. A cop, guard, correctional officer.

badge heavy. Describing a self-important cop; or one who gets carried away with his or her authority.

bag. (1) Police term for a uniform; to be sent back to the uniformed ranks after being a plainclothes officer is known as going back "into the bag." (2) To arrest, as in "bag him."

B&W/black and white. Police car. This term varies from city to city, as police colors change.

banger. A knife. Also called a burner or a shank.

baton. Nightstick.

beagle. A detective.

beat. Diluted, as in a "beat drug," which has been cut.

beat the bricks. To get out of prison.

belch. To inform or testify.

big con. Confidence game or trick, normally requiring an elaborate setup, that nets the con artist big money.

bit. A prison sentence.

blaster. Gunman.

blotter. Police station-house ledger.

blue flu. A police sick-out; a job action in which police call in with false illnesses.

body pack. More than three dead bodies to a cop.

bolo. Police shorthand for "be on the lookout for."

bonaroo. One's best clothes in prison parlance. "I've got my bonaroos all ready for my next visit."

bones. Dominoes, the popular prison game.

boneyard. The family (conjugal) visiting area in prison talk.

book. (1) Life sentence (in the sense that one has had the book thrown at him). (2) To arrest.

boost. To shoplift.

boss. A guard to prison inmates—some say it is "sorry son of a bitch" spelled backward.

bottle baby. Derelict.

bounce. Police vernacular for a brainstorming session.

bow-and-arrow squad. A police unit not allowed to carry firearms.

breakdown. Shotgun.

bricks. The outside, on the outside, as in "on the bricks."

bridal suite. Room where police who work late or extra shifts can take a nap.

broadway. The first floor of some tiers of cells in prison. A wide area where inmates come and go—and occasionally may be housed if the prison is particularly crowded.

broom. Cop who keeps the station house clean and acts as an errand boy.

brownie. A traffic cop, in the eyes of the police who deal with crime.

bubs. The blue flashers or bubbles on the top of police cars.

bucket, the. Jail.

bucket of blood. Violent tavern requiring routine police visits.

bug. (1) Police term for a criminal without compassion or empathy. (2) A crazy person in prison talk.

buggin'. Cop slang for playing around.

bull. Guard, in "slammerese."

bunkie. The person with whom a prisoner shares a bunk bed in slammerese.

burn. To shoot.

bush gang. Prison gang that works outside cutting brush and doing other jobs. It has been termed a chain gang without the chains.

buy down. Term for convicted criminals to forfeit as much of their ill-gotten estate as possible to the authorities in hopes of getting a reduced sentence.

buy you a suit. Phrase used to tell a police officer that a bribe is forthcoming if a violation is overlooked. It is also phrased as "give you a hat."

 C

Cadillac. Prison coffee with cream and sugar; smooth, rich, and creamy.

cage. Prison cell.

calendar. A year in prison talk.

canned. Imprisoned.

cannon. A pickpocket.

cap. The amount of marijuana that fits into a Chap Stick cap in the lingo of prison inmates.

carry-out rape. Police term for abduction and rape.

catcher. Sexually passive or submissive prison inmate, often victimized.

celly. One's cellmate.

chalk. Homemade alcohol, or PRUNO.

chester. Child molester in the vernacular of prison inmates.

chicken hawk. Child molester.

chill. Kill.

chinaman. Inmate washing his clothes in the sink, instead of using the prison laundry.

chop shop. Garage in which stolen cars are disassembled in preparation for the used-parts market.

clavo. A prison stash or collection. "He has a huge clavo of jelly beans."

Club Fed. Federal penitentiaries, especially to inmates of other institutions.

code 7. Work break or meal to most police.

coin wrestler. One who dives into public fountains for coins thrown by tourists for luck: usually homeless men working late at night.

cold gun. A gun that has been worked on to disguise its origins, as opposed to a hot or stolen gun.

collar. To arrest.

collars for dollars. When corrupt police purposely wait until a shift's end to make an arrest. The time it takes to process a suspect can guarantee as much as twenty-four hours of overtime pay.

convict. Career criminal to a fellow inmate.

cooping. Police sleeping or relaxing on the job.

cop killer. Armor-piercing bullets.

corner. In prison a corner is de-

SAY WHAT?

Caveat

*C*onvict vs. inmate: Even though the terms are interchangeable, in many systems *inmate* carries a negative connotation, while *convict* implies a career criminal or one who is attuned to the nuances of prison life. This is called being down—"Bob is a real down dude."

The importance of words is never more obvious than in prison—the wrong word, or even saying one the wrong way, can get an inmate killed.

—Letter from Colorado inmate to author, September 3, 1991.

fined by who a man hangs out with. Quoting directly from Fannie Martin's *Committing Journalism,* "Lots of times, even a loner is hooked to a certain corner, so within that you've got 'strong corners,' 'weak corners,' etc. Once you know all the corners, where they are, and what their guidelines are, then you get an easy feel for the pulse of a prison."

corset. Bulletproof vest.

crate. A carton of cigarettes in prison.

crib. In prison, one's cell.

crib burglar. One who breaks in and robs from homes and apartments.

cut. To attempt suicide behind bars.

 D

daddy. Pimp.

dance hall. Execution chamber.

dead presidents. Money in bills: "Open your wallet and show me some dead presidents."

dead time. Time spent in jail that does not count against a sentence. For instance, time spent for contempt or not cooperating with a grand jury is often dead time.

deck. A pack of cigarettes to a prison inmate.

Deuce, the. The block of Forty-second Street between Seventh and Eighth Avenues in New York City, to police and criminals alike. This may be the highest area of crime concentration in the nation.

deuce-deuce. A .22-caliber gun.

devastator. An exploding small-caliber bullet.

digger. A pickpocket.

dime/dime ya. To inform; to DROP A DIME.

dimed out. (prison) Telling on someone. "The rat, he dimed me out."

dinger. Burglar alarm.

dip. In a pickpocket operation, this is the person who removes the wallet. The setup on the other hand is the person who prepares the victim, usually by bumping into him.

dirty. Describing a bad prison reputation.

divorce. To police, a domestic shooting.

DMZ. Street or area of a city that demarks a high-crime area from one with an average or low crime rate. In New York City, the DMZ of the Upper East Side is Ninety-sixth Street. DMZ is an acronym for *demilitarized zone.*

do a piece of work. Whack, hit, or pop in gangland.

dog house. Prison watchtower.

doin' doors. Corrupt-cop talk for kicking in doors at known drug locations without a warrant solely to steal cash and drugs. Also known as hittin' spots or a drug raid.

drive-by. Committing crime from a moving vehicle, such as a drive-by shooting.

drop a dime. (1) Police term for calling in information on a specific crime. (2) In prison, to inform on someone. "He dropped a dime on his bunkie."

drum. Jail cell.

dumping ground. A police precinct, usually in a poor, crime-ridden neighborhood, where the department sends officers with discipline problems.

dump truck. A lawyer who makes an easy deal at the expense of the client.

* E

85. Police slang/code for a girlfriend.

equalized. Armed.

eyeball van. Police term for surveillance vehicle with one-way glass.

* F

fade the heat. To take responsibility, in prison parlance.

feero. Firebug; an arsonist.

fence parole. Escape in slammerese.

56. Police term for time off.

finger. (1) Police informer. (2) To identify someone as a suspect; to inform on someone.

fireworks. Gunplay; shoot-out.

fish. A new prisoner.

five-finger discount. Shoplifting.

five-O. Street slang for cops, taken from the television show *Hawaii Five-O.*

fix. (1) A stationary post for a police officer. (2) Trouble (to be in a fix).

flake. To plant false evidence.

flip. To turn on; to give evidence to the police or to prison authorities.

floater. Police term for a body found in water.

fly. To escape from prison.

fooled out. To make a mistake.

four-five. A .45-caliber gun.

four-to-four. Police beat from four in the afternoon until midnight, but which may also include time to unwind at a bar that closes at four A.M. In *One Police Plaza*, William J. Caunitz describes one of these shifts and adds, "The session lasted until four in the morning. Policemen's wives have dubbed these tours the 'four-to-fours.' "

freeway dancer. Police term for people who dash across major highways in the dark.

freeworld. (1) The outside to a prisoner. (2) mass-made cigarettes—as opposed to hand-rolled "tailor-made."

fresh kills. New homicides to a detective.

∗ G

gat. Gun.

gauge, the. Shotgun, especially to police.

gee. A guy in prison.

get busy. Street slang: to rob someone.

get paid. Street slang for committing a successful robbery.

get small. To get away; to disappear, especially as a suspect is getting away ("He got small in a hurry.").

gimmie. Handgun to police—from the robber's demand "to gimme . . ."

G-joint. Federal prison.

gladiator fight. Prison fighting staged for the benefit of others such as guards.

gladiator school. Maximum-security prison.

glass beat/glass post. Police term for a beat with a lot of stores with large plate-glass windows.

gold tin. Detective's badge, as opposed to *tin*, which is the name for a uniformed police badge. To "get the gold tin" is to be promoted to detective.

gonzales. Blackjack.

gooners. Corrections officers to prisoners.

go on the box. To take a lie detector test.

Gray Bar Motel. Jail.

grounder. In his book *Close Pursuit: A Week in the Life of an NYPD Homicide Cop*, Carsten Stroud says that this term is used by the New York Police Department for "a homicide case that can be solved with relative speed and simplicity." The opposite of a grounder is a *mystery* or a *queer one*.

∗ H

hair bag. (1) Veteran cop to other cops. (2) a PERP, especially since *Hill Street Blues*.

hard time. (1) Sentence with no parole in sight. (2) Sentence to hard labor.

heat. (1) Gun. (2) Pressure.

heeled. Carrying a gun.

he/she. Transvestite to the police.

hit. Shoot.

hitch. Prison sentence.

hit man. Gang assassin.

hold your mud. Criminal talk for not blabbing to the police or feds when arrested; one who does not rat on others. In James Mills's *Underworld Empire* a man is described as "an old-time crook, who holds his mud."

hole, the. (1) Solitary confinement. (2) The subway to an urban cop in a city with an underground.

hook down. "The guard is coming" in prison talk.

hook 'n' bookin. Handcuffing and arresting in cop talk.

horse. Person who smuggles money or drugs into prison. Also known as a MULE.

Horsemen. The Royal Canadian Mounted Police in Canada.

hot. Stolen.

hot prowl. Police talk for a prowler in an occupied home.

hot shot. Police emergency call meaning "shots fired."

house. Prison cell.

hugger-mugger. A man who, according to Joseph Wambaugh in *Echoes in the Darkness*, "picks on plain or homely women, turns on the charm, and gives them some cuddles while he picks their purses."

husher. Device used to mask conversation between judge and attorneys in jury trials.

I

IBM. For *Italian businessman,* in the parlance of the FBI and other law enforcement groups. It refers to someone associated with the Mafia.

in a crack. In trouble, especially in prison.

in-house lawyer. Inmate paralegal.

ink. Tattooes in jail.

inside/outside. Inside and outside the walls of a prison.

in the free. Prison term for out of jail; on the street.

J

jacket. (1) A criminal record. (2) The reputation (good or bad) of a prisoner or inmate.

jade squad. Special police unit used to thwart the efforts of Asian crime syndicates.

jailhouse lawyer. A prisoner who assists others in filing legal actions. As explained on an inmate-controlled Internet site devoted to prison slang, "Some are quite knowledgeable, others know enough to get themselves or others into trouble. Jailhouse lawyers are important because most prisoners have limited access to law libraries, little legal knowledge, and there are all too few lawyers able to assist prisoners."

jailin'. (1) Someone who's in the hole (aka in jail). (2) Prison style: Seth Morgan in his book *Homeboy* writes, "Jailin' was an art form and lifestyle both. The style was walkin' slow, drinkin' plenty of water, and doin' your own time; the art was lightin' cigarettes from wall sockets, playin' the dozens, cuttin' up dream jackpots, and slowin' your metabolism to a crawl, sleepin' twenty-four hours a day. Forget the streets you won't see for years. Lettin' your heart beat the bricks with your body behind bars was hard time. Acceptin' the jailhouse as the only reality was easy time."

jakes. Police term for uniformed police.

jocker. Aggressive homosexual male prisoner.

John Law. The police.

joint. Prison.

jug. (1) To attempt to cut the jugular vein. (2) Jail; the joint.

juice. Good prison connections; penitentiary pull.

jumpouts. Teams of arresting officers who commonly jump out of hiding or out of a patrol car.

 K

kazoonie. Passive homosexual male prisoner.

keep. Prison.

keeping six. Safecracker's code for a lookout; one who watches for the police and other interlopers.

keeping the peek. (prison) A lookout, watching for the guards, etc.

keester. To hide contraband in the rectum. Prisoners keester money, drugs, and even weapons.

K.G. (police) Known gambler.

kick 'em. To release a suspect, in police talk.

kit. Items for taking drugs, in prison talk.

kite. Letter to, from, or within prison; for example, "to float a kite."

klepto. Kleptomaniac.

knocked. Arrested.

Kojak light. Portable flashing red light that police can throw up on the roof of an unmarked car to mark it. The term comes from the television cop Kojak, who used such a light.

 L

lajaras. Hispanic street slang for New York cops. Carsten Stroud points out that it derives from the name O'Hara.

launder. Legalize.

lay chickie. To act as a lookout.

laying paper. Passing worthless checks.

laying the track. Having sex, in the lingo of prisoners.

lemac. A camel cigarette in slammerese. It is the word *camel* spelled backward.

lockdown. The policy of confining a group of prisoners or an entire prison to cells. Generally done in response to unrest or emergency—although some lockdowns are instituted for extended periods.

loid. To open a lock with a credit card or other piece of plastic. The term predates credit cards and harks back to the time when burglars used thin strips of celluloid.

 M

mafias. Dark sunglasses in the lingo of prison.

mainline. The general population—prison talk.

man, the. The warden.

mark. (1) Victim. (2) Someone who wants to be a gang member.

maxin'. Prison slang for serving maximum time. By extension, hanging out, as one must do while serving a long sentence.

maytag. Prison slang for a male inmate unable to protect himself from rape.

minute. Short sentence in the language of prisoners, who refer to a life sentence as ALL DAY.

Mirandize. To warn a suspect of his or her constitutional rights under the Supreme Court's Miranda decision.

moe. Married homosexual in prison.

mole. Inmate secretly working for the man.

money bus. Armored truck.

monster, the. HIV in prison, as in, "He has the monster."

mooch. Target of scam.

mooner. Person who gives police a hard time and is believed to be most pesky during a full moon.

mother's day. Day on which welfare checks arrive and women are more vulnerable to robbery.

motor. Tattoo gun in prison.

mug. (1) Rob and beat. (2) To take a police or prison photo, or mug shot.

mug shot. A police or prison photo.

mule. (prison) A person who carries things for others; either around the prison or in prison—usually contraband. See HORSE.

mushfake. Contraband in prison.

mustard chucker. Pickpocket who, according to an article in the *New York Times* (July 13, 1989) on criminals who prey on tourists, "sprays a victim with mustard. He apologizes profusely and helps to remove it while an accomplice steals the victim's wallet."

Mutt and Jeff act. Interrogation technique in which one cop is the bad cop (heavy and hostile) and the other good (good-natured and friendly).

 N

ninja rock. A three-eighths-inch-thick, cube-shaped piece of white procelain used, first by Southeast Asian gangs, to break into cars. Thrown at a moderate speed, it will break or shatter glass making little or no sound. Nearly undetectable at the crime scene.

 O

off. Kill.

one-percenters. Term used by outlaw/outcast bikers (motorcyclists) to show that they represent the worst 1 percent of the population.

on ice. In the morgue.

on the arm. A free meal or other item, in police terminology. Writing in the *New York Times* (February 15, 1970), David Burham said that this expression "might be a play on the expression 'the long arm of the law.'" A character in Vincent Patrick's *Pope of Greenwich Village* says, "He wasn't that greedy at all. He was putting next to nothing into his pocket. It was all bar bills and seven-course dinners on the arm."

on the grain and drain train. To be in solitary confinement in prison. It comes from the old notion of bread and water, or grain and drain.

on the muscle. Said of a nervous suspect by police.

 P

paper. (1) Parking ticket. (2) To issue a ticket. (3) Acid (LSD) in drug parlance.

paper hanger. Check forger to police: a bad-check passer.

patch. The proceeds of a crime that are given to corrupt police to keep from going to jail. A patch is much more costly than a simple bribe or payoff since it involves the total haul.

pavement princess. Prostitute.

perp. Perpetrator.

phone's off the hook. Inmate talk for "the guard is listening."

phony collar. Unjust arrest.

PI. Prison industries.

piddling. Crafting items out of matchsticks, toothpicks, and other humble objects in prison. An item in the *Houston Post* for March 23, 1989, speaks of a death-row inmate known for his piddling ability.

piece. A revolver.

pile. Weights in prison, as in the iron pile.

pine-box parole. Prison term for dying in the joint.

pinner. In slammerese, a marijuana cigarette the size of a toothpick.

pitcher. Sexually dominant, aggressive, in the lingo of prison.

place, the. Prison.

plant. Police stakeout.

playing on ass. Gambling without money—if a prisoner loses "it's his ass."

pocket man. Criminal holding the money after a robbery or other crime.

pop caps. To open fire, in police parlance.

popcorn machine. Light(s) on top of a police car.

potty watch. Special prison watch when someone is suspected of eating drugs or other contraband items, such as money.

pp. Short for penitentiary pull; influence in prison.

present the bill. Nicaraguan slang for a death threat—to government deputies in the National Assembly.

press your bunk, punk. Prison command meaning "lie down on your bed and shut up."

priors. Previous prison terms, enhancing one's sentence.

pruno. Homemade alcohol, fermented juice, the classic prison drink.

pulling someone's card. Finding out about another prisoner in prison talk.

punch job. Safecracking in which the dial of the safe has been removed.

punk. Prison talk: (1) To sodomize. (2) Victim or willing partner in a homosexual arrangement.

put his papers in. For a policeman to retire.

put your pen to the wind. By inmates, to tell an officer to go ahead and write a disciplinary report. By officers, to tell prisoners to go ahead and file a grievance.

* R

rabbit. An inmate who has escaped or is planning to.

raisin jack. Homemade booze in prison.

rap. Talk, especially in prison.

rap sheet. Criminal record.

reefer. (police) The six-button tunic worn by police in cold weather.

ride on. A drive-by shooting.

ride-out. Automotive scam in which the perp intentionally slams into the car of an apparently wealthy person in hopes of making an injury claim and getting a fat settlement.

road dog. Prison term for a good friend made in prison.

roll. (police) To take fingerprints.

roscoe. Gun. This term is dated, common to gangster movies of the 1940s, but still used with tongue in cheek. (There is a sizable slang vocabulary from these movies, which is still toyed with—among others, *shamus* for private eye, *mug* for man or his face, *big house* for prison, etc.)

rough off. To steal; to rip off.

rounder. Street criminal who operates around bars, clubs, and hotels, selling drugs, setting up high-stakes poker games, etc. So called because they are always *around* to make the deals.

∗ S

safe. The vagina, where women prisoners may hide contraband.

S&J. Sentence and judgment.

S&W. Short for Smith and Wesson.

satch. Paper that has been impregnated with heroin or LSD and mailed into prison in an envelope.

Saturday night special. Cheap handgun.

screw. Prison guard.

SCUM. Semi-acronym for *street crimes unit.*

second-story man. Burglar.

set-up. The person who sets up a pickpocketing—the DIP is the one who actually takes the wallet.

shakedown. Search in prison.

shank. (1) Handmade prison weapon—generally a stabbing instrument. (2) To stab.

shine on. To ignore, in prison parlance.

shiv. Knife.

shoe. Plainclothes detective.

short. Describing somebody with little prison time to do.

short con. A confidence game requiring little preparation and involving small stakes.

shot. Friend in prison.

signal 12. Someone who is dead in police parlance.

size the vic. To observe, or size up, a victim from a distance.

skell. Police name for a derelict or habitual drunk.

skinner-diddler. Prison slang for a person who has committed a sex crime, usually against a child. Also *hedge-hopper, child-lover,* and more.

slammer. (1) Prison. (2) In illegal boiler-room sales swindles, the high-pressure salesperson who gets the mark to part with his money.

slim-jim. Thin, limber strip of metal used by car thieves to yank open the lock on a car door.

smurfing. Money-laundering procedure by which currency is exchanged at various banks in amounts slightly less than those that must be reported to federal authorities. These amounts change, but when all transactions of $10,000 or more had to be reported, many transactions took place involving $9,999.

snitch. An informant: a rat.

songbird. Informer.

spit on the sidewalk. To commit a minor crime.

spitter. Police slang for a pickpocket.

squat. An intentional accident in which two cars bump each other so that a fraudulent injury claim can be made.

squeal. Complaint, in police parlance.

stall. Person who distracts a victim in a robbery. The *hook* is a person who takes the money or goods.

staties. State police.

stay down. Engage in a fight to prove one's manhood, in Texas prison talk.

step back. Incarceration. A prosecutor may waive "step back" in certain arraignments. It comes from the words of judges who tell some defendants to step back and be escorted to prison.

stepson. Inmate under the control of another.

stinger. Prison inmate's appliance used to heat water, which may be created by attaching live electrical wires to a metal plate.

stir. Prison.

stooge. A person working for the prison administration.

straight eight. Tour in which patrolman puts in eight hours with no overtime.

strapped. Armed in the parlance of street gangs.

straps. Street slang for guns.

street. The outside world, as in "on the street."

swag stuff. (partial acronym) Stuff stolen without a gun—in cop talk.

swallow. Female operative who obtains secrets for sex.

swap paint. What one car does to another when it is sideswiped.

system, the. The entire corrections, jurisprudence bureaucracy; to inmates it is the enemy.

* T

10/13. Police radio code for an officer in trouble who needs immediate help. This is part of a set of radio 10 codes: for instance, 10/6 stands for "Shut up, you're jamming the frequency," and 10/98 means "This car is ready for a new assignment."

Thirsty Third, the. New York police nickname for the Forty-sixth Precinct's Third Squad in recognition of its members' penchant for drinking on the job.

13½. The total of twelve jurors, one judge, and one-half chance, often featured in tattoos seen in prison.

three hots and a cot. In the lingo of the streets, the food and lodging afforded by jail.

throwaway. Clothing worn by a mugger and discarded immediately after commission of a crime, to confuse pursuers.

throw bricks. Commit a felony.

tin. Policeman's badge; by extension, a policeman. See also GOLD TIN.

tree jumper. Rapist in the lingo of prison.

trey-eight. A .38-caliber gun.

turn. To change sides from gangster to informer.

turnkey. In prison talk, a guard who is there just to open doors, who cares about nothing other than doing his or her shift.

turn out. To rape or make into a "punk" in the language of prison.

24/24. Prison slang for all day.

24/24 rule. (police homicide) Explained by Carsten Stroud in *Close Pursuit: A Week in the Life of an NYPD Homicide Cop:* "It means that the most important hours in the investigation of any murder are the last twenty-four hours in the victim's life and the first twenty-four hours after the body has been discovered."

 V

vesting. Process by which an inmate's good time for good behavior becomes irrevocable and cannot be taken.

vic. A duped customer, such as one to which a bogus drug has been sold.

 W

wad cutter. Bullet.

wagger. Flasher, to police.

Waldorf-Astoria. Solitary confinement in prison.

walkalone. A prisoner who cannot exercise in a yard with other prisoners. San Quentin's death row has a yard for walkalones to exercise together.

walls. The joint; prison.

waste. Kill.

whack/whack in the mouth. To execute, in gangland.

wire. The fence surrounding a prison.

wired. (1) Carrying a recording device or microphone. (2) Armed.

 Y

yard hack. Guard in a prison yard.

yellow sheet. Same as RAP SHEET.

yoking. A form of mugging in which a male victim is grabbed from behind, put in a headlock, and has his wallet taken from his jacket pocket.

 Z

zippers. Scars.

zip to five. Parole time of zero to five years.

SOURCES

The Tamony Collection greatly aided this glossary, as did the eagle-eyed Joseph C. Goulden, who scanned many a newspaper cop story for examples. Among other things, he sent along a circa 1961 carbon of a piece he did for the *Dallas News* on South Dallas cop/perp slang. Russell Mott, Charles D. Poe, Edward O'Brien, Mike Stackpole, and Suzy Nace were all of great help. Letters from inmate #63760 at the Colorado Department of Corrections, #80535 at the Louisiana State Prison in Angola, Louisiana, #381867 in the Texas Department of Criminal Justice in Amarillo, and several other insiders were most helpful, as was an Internet inmate slang glossary updated through August 10, 1996.

It should be noted that a particularly useful and fascinating glossary of police terminology appears in the back of Carsten Stroud's *Close Pursuit: A Week in the Life of an NYPD Homicide Cop* (Bantam, 1987). A particularly good article on Los Angeles Police Department slang by Chip Johnson appeared in the *Los Angeles Times* of December 19, 1994.

11

THE DRUG TRADE

The Spacey Talk of the Junkie, Cokie, Druggie, and Pothead

. . . to which we must now add drugs.

—Anthony Burgess's reaction to the old
assertion that slang's chief stimuli are liquor,
money, and sex. The London *Times Literary
Supplement,* December 5, 1986

Little is subtle about today's drug trade. The same is true about the slang used in that realm, which is at once direct, street-smart, and composed of a vast collection of synonyms.

What follows is a major haul of drug slang combining a number of sources, of which the major one has been a periodic "street terms" list compiled by the Federal Drugs and Crime Data Clearinghouse and distributed by mail and over the Internet (askjncjrs@ncjrs.aspensys.com).

The list, which is far from complete, underscores the level to which the drug culture has made itself known in the larger culture.

✳ A

A. (1) LSD. (2) Amphetamine.

ab. Short for *abscess*—the result of using dirty needles and/or adulterated drugs.

Abe. Five dollars' worth of drugs.

Abe's cape. Five-dollar bill, an allusion to the fact that Abraham Lincoln is on it.

Abolic. Veterinary steroid.

Acapulco gold. Powerful marijuana from southwest Mexico, somewhat gold in color.

ace. (1) A single pill. (2) marijuana; PCP.

acid. LSD

acidhead. LSD user.

AD. Short for drug addict. According to Jonathan Green in his *Dictionary of Contemporary Slang,* this initialism has been reversed to avoid confusion with the law's *DA* for district attorney.

Adam. Methylendioxy-methamphetamine or MDMA.

African black/African bush/African woodbine. Marijuana cigarette.

agonies. Withdrawal symptoms.

a-head. Amphetamine user.

Ah-pen-yen. Opium.

aimies. Amphetamine; amyl nitrite.

AIP. Heroin from Afghanistan, Iran, and Pakistan.

air blast. Inhalant.

airhead. Marijuana user.

airplane. Marijuana.

Alice B. Toklas. Marijuana brownie, named for Gertrude Stein's companion, who was renowned for this dopey confection.

all-American drug. Cocaine.

all lit up. Under the influence of drugs.

all-star. User of multiple drugs.

alpha-ET. Alpha-ethyltyptamine.

Ames. Amyl nitrite.

amidone. Methadone.

amoeba. PCP.

amp. Amphetamine.

amped-out. Fatigue after using amphetamines.

amping. Accelerated heartbeat.

amp joint. Marijuana cigarette laced with some form of narcotic.

amt. Dimethyltryptamine.

Anadrol. Oral steroid.

anatrofin. Injectable steroid.

Anavar. Oral steroid.

angel dust/angel hair/angel mist. PCP.

Angie. Cocaine.

Angola. Marijuana.

animal. LSD.

animal trank/animal tranquilizer. PCP.

antifreeze. Heroin.

ant trafficker. One dealing in small quantities.

anywhere. Holding or possessing drugs, as in the query "Are you anywhere?"

apple jacks. Crack.

Aries. Heroin.

aroma of men. Isobutyl nitrite.

artillery. Equipment for injecting drugs.

ashes. Marijuana.

assassin of youth. Marijuana, from the 1930s film of the same name.

asskash. Narcotics concealed in the rectum, usually in a condom or metal capsule. Blend of *ass* + *cache*.

atom bomb. Heroin mixed with marijuana.

atshitshi. Marijuana.

attic. Slurred rhyme of *addict*.

Aunt Hazel. Heroin.

Aunti/Aunt Emma. Opium.

Aunt Mary. Marijuana.

Aunt Nora. Cocaine.

aurora borealis. PCP.

b/B. (1) Benzedrine. (2) Amount of marijuana to fill a matchbox.

babe. Drug used for detoxification.

baby/baby bhang. Marijuana.

baby habit. Occasional use of drugs.

babylon. The outside world. (A Rastafarian term used primarily by members of Jamaican gangs.)

baby-sit. Guide someone through first drug experience.

baby T. Crack.

backbreakers. LSD and strychnine.

back door. Residue left in a pipe.

back in the box. To be back in operation again after being arrested on a drug charge. (A Rastafarian term used primarily by members of Jamaican gangs.)

backjack. Injecting opium.

back-to-back. Smoking crack after injecting heroin or heroin used after crack.

backtrack. Allow blood to flow back into a needle during injection.

backup. Prepare vein for injection.

backwards. Depressant.

bad. Crack.

bad bundle. Inferior-quality heroin.

bad go. Bad reaction to a drug.

bad seed. Peyote, heroin, marijuana.

bag. (1) A measure of narcotics determined by retail value; hence, a nickel bag is a $5 amount. (2) Container for drugs.

bag bride. Crack-smoking prostitute.

baggies. Plastic bag for small quantities of narcotics.

bagging. Using inhalant.

bagman. Person who transports money.

baldhead. Undesirable; outsider.

bale. Marijuana.

ball. Crack.

balling. Vaginally implanted cocaine.

balloon. Heroin supplier.

ballot. Heroin.

bam. Depressant; amphetamine.

bamblacha. Marijuana.

bambs. Depressant.

bang. To inject a drug; inhalant.

bank. Money. To say that one has bank is to say that one has a lot of money.

bank bandit pills. Depressant.

bar. Marijuana.

barb. Depressant.

Barnes man. New York street slang for a major drug dealer. According to Carsten Stroud in *Close Pursuit: A Week in the Life of an NYPD Homicide Cop,* the term comes from the name of a famous Harlem dealer, Nicky Barnes.

barrels. LSD.

base. (1) Freebase. (2) Cocaine, crack.

baseball. Crack.

base crazies. Searching on hands and knees for crack.

basehead/base head. (1) One addicted to the freebasing of cocaine. In his autobiography, *Long Time Gone,* musician David Crosby described himself as a basehead for fifteen harrowing years of his life. (2) Person who bases.

bash. Marijuana.

basuco. Cocaine; coca-paste residue sprinkled on a marijuana or regular cigarette.

bathtub speed. Methcathinone.

batt. IV needle.

battery acid. LSD.

bazooka. (1) Cocaine paste or coke paste that's said to have an "explosive" effect on the user. (2) Synthetic drug. (3) Cocaine; crack.

bazuco/bazko. Highly addictive powder containing cocaine, kerosene, ether, and sulfates that can be rolled into a cigarette for smoking.

bazulco. Cocaine.

beamer. Crack user.

beam me up, Scotty. (1) Mixture of PCP and crack, from the original *Star Trek* line calling for transmogrification back to the ship. (2) Crack dipped in PCP.

beans. Amphetamine; depressant; mescaline.

beast. (1) Police. (2) LSD. (3) Heroin.

beat artist. Person selling bogus drugs.

beat bag. Quantity of heavily cut (diluted) narcotics.

beat vials. Vials containing sham crack to cheat buyers.

beautiful boulders. Crack.

bebe. Crack.

bedbugs. Fellow addicts.

beemers. Crack.

beeper boy. Dealer using electronic equipment in sales effort.

B-40. Cigar laced with marijuana and dipped in malt liquor.

behind the scale. To weigh and sell cocaine.

beiging. Chemicals altering cocaine to make it appear a higher purity.

belly habit. The stomach pains that accompany withdrawal from continued heroin use.

belt. (1) The "kick" of a narcotic. (2) Effects of drugs.

Belushi cocktail. A mixture of cocaine and heroin (and an obvious reference to the late comedian John Belushi, who was killed with such a mixture).

belyando spruce. Marijuana.

bender. Drug party.

bennies. (1) Benzedrine. (2) Amphetamine.

benz/benzo. (1) Mercedes-Benz. (2) Amphetamine.

be off. To abstain: to be off drugs.

Bernice/Bernie/Bernie's flakes/Bernie's gold dust. Cocaine.

Bhang. Marijuana, Indian term.

big bag. Heroin.

big bloke/big C. Cocaine.

big D. LSD.

big 8. One-eighth kilogram of crack.

big flake. Cocaine.

big H./big Harry. Heroin.

big man. Drug supplier.

big O. Opium.

big rush. Cocaine.

biker's speed. Methamphetamines.

Bill Blass. Crack.

Billie hoke. Cocaine.

bindle. (1) Paper in which drugs are wrapped and folded. It comes from hobo slang in which a bindle is a bedroll carried folded up. A once common term for a tramp was a *bindle stiff*. (2) Small packet of drug powder; heroin.

bing. Enough of a drug for one injection.

bingers. Crack addicts.

bingo. To inject a drug.

bings. Crack.

birdie powder. Heroin; cocaine.

bird's-eye. A small amount of narcotics.

biscuits. (1) Methadone. (2) Fifty rocks of crack.

bite. Arrest.

bite one's lips. To smoke marijuana.

biz. Bag or portion of drugs.

B.J.'s. Crack.

black. Opium.

black acid. LSD; LSD and PCP.

black and white. Amphetamine.

black bart. Marijuana.

black beauties. Depressant; amphetamine.

black birds. Amphetamine.

black ganga/black gold. High-potency marijuana.

black gungi. Marijuana from India.

black gunion. Marijuana.

black hash. Opium mixed with hashish.

black mo/black moat. Highly potent marijuana.

black mollies. Amphetamine.

black mote. Marijuana mixed with honey.

black pearl. Heroin.

black pill. Opium pill.

black rock. Crack.

black Russian. Hashish mixed with opium.

blacks. Amphetamine.

black star. LSD.

black stuff. Heroin.

black sunshine/black tabs. LSD.

black tar. (1) Heroin. (2) Potent Mexican heroin with a tarry look.

black whack. PCP.

black widow. Black capsule carrying amphetamines.

blanco. Heroin.

blanket. Marijuana cigarette.

blanks. Low-quality drugs.

blast. (1) A line or snort of cocaine. (2) To smoke marijuana; to smoke crack.

blast a joint/blast a roach/blast a stick. To smoke marijuana.

blasted. Under the influence of drugs.

blizzard. White cloud in a pipe used to smoke cocaine.

block. Marijuana.

blockbusters. Depressant.

blonde. Marijuana.

blotter/blotter acid/blotter cube. LSD.

blow. (1) Cocaine; to inhale cocaine; to smoke marijuana. (2) A snort or sniff of cocaine.

blow a fix/blow a shot. Injection misses the vein and is wasted in the skin.

blow a stick. To smoke marijuana.

blow blue. To inhale cocaine.

blowcaine. Crack diluted with cocaine.

blow coke. To inhale cocaine.

blowing smoke. Marijuana.

blow one's roof. To smoke marijuana.

blowout. Crack.

blow smoke. To inhale cocaine.

blow the vein. (1) To use too much pressure on a weak vein, causing it to rupture. (2) Injection misses the vein and is wasted in the skin.

blow up. Crack cut with lidocaine to increase size, weight, and street value.

blue. Depressant; crack.

blue acid. LSD.

blue angels. Depressant.

blue barrels. LSD.

blue birds. Depressant.

blue boy. Amphetamine.

blue bullets. Depressant.

blue caps. Mescaline.

blue chairs/blue cheers. LSD.

blue de hue. Marijuana from Vietnam.

blue devil/blue dolls. Depressant.

SAY WHAT?

How many ways are there to smoke a marijuana cigarette? For starters:

Be in tweeds; bite one's lips on bamblachas; blast Mary Jane to kingdom come; blast the reefers; blast the weed; bounce the goof balls; break a stick; burn Indian hay; drink Texas tea; go loco; hit the hay; hunt in the sage; kiss Mary Jane; lie in state with the girls; puff the dust; send up smoke rings; twist a giraffe's neck; vipe.

blue heaven/blue microdot/blue mist/ blue moons. LSD.

blue sage. Marijuana.

blue sky. Heroin.

blue sky bond. High-potency marijuana from Columbia.

blue tips. Depressant.

blue vials. LSD.

blunt. Marijuana inside a cigar; marijuana and cocaine inside a cigar.

boat. Marijuana laced with PCP.

bo-bo. Marijuana

bobo. Crack.

bobo bush. Marijuana.

body packer/body stuffer. Person who ingests crack or cocaine to transport it, or to avoid prosecution.

Bogart a joint. Salivate on a marijuana cigarette; refuse to share a marijuana cigarette.

bohd. Marijuana; PCP.

Bolasterone. Injectable steroid.

Bolivian marching powder. Cocaine.

bolo. Crack.

bolt. Isobutyl nitrate.

bomb. Crack; heroine; large marijuana cigarette; high-potency heroin.

bomber. Marijuana cigarette.

bombido. Injectable amphetamine; heroin; depressant.

bombita. Amphetamine; heroin; depressant.

bombs away. Heroin.

bomb squad. Crack-selling crew.

bone. Marijuana; $50 piece of crack.

bonecrusher/bones. Crack.

bong. Type of pipe used to smoke marijuana.

Bonita. Heroin.

boo/boom. Marijuana.

boom car. Drug dealer's car with loud, expensive stereo system.

boomers. Psilocybin/psilocin.

boopers. Amyl nitrite.

boost. To inject a drug; to steal.

boost and shoot. Steal to support a habit.

booster. To inhale cocaine.

boot. To inject a drug.

booted. Under the influence of drugs.

boot the gong. To smoke marijuana.

botray. Crack.

bottles. Crack vials; amphetamine.

boubou. Crack.

boulder. Crack; $20 worth of crack.

boulya. Crack.

bouncing powder. Cocaine.

boxed. In jail.

boy. Heroin.

bozo. (1) Ration of drugs: often an ounce. (2) Heroin.

brain ticklers. Amphetamine.

breakdowns. Forty-dollar crack rock sold for $20.

break night. Staying up all night until daybreak.

brewery. Place where drugs are made.

brick. One kilogram of marijuana; crack.

brick gum. Heroin.

bridge up or **bring up.** Ready a vein for injection.

broccoli. Marijuana.

broker. Go-between in a drug deal.

brown. Heroin; marijuana.

brown bombers/brown dots. LSD.

brown crystal/brown rhine/brown sugar. Heroin.

brownies/browns. Amphetamine.

bubble gum. Cocaine; crack.

buck. Shoot someone in the head.

bud. Marijuana. One expensive strain of California pot is known as mendo bud. This term came into vogue during the countercultural era.

buda. A high-grade marijuana joint filled with crack.

Buddha grass. Strong marijuana sold by bar girls in Saigon during the Vietnam War.

buffer. Crack smoker; a woman who exchanges oral sex for crack.

bugged. Annoyed; to be covered with sores and abscesses from repeated use of unsterile needles.

bule. Marijuana.

bull. Narcotics agent or police officer.

bullet. (1) A line or snort of cocaine. (2) Isobutyl nitrite.

bullet bolt. Inhalant.

bullia capital/bullion. Crack.

bullyon. Marijuana.

bumblebees. Amphetamine.

bump. Crack; fake crack; boost a high; hit of ketamine.

bundle. Heroin.

bunk. Fake cocaine.

burese. Cocaine.

burn. To cheat; to sell bogus drugs. A source who knows about such things says, "a burn artist is a dope dealer who consistently sells catnip for pot, Accent [the commercial flavor enhancer] for speed, coffee for heroin, etc. Don't take up the trade; you could get shot."

burn bag. Quantity of bogus drugs sold as real.

burned. To purchase fake drugs.

burned-out. Collapse of veins from repeated injections; permanent impairment from drug abuse.

burner. Gun, usually a handgun.

burnese. Cocaine.

burnie. (1) Half-smoke marijuana cigarette. (2) Marijuana.

burn one. To smoke marijuana.

burnout. (1) One addled by and dependent on marijuana. (2) Heavy abuser of drugs.

burn the main line. To inject a drug.

burros. Derogatory but common name given to people who carry cocaine and other drugs across the Mexican border on their persons.

bush. Cocaine; marijuana.

businessman's LSD/businessman's

trip/businessman's special. Dimethyltryptamine.

bust caps. To inject a narcotic. (In military jargon, the same term is used for firing a weapon.)

busted. Arrested.

busters. Depressant.

busy bee/butt naked. PCP.

butter. Marijuana; crack.

butter flower. Marijuana.

buttons. Mescaline.

butu. Heroin.

buzz. (1) High on marijuana. (2) Under the influence of drugs.

buzz bomb. Nitrous oxide.

* C

C/C. Cocaine.

C, the. Methcathinone.

caballo. Heroin.

cabello. Cocaine.

caca. Heroin.

cactus/cactus buttons/cactus head. Mescaline.

cad/Cadillac. One ounce.

Cadillac. PCP.

Cadillac cops. DEA and other enforcers who drive rental luxury cars.

Cadillac express. Methcathinone.

caine. Cocaine; crack.

cakes. Round discs of crack.

cali. Marijuana.

California cornflakes. Cocaine.

California sunshine. LSD.

Cambodian red/cam red. Marijuana from Cambodia.

cam trip. High-potency marijuana.

can. One ounce of marijuana.

Canadian black/canamo/canappa. Marijuana.

canceled stick. Marijuana cigarette.

c&m/C&M. Cocaine and morphine.

candy. Cocaine; crack; depressant; amphetamine.

candy bar. Cocaine joint.

candy c. Cocaine.

cannabinol. PCP.

cannabis tea. Marijuana.

cap. Crack; LSD.

capital H. Heroin.

caps. Crack; heroin; psilocybin/psilocin.

cap up. Transfer bulk-form drugs to capsules.

carburetor. Crack-stem attachment.

carga. Heroin.

carmabis. Marijuana.

carne. Heroin.

carnie. Cocaine.

carpet patrol. Crack smokers searching the floor for crack.

carrie/carrie nation. Cocaine.

cartucho. Package of marijuana cigarettes.

cartwheels. Amphetamines. A cartwheel is also a feigned illness, fit, or spasm enacted by an addict to get drugs legally from a physician.

Casper the ghost. Crack.

cat. Methcathinone.

catch a buzz. Smoking marijuana.

catnip. Marijuana cigarette.

cat valium. Ketamine.

caviar. Crack.

cavite all-star. Marijuana.

C-dust/Cecil/C-game. Cocaine.

chalk. Methamphetamine; amphetamine.

chalked up. Under the influence of cocaine.

chalking. Chemically altering the color of cocaine so it looks white.

chandoo/chandu. Opium.

channel. Vein into which narcotic is injected.

channel swimmer. One who injects heroin.

charas. Marijuana from India.

charge. Marijuana.

charged up. (1) Marijuana intoxification. (2) Under the influence of drugs.

Charley. Heroin.

Charlie. Cocaine.

chase. To smoke cocaine; to smoke marijuana.

chaser. Compulsive crack user.

chasing the dragon. (1) Smoking a mixture of heroin and cocaine. (2) Crack and heroin.

chasing the tiger. To smoke heroin.

chasing the white nurse. Addicted to morphine or cocaine.

cheap basing. Crack.

check. Personal supply of drugs.

cheeba/cheeo. Marijuana.

chemical/chewies. Crack.

chiba chiba. High-potency marijuana from Columbia.

Chicago black/Chicago green. Marijuana.

chicken powder. Amphetamine.

chicken scratch. Searching on hands and knees for crack.

chicle. Heroin.

chief. LSD; mescaline.

chieva. Heroin.

China cat. High-potency heroin.

China girl/China town/China white. Fentanyl.

Chinese molasses/Chinese tobacco. Opium.

Chinese #3. Variety of heroin processed in Hong Kong and sold by Chinese merchants.

Chinese red. Heroin.

chip. Heroin.

chipper. Weekend junkie.

chipping. Using drugs occasionally.

chippy. Cocaine.

chippying. Light narcotic sampling.

chira. Marijuana.

chocolate. Opium; amphetamine.

chocolate chips. LSD.

chocolate ecstasy. Crack made brown by adding chocolate milk powder during production.

cholly. Cocaine.

chorals. Depressant.

Christina. Amphetamine.

Christmas rolls. Depressant.

Christmas tree. Marijuana; marijuana mixed with crack; depressant; amphetamine.

chronic. Marijuana. From the concept "chronic user."

chucks. Hunger following withdrawal from heroin.

churus. Marijuana.

cid. LSD.

cigarette paper. Packet of heroin.

cigarrode cristal. PCP.

citrol. High-potency marijuana, from Nepal.

CJ. PCP.

C joint. Place where cocaine is sold.

clap. Shoot.

clear up. Stop drug use.

clicker. Crack and PCP.

climax. Crack; isobutyl nitrite; heroin.

climb. Marijuana cigarette.

clips. Rows of vials heat-sealed together.

closet baser. User of crack who prefers anonymity.

cloud/cloud nine. Crack.

cluck. Crack smoker.

coasting. Under the influence of drugs.

coasts to coasts. Amphetamine.

coca. Cocaine.

cocabucks. Cocaine money, in the same sense that oil money has been called petrodollars.

cocaine blues. Depression after extended cocaine use.

cocaine industrial park. State-of-the-art facility for the manufacture and distribution of cocaine.

cochornis. Marijuana.

cocktail. Cigarette laced with cocaine or crack; partially smoked marijuana cigarette inserted in regular cigarette.

cocoa puff. To smoke cocaine and marijuana.

coconut/coconuts. Cocaine.

coco rocks. Dark brown crack made by adding chocolate pudding during production.

coco snow. Benzocaine used as cutting agent for crack.

coffee. LSD.

coke. Cocaine; crack.

coke bar. Bar where cocaine is openly used.

coke bugs. Nickname for cocaine hallucination in which bugs infest the user's body.

coked. Under the influence of and/or addicted to cocaine.

coke oven. Drug joint.

cokie. Cocaine user.

cola. Cocaine.

cold turkey. (1) Completely and suddenly quitting drugs—the term is also used for getting off tobacco, alcohol, etc. (2) Sudden withdrawal from drugs.

coli/coliflor tostao/colly weed/Colorado cocktail/Columbian. Marijuana.

columbo. PCP.

Columbus back. Marijuana.

comeback. Benzocaine and mannitol used to adulterate cocaine for conversion to crack.

come down. For the effect of a drug to wear off.

come home. End a "trip" from LSD.

conductor. LSD.

connect. Purchase drugs; supplier of illegal drugs.

contact lens. LSD.

convert. One newly addicted to drugs.

cook. Mix heroin with water; heating heroin to prepare it for injection.

cook down. Process in which users liquefy heroin to inhale it.

cooker. (1) A receptacle in which drugs are heated before injection. (2) To inject a drug.

cookies. Crack.

cooler/coolie. Cigarette laced with cocaine.

coolie mud. Cheap grade of opium or heroin, often derived from residues.

cop. (1) To buy drugs. (2) To obtain drugs.

copilots. Amphetamines, so called

because of truck drivers who have been known to use them on long trips.

copping zones. Specific areas where buyers can purchase drugs.

coral. Depressant.

coriander seeds. Cash.

cork the air. To inhale cocaine.

corn. Marijuana.

Corrinne. Cocaine.

cosa. Marijuana.

coso. Small package of BAZUCO.

'cotics/cotics. (1) *Narcotics* for short. (2) Heroin.

cotton. Currency.

cotton brothers. Cocaine, heroin, and morphine.

courage pills. Heroin; depressant.

course note. Bill larger than $2.

cozmo's. PCP.

crack. Form of cocaine that is highly addictive, relatively cheap, and is smoked by the user.

crack attack. Craving for crack.

crack back. Crack and marijuana.

crack cooler. Crack soaked in wine cooler.

cracker jacks. Crack smokers.

crackers. LSD.

crack gallery/crack spot. Place where crack is sold.

crackhead. One addicted to crack.

crack house. Building in which crack cocaine is sold and consumed.

crank. Meth or methamphetamines; amphetamine; methcathinone.

cranking up. To inject a drug.

cranny. Marijuana.

crap/crop. Low-quality heroin.

crash. (1) To collapse in exhaustion after a bout of heavy drug use—especially amphetamines. (2) Sleep off the effects of drugs.

crazy weed. Marijuana.

credit card. Crack stem.

crib. Crack.

crimmie. Cigarette laced with crack.

crink. Methamphetamine.

cripple. Marijuana cigarette.

cris/crisscross/Cristina. Methamphetamine.

croak. Crack and methamphetamine.

Crop, the. The agricultural side of the marijuana business. As one close observer writes from his rural northern-California home, "When people in the Emerald Triangle speak of the Crop, they do it reverently, and they ain't talkin' about apples, grapes, or corn."

cross tops/crossroads. Amphetamine.

crown crap. Heroin.

crumbs. Tiny pieces of crack.

crunch and munch. Crack.

crying weed. Marijuana.

crypto. Methamphetamine.

crystal/crystals. Methamphetamines in crystalline form; PCP; amphetamine; cocaine.

crystal joint. PCP.

crystal meth. Methamphetamine.

crystal tea. LSD.

cube. One ounce; LSD.

cubes. (1) Demerol. (2) Marijuana tablets.

culican. High-potency marijuana from Mexico.

cupcakes. LSD.

cura. Heroin.

cushion. Vein into which narcotics are injected.

cut. Adulterate drugs.

cut-deck. Heroin mixed with powdered milk.

cyclones. PCP.

✳ D

D. LSD.

DA. Drug addict. See also **AD**.

dabble. (1) To experiment with drugs: to be in the early stages of addiction. (2) To use drugs occasionally.

dama blanca. Cocaine.

dance fever. Fentanyl.

dawamesk. Marijuana.

Dead-head. Heavy marijuana user who is a follower of the Grateful Dead.

dead on arrival. Heroin.

Deca-Duabolin. Injectable steroid.

deck. One to fifteen grams of heroin, also known as a bag; packet of drugs.

deeda. LSD.

Delatestryl. Injectable steroid.

demo. Crack stem; a sample-size quantity of crack.

demolish. Crack.

DET. Dimethyltryptamine.

detox. *Detoxification* for short; getting off drugs, even if only temporarily.

Detroit pink. PCP.

deuce. Two dollars' worth of drugs; heroin.

devil, the. Crack.

devil's dandruff. Crack.

devil's dick. Crack pipe.

devil's dust. PCP.

devilsmoke. Crack.

dew. Marijuana.

dews. Ten dollars' worth of drugs.

dexies. Amphetamine.

diambista. Marijuana.

Dianabol. Veterinary steroid.

diet pills. Amphetamine.

Dihydrolone. Injectable steroid.

dimba. Marijuana from West Africa.

dime. Crack; $10 worth of crack.

dime bag. Ten dollars' worth of drugs.

ding. Marijuana.

dinkie dow. Marijuana.

dip. (1) A small amount: a single dose. (2) Crack.

dipping out. Crack runners taking a portion of crack from vials.

dirt. Heroin.

dirt grass. Inferior-quality marijuana.

dirty basing. Crack.

disco biscuits. Depressant.

disease. Drug of choice.

ditch. Marijuana.

ditch weed. Marijuana of inferior quality, Mexican.

Dixie-cup people. Those workers and couriers in the international drug trade with so little importance that they can be used once and thrown away like a paper drinking cup.

djamba. Marijuana.

DMT. Dimethyltryptamine.

do. Consume a given drug; to "do" amphetamines, for example.

DOA. PCP; crack.

do a joint. To smoke marijuana.

do a line. To inhale cocaine.

do a number. Make and smoke a marijuana cigarette.

doctor-shop. To try to get drugs legally by prescription.

dog. Good friends.

dog food/doggie. Heroin.

dollar. One hundred dollars' worth of drugs.

dolls. Depressant.

domes. LSD.

domestic. Locally grown marijuana.

domex. PCP and methylenedioxymethamphetamine or MDMA.

dominoes. Amphetamine.

Don Jem/Dona Juana/Dona Juanita. Marijuana.

doobie/dubbe/duby. Marijuana cigarette, as in, "He taught her to roll doobies." The seventies rock group the Doobie Brothers took its name from this slang term. In 1993 the former drummer for the group, John Hartman, launched a lawsuit against twenty police departments in California that had turned him down for employment because of his former drug use. He lost and was clearly not aided in his effort by the name of the group.

doogie/doojee/dugie. Heroin.

dooley. Heroin.

dope. Heroin; marijuana; any other drug.

dope fiend. Crack addict.

dope smoke. To smoke marijuana.

dopium. Opium.

doradilla. Marijuana.

dose/dots. LSD.

doub. Twenty-dollar rock of crack.

double bubble. Cocaine.

double clutch. To take more than one's share of a communally shared marijuana cigarette.

double cross. Amphetamine.

double dome. LSD.

double rock. Crack diluted with procaine.

double trouble. Depressant.

double ups. A $20 rock that can be broken into two $20 rocks.

double yoke. Crack.

dove. Thirty-five-dollar piece of crack.

dover's powder. Opium.

downer/downers. (1) Barbiturates. Any drug used to slow the nervous system. Sometimes used to bring user down from a high. (2) Depressant.

downie. Depressant.

draf weed/drag weed. Marijuana.

draw up. To inject a drug.

dream. Cocaine.

dreamer. Morphine.

dream gum/dream stick. Opium.

dreams. Opium.

dreck. Heroin.

dropper. To inject a drug.

drowsy high. Depressant.

druggie. User.

dry high. Marijuana.

duct. Cocaine.

due. Residue of oils trapped in a pipe after smoking base.

duji. Heroin.

dummy. PCP.

Durabolin. Injectable steroid.

durog/duros. Marijuana.

dust. Heroin; cocaine; PCP; marijuana mixed with various chemicals.

dust bunny. Person showing effects of angel dust.

dusting. Adding PCP, heroin, or another drug to marijuana.

dust of angels/dusted parsley. PCP.

Dymethzine. Injectable steroid.

dynamite. (1) Powerful narcotic. (2) Heroin and cocaine.

dyno/dyno-pure. Heroin.

 # E

early girl. Marijuana that comes in before the main crop.

earth. Marijuana cigarette.

easing powder. Opium.

eastside player. Crack.

easy score. Obtaining drugs easily.

eating. Taking a drug orally.

ecstasy. Methylendioxy-methamphetamine or MDMA.

egg. Crack.

eight ball. One-eighth-ounce quantity of drugs/methamphetamines (CRANK).

eightball. Crack and heroin.

eighth. Heroin.

eight-track. Two and a half grams of cocaine.

el diablito. Marijuana, cocaine, heroin, and PCP.

electric kool aid. LSD. This term came into play in Tom Wolfe's book *The Electric Kool-Aid Acid Test,* which featured a group of LSD consumers known as the Merry Pranksters.

elephant. PCP.

embalming fluid. PCP.

emergency gun. (1) Homemade hypodermic syringe often composed of a pointed medicine dropper or a medicine dropper tipped by a pin. (2) Instrument used to inject other than a syringe.

Emm. Morphine.

emsel. Morphine.

endo. Marijuana.

Enoltestovis. Injectable steroid.

Ephedrone. Methcathinone.

Equipose. Veterinary steroid.

erth. PCP.

esra. Marijuana.

estuffa. Heroin.

ET. Alpha-ethyltryptamine.

eve. MDEA.

evil. Cocaine.

explorers club. Group of LSD users.

eye-opener/eye opener. (1) First ingestion or injection of the day. (2) Crack; amphetamine.

F

faith. Addiction.

fall. Arrested.

Fallbrook redhair. Marijuana, term from Fallbrook, California.

famous dimes. Crack.

fantasia. Dimethyltryptamine.

farm-to-arm. Describing an operation in which the same people grow, process, and sell a drug. For instance, a Mexican heroin grower who controls the pushers who retail it on the streets of Chicago.

fat bags. Crack.

fatty. Marijuana cigarette.

feed bag. (1) Taking narcotics by mouth as opposed to injection. (2) Container for marijuana.

ferry dust. Heroin.

fi-do-nie. Opium.

fields. LSD.

fiend. Someone who smokes marijuana alone.

fifteen cents. Fifteen dollars' worth of drugs.

fifty-cent bag. Fifty-dollar quantity of drugs.

fifty-one. Crack.

finajet/Finaject. Veterinary steroid.

fine stuff/finger/fir. Marijuana.

fire. To inject a drug; crack and methamphetamine.

fire it up. To smoke marijuana.

first line. Morphine.

fish scales. Crack.

five-cent bag. Five dollars' worth of drugs.

five-C note. Five-hundred-dollar bill.

five-dollar bag. Fifty-dollars' worth of drugs.

fives. Amphetamine.

fix. (1) An injection of narcotics. (2) To inject narcotics.

fizzies. Methadone.

flake. Cocaine.

flame cooking. Smoking cocaine base by putting the pipe over a stove flame.

flamethrowers. Cigarette laced with cocaine and heroin.

flash/flat blues. LSD.

flat chunks. Crack cut with benzocaine.

flea powder. Low-purity heroin.

Florida snow. Cocaine.

flower/flower tops. Marijuana.

fly Mexican airlines. (1) To smoke marijuana while flying. (2) Under the influence of drugs.

following that cloud. Searching for drugs.

food. Marijuana.

foo-foo dust. Cocaine.

foolish powder. Heroin; cocaine.

footballs. Amphetamine.

forty-five-minute psychosis. Dimethyltryptamine.

forwards. Amphetamine.

fraho/frajo. Marijuana.

freebase. (1) To purify cocaine with the aid of ether. (2) To smoke the pure cocaine thus produced. (3) Smoking cocaine; crack.

freeze. Cocaine; renege on a drug deal.

French blue. Amphetamine.

French fries/fries. Crack.

frios. Marijuana laced with PCP.

Frisco special/Frisco speedball. Cocaine, heroin, and LSD.

friskie powder. Cocaine.

frosty. High.

fry. Crack.

fry daddy. Crack and marijuana; cigarette laced with crack.

fu. Marijuana.

fucked-up. Extremely intoxicated from drug use.

fuel. Marijuana mixed with insecticides; PCP.

fuete. Hypodermic needle.

fuma d'angola. Marijuana, Portuguese term.

✳ G

G. One thousand dollars or one gram of drugs; term for an unfamiliar male.

gaffel. Fake cocaine.

gaffus. Hypodermic needle.

gage/gauge. Marijuana.

gagers/gaggers. Methcathinone.

galloping horse. Heroin.

gamot. Heroin.

gange/gangster. Marijuana.

gangster pills. Depressant.

ganja. Marijuana from Jamaica.

gank. (1) Bad drugs. (2) Fake crack.

garbage. Inferior-quality drugs.

garbage heads. Users who buy crack from street dealers instead of cooking it themselves.

garbage rock. Crack.

gash. Marijuana.

gasper/gasper stick. Marijuana cigarette.

gate. House or apartment.

gato. Heroin.

gauge butt. Marijuana.

GB. Depressant.

gee. Opium.

geek. (1) Crack addict. (2) Crack and marijuana.

geeze. (1) To inject narcotics. (2) To inhale cocaine.

geezer. To inject a drug.

geezin' a bit of dee gee. (1) Injecting smack. (2) Heroin.

geronimos. Barbiturates.

get a gage up. To smoke marijuana.

get a gift. Obtain drugs.

get down. To inject a drug.

get high. To smoke marijuana.

get lifted. Under the influence of drugs.

get off. To inject a drug; get high.

get one's wings. To start using heroin.

get the wind. To smoke marijuana.

get through. Obtain drugs.

Ghana. Marijuana.

GHB. Gamma hydroxy butyrate.

ghost. LSD.

ghost busting. Smoking cocaine; searching for white particles in the belief that they are crack.

gick monster. Crack smoker.

gift-of-the-sun. Cocaine.

giggle smokes. Marijuana cigarettes.

gimmick. Drug-injection equipment.

gimmie. Crack and marijuana.

gin. Cocaine.

girl. Cocaine; crack; heroin.

girlfriend. Cocaine.

give wings. Inject someone or teach someone to inject heroin.

glading. (1) The inhalation of easily obtainable household and industrial products, such as Glade, from which the term gets its name. Also known as huffing and bagging. (2) Using inhalant.

glad stuff. Cocaine.

glass/glass gun. Hypodermic needle.

glassines. Heroin.

glo. Crack.

gluey. Person who sniffs glue.

God's flesh. Psilocybin/psilocin.

God's medicine. Opium.

go-fast. Methcathinone.

gofer. Person paid to pick up drugs.

go into a sewer. To inject a drug.

gold. Marijuana; crack.

gold dust. Cocaine.

golden dragon. LSD.

golden girl. Heroin.

golden leaf. High-quality marijuana.

gold star. Marijuana.

golf ball. Crack.

golf balls. Depressant.

go loco. To smoke marijuana.

go on a sleigh ride. To inhale cocaine.

golpe. Heroin.

goma. Opium; black-tar heroin.

gondola. Opium.

gong. (1) Gun. (2) Marijuana; opium.

goob. Methcathinone.

good and plenty. Heroin.

good butt. Marijuana cigarette.

good fellas. Fentanyl.

good giggles. Marijuana.

good go. Proper amount of drugs for the money paid.

goods. Drugs.

goofball. Cocaine and heroin; depressant.

goofers. Depressant.

goofy's. LSD.

goon/goon dust. PCP.

goric. Opium.

gorilla biscuits. PCP.

gorilla pills. Depressant.

got it going on. Fast sale of drugs.

graduate. Completely stop using drugs or progress to stronger drugs.

gram. Hashish.

grape parfait. LSD.

grass/grass brownies/grata. Marijuana.

gravel. Crack.

gravey. To inject a drug; heroin.

grease. Currency.

great tobacco. Opium.

green. Inferior-quality marijuana; PCP; ketamine.

green double domes. LSD.

green dragons. Depressant.

green frog. Depressant.

green goddess. Marijuana.

green gold. Cocaine.

green goods. Paper currency.

green leaves. PCP.

greens/green stuff. Paper currency.

green single domes/green wedge. LSD.

greeter/greta. Marijuana.

grey shields. LSD.

griefo/griff/griffa/griffo. Marijuana.

grit/groceries. Crack.

G-rock. One gram of rock cocaine.

ground control. Guide or caretaker during a hallucinogenic experience.

G-shot. Small dose of drugs used to hold off withdrawal symptoms until full dose can be taken.

gum/guma. Opium.

gumdrop. Barbiturate.

gun. (1) Hypodermic syringe. (2) To inject a drug; needle.

gungun. Marijuana.

gutter. A vein into which a drug is injected. (2) A vein to a heroin addict.

gutter junkie. Addict who relies on others to obtain drugs.

gyve. Marijuana cigarette.

 H

H. Heroin.

habit. Addiction.

hache. Heroin.

hail. Crack.

hairy. Heroin.

half/half piece. Half ounce.

half a C. Fifty-dollar bill.

half a football field. Fifty rocks of crack.

half G. Five hundred dollars.

half load. Fifteen bags (decks) of heroin.

half moon. Peyote.

half piece. One-half ounce of heroin or cocaine.

half track/hamburger helper. Crack.

H&C. Heroin and cocaine.

hand-to-hand. Direct delivery and payment.

hand-to-hand man. Transient dealers who carry small amounts of crack.

hanhich. Marijuana.

happy cigarette. Marijuana cigarette.

happy dust. Cocaine.

happy flakes. Any powdered narcotic.

happy powder/happy trails. Cocaine.

hard candy. Heroin.

hard line/hard rock. Crack.

hard stuff. Opium; heroin.

hardware. Isobutyl nitrite.

harpoon. Hypodermic syringe.

Harry. Heroin.

has. Marijuana.

hash. Hashish.

hash bash. Rally or event for the legalization of marijuana.

hats. LSD.

have a dust. Cocaine.

haven dust. Cocaine.

have the slows. To be very high.

Hawaiian. High-potency marijuana.

Hawaiian sunshine. LSD.

hawk. LSD.

hay. Hashish/marijuana.

hay burner. Smoker of marijuana.

hay but/hay butts. Marijuana cigarettes.

haze. LSD.

Hazel. Heroin.

H caps. Heroin.

HCP. PCP.

head drugs. Amphetamine.

headlights. LSD.

heart-on. Inhalant.

hearts. Amphetamine.

heaven dust. Heroin; cocaine.

heavenly blue. LSD.

heeled. Having plenty of drug money.

Helen/hell dust. Heroin.

he-man. Fentanyl.

hemp. Marijuana.

henpicking. Searching on hands and knees for crack.

Henry. Heroin.

Henry VIII. Cocaine.

her. Cocaine.

herb. Marijuana.

Herba. Marijuana.

Herb and Al. Marijuana and alcohol.

hero/heroina/herone/hero of the underworld/hessle. Heroin.

high beams on/highbeams. (1) High on cocaine. (2) The wide eyes of a person on crack.

hikori/hikuli. Peyote.

him. Heroin.

Hinckley. PCP, an allusion to the craziness of John Hinckley, the man who shot Pres. Ronald Reagan.

hippie crack. Inhalant.

his. Heroin sold in a straw. The powder is tapped into the straw, which is then heat-sealed at either end.

hit. (1) A puff, injection, swallow, or snort that gets a drug into one's system. (2) To adulterate drugs prior to selling them. (3) A purchase. (4) Crack; marijuana cigarette; to smoke marijuana.

hit the hay. To smoke marijuana.

hit the main line/hit the needle/hit the pit. To inject a drug.

HMC. (1) Her Majesty Cocaine. (2) Mix of heroin, morphine, and cocaine.

hocus. Opium; marijuana.

hog. PCP.

holding. Possessing drugs. The mid-1960s rock group Big Brother and the Holding Company used the word in this sense. The band was Janis Joplin's vehicle to fame and glory.

hombre. heroin.

homegrown. Marijuana.

honey. Currency.

honey blunts. Marijuana cigars sealed with honey.

honeymoon. Early stages of drug use before addiction or dependency develops.

honey oil. Ketamine; inhalant.

hong-yen. Heroin in pill form.

hooch. Marijuana.

hook/hooked. To addict to drugs.

hooter. Marijuana; cocaine.

hop/hops. Opium.

hophead. Heroin addict.

hopped up. Under the influence of drugs.

horn. To inhale cocaine; crack pipe.

horning. Heroin; to inhale cocaine.

horse. Heroin.

horse heads. Amphetamine.

horse tranquilizer. PCP.

hotcakes. Crack.

hot dope. Heroin.

hot heroin. Poisoned to give to a police informant.

hot load/hot shot. (1) A potent dose of heroin that may be lethal. (2) Lethal injection of an opiate.

hot stick. Marijuana cigarette.

house fee. Money paid to enter a crack house.

house piece. Crack given to the owner of a crack house or apartment where crack users congregate.

how do you like me now. Crack.

hows. Morphine.

HRN. Heroin.

hubba/hubba, I am back. Crack.

hubba pigeon. Crack user looking for rocks on a floor after a police raid.

hubbas. Crack, term from northern California.

huff. Inhalant.

huffer. (1) Person who inhales vapors from solvents and other chemical compounds to get high. (2) Inhalant abuser.

hulling. Using others to get drugs.

hunter. Cocaine.

hustle. Attempt to obtain drug customers.

hustler. Seller.

hyatari. Peyote.

hype. (1) Hypodermic syringe. (2) Heroin addict; an addict.

hype stick. Hypodermic needle.

 I

I am back. Crack.

ice. (1) A smokable form of amphetamines that first hit the streets of Hawaii and California in the latter half of 1989. It is similar to crack, but the high lasts longer and would appear to be even more addictive. (2) Cocaine; methamphetamine; methylendioxy-methamphetamine or MDMA.

ice cream habit. (1) A state of minimal addiction; nonsevere habit. (2) Occasional use of drugs.

ice cube. Crack.

ice-tong doctor. Physician who prescribes or sells narcotics illegally.

icing. Cocaine.

idiot pills. Depressant.

ily. Marijuana.

in. Connected with drug suppliers.

in-betweens. Depressant; amphetamine.

Inca message. Cocaine.

Indian boy/Indian hay. Marijuana from India.

Indica. Species of cannabis, found in hot climate. Grows three and a half to four feet tall.

indo. Marijuana, a term from northern California.

Indonesian bud. Marijuana; opium.

inner itch. To have a craving for narcotics.

instant zen. LSD.

interplanetary mission. Travel from one crack house to another in search of crack.

iron cure. Treatment of narcotic addiction by unyielding regime of abstinence.

isda. heroin.

issues. Crack.

* J

J. Marijuana cigarette.

jab job. To inject heroin into the blood.

jab stick. Syringe.

jack. Steal someone else's drugs.

jackpot. Fentanyl.

jack-up. To inject a drug.

jag. Keep a high going.

jam. (1) Overdose. (2) Amphetamine; cocaine.

jam cecil. Amphetamine.

Jane. Marijuana.

jar wars. Controversy over drug testing, which requires urine samples.

jay/jay smoke. Marijuana cigarette.

jee gee. Heroin.

Jefferson airplane. Used match cut in half to hold a partially smoked marijuana cigarette, an allusion to the band and the fact that the split match looks a bit like an airplane.

jellies. Depressant.

jelly. Cocaine.

jelly baby/jelly bean. Amphetamine; depressant.

jelly beans. Crack.

jet. Ketamine.

jet fuel. PCP.

Jim Jones. (1) Marijuana cigarette dipped in PCP, from the name of the crazed cult leader. (2) Marijuana laced with cocaine and PCP.

jive. Heroin; marijuana; drugs.

jive doo jee. Heroin.

jive stick. Marijuana.

Johnson. Crack.

joint. Marijuana cigarette.

jojee. Heroin.

jolly bean. Amphetamine.

jolly green. Marijuana.

jolly pop. Casual user of heroin.

jolt. (1) Cocaine. (2) To inject a drug; strong reaction to drugs.

Jones. Heroin.

Jonesing. Need for drugs.

joy flakes. Heroin.

joy juice. Depressant.

joy plant. Opium.

joy pop. To inject a drug.

joy popper/joy popping. Intermittent user of hard drugs.

joy powder. Heroin; cocaine.

joy smoke. Marijuana.

joy stick. Marijuana cigarette.

Juan Valdez/Juanita. Marijuana.

juggle. Sell drugs to another addict to support a habit.

juggler. Teenaged street dealer.

jugs. Amphetamine.

juice. (1) PCP. (2) Steroids.

juice joint. Marijuana cigarette sprinkled with crack.

ju-ju. Marijuana cigarette.

juke. Holdup.

jum. Sealed plastic bag containing crack.

jumbos. Large vials of crack sold on the streets.

junk. (1) Addictive narcotics. (2) Cocaine; heroin.

junkie/junky. An addict.

* K

kabayo. Heroin.

kabuki. Crack pipe made from a plastic rum bottle and a rubber spark-plug cover.

kali. Marijuana.

kangaroo. Crack.

kaps. PCP.

karachi. Heroin.

kaya. Marijuana.

Kentucky blue. Marijuana.

keyster plant. Drugs hidden in person's rectum.

KGB (killer green bud). Marijuana.

K-hole. Periods of ketamine-induced confusion.

kibbles and bits. (1) A combination of the stimulant Ritalin and the painkiller Talwin. It is, of course, a reference to a heavily advertised dog food called Kibbles'n Bits. (2) Cocaine scraps. (3) Small crumbs of crack.

kick. Getting off a drug habit; inhalant.

kicked by the horse. Addicted to heroin.

kick stick. Marijuana cigarette.

kiddie dope. Prescription drugs.

kiff. Marijuana.

killer/killer weed. Marijuana and PCP.

kilo. 2.2 pounds.

kilter. Marijuana.

kind. Marijuana.

king ivory. Fentanyl.

King Kong pills. Depressant.

king's habit. Cocaine.

kit. Equipment used to inject drugs.

KJ. PCP.

kleenex. Methylendioxy-methamphetamine or MDMA.

klingons. Crack addicts.

knocker. Addict: one who knocks him- or herself out with narcotics.

kokomo/kryptonite. Crack.

kumba. Marijuana.

KW. PCP.

✳ L

L. LSD.

LA. Long-acting amphetamine.

lace. Cocaine and marijuana.

lady/lady caine/lady snow. Cocaine.

lakbay diva. Marijuana

Lamborghini. Crack pipe made from plastic rum bottle and a rubber spark-plug cover.

lason sa daga. LSD.

laugh and scratch. To inject a drug.

laughing gas. Nitrous oxide.

laughing grass/laughing weed. Marijuana.

lay. An ounce of narcotics.

lay back. Depressant.

lay-out. Equipment for taking drugs.

LBJ. LSD; PCP; heroin.

leaf. Marijuana; cocaine.

leapers. Amphetamine.

leaping. Under the influence of drugs.

lemonade. Heroin; poor-quality drugs.

lens. LSD.

lib (Librium). Depressant.

lid. One ounce of marijuana.

lid poppers. Amphetamine.

lightning. Amphetamine.

light stuff. Marijuana.

lima. Marijuana.

lime acid. LSD.

line. Cocaine.

Lipton tea. Inferior-quality drugs.

lit/lit up. Under the influence of drugs.

little bomb. Amphetamine; heroin; depressant.

little smoke. Marijuana; psilocybin/ psilocin.

LL. Marijuana.

llesca. Marijuana.

load. Twenty-five bags of heroin.

loaded. High.

loaf/lobo. Marijuana.

locker room. Isobutyl nitrite.

locoweed. Marijuana.

log. PCP; marijuana cigarette.

logor. LSD.

loused. Covered by sores and abscesses from repeated use of unsterile needles.

love. Crack.

love affair. Cocaine.

love boat/lovely. (1) PCP. (2) Marijuana dipped in formaldehyde.

love drug. Methylendioxy-methamphetamine or MDMA; depressant.

lovelies. Marijuana laced with PCP.

love pearls/love pills. Alpha-ethyltryptamine.

love trip. Methylendioxy-methamphetamine or MDMA and mescaline.

love weed. Marijuana.

LSD. Lysergic acid diethylamide.

lubage. Marijuana.

Lucy in the sky with diamonds. LSD.

luded out. Showing the effects of quaaludes.

ludes/luding out/luds. Depressant.

'ludes. Quaaludes.

* M

M. (1) Morphine. (2) Marijuana.

machinery/macon. Marijuana.

magic dust. PCP.

magic mushroom. Psilocybin/psilocin.

magic smoke. Marijuana.

mainline. To inject a drug.

mainliner. Person who injects into the vein.

make up. Need to find more drugs.

mama coca. Cocaine.

M&C. Mix of morphine and cocaine.

M&M. Depressant.

Manhattan silver. Marijuana.

marahoochie. Marijuana.

marathons. Amphetamine.

mari. Marijuana cigarette.

marshmallow reds. Depressant.

Mary/Mary and Johnny/Mary Ann/ Mary Jane/Mary Jonas/Mary Johanna/ Mary Warner/Mary Weaver. Marijuana.

Maserati. Crack pipe made from a plastic rum bottle and a rubber spark-plug cover.

matchbox. One-quarter ounce of marijuana or six marijuana cigarettes.

matsakow. Heroin.

Maui Wowie/Maui Wauie. Marijuana strain that may or may not have come from Hawaii.

Max. Gamma hydroxy butyrate dissolved in water and mixed with amphetamines.

Maxibolin. Oral steroid.

mayo. Cocaine; heroin.

MDA. Miracle drops of acid, actually methylendioxy-methamphetamine.

MDM/MDMA. Methylendioxy-methamphetamine.

Medusa. Ethyl chloride.

meg/meggie. Marijuana.

megg. Marijuana cigarette.

mellow yellow. LSD.

merchandise. Drugs.

merk. Cocaine.

mesc/mescal/mese. Mescaline.

messorole. Marijuana.

meth. Methamphetamine.

Methatriol. Injectable steroid.

meth head. Regular user of methamphetamine.

meth monster. Person who has a violent reaction to methamphetamine.

methyltestosterone. Oral steroid.

Mexican brown. Heroin; marijuana.

Mexican horse/Mexican mud. Heroin.

Mexican mushroom. Psilocybin/psilocin.

Mexican red. Marijuana.

mezc. Mescaline.

Mickey Finn/Mickeys. Depressant.

microdot. LSD.

midnight oil. Opium.

Mighty Joe Young. Depressant.

Mighty mezz. Marijuana cigarette.

Mighty Quinn. LSD.

mind detergent. LSD.

minibennie. Amphetamine.

Mira. Opium.

miss. To inject a drug.

Miss Emma. Morphine.

missile basing. Crack liquid and PCP.

mission. Trip out of the crack house to obtain crack.

mist. PCP; crack smoke.

mister blue. Morphine.

MJ./MO./MU. Marijuana.

modams/mohasky. Marijuana.

mojo. Cocaine; heroin.

monkey. Drug dependency; cigarette made from cocaine paste and tobacco.

monkey dust/monkey tranquilizer. PCP.

monos. Cigarette made from cocaine paste and tobacco.

monte. Marijuana from South America.

mooca/moocah. Marijuana.

moon. Mescaline.

moonrock. Crack and heroin.

mooster/moota/mooters/mootie/mootos/mor a grifa/mota/mother/moto/mutah. Marijuana.

more. PCP.

morf. Morphine.

morning glory. First hit of the day.

morning wake-up. First blast of crack from the pipe.

morotgara. Heroin.

mortal combat. High-potency heroin.

mosquitoes. Cocaine.

mother's helper/mother's little helper. (1) Valium. (2) Depressant.

mouth worker. One who takes drugs orally.

movie-star drug. Cocaine.

mow the grass. To smoke marijuana.

MS. Morphine.

mud. Opium; heroin.

muggie/muggle. Marijuana.

mujer. Cocaine.

mule. Carrier of drugs.

munchies. Hunger attack after marijuana use.

murder eight. Fentanyl.

murder one. Heroin and cocaine.

mush mind. Marijuana user whose mind has become muddled by it.

mushrooms. (1) Psilocybin/psilocin. (2) Name for innocent bystanders who sometimes get hurt or killed in inner-city drug shoot-outs.

mutha. Marijuana.

muzzle. Heroin.

 N

nail. (1) Hypodermic needle. (2) Marijuana cigarette.

nailed. Arrested.

nebbies. Depressant.

nemmies/nimbies. (1) Nembutal. (2) Depressant.

new jack swing. Heroin and morphine.

new magic. PCP.

New York barricade. A two-by-four nailed across the door of a crack house.

nice and easy. Heroin.

nickel/nickel bag. (1) Five dollars' worth of drugs. (2) Heroin.

nickel deck. Heroin.

nickel note. Five-dollar bill.

nickelonians. Crack addicts.

niebla. PCP.

nimbies. Depressant.

nix. Stranger among the group.

nod. Effects of heroin.

noise. Heroin.

nontoucher. Crack user who doesn't want affection during or after smoking crack.

nose. Heroin.

nose candy/nose powder/nose stuff. Cocaine.

nose drops. Liquefied heroin.

nubs. Peyote.

nugget. Amphetamine.

nuggets. Crack.

number. Marijuana cigarette.

number 8. Heroin.

number 3. Cocaine.

 O

O. Opium.

ogoy/oil/old Steve. Heroin.

OJ. Marijuana.

on a mission. Searching for crack.

on a trip. Under the influence of drugs.

one and one. To inhale cocaine.

one box tissue. One ounce of crack.

one fifty-one. Crack.

one way. LSD.

on ice. In jail.

on the bricks. Walking the streets.

on the nod. Under the influence of narcotics or depressants.

on the pipe. Freebasing cocaine.

OP. Opium.

ope. Opium.

optical illusions. LSD.

orange barrels/orange cubes/orange haze/orange micro/orange wedges. LSD.

oranges. Amphetamine.

outerlimits. Crack and LSD.

owsley/owsley's acid. LSD.

Oz. Inhalant.

ozone. PCP.

 P

P. Peyote.

pack. Heroin; marijuana.

pack of rocks. Marijuana cigarette.

pakalolo/Pakistani black/Panama cut/ Panama gold/Panama red. Marijuana.

panatela. Large marijuana cigarette.

pane. LSD.

pangonadalot. Heroin.

panic. (1) Shortage of heroin— "There's panic in Needle Park." (2) Drugs not available.

paper/paper acid. LSD.

paper bag. Container for drugs.

paper blunts. Marijuana within a paper casing rather than a tobacco-leaf casing.

paper boy. Heroin peddler.

Parabolin. Veterinary steroid.

parachute. Crack and PCP smoked; heroin.

paradise/paradise white. Cocaine.

parlay. Crack.

parsley. Marijuana.

paste. Crack.

pat. Marijuana.

patico. Crack (Spanish).

PCP. Phencyclidine.

P-dope. Twenty–thirty percent pure heroin.

peace/peace tablets. LSD.

peace pill/peace weed. PCP.

peaches. Amphetamine.

peanut. Depressant.

pearls. Amyl nitrite.

pearly gates. LSD.

pebbles. Crack.

peddler. Drug supplier.

peewee. Crack; $5 worth of crack.

peg. Heroin.

pellets. LSD.

pen yan. Opium.

pep pills. Amphetamine.

Pepsi habit. Occasional use of drugs.

perfect high. Heroin.

perico. Cocaine.

perks. Percodan.

perp. Fake crack made of candle wax and baking soda.

Peruvian/Peruvian flake/Peruvian lady. Cocaine.

peth. Depressant.

peyote. Mescaline.

P-funk. (1) A synthetic form of heroin that was first discussed for a national audience in front of the Senate Judiciary Committee in September 1989 hearings on new trends in narcotics. (2) Crack and PCP.

phennies/phenos. Depressant.

pianoing. Using the fingers to find lost crack rocks, which might remind one of someone playing the piano.

piddle. Hospital, especially one used to treat addicts. The term is an old one and is based on a slurred pronunciation of *hospital.*

piece. One ounce; cocaine; crack.

piedras. Crack (Spanish for rocks).

piles. Crack.

pillow. Any opiate.

pimp. Cocaine.

pimp your pipe. Lending or renting your crack pipe.

pin. Marijuana.

ping-in-wing. To inject a drug.

pin gon/pin yen. Opium.

pink blotters/pink robots/pink wedge/ pink witches. LSD.

pink hearts. Amphetamine.

pink ladies. Depressant.

pipe. Crack pipe; marijuana pipe; vein into which a drug is injected; mix drugs with other substances.

pipero. Crack user.

pit. PCP.

pixies. Amphetamine.

plant. Hiding place for drugs.

pocket rocket/pod. Marijuana.

poison. Heroin; fentanyl.

poke. Marijuana.

polvo. Heroin; PCP.

polvo blanco. Cocaine.

pony. Crack.

poor man's pot. Inhalant.

pop. To inhale cocaine.

poppers. Isobutyl nitrite; amyl nitrite.

poppy. Heroin.

posse. Jamaican gang often dealing in marijuana, crack, or both.

pot. Marijuana.

potato. LSD.

potato chips. Crack cut with benzocaine.

pothead. Regular marijuana user; one who has become addled by the weed.

potten bush. Marijuana.

powder. Heroin; amphetamine.

powder diamonds. Cocaine.

power puller. Rubber piece attached to crack stem.

pox. Opium.

PR. (Panama red). Marijuana.

prescription. Marijuana cigarette.

press. Cocaine; crack.

pretendicia/pretendo. Marijuana.

primo. Crack; marijuana mixed with crack.

Primobolan. Injectable and oral steroid.

primos. Cigarettes laced with cocaine and heroin.

Proviron. Oral steroid.

pseudocaine. Phenylpropanolamine, an adulterant for cutting crack.

puffer. Crack smoker.

puff the dragon. To smoke marijuana.

pulborn. Heroin.

pullers. Crack users who pull at parts of their bodies excessively.

pumping. Selling crack.

puppy. Gun.

pure. Heroin.

pure love. LSD.

purple. Ketamine.

purple barrels/purple flats/purple haze/purple ozoline. LSD.

purple hearts. Phenobarbital; LSD; amphetamine; depressant.

push. Sell drugs.

pusher. (1) One who sells drugs. (2) Metal hanger or umbrella rod used to scrape residue in crack stems.

push shorts. To cheat or sell short amounts.

 Q

Q. Depressant.

quacks. Quaaludes.

quad. Depressant.

quarter/quarter bag. Twenty-five dollars' worth of drugs.

quarter moon. Hashish.

quarter piece. One-quarter ounce.

quas. Depressant.

Queen Anne's lace. Marijuana.

quicksilver. Isobutyl nitrite.

quill. Methamphetamine; heroin; cocaine.

Quinolone. Injectable steroid.

 R

racehorse charlie. Cocaine; heroin.

rad weed. Marijuana.

ragweed. Inferior-quality marijuana; heroin.

railroad weed. Marijuana.

rainbows. Depressant.

rainy-day woman. Marijuana.

Rambo. Heroin.

rane. Cocaine; heroin.

rangood. Marijuana grown wild.

rap. (1) Criminally charged. (2) To talk with someone.

raspberry. Female who trades sex for crack or money to buy crack.

rasta weed. Marijuana.

ratboy. Street slang for a human laboratory rat who is skilled at testing the strength of various drugs.

rave. Party drug designed to enhance a hallucinogenic experience.

raw. Crack.

razed. Under the influence of drugs.

ready rock. Cocaine; crack; heroin.

recompress. Change the shape of cocaine flakes to resemble "rock."

recycle. LSD.

red. Under the influence of drugs.

red and blue/red bullets. Depressant.

red caps. Crack.

red chicken. Heroin.

red cross. Marijuana.

red devil. (1) Seconal. (2) Depressant.

red dirt. Marijuana.

red dragon. Opium. This term emerged from Chinese American gang slang.

red eagle. Heroin.

red flag. Method of injecting heroin in which the needle is put into a vein and is allowed to expand until blood is drawn into the bulb. This ensures a hit in the vein rather than in the muscle.

red phosphorus. Smokable speed.

Red Rum. Powerful brand of heroin that killed rock musician Jonathan Melvoin of the group Smashing Pumpkins in July 1996. Red Rum is *murder* spelled backward. The weekend after Melvoin's death, packets stamped Red Rum were in high demand on Manhattan's Lower East Side. Rather than scare potential buyers, a heroin death will signal other users that the brand in question is of high purity.

reds. Depressant.

reefer. Marijuana.

regular P. Crack.

reindeer dust. Heroin.

Rhine. Heroin.

rhythm. Amphetamine.

riding the wave. Under the influence of drugs.

rig. Paraphernalia for injecting or smoking drugs.

righteous bush. Marijuana.

ringer. Good hit of crack.

rings. Guns and bullets.

rippers. Amphetamine.

roach. Butt of marijuana cigarette.

roach clip. Holds partially smoked marijuana cigarette.

road dope. Amphetamine.

roca. Crack (Spanish).

rock/rock attack/rocks/rocks of hell/ Rocky III. Portion of crack cocaine, as in, the boy had twenty-one rocks of cocaine in his possession with a street value of $1,050.

rocket caps. Dome-shaped caps on crack vials.

rocket fuel. PCP.

rockets. Marijuana cigarette.

rockette. Female who uses crack.

rock house. Place where crack is sold and smoked.

rock star. Female who trades sex for crack or money to buy crack.

roid rage. Aggressive behavior caused by excessive steroid use.

roller/rollers. (1) Police, from the fact patrol cars roll through open-air drug markets slowly. (2) Vein that will not stay in position for injection. (3) To inject a drug.

rolling. Methylendioxy-methamphetamine or MDMA.

roofies. Rohypnol, a powerful prescription sedative, known as the date-rape drug because it can cause blackouts with complete loss of memory.

rooster. Crack.

root. Marijuana.

rope. (1) Marijuana. (2) Marijuana cigarette. (3) Rohypnol.

rosa. Amphetamine.

rose marie. Marijuana.

roses. Amphetamine.

Rox/Roxanne. Cocaine; crack.

royal blues. LSD.

roz. Crack.

R's and T's. A combination of the stimulant Ritalin and the painkiller Talwin.

ruderalis. Species of cannabis, found in Russia, grows to one to two and a half feet.

runners. People who sell drugs for others.

running. Methylendioxy-methamphetamine or MDMA.

rush. (1) Intense orgasmlike sensation that follows an intravenous injection. (2) Isobutyl nitrite.

rush snappers. Isobutyl nitrite.

Russian sickles. LSD.

✳ S

sack. Heroin.

sacrament. LSD.

salt. Heroin.

salt and pepper. Marijuana.

Sam. Federal narcotics agent.

sancocho. To steal (Spanish).

sandoz. LSD.

sandwich. Two layers of cocaine with a layer of heroin in the middle.

Santa Marta. Marijuana.

sasfras. Marijuana.

Satan's secret. Inhalant.

satch. Papers, letters, cards, clothing, etc., saturated with drug solution (used to smuggle drugs into prisons or hospitals).

satch cotton. Fabric used to filter a solution of narcotics before injection.

sativa. Species of cannabis, found in

cool, damp climate, grows up to eighteen feet tall.

scaffle. PCP.

scag/scat/scate. Heroin.

schmeck/schoolboy. Cocaine.

scissors. Marijuana.

score. Purchase drugs.

scorpion. Cocaine.

Scott. Heroin.

Scottie/Scotty. Cocaine; crack; the high from crack.

scramble. Crack.

scrambler. Street term for a hustler or, occasionally, a drug dealer.

scratch. Money.

script. A prescription given to a drug user who has faked physical illness or emotional distress to get it.

scruples. Crack.

seccy. Depressant.

seeds. Marijuana.

seggy. Depressant.

sen. Marijuana.

seni. Peyote.

sernyl. PCP.

serpico 21. Cocaine.

server. Crack dealer.

servin'. Selling, as in "servin' " rock.

sess. Marijuana.

sevenup. Cocaine; crack.

sewer. Vein into which a drug is injected.

sezz. Marijuana.

shabu. Ice.

shake. Useless or poor-quality leaves of a marijuana plant.

shaker/baker/water. Materials needed to freebase cocaine; shaker bottle, baking soda, water.

sharps. Needles.

she. Cocaine.

sheet rocking. Crack and LSD.

shermans/sherms. PCP; crack.

shit. Heroin.

shmeck/schmeek. Heroin.

shoot/shoot up. To inject a drug.

shooting gallery. Place where drugs are used.

shoot the breeze. Nitrous oxide.

shot. To inject a drug.

shot down. Under the influence of drugs.

'shrooms. Psilocybin/psilocin—short for *mushrooms*.

siddi. Marijuana.

sightball. Crack.

silly putty. Psilocybin/psilocin.

silver bike. Syringe with chrome fittings.

simple simon. Psilocybin/psilocin.

sinse. Marijuana.

sinsemilla. (1) Seedless, as applied to marijuana, specifically the unpollinated female plants. (2) The name of the powerful northern-California seedless variety of marijuana.

sixty-two. Two and one-half ounces of crack.

skee. Opium.

skeegers/skeezers. Crack-smoking prostitute.

skid. Heroin.

skid drop. A large load of drugs dropped from the air by means of a cargo skid attached to a parachute.

skied. Under the influence of drugs.

skin popping. Injecting drugs under the skin.

skunk. Marijuana.

slab. Crack.

slam. To inject a drug.

slanging. Selling drugs.

sleeper. Heroin; depressant.

sleet. Crack.

sleigh ride. Drug spree.

slick superspeed. Methcathinone.

slime. Heroin.

smack. Heroin.

smack weed. Pot cured in heroin.

smears. LSD.

smoke. Heroin and crack; crack; marijuana.

smoke Canada. Marijuana.

smoke-out. Under the influence of drugs.

smoking gun. Heroin and cocaine.

snap. Amphetamine.

snappers. Isobutyl nitrite.

sniff. To inhale cocaine; inhalant; methcathinone.

snop. Marijuana.

snort. To inhale cocaine; use inhalant.

snot. Residue produced from smoking amphetamine.

snot balls. Rubber cement rolled into balls and burned.

snow/snow bird/snow cones/snow soak/snow white. Cocaine.

snowball. Cocaine and heroin.

snow pallets. Amphetamine.

snow seals. Cocaine and amphetamine.

society high. Cocaine.

soda. Injectable cocaine used in Hispanic communities.

softballs. Depressant.

soles. Hashish.

soma. PCP.

sopers. Depressant.

space base. Crack dipped in PCP; hollowed-out cigar refilled with PCP and crack.

space cadet/space dust. (1) Mixture of PCP and crack. (2) Crack dipped in PCP.

spaceship. Glass pipe used to smoke crack.

spark it up. To smoke marijuana.

sparkle plenty/sparklers. Amphetamine.

Special K/special la coke. Ketamine.

speed. Methamphetamine; amphetamine; crack.

speedball/speed ball. (1) A mix of heroin and cocaine. The instrument that killed twenty-three-year-old actor

River Phoenix in 1993 was a speed-ball. (2) Amphetamines in the sense of an enhancer of personal perfor-mance. Lines from Jay Richard Kennedy's novel *The Chairman* illustrate: "Getting there by copter he would only have to swim one way, cutting time in half. With the aid of a speed ball and flippers, he could improve that by 25 percent."

speed boat. Marijuana; PCP; crack.

speed for lovers. Methylendioxy-methamphetamine or MDMA.

speed freak. Habitual user of meth-amphetamine.

spider blue. Heroin.

spike. To inject a drug; a needle.

splash. Amphetamine.

spliff. (1) A joint or portion of mari-juana. (2) Marijuana cigarette.

splim. Marijuana.

split. Half and half or to leave.

splivins. Amphetamine.

spoon. One-sixteenth ounce of her-oin; paraphernalia used to prepare heroin for injection.

sporting. To inhale cocaine.

spray. Inhalant.

sprung. Person just starting to use drugs.

square grouper. A bale of marijuana in south Florida.

square mackerel. Marijuana, term from Florida.

square time Bob. Crack.

squirrel. Smoking cocaine, mari-juana, and PCP; LSD.

SS. Skin shot: injection into skin rather than directly into the vein.

stack. Marijuana.

star. Methcathinone.

star dust/star-spangled powder. Co-caine.

stash. Place to hide drugs.

stash areas. Drug storage and distri-bution areas.

steerer. One who does not sell drugs but guides or steers potential buyers to places where they are sold.

stem. (1) Glass pipe for smoking crack or ICE. (2) Cylinder used to smoke crack.

stems. Marijuana.

step on. (1) To cut or adulterate a drug, by doubling its weight (and halving its purity). If fifteen pounds of a drug is stepped on twice, it be-comes sixty pounds. (2) Dilute drugs.

stick. Marijuana cigarette.

stickup boys. Those who rob drug dealers.

stink weed. Marijuana.

stoned. Under the influence of drugs.

stones. Crack.

stoppers. Depressant.

STP. PCP.

straw. Marijuana cigarette.

strawberry. (1) Prostitute who will trade sex for cocaine. (2) Female who trades sex for crack or money to buy crack.

strawberry fields. LSD, an allusion to

the Beatles song "Strawberry Fields."

strung out. (1) Condition resulting from habitual use of drugs. (2) Heavily addicted to drugs.

stuff. Heroin.

stumbler. Depressant.

sugar. Cocaine; LSD; heroin.

sugar block. Crack.

sugar cubes/sugar lumps. LSD.

sugar weed. Marijuana.

sunshine. LSD.

superacid. Ketamine.

super C. Ketamine.

sweet Jesus. Heroin.

sweet Lucy. Marijuana.

sweets. Amphetamine.

sweet stuff. Heroin; cocaine.

swell up. Crack.

* T

T. Cocaine; marijuana.

tab/tabs/taillights. A dose of LSD.

taima. Marijuana.

taking a cruise. PCP.

takkouri. Marijuana.

tamal. Small packet of the drug bazuco.

tango & cash. Fentanyl.

tar. Opium; heroin.

tardust. Cocaine.

tarred and feathered. Addicted.

taste. Heroin; small sample of drugs.

taxing. (1) Price paid to enter a crack house. (2) Charging more per vial depending on the race of a customer or if not a regular customer.

tea/tea 13. Marijuana. Why 13? In her trendy, punky *Modern English,* Jennifer Walters asserts that the number 13 alludes to the fact that *M,* for *marijuana,* is the thirteenth letter of the alphabet.

tea party. To smoke marijuana.

teardrops. Dosage units of crack packaged in the cutoff corners of plastic bags.

tecate. Heroin.

tecatos. Hispanic heroin addicts.

teeth. (1) Bullets. (2) Cocaine; crack.

tension. Crack.

Tex-Mex/Texas pot/Texas tea. Marijuana.

Thai sticks. Bundles of marijuana soaked in hashish oil; marijuana buds bound or short sections of bamboo.

THC. Tetrahydrocannabinol.

thing. Heroin; cocaine; main drug interest at the moment.

thirst monsters. Heavy crack smokers.

thirteen. Marijuana.

thoroughbred. Drug dealer who sells pure narcotics.

thrust. Isobutyl nitrite.

thrusters. Amphetamine.

thumb. Marijuana.

ticket. LSD.

ticket agent. Dealer in hallucinogenic drugs.

tic tac. PCP.

tie. To inject a drug.

tin. Container for marijuana.

tissue. Crack.

T-man. Federal narcotics agent.

TNT. Heroin; fentanyl.

toilet water. Inhalant.

toke/toke up. To inhale cocaine; to smoke marijuana.

tolly. Street name for toluene, a hydrocarbon solvent that is inhaled by HUFFERS.

toncho. Octane booster that is inhaled.

tool. Gun.

tooles. Depressant.

tools. Equipment used for injecting drugs.

toot. Cocaine; to inhale cocaine.

tooties. Depressant.

tootsie roll. Powerful form of Mexican heroin.

top gun. Crack.

topi. Mescaline.

tops. Peyote.

torch. Marijuana.

torch cooking. Smoking cocaine base by using a propane or butane torch as a flame.

torch up. To smoke marijuana.

torpedo. Crack and marijuana.

toss up. Female who trades sex for crack or money to buy crack.

totally spent. Methylenedioxy-methamphetamine or MDMA hangover.

toucher. User of crack who wants affection before, during, or after smoking crack.

tout. Person who introduces buyers to sellers.

toxy. Opium.

toy. Container for narcotics.

toys. Opium.

track. To inject a drug.

tracks. Marks left in the skin from continued injection of drugs into the veins.

tragic magic. (1) Mixture of PCP and crack. (2) Crack dipped in PCP.

trails. LSD-induced perception that moving objects leave multiple images or trails behind them.

tranqu. Depressant.

trap. Hiding place for drugs.

travel agent. LSD supplier.

trays. Bunches of vials.

trey. Three bucks' worth of drugs, often a half-inch vial of crack.

trip. LSD; alpha-ethyltryptamine.

triple-nine. A form of morphine base.

troop. Crack.

Trophobolene. Injectable steroid.

TR-6s. Amphetamine.

truck drivers. Amphetamine.

tubo. Crack and marijuana.

tuie. Depressant.

turd. Secreted narcotics, usually hidden in the rectum.

turf. Place where drugs are sold.

turkey. (1) A fake capsule containing only sugar or chalk, but which is sold as a powerful drug. (2) Cocaine; amphetamine.

turnabout. Amphetamine.

turned on. Introduced to drugs; under the influence.

tutti-frutti. Flavored cocaine developed by a Brazillian gang.

tweaker. Crack user looking for rocks on the floor after a police raid.

tweaking. Drug-induced paranoia.

tweak mission. On a mission to find crack.

tweek. Methamphetamine-like substance.

tweeker. Methcathinone.

twenty. Twenty-dollar rock of crack.

twenty-five. LSD.

24/7. Alluding to drugs available twenty-four hours a day, seven days a week.

twist-twistum. Marijuana cigarette.

two for nine. Two $5 vials or bags of crack for $9.

 U

ultimate. Crack.

uncle. Federal narcotics agent.

Uncle Milty. Depressant.

unkie. Morphine.

unmarried. Addict with no regular connection.

up against the stem. Addicted to smoking marijuana.

uppers/uppies/ups. Amphetamines. Drugs used to stimulate the nervous system.

ups and downs. Depressant.

using. Taking narcotics.

utopiates. Hallucinogens.

uzi. Crack; crack pipe.

 V

V. The depressant Valium.

vipe. To inhale marijuana smoke.

viper. Marijuana smoker.

viper butts/viper's weed. Marijuana.

vitamin A/vodka acid. LSD.

VS. Vein shooter.

 W

wac. Mixture of PCP on marijuana.

wack. PCP.

wacky weed. Marijuana.

wake ups. Amphetamine.

wasted. Under the influence of drugs; murdered.

water. (1) PCP. (2) Methamphetamine.

wave. Crack.

wedding bells. LSD.

wedge. LSD.

weed. Marijuana.

weed hound. Since the 1920s, one with a craving for marijuana.

weed tea. Marijuana.

weightless. High on crack.

wheat. Marijuana.

when-shee. Opium.

whippets. Nitrous oxide.

white. Amphetamine.

white ball. Crack.

white boy. Heroin.

white Christmas. Cocaine.

white cloud. Crack smoke.

white cross. Methamphetamine; amphetamine.

white dust. LSD.

white ghost. Crack.

white girl. Cocaine; heroin.

white-haired lady. Marijuana.

white horizon. PCP.

white horse. Cocaine.

white junk/white lady. Cocaine; heroin.

white lightning. LSD, a term borrowed from alcohol, where it was a name for powerful homemade booze or moonshine.

white mosquito. Cocaine.

white nurse. Heroin.

whiteout. Isobutyl nitrite.

white owsleys. LSD.

white powder. Cocaine; PCP.

white-powder bar. Collective term for lawyers representing the higher level of drug sellers.

whites. Amphetamine.

white snow. Powder cocaine; the kind that is snorted.

white stuff. Heroin.

white sugar/white tornado. Crack.

whiz bang. Cocaine and heroin.

wild cat. Methcathinone and cocaine.

window glass/windowpane. LSD.

wings. Heroin; cocaine.

wisdom weed. Marijuana.

witch/witch hazel. Heroin; cocaine.

wollie. Rocks of crack rolled into a marijuana cigarette.

wonder star. Methcathinone.

woolah. A hollowed-out cigar refilled with marijuana and crack.

woolas. Cigarette laced with cocaine; marijuana cigarette sprinkled with crack.

woolies. Marijuana and crack or PCP.

wool the jacket. To become addicted.

wooly blunts. Marijuana and crack or PCP.

working. Selling crack.

working half. Crack rock weighing a half gram or more.

works. Drug user's equipment for injecting drugs.

wrecking crew. Crack.

X

X. (1) Narcotic injection. (2) Marijuana; methylendioxy-methamphetamine or MDMA; amphetamine.

X-arm. Arm preferred by addict for injection.

X-ing. Methylendioxy-methamphetamine or MDMA.

Xmas. Period of euphoria following narcotic ingestion.

XTC. Methylenedioxy-methamphetamine or MDMA.

 Y

yahoo/yeaho. Crack.

Yale. Crack.

yeh. Marijuana.

yellow/yellow bullets. LSD; depressant.

yellow bam. Methamphetamine.

yellow dimples. LSD.

yellowjackets/yellow jackets. (1) Barbiturates. (2) Depressant.

yellow submarine. Marijuana.

yellow sunshine. LSD.

yen. Opium.

yen pop. Marijuana.

yen shee suey. Opium wine.

yen sleep. Restless, drowsy state after LSD use.

Ye Olde Peruvian Marching Powder. Mock-elegant nickname for cocaine.

yerba. Marijuana.

yerba mala. PCP and marijuana.

yesca/yesco. Marijuana.

yeyo. Cocaine, Spanish term.

yimyon. Crack.

 Z

Z. One ounce of heroin.

zacatecas purple. Marijuana from Mexico.

zambi. Marijuana.

zen. LSD.

zeppelin. Cigar containing secreted narcotics.

zero. Opium.

zigzag man. LSD; marijuana; marijuana rolling papers.

zip. Cocaine.

zol. Marijuana cigarette.

zombie. (1) Heavy marijuana user. (2) PCP. (3) Heavy user of drugs.

zooie. Holds butt of marijuana cigarette.

zoom. (1) Marijuana. (2) Mixture of PCP and marijuana.

zoomar. Powerful narcotic.

zoomers. Individuals who sell fake crack and then flee.

*

SOURCES

Esther and Albert Lewin's *Thesaurus of Slang* (Facts on File, 1988) and J. E. Schmidt's *Narcotics Lingo and Lore* (Charles C. Thomas, 1959) were most useful in the preparation of this listing, as was *Modern English* by Jennifer Walters. An anonymous Californian helped authenticate some of this, the late Charles D. Poe located many references in newspapers and novels, Joe McCabe was the first to point out that the Justice Department was compiling these terms, and the Tamony Collection provided many examples. Virginia Scallis also contributed.

12

FANTASY, THE FUTURE, SCIENCE FICTION, AND CYBERPUNK

Coming to Terms With Parallel Worlds

. . . listen to a fan's speech. It's a foregone conclusion if he uses words such as *faned, fapan, fanac, sercon, Neffer, vombic, fout, slan, neohood, grok.* By the way, a female fan is a *fanne.*

—From the "Amazing World of the Fen," *San Francisco Examiner*, October 13, 1968. Most of these science fiction terms are now archaic.

Bink, dweezle, frakkin' geek, scrod, skag, skeekin', sokkin', dithead.

—Selected cyberpunk swearwords from an Internet "Glossary of Slang in 2054," courtesy World Wide Word Watch.

Most slang concerns itself with the real world, of what is or what was. However, a small corner of the slang universe is reserved for what will be or could conceivably be. It is the realm of science fiction, futurism, fantasy, and cyberpunk—the newest and determinedly nasty bastard child of science fiction and the Net—each of which generates its own odd terminology. Here is a smattering from all of those netherworlds with the hard-edged slang of the cyberpunk marked as such.

* A

ace of spades. (cyberpunk) Solo term for death in combat. To "draw the ace" is to die in battle. "Drawing the ace" is a shorthand expression with the same meaning.

ALF. Alien life-form. Presumably the Alf of television fame was named with this science fiction acronym in mind.

APA/-apa. (1) Amateur Press Association or Amateur Press Alliance, which are cooperative efforts to publish FANZINES, or in this case, **apazines.** As one versed in APA ways explains, "Minac [minimum activity] is generally two pages per issue. Each author pays to print his pages, and the OE [official editor] collates and distributes the APA when each issue is ready." (2) As a suffix, it is used in constructions like *Bobapa,* for an APA where all discussion relates to Bob.

apazine. See APA.

apogee. (cyberpunk) The best. The greatest.

 ## B

bakebrain. (cyberpunk) General-purpose derogatory term indicating someone with limited or damaged mental faculties (frequently due to excessive use of neural cyberware).

BEM. The *bug-eyed monster* of science fiction. The bible of BEMs is *Barlowe's Guide to Extra-Terrestrials,* by Wayne Barlowe and Ian Summers, which contains such fine examples as the Abyormenite, Denu, Ixtl, Pnume, Thrint, and Unhjinian.

Benji. (cyberpunk) A robot dog or robohound.

big crunch. The hypothesized contracting of the universe by implosion and the flip side of the "big bang" of creation. The general estimate is that if it takes place, it is still some 110 billion years off.

big dark. (cyberpunk) Space.

biosoft. (cyberpunk) Software that can plug straight into a jack that goes into a person's head, to give them, for example, fluency in Spanish or an understanding of electronics.

bitty box. (cyberpunk) A primitive, underpowered, or generally useless computer or other electronic device.

biz. (cyberpunk) Crime.

black clinic. (cyberpunk) A medical facility that specializes in the implant of illegal or unregistered cyberware.

black ice. (cyberpunk) Illegal countermeasure software that causes physical harm or death to an intruder.

bloc. (cyberpunk) A powerful group with universal grasp, e.g., the aerospace bloc, the pharmaceutical bloc, etc.

BNF. Big-name fan; one known in fannish circles.

booper. (cyberpunk) A robot.

booster. (cyberpunk) Any member of a gang that affects cyberware, leather clothing, and random violence.

Boswash. Futurists' term for the emerging supercity sprawling between Boston and Washington. For those who believe the city will stretch from Portland, Maine, to Portsmouth, Virginia, the name is Portport. The Chicago-to-Pittsburgh supercity has been called Chipitts, and the sprawl from San Francisco to San Diego, Sansan.

bount. (cyberpunk) Bounty hunter.

braindance. (cyberpunk) A direct connection to a virtual reality via neural link. Used for re-creation, criminal rehabilitation, and training exercises.

brain potato. (cyberpunk) A braindance addict.

bruce. (cyberpunk) Pronunciation of the hacker acronym BRS (big red switch), used (1) to deactivate a machine; (2) to kill someone or render them senseless.

BTL chip. (cyberpunk) A *better than life* chip (also called dreamchips). An illegal cyberdata chip that provides the user a combination of artificial reality coupled with direct stimulation of different centers of the brain.

buttonhead. (cyberpunk) A person addicted to stimulating the pleasure centers through interface sockets.

∗ C

CE. A close encounter. A CE3 is a close encounter of the third level, celebrated in the film *Close Encounters of the Third Kind,* which according to this scale is a contact with a UFO and its occupants. CE2s involve UFOs that interact with the environment, and CE1s are encounters that are close and detailed enough to rule out misinterpretation of some other stimuli.

cement poisoning. (cyberpunk) What a person dies of after being pushed off a multistory building and hitting the sidewalk. Also known as deceleration trauma.

character. The playing piece that most people use in role-playing games. "You enter these games through the persona of a character," says writer and fantasy-game designer Mike Stackpole. "If you play well, your character will develop into a 'real' person who will leave you no doubt about how he or she would handle a situation."

Chinese takeout. (cyberpunk) Anything extremely jumbled or messy (e.g., "That riot gun made his chest look like Chinese takeout").

chit. Playing piece in role-playing games.

choob. (cyberpunk) Jerk, nerd, weirdo.

chopping. (cyberpunk) Cracking a stolen *credcard* or *credchip*—punkese for "credit card" or "credit chip."

chrome. (cyberpunk) (1) Flash, glitter, bells and whistles, tinsel. Material used to spice up the appearance of something. (2) Sexy features on a program, not needed for functionality but radiating style (e.g., a guillotine instead of a trash-can icon). (3) Generic reference to cyberware.

clamhead look. Describing Star Trekkers who wear Klingon haircuts.

clubzine. Fanzine published by a science fiction club.

combat drugs. (cyberpunk) Designer drugs for military use.

-con. A science fiction convention.

It is almost always applied as a suffix. Examples include Worldcon, Lunacon, Swampcon (in Baton Rouge), Amigocon (El Paso), Onceuponacon, Kublacon, Deepsouthcon, Mythcon, Loscon (Los Angeles), Mythcon, Okcon (Tulsa), Armadillocon (Austin), and Pretty Goodcon. The names of these conventions underscore the urge to pun and play with words that is at work in organized science fiction fandom. See also NONCON.

cortex bomb. (cyberpunk) A small, implanted explosive device (usually in the skull) that detonates in response to a timer or remote signal. Usually implanted against the wearer's will to keep him or her under control. Most cortex bombs will detonate automatically if tampered with.

crudzine. "A worthless fanzine," according to Robert Runte's *Fanspeak Glossary.*

cyberaxe. (cyberpunk) Any musical instrument—although typically a guitar—that is equipped with a cybernetic interface.

cyberculture. Society served by automation.

cybermetrician. Person with a highly advanced level of rapport with computers.

cyperpsychosis. (cyberpunk) A psychotic aberration suffered by excessive users of cyberware.

cyberpunk. A science fiction movement lead by a group of young writers who, according to Michael Dirda, writing in the *Washington Post,* "share a liking for hard-edged, high-tech, razzle-dazzle visions of the future, especially a grim future where computers, drugs, and cybernetics rule." The dust jackets on recent editions of Rudy Rucker's 1982 novel *Software* contain this claim: "The astonishing cyberpunk novel that started it all." By most accounts the best example of the genre is Bill Gibson's *Neuromancer.*

cyborg. Human fitted with electronic parts.

cybot. Cybernetic robot; a robot capable of making decisions.

* D

daddy/daddie. (cyberpunk) According to Jes Wulfsberg Nielsen's "Shadowrun & Cyberpunk Glossary" on the Internet: an "add-on" chip; a cyberdata chip containing a programmed skill that augments existing skills or provides new ones. These chips provide "instant" training of a normally unknown ability (e.g., flying a jet).

D&D. The game Dungeons & Dragons.

derms. Dermal patches that introduce drugs into a person's system; a term with ties to CYBERPUNK.

die of the measles. (cyberpunk) In military parlance, an assassination that makes the death appear to be of natural causes.

dirtgirl. (cyberpunk, derogatory) An earth woman.

DM. Dungeon master; in D&D, the

✳

SUP ZOMBIE?

Cyberpunk has its own sublingo that goes beyond such terms as *derms, flatline, meat puppet, razor boy/girl, sensetapes,* and others listed in this glossary. Also part of it is a motley assortment of gang and cop slang, motorcycle slang, some of the slang of the military, French slang, Russian cant, nonstandard Spanish, and Japanese slang of all sorts, but especially motorcycle slang. Thus, *ammo* (ammunition), *bakuto* (Japanese: gambler), *B&E* (cop slang for breaking and entering), *organiskaya* (the Russian Mafia), *boga* (in vogue from Spanish), *'ricain* (French slang for American), and *bourgie* (low class from the French *bourgeoisie*) are all part of the lingo. There are many terms for low-life scum, including *yono* (from the Korean *yonomoseki*), and garbage, including *gomo* (from the Japanese). The cyberpunks even have their own term for *nihilist,* which is *zombie*—about the closest that this hard-edged subculture gets to humor.

---

person who designs adventures for others to engage in.

dock. (cyberpunk) (1) To meet someone. (2) To have sex.

'dorph. (cyberpunk) (1) Street slang for synthetic endorphins, a designer drug that increases healing powers, limits fatigue, and produces a "rush" similar to a second wind. (2) A synthetic analogue for endorphins (organic painkillers produced naturally by the human body). Used to suppress pain and shock. Addictive.

doughboy/girl. (cyberpunk) Someone who is wearing too much armor.

dozmo. Irritating or boorish science fiction fan.

drek. (cyberpunk) Common curse word (archaic: *shit*). Adjective: *drekky.*

drig. (cyberpunk) Copulation. Expletive.

drobe. One who attends science fiction conventions in costume.

DSPSG. Trekker abbreviation for "disgusting, slobbering Patrick Stewart groupie," alluding to the commander in *Star Trek: The Next Generation,* Jean-Luc Picard, played by Patrick Stewart.

duck. (cyberpunk) A person who carries more weapons than could possibly be needed.

dweegs. Dorks with guns—fan David C. Kopaska-Merkel says that this is a reference to "pubescent males or those with arrested development who brandish weapons (more often than not fakes) at conventions, angering the management, and commonly causing the convention to be banned from the only good convention hotel in town." Extremely pejorative.

 E

earth grazer. Asteroid that comes close—that is, within several million miles—of earth.

egoboo. Ego boost, in the world of science fiction.

encounter. In the realm of UFOLOGY, one of three levels of extraterrestrial contact. See CE.

ETI. Extraterrestrial intelligence.

exobiota. Extraterrestrial life.

exosociology. Futurists' term for that aspect of sociology dealing with extraterrestrial civilization.

exotic. (cyberpunk) An obviously biosculpted individual, usually with nonhuman features (fangs, fur, tail, etc.).

F

faaan. A fanatical science fiction devotee. Written as *faaan*, it is often called a "triple-A fan."

'face/face/eye-face/I-face. (cyberpunk) The interface. Jacking into the Net.

FAFIA. Forced away from it all. A fan may fafiate from fannish activities because of bad press or any of a hundred other reasons. See also GAFIA.

fanac. Fan activity (*fan* and *activ-*

ity—pronounced *FAN-ac*) in the realm of science fiction. A prime example of fanac is publishing a FANZINE.

fandom. The science fiction subculture.

faned. *Fan editor* for short.

fannish. Relating only to science fiction fans; of the realm.

fanspeak. How science fiction fans speak.

fanzine. A blend of *fan* and *magazine*, these are simple science fiction periodicals that may be stenciled or photocopied.

fate meat. (cyberpunk) Someone bound for the body banks. "It is his fate to be meat."

fen. Plural of *fan*. Some say that this term is obsolete, but it still shows up in print.

FIAWOL. Fandom is a way of life; science fiction initialism for one of the two camps of fandom. The second camp is represented by the idea of:

FIJAGH. Fandom is just a goddamned hobby.

fixed pie. The view of the earth's future that contends there is a known limit to the planet's resources.

flatline. To be slain while hacking into a system in cyberspace. This is the most severe form of dealing with an intruder.

fletcher. (cyberpunk) A flechette pistol, or rifle.

flickercladding. (cyberpunk) A synthetic plastic material impregnated with fiber optics and temperature gauges designed to respond to skin temperature, a twenty-first-century version of the mood ring, but is worn as clothing—according to the Jes Wulfsberg Nielsen's "Shadowrun & Cyberpunk Glossary" on the Internet.

fossil. (cyberpunk) (1) An elderly person. (2) Someone who refuses to give up old ways. (3) Any old or obsolete item.

foxtrot uniform. (cyberpunk) Fucked up.

frob. (cyberpunk) To alter control settings in a random or mischievous fashion.

FRP. Fantasy role-playing. Expert Michael Stackpole says, "This is the generic term used to describe all of the role-playing games, though purists stick to *RPG* for that designation."

FTL. Faster than light (travel.)

* G

GAFIA. Getting away from it all. "To gafiate means to abandon science fiction and return to the mundane world," writes Michael Dirda in the *Washington Post.*

gamer. One who plays role-playing games.

geek. (cyberpunk) To kill or die.

get-a-lifer. Hard-core *Star Trek* fan; one needing to get a life.

GM. Game master, the director of role-playing games. A definition given by Chaosium, Inc., a distributor of such games, says that the GM "is one player who acts as the story's narrator and coordinator, describing the game world to the players, presenting the evening's objective, and controlling the actions of all the bad guys."

go-go-gang. (cyberpunk) A biker gang.

Golden Age. The period in which some of the greatest science fiction writers (Arthur C. Clarke, Isaac Asimov, and Robert Heinlein) were writing their classics. The 1940s and early 1950s.

goto. (cyberpunk) A dossier, usually illegally compiled.

grab gee. (cyberpunk) To spend time in a gravity field.

grav or **gee.** (cyberpunk) (1) Gravity. (2) Weight. (3) A measure of importance.

grok. To be, to love, to understand, to have cosmic awareness, etc. The verb is Martian and comes from Robert A. Heinlein's *Stranger in a Strange Land.* The term has spread outside the realm of science fiction, where it is still used but considered passé.

gumby from Monty Python. (cyberpunk) An act of minor but conspicuous stupidity (e.g., "pulling a gumby").

* H

hard. (cyberpunk) (1) A flattering term, like *cool, hip, touch,* etc. (2) A target wearing an exoskeleton.

(3) Any heavily armored object or position.

hard science/hard SF/hard. Science fiction that is hardware intensive or in which the magic and fantasy obey the laws of science. With the advent of the NEW WAVE of the 1960s, hard science fiction was deemed to be conservative and "Old Wave."

heroic fantasy/heroic fiction or **HF.** A genre of fantasy fiction that mixes monsters, barbarians, and pretty women. It is also known as S&S.

hexed. (cyberpunk) (1) Having cyberpsychosis. (2) Being obsessed with the Net.

hibernaculum. Place where a human is put into artificial hibernation for travel into deep space.

high frontier. Term characterizing space as a vast human habitat.

hotdogger. (cyberpunk, derogatory) Inexperienced netrunners.

Hugo. The most famous award in the world of science fiction, it is awarded by the World Science Fiction Convention and is voted on by members of that convention. It is named after Hugo Gernsback, the "father of modern science fiction."

hyperspace. Space containing more than three dimensions. A realm in which vehicles move faster than light. It was made popular in the movie *Star Wars.*

 I

IDIC. Infinite diversity in infinite combination—a Star Trekker tenet of life.

ish. In science fiction literature, this means "issue" and is often used as a suffix. Nextish, for instance, is the next issue of a FAN-ZINE.

 J

jack. (cyberpunk) (1) Jack in, or enter cyberspace. Jack out, or leave cyberspace. (2) A direct neural interface connection (usually in the skull) for a cyberdeck.

jander. (cyberpunk) To walk in a casual or arrogant manner, to strut.

jazzed. (cyberpunk) Equipped with reflex-enhancing cyberware.

 K

kibble card. (cyberpunk) Government food ration card. Kibble is a food product of the future resembling dry cat or dog food, hence the name.

kleptoid. (cyberpunk) Thief or prowler.

Klingon. Language of about two thousand words created by Marc Okrand, a writer. It is the language of the alien Klingons of *Star Trek,* and there are now Klingon language camps for those hoping to master the guttural, totally fabricated tongue. Here is a bit of Klingon from Ian Spelling's "Inside Trek" column in the *Washington Times* for October 10, 1994: "Ja'-chuqmeH roj-Hom neH jaghla'," which in English would be "The enemy commander wishes a truce [in order] to confer."

kranston maneuver. (cyberpunk) To become spacesick to the point of vomiting.

 L

leash. (cyberpunk) A corporate safeguard implanted into an employee to ensure loyalty and continued service. Cortex bombs and sabotaged chipware are common examples.

LGM. Little green men.

lifeboat ethic. The moral code based on the belief that an individual or nation can justify not aiding less fortunate individuals or nations because of widespread shortage and deprivation. Some believe that holding on to this "ethic" will lead to wars of redistribution.

light sailing. A means of spaceship propulsion in which a giant sail is used to catch powerful solar winds.

lizard brain. (cyberpunk) A cold, calculating, unemotional person, somebody always running in pure floating-point mode (e.g., Mr. Spock of *Star Trek* as viewed by the cyberpunks).

✳ M

Martian Statue of Liberty. An idea that first appeared in Arthur C. Clarke's *Profiles of the Future*. The inscription on the base of this imaginary structure reads: "Give me your nuclear physicists, your chemical engineers, your biologists and mathematicians."

matchbox. (cyberpunk) A sleep cube or coffin.

meatball. (cyberpunk) Someone augmented with grafted muscle.

meat puppet. (cyberpunk) a person who has had a neural cutout so as not to be conscious of what is happening to his or her body. Generally used to describe prostitutes, who use the cutouts to be "elsewhere" while their johns thrill themselves. In Ocelot's *Definition of Slang Used in Cyberpunk:* "A prostitute whose consciousness is wired into a braindance/simstim unit while customers have sex with her."

megacharacters. Characters in a role-playing game who have become "too tough" and possess many weapons and powers.

metalhead. (cyberpunk) A full 'borg conversion.

monkey. (cyberpunk) The business term for an expendable person.

monkey trick. (cyberpunk) A job in which a monkey—an expendable person—is not expected to survive.

monster fodder. A role-playing-game term for characters who are often used as guinea pigs to test traps and other hazards.

monty haul. Derogatory term for a role-playing game in which there are incredible rewards for trivial actions. It is a play on the name of Monty Hall, host of the once-popular *Let's Make a Deal* television quiz show.

moontel. Lodging on the moon.

mother ship. Term used in science fiction and UFO writing for a large spaceship from which smaller craft emerge.

mudboy. (cyberpunk, derogatory) An Earth man.

munchkin. Derogatory role-playing-game term for immature players who dwell on boring war stories.

mundane. A person with no knowledge of science fiction; nonfan. Interestingly, one of the cyberpunk dictionaries defines this as "a non-magician, or nonmagical."

Nebula. The second most famous award in the world of science fiction (after the HUGO). It is awarded by and voted on by members of the Science Fiction Writers of America (SFWA).

neofan. A new science fiction fan who sometimes displays excessive enthusiasm.

netfet/Net fetishist. (cyberpunk) Derogatory term for a netrunner who can only relate to life in the Net.

New Wave. Label for the "soft" science fiction of the 1960s, which deemphasized science and technology and emphasized values, politics, sociology, psychology, and social experimentation.

nextish. See ISH.

noncon. A "nonconvention"—a sci-

ence fiction gathering that is too small to be a convention.

normals. Fantasy gaming for characters without special powers who must constantly be rescued. Akin to MONSTER FODDER.

NPC. A *non-playing character* in fantasy gaming. "The players may interact with this character, in most cases to resort to combat, hence initiating role-playing," says Michael Stackpole, who adds, "Munchkins kill NPCs."

one and twenty, the. (cyberpunk) The twenty-first century.

output. (cyberpunk) Boyfriend.

overcook. (cyberpunk) To go too fast.

parallel world. Science fiction setting/premise in which the world is presented as it would be if a key historical or biological event had gone differently.

parsec. A parallax second, which is the equivalent to 3.26 light-years.

planet X. A tenth planet in the solar system, which was once suspected but not proven. It is now used in a mocking, tongue-in-cheek context. Futurist Ralph Hamil has this to say about a name for planet X: "Over the years, astronomers have postulated a 'Hades' and an 'Oceanus' among other names suggested for the hypothetical planet. 'Charon' and 'Prosperine' are other alternatives from science fiction." Martin Kottmeyer adds that "Nemesis" is the hypothetical planet involved in dinosaur-extinction theories.

popsicle. (cyberpunk) A frozen corpse, usually found in a drifting space wreck.

porky. (cyberpunk) Someone who loves or collects weapons; a "porcupine."

posergang. (cyberpunk) Any group whose members affect a specific look or bodysculpt job.

propars. Futurists' blend word for *pro*fessional *par*ents.

prozine. A commercial science fiction magazine, published to make money—a blend of *pro*fit and magazine. Longtime fan David C. Kopaska-Merkel adds, "Not all are published by major publishing houses (e.g., *Aboriginal SF*), but all have slick covers, advertising, and at least purport to make a profit."

puppets. (cyberpunk) Street-gang members who have, overtly or covertly, sold out to a major corporation or organized crime syndicate.

 Q

quakers. (cyberpunk) Missiles or rockets.

 R

rad. (cyberpunk) (1) Radiation. (2) A dose of radiation.

railway thinking. That way of thinking about the future in which events repeat themselves.

ramscoop. A spacecraft that operates on hydrogen, which it scoops up in space and converts to energy.

razor boy/girl. (cyberpunk) A cybernetically augmented thug. The name comes from the addition of razor-blade claws (retractable or not) in the fingers. Augmentation includes eye replacement for sighting, direct computer links, etc.

reality junkies. (cyberpunk) Addicts of virtual reality, braindance, the Net, or video games.

recycling. (cyberpunk) Environmentally friendly act of killing someone and taking the corpse to a body bank.

rimbo. (cyberpunk) A gun-toting sex kitten (a Rambo-bimbo).

rin tin tin. (cyberpunk) A robohound, especially a police K9.

ripperdoc. (cyberpunk) Surgeon specializing in implanting illegal cyberware.

rockerboy/ -girl. (cyberpunk) A musician or performer who uses his or her art to make political or social statements.

RPG. Role-playing game. Literature from Palladium Books of Detroit, distributor of the "megapopular" *Teenage Mutant Ninja Turtles* game defines an RPG in its sales literature this way: "An RPG is not a traditional board game. In fact, it has no playing board, no deck of cards, no spinner, nor even playing pieces. Instead the players have a book of rules with background information about adventure in a fictional world." See also FRP.

rules lawyer. Derisive role-playing-game term for a player who memorizes rules so carefully that he or she can cite verbatim specifics in arguments.

 S

S&S. Short for swords and sorcery, a genre of fantasy fiction that mixes monsters, barbarians, and pretty women. It is also known as HF, heroic fiction, or HEROIC FANTASY. The Conan the Barbarian series epitomizes this science fiction format.

saving roll/saving throw. The use of dice to simulate fate in role-playing games.

sci-fi. What science fiction is called outside the world of science fiction. *Sci-fi*, pronounced *sigh-fi*, is used by fans with irony. Science fiction fans say science fiction or SF.

screamsheet. (cyberpunk) A slick, flimsy newspaper printed at a data terminal.

sensetapes. (cyberpunk) The equivalent of videotapes, which allow the user to get the sensations of actors within the teleplay. Most tapes represent rich, upper-class life situations so the hopeless can experience what they will never know in life.

sercon. Science fiction fan term for *ser*ious and *con*structive.

SETI. Search for extraterrestrial life.

SF. *Science fiction* for short, although some insist that it stands for *speculative fiction* or *science fantasy.* The faithful say SF rather than sci-fi and pronounce it *ess-eff.*

shortwire. (cyberpunk) To burn out, flame out, splash down and generally crash mentally.

shredder. (cyberpunk) A minigun or auto-cannon.

sidewalk outline. (cyberpunk) A recently deceased person or one who expected to die soon. The reference is to the chalk outline drawn around a dead body at a murder scene by the police.

skeleton. (cyberpunk) All the collected electronic records kept on a person; their electronic identity.

skiffy. Sci-fi.

skyball. (cyberpunk) A satellite (usually surveillance).

slam. (cyberpunk) To assault or beat up (e.g., "Let's go slam some 'dorphers").

slammit on. (cyberpunk) (1) To get violent. (2) To attack someone without reason.

slash and hack. Term used in role-playing-game circles for the play of beginners whose characters turn into traveling butchers who kill monsters and take treasure. Also known as shoot and loot or trash for cash.

slice 'n' dice. (cyberpunk) A monofilament cyberweapon not unlike the suburban Weedwacker, usually mounted in the tip of a finger, that is used as a garrote or whip. It will cut through almost all organic material and most plastics.

smof. FANNISH word created from acronym of *secret master of fandom.* Defined by an insider: "Mysterious and shadowy, but not as much as they might like, smofs supposedly run fan groups and put on conventions. It has either complimentary or pejorative connotations, depending on usage."

solar wind. (cyberpunk) Hot air, i.e., something that is pretty much bullshit.

solo. Role-playing game that can be played by one person working against a programmed text.

space opera. A science fiction story written especially for action and excitement—intergalactic adventure. It is comparable to calling old-fashioned cowboy movies horse operas.

spaceship ethic. The moral code based on the concept that the earth is a large vehicle or spacecraft whose survival depends on cooperation by the passengers.

spill. (cyberpunk) (1) To spend money. (2) To confess or inform on others.

splatterpunk. SF/horror genre movement that unites the nihilism of punk with hyperviolent action.

suitcase war. One waged by people leaving small thermonuclear devices in other people's countries.

system hacker. A role-playing-game participant who uses loopholes and words like *sometimes* in the rules to do outlandish things. "You can generally see them coming and can modify situations to disallow most of their nonsense," says Mike Stackpole.

✳ T

tachyon. Theoretical particle that fuels much science fiction in that it moves faster than light and cannot go any slower.

tag. (cyberpunk) (1) Name, handle, or trademark. (2) To grab or take something.

taking sake. (cyberpunk) Working for Japanese business or criminal concerns.

terraforming. Reengineering the atmosphere or terrain of planets to make them ready for human habitation.

third industrial revolution. That which frees us from the confines of earth. The first two freed us from physical slavery and repetitive tasks.

tiger team. (cyberpunk) Computer experts who test system security by attempting penetration.

Titanic analogy. False perception of the earth as "unsinkable," in the sense that the *Titanic* was regarded as unsinkable before it sank.

transphotic. Describing faster-than-light travel.

Trekker. *Star Trek* fan. In his *Fan-*

speak Glossary, Robert Runté points out that this term is used for more restrained or older fans, while the next, TREKKIE, tends to be used for the more fanatical or young fan.

Trekkie. Fan of the *Star Trek* phenomenon, four television series, seven movies, books, etc. Hotter than ever!

trid. (cyberpunk) 3-D successor to video.

trog. (cyberpunk) Short for *troglodyte*. A derogatory term meant to indicate that an individual is subhuman or extremely ugly or misshapen.

twitcher/twitchers. (1) Fantasy gamer who is so excited by a subject that he explodes with energy and chatter, given to long, one-sided conversation. (2) (cyberpunk) Taser and, by extension, any electricity-based weapon.

* U

ufology. The study of unidentified flying object (UFO) reports.

uforia/ufomania. Zest for UFOs and/or conviction that aliens are visiting our world.

user interface. (cyberpunk) Anything used to snort, inject, or otherwise apply drugs, a play on the term that is so key to straight computer use.

* V

VRcade. (cyberpunk) A virtual reality, braindance, and/or video game arcade or parlor.

* W

waldo. Mechanical hands, coined by Robert A. Heinlein in a story of the same name. The main character was named Waldo, who had severe physical disabilities so he needed several "waldoes" to keep him going.

weefle. (cyberpunk, derogatory) An inexperienced netrunner.

wetwork. (cyberpunk) Assassination.

white hole. The hypothetical vehicle from which matter and energy emerge after being sucked into a black hole.

Whovian. Fan of the long-running British science fiction television series *Dr. Who*. A television special on the phenomenon contained this comment: "Denver is the center of Whovian activities in America."

wild card. Futurists' term for an event that defies conventional forecasting; for instance, the emergence of AIDS.

Wilson. (cyberpunk, derogatory) Netrunner slang for someone who you consider stupid, crazy, or a screwup.

wizworm. (cyberpunk) Slang for a dragon.

* X

xenology. The study of extraterrestrials.

Z

zine. Small magazine.

zonedance. (cyberpunk) As explained in the *Definition of Slang Used in Cyberpunk,* compiled by Ocelot, "Dancing turned into a dominance game. The dancer tries to persuade, by charisma, talent, or violence, other dancers within his zone to conform to his movements. Challenging because other dancers are often listening to other music via cyberaudio."

SOURCES

Earthlings who helped with this glossary are writer and game designer Mike Stackpole, futurist Ralph Hamil, and book editor Michael Dirda. Many of Stackpole's definitions have been quoted in their entirety, especially those from his memos on game and cyberpunk terminology. Martin Kottmeyer of Carlyle, Illinois, read the original version of this glossary and made important suggestions for its improvement.

The second edition of Robert Runté's *Fanspeak Glossary* (which is sold by the author at P.O. Box 4655, Postal Station South Edmonton, Edmonton, Alberta T6E 5G5), and a fanzine glossary produced by Mike Gunderloy, editor of *Factsheet Five,* of Rensselaer, New York, were useful in decoding SF talk.

David C. Kopaska-Merkel of Tuscaloosa, Alabama, suggested and defined more than a dozen terms that were not in the earlier version of this list.

A series of glossaries pulled from the Internet by Tom Dalzell were used for most of the cyberpunk entries. Of these, the best are Jes Wulfsberg Nielsen's "Shadowrun & Cyberpunk Glossary," the *Definition of Slang Used in Cyberpunk* compiled by Ocelot, also known as HighRider, and "Glossary of Slang in 2054" courtesy of the World Wide Word Watch.

13

FOOD AND DRINK
Words and Phrases to Fill a Doggie Bag

Ah, the menu—what contortions of language it embodies, what culinary sleights of hand it conceals, what glories of the kitchen it celebrates, and how mysterious it can be.

—Stanley Dry in *Food & Wine* magazine,
March 1984

"Couple a blues with," says Pete the counterman and owner of the Deluxe Diner in Rumford, Maine.

"Couple a blues comin' up," says a female voice from the kitchen. As Pete draws coffee from a forty-year-old coffee machine that he fired up at three that morning (for his 4 A.M. customers), the waitress Rose arrives with two monster, homemade blues—blueberry muffins and several pats of real butter.

On this summer morning the blues are selling well, and a few minutes later Pete asks for one "with wheels"—which means that it is to be put in a paper bag "to go."

There are a lot of good reasons to stop at this diminutive diner that is tucked into a tiny lot on Oxford Street. The food is first-rate, the prices are what big-city folk payed in the 1970s, and Pete Duguay, the owner, makes sure you feel at home even when it's early and the sky is as black as his coffee.

What makes it an oasis for this diner lover (who loves the Jersey Turnpike not for itself but for what is just off it) is that the atmosphere is just about as traditionally dinerish as you can find—that is, it is as dinerish as, say, O'Rourkes in Middletown, Connecticut, or Barb and Bob's Salem Oak Diner in Salem, New Jersey—and is much the same place it was when Eisenhower was in the White House.

Part of what gives it that dinerishness is that it sounds like a diner from the sizzle of the ancient grill, to the banter behind the man at the stools and the waitress who trades barbs and pleasantries with the largely male crew who line the row of stools. Then there are the calls—or abbreviated orders—which are hurled about and are as much a part of the diner culture as bread pudding, squeaky stools, and neon-rimmed clocks.

Calls are those distinct forms of communication that allow those behind the counter to pass orders around with a degree of efficiency and good humor that is typically American. The rules are easy: make it flip and make it easy to hear so there is no confusion and no need to repeat. For this reason, DOWN means toasted, and there is no such thing as mayonnaise in a diner (except on the menu)—it is always *mayo*. Odd sound effects are allowed. I ordered a turkey sandwich in a Delaware diner not long ago and the waitress passed on the order by making loud gobbling noises to her cook.

Gobbles notwithstanding, short-order calls can be disconcerting if one is not prepared for them. A friend who was born in Scotland and moved to the United States as a young man loves to tell the story of the first time he ate in an American diner and heard a waitress call across the room and tell her counterman to "burn the British." He recalls, "I didn't realize she was asking for a toasted English muffin, and for one very quick moment I thought I'd stumbled on some hotbed of anti-British feeling."

The lingo is fairly easy to master, and here are just a few examples (heard at the Deluxe and other favorite diners) that are easily heard if you get off the interstates. Consider this as a very basic intro. *A.C.* stands for American cheese, as opposed to SC or Swiss; *all the way* means a sandwich served with all the fixin's; *back* is on the side; *B&B* is not bed and breakfast but bread and butter; *behind the stick* is to operate a beer or soft-drink tap; *black* is black coffee; and a *bowl of red* is chili con carne. A *burger* is a hamburger, but *CB* is your cheeseburger, while your double cheeseburger is *CB2*.

Damages is what you call a bill; *easy over* means once over easy; and *86* is to be out of something, as in "Eighty-six on the lemon pie." This is one of the few survivors of an elaborate diner and lunch-room code that obtained before World War II. For instance, *95* stood for a customer leaving without paying, and *400W* stood for maple syrup.

FBI stands for franks and beans. The *five B's* is the name used in parts of New England for Boston baked beans and brown bread; a *full house* is lettuce, tomato, and mayonnaise; *GJ* is grapefruit juice; *to go* describes food that is taken out of the restaurant; and *to hold* is to withhold in a restaurant order, as "BLT, hold the mayo." *OJ* is short for orange juice; *once over easy* is to turn over and cook lightly on the other side, usually applied to fried eggs; and *on wheels* is said of a diner order that is to go. It is sometimes stated as "put wheels on that."

Repeaters are beans; *to smother it* is to cover as with gravy; and a *stack* is a pile of pancakes or toast. *Sunny-side up* refers to eggs that are fried with their yokes up and fully cooked on one side; a *tube steak* is one of a number of calls for a hot dog; and to *wreck* is to scramble, as in "wreck two" for two scrambled eggs.

These calls were born of an earlier America and nurtured in diners, lunch counters, and soda fountains and hang on in the older traditional diners, but are much less commonly heard than in earlier decades of this century. Perhaps because these terms were colorful and not always that appetizing, they became increasingly unwelcome. As John F. Mariani explains about diner and lunch-counter slang in his *Dictionary of American*

Food and Drink, "The vitality of lunch-counter speech—*cat's eye* for tapioca, *baby* for glass of milk, *jerk* for ice cream soda, and *Adam and Eve on a raft* for fried eggs on toast—had a raciness about it that many people sought to put an end to in the 1930s."

Fact is, much of the lingo survived the 1930s, as did places like the Deluxe Diner, which has been on the same spot since 1928 when it was delivered from the Worcester Dining Car Company factor. Just consider how much time has been saved in all those years by being able to make calls that were short, colorful, and to the point.

Diner slang is just a small part of a much richer brew—food slang from all over the world. English is a liberal language that seems predisposed to welcoming words from other languages. One can make a game of coming up with strings of these immigrants. Think of an intensely masculine, hungry, highly qualified public advocate, and you have your basic *macho ombudsman extraordinaire,* who, when hungry, may *nosh* on *dim sum.*

The point at which we speakers of American English are most open-minded would seem to be when we are most open-mouthed. We devour words like *pasta, empanadas, souvlakia, quiche lorraine, Havarti, caldo verde, tabbouleh, yakitori,* and *osso bucco.*

The reason for this linguistic liberalism, which has been especially strong since World War II, is simple. Some things are better said with a word or phrase that is or approximates the original. A wok is a wok and to call it "a shallow pan used for quick stir-frying" is to define rather than describe it.

Because of this international stew, a large amount of new food terminology is neither English nor American slang.

Another factor in all of this has been the rise in processed store food and fast-food restaurants. In a world of bottled salad dressings and nationally franchised drive-in restaurants, we get new terms like *Green Goddess* and *Big Mac,* but these are carefully selected product names and not slang. *Junk food* is a slang term, and people in the fast-food business would just as soon lose the adjective *junk.*

Here is the slang of food and drink—some old, some new—all in use.

A

A.C. American cheese.

all the way. A sandwich served with all the fixin's; lettuce, mayo, onion, etc.

amateur night. To heavy drinkers, this is New Year's Eve.

antifreeze. Alcohol (illegal or legal).

apron. A bartender.

B

BB. Back booth in a restaurant.

baby. Menuese for young, as in "baby kiwi" or "baby bok choy."

back. On the side. "Scotch, soda back" would be straight scotch with soda water on the side.

B&B. (1) Bed and breakfast. (2) Bread and butter.

bang/banger. Straight booze, usually vodka, on ice, which the bar customer bangs ceremoniously on the bar before downing.

barfly. One who spends much time at a bar drinking.

barista. Server at an espresso bar.

barkeep. Bartender.

beer goggles. Perception influenced by the consumption of alcohol. "He was handsome, but I was wearing beer goggles."

behind the stick. To tend bar.

big three. In the burger realm, McDonald's, Burger King, and Wendy's.

binder. Constipating food.

bite. Small meal or snack.

BJ. Bug juice—any sugary, noncarbonated fruit drink.

black. Black coffee.

blind pig. Tavern that opens after the legal closing hour; any illegal bar.

blues. (1) Bluefish. (2) Blue crabs.

bootie food. Food that goes right straight to the butt.

booze. Liquor, an old slang term that is as commonly used today as it ever was.

booze cruise. Short boat trip on which there is plenty of music and drinking.

bouncer. (1) Bad check to a restaurant. (2) Person employed to keep order in a bar or nightclub.

bowl of red. Chili con carne.

branwagon. The drive toward healthier eating, an allusion to both bran (as in oat or wheat) and bandwagon.

brew-ha. Beer.

brewpub. A bar/restaurant where beer is brewed on the premises.

brewsky. Beer.

brown bag. (1) Paper bag or wrapping for a meal. (2) To bring one's lunch in a brown paper bag, as in, "Let's brown-bag it tomorrow and go to the park."

bubble and squeak. Mashed potatoes and shredded beef.

bucket o' blood. Tough bar or saloon.

Budhead. Beer drinker.

bug juice. Noncarbonated fruit drink.

bullshot. Vodka mixed with beef broth.

burger. Hamburger.

burger joint. Place where the specialty is hamburgers.

bust some suds. To drink some beer.

buzzmaker. A particularly potent mixed drink, often a SHOOTER.

 C

campers. Slow-eating restaurant patrons.

cancer ward. Smoking section of an eating establishment.

carryout. Place that sells food to be taken from the premises.

cattle fries. Fried bull testicles in Texas.

CB. Cheeseburger.

chaser. Hard liquor thrown back after a beer or other less potent drink.

chicken-fried. Describing a flour-covered steak or other piece of beef that has been cooked in deep, hot fat, in the manner of fried chicken.

chili mac. Chili con carne mixed with macaroni (mac) or other pasta.

chilly. A beer.

chocoholic. Person with a passion for anything chocolate.

chow down. To eat.

chugalug. To drink without pausing to finish a gulp.

church key. Beer-can opener. This term is at least thirty-five years old and should have been eliminated by the pop-top can, but it is still heard.

comfort food. Food with nostalgic, pleasant overtones: mashed potatoes for some, chicken soup for others.

cooler. (1) A wine concoction, usually combining wine, carbonated water, and fruit juice. (2) A bouncer—one who throws unruly patrons out of bars and clubs.

country style. All-you-can-eat from central bowls. Let's go to the menu from Country Line Barbecue: "You get a big platter of meat (beef, ribs, brisket, and sausage), and generous bowls potato salad, coleslaw, and beans. It's all for one and one for all."

cowboy. Short-order-cook slang for a western omelet.

crack a tube. To open a beer can.

crispy. Hungover.

cuke. Cucumber.

* D

dagwood. Enormous sandwich from the multilayered constructions of Dagwood Bumstead of comic-strip fame.

damages. The bill in a restaurant.

DD. Designated driver.

DDK. Designated drunk.

dead one. An empty beer or liquor bottle.

deli. (1) Delicatessen. (2) In the style of a delicatessen, such as deli-sized sandwiches.

demi-veg. Part-time vegetarian.

designer ketchup. Those based on everything from cranberries to plums and mushrooms. A 1991 *Boston Globe* blind tasting of designer ketchups yielded a winner: Heinz tomato ketchup. A plum ketchup was adjudged to taste like "sweet black mud."

doggie bag/doggy bag. A bag provided by restaurants to hold a patron's leftovers. Despite the face-saving name, the contents of a doggie bag are usually destined for human as opposed to canine consumption.

do lunch. Have lunch.

down. Anything toasted in short-order-cook slang. "Whiskey down" is slang for toasted rye (a play on rye whiskey).

DQ. Dairy Queen, for short.

draggings. What the waitstaff term diners who linger at the table.

dry. Beer term for a brew with higher alcohol content.

 E

early-bird special. Restaurant meals that are reduced in price for those who are seated early.

easy over. See ONCE OVER EASY.

86. To be out of something; "Eighty-six on the lemon pie." This is one of the few survivors of an elaborate restaurant code that obtained before World War II. For instance, *95* stood for a customer leaving without paying, and *400W* stood for maple syrup.

em. An empty beer, wine, or liquor bottle.

empty calories. Term used to describe foods with little nutritional value.

eyetalian. See ITALIAN.

 F

fast food. Food that is cheap, standardized, and quickly dispensed.

Most fast-food restaurants are chains with plenty of parking.

fat farm. Camp or resort where one goes to diet and exercise.

fat pill. A pastry or other food that is high in calories and seemingly has the effect of a pill taken to make one fatter.

FBI. Franks and beans in short-order-cook slang. What does the *I* stand for? Nothing. FBI sounds better than FB.

fern bar. Establishment characterized by light wood, hanging plants, and good illumination.

FGTs. Fried green tomatoes in short-order-ese.

five B's. Name used in parts of New England for Boston baked beans and brown bread.

flatlined. To be totally drunk.

flight. Three different samplings (2.5 ounces) of wine offered for a flat price. Trendy way of getting a sip of three expensive wines.

fluff and fold. In restaurant parlance this is an injunction to take special care of a patron or tableful of patrons.

foam. Beer.

foodie. The food trendy of the eighties; one who was quick to discover GRAZING, talks about "food as fashion," and is among the first to try out new restaurants.

fool. A pureed fruit dessert mixed with sugar and cream.

free-range. Describing a chicken or other fowl that is raised outside rather than in a closed coop. These birds are preferred by people who have ethical problems with the treatment of fowl in factory-like coops. Free-range eggs are the eggs laid by these fowl.

frickles. Fried pickles, a dish with a following in parts of the South.

frog's eyes. Tapioca pudding.

front-loading. Drinking a lot in a short period of time before going to an event where liquor will not be served, such as the ballet.

froth. Beer.

full house. Lettuce, tomato, and mayo.

 G

garbage. Restaurant adjective for that which is left over from one dish and used in the next. It is not as nasty as it sounds: a *USA Today* article on the new California cuisine featured a restaurant specializing in "garbage salads" (based on leftover shrimp, avocados, etc.).

getting stiffed. Waiter/waitress term describing a party that leaves no tip or a small tip.

gin 'n It. This is a British drink; two parts gin to one part Italian vermouth, served at room temperature. In other words, a lukewarm martini.

give good wrist. To pour generous drinks.

GJ. Grapefruit juice.

go, to. Food that is taken out of the restaurant for consumption elsewhere.

going all the way. Chocolate cake with chocolate ice cream.

gorp. A "trail mixture" of peanuts, raisins, candy, and grain. It has been claimed that the term began as an acronym for *good old raisins and peanuts,* but many would side with William Safire, who thinks that the acronym story is bunk. Safire has written, "To me, the word seems formed like Lewis Carroll's creation of *chortle* by combining *chuckle* with *snort; gorp* is a wedded *snort* and *gulp.*"

grapes of wrath. Wine.

grazing. Ordering a series of small entrée portions rather than one large entrée. One can graze a meal's worth at a single restaurant or at several.

greasy spoon. Restaurant at the low end of the scale in terms of food, cleanliness, and decor; a dive.

green chop. Coleslaw in some rural regions of Maryland.

greenhouse look. Restaurant or bar with immense windows and lots of greenery.

grinder. Sandwich served on Italian bread sliced sideways. This is one of a number of names for the same thing, with this one being popular in parts of southern New England. Other names, in other regions, include HERO, HOAGIE, ITALIAN, TORPEDO, SUBMARINE, and WEDGE.

ground hog. Today as always, the preferred nickname for a steam-operated still.

gumbo. A tasty stew of okra, vegetables, and meat or seafood.

* H

happy camper. In the context of bars and restaurants, this term refers to one who is intoxicated; however, someone who is "not a happy camper" is an angry customer.

happy hour. Period before dinner during which bars attempt to promote themselves, often with reduced drink prices.

harmless. Latte made with decaf espresso.

hero. Sandwich served on Italian bread sliced sideways. The term was invented in the 1930s by the legendary food writer Clementine Paddleford of the *New York Herald Tribune,* who insisted that you had to be a hero to eat one. But wordsmith Bruce Boston says *hero* is actually the Greeks' pronunciation of their own stacked sandwich: the giro.

hoagie. The same thing as a HERO, SUBMARINE, TORPEDO, etc.

hold. To withhold in a restaurant order: "Roast beef, hold the gravy."

hooter. Same as SHOOTER.

hopping. Moving around in search of food, restaurant hopping; drink, bar hopping; or companionship, as in table hopping.

hungchow. Any food that is constipating: a binder.

hush puppy. Deep-fried cornmeal dumpling.

* I

idiot oil. Booze.

in-and-out. Martini created by pouring a small amount of vermouth into the pitcher, swizzling it around, pouring it out, and adding gin.

inhale. To eat quickly, as if one is breathing in air.

in the ozone. Restaurant term describing a table where the patrons have had too much to drink.

in the trees/in the weeds. Describing a kitchen that is running way behind.

Irish sweetener. Alcoholic substance added to coffee—often Irish whiskey or brandy.

Italian. Long sandwich served on Italian bread. In the upper Northeast it is often pronounced *eye-talian.*

* J

jew stew. Chicken soup.

jigger. Bar glass holding one and a half ounces of liquor and used for measurement.

junque food. So-called adult fast food, a $7.95 hamburger touted as "our deluxe, gourmet burger."

*

SAY WHAT?

Franchising has made *pancakes* the preferred term for flat cakes of batter fried on a griddle or pan, but you can still spot several variations. Some people from the Northeast will respond with *griddle cakes,* which sounds much tastier, but less often with *hotcakes,* although other regions still cling to this expression. And *flapjacks* is holding its own in the South and West. Lastly, in the North's upper tier, they are *wheat cakes.*

Doughnuts are another giveaway. Ask people what they call a small ring-shaped cake fried in deep fat and some natives of New York and New England will use the Dutch term *cruller,* blissfully ignorant of the usual understanding of that word as a twisted cake without a hole, meant by God to be dipped into coffee. (A *French cruller* is the same thing, only with a little more class.) A Chicagoan might knock you over with *crawler.*

Farther inland, still in the North, a doughnut becomes a *friedcake.* But if you ask someone from Pottsville, Pennsylvania, in the heart of Pennsylvania Dutch country, the answer might be *fassnacht* or *fatcake.* By the way, a doughnut hole in Berlin, New Hampshire, may still be called a *comfy.*

Speaking of calories, what do you call a rich, flaky pastry filled with fruit or soft cheese and topped with icing? A *Danish pastry,* right? Well, don't be too sure. In New York City, which has the best, it's more likely to be simply *Danish.* But ask someone from the West, and you might well hear *bear claw,* or, from the Northwest, *maple bar.* But your favorite, dropped like deep-fried dough from the lips of a Midwesterner, is likely to be *Bismarck.* Our guess is that it is linked more closely to the capital of North Dakota than to the Prussian chancellor.

If you cut a potato into long strips and deep fry them, there's little disagreement about what you call the result. But ask people what they call potatoes sliced into flat circles and perhaps fried up with eggs and it's a different story. In the lower North they are *fresh fries,* while in the Northeast they are *home fries* or sometimes *pan fries.* But someone from an upper Midwest state such as Minnesota might come out with *American fries.*

A quick and dirty way to tag a New Yorker is to ask what he or she requests at a place that sells pizza by the slice. A *slice,* of course. As in, "Lemme have a soda and a slice."

You order ice cream in the town or city where you grew up and ask for a cone dipped in tiny, multicolored (or chocolate) flecks of candy. How exactly do you place your order?

The answers here are proof positive of the nation's enduring diversity. They are *jimmies* in Boston and northern New England, *sprinkles* in New York and Connecticut, *ants* in Rhode Island, and west of the Hudson they have several names including *shots* and *cake* decorations. In the United Kingdom, folks call them *hundreds and thousands.*

∗ K

kittie bag. Same as doggy bag only more petite.

knock back. To drink aggressively.

∗ L

leaded. Caffeinated coffee.

liquid bread. (drink) Beer.

lite. Low in calories; lighter than normal.

little ears. A pasta called orecchiette.

lo-cal. Low in calories.

long list. A restaurant's full listing of wines in stock.

long neck. A beer bottle with a long neck. A certain bravado is associated with carrying one around a bar, especially a Lone Star long neck in Texas.

∗ M

martooni. (drink) Martini.

mayo. Mayonnaise.

meat market/meat rack. (drink) Singles bar where the primary objective seems to be to get laid.

medley. Upscale MENUESE for a mixture or combination, as in a medley of baby vegetables.

megadiner. One of the new breed of diners that can seat as many as five hundred—in contrast to the classic forty-seaters built in the 1930s through the 1950s.

menuese. Derogatory term for the overblown descriptions of simple food found in some menus. Here is an example from a real menu: *"Fresh Fruit Salad*—transported in a pineapple boat for the highest vibration, and your transmutation with yogurt on the side for accent, or dressing sprinkled with coconut . . . $6.35."

merry Christmas. In short-order-cook slang this is tuna on toast with lettuce and tomatoes.

microbrew. Beer produced by a small brewery producing beer for local consumption.

mud pie. An ice cream concoction that is intensely chocolate.

munchies. Craving for food.

mystery meat. Food, usually from an institutional cafeteria, that defies identification.

∗ N

neat. Straight liquor, not on the rocks.

nibbling. Sipping slowly.

nightcap. Drink taken late at night.

nosh. To munch or snack; a Yiddish Americanism.

noshery. Delicatessen or snack bar where one goes for appealing food.

∗ O

OD. To overeat; from the drug initialism for overdose.

OJ. Orange juice.

once over easy. To turn over and cook lightly on the other side, usually applied to fried eggs. Eggs can also be *medium, over hard,* and other variations.

on the rocks. With ice.

on wheels. Said of a restaurant order that is to go. Sometimes stated as "put wheels on that."

open dating. Products with an easily read date telling when it was packed and when it must be pulled from the shelf.

* P

PB. Peanut butter.

PBD. Peanut butter and dill pickle sandwich.

PBJ. Peanut butter and jelly. In some parts of the South a popular drink is the *PBJ shake,* a peanut butter and jelly milkshake.

pig out. To overeat.

pistol. Pastrami in short-order-cook slang.

pit stop. Place where one goes for food and a rest room on a car trip.

pop. Soft drink.

pork out. To overeat, to pig out.

pot luck. (1) Meal made of what is on hand. (2) A dinner to which everyone brings a dish.

power breakfast/power lunch. A meeting at which policy makers discuss business or politics over food.

* R

rabbit food. Raw vegetables.

repeaters. Beans.

rinse. Chaser.

roach coach. Small truck selling prepared food; common around industrial areas where there are no cafeterias.

road ribber. Those who go on the road to sell barbecue ribs at chili cook-offs, barbecue festivals, and the like. According to an article in the December 1992 *Food Arts* magazine, some road ribbers can make up to $20,000 a weekend.

rocks glass. Old-fashioned glass.

Rocky Mountain oysters. Testicles of a bull or other male animal that have been breaded and fried.

roots and berries. Derogatory characterization of natural foods and/or vegetarianism.

ruckus juice. Moonshine.

* S

sack. A bag of ten—count 'em, ten—burgers from the White Castle chain of stores.

scarf. To eat quickly. The term is often used in connection with fast food. William Safire believes that this verb came from the 1930s black-English word *scoff,* for food.

schizo. (coffeehouse) A half-leaded (caffeinated), half-unleaded (decaffeinated) drink.

shooter. (1) Straight shot meant for

POP QUIZ

What would you ask for if you wanted a carbonated beverage and to be regionally correct in various parts of the United States? A *soda* puts you in the Northeast, *pop* in the North from New Hampshire to Washington State, but especially in the Midwest where it is *pahp*. It is *tonic* in eastern New England, perhaps in Springfield, Massachusetts, or Manchester, New Hampshire; but a plain old *cold drink* will do just fine in the South. An older person from the Mid-Atlantic might call it *dope*. Soda pop? *Coke,* not the brand name, is generic for any *soft drink* in Oklahoma and parts of Tennessee.

SAY WHAT?

Restaurant testicles require a certain dressing up for the menu. Here are a few possibilities beyond the traditional ROCKY MOUNTAIN OYSTERS to have graced American menus:

- bull fries
- cattle fries (term preferred in Texas)
- prairie oysters
- swinging steaks

If one were giving a prize for this kind of naming, it would have to go to the owners of Bruce's in—hold on!—Severence, Colorado, where, according to *Travel Matters* magazine, they let their patrons believe that they are getting "headless and tailless shrimp."

consuming in one gulp. (2) House drink that is usually sweet and easy to consume quickly. These shooters are common to summer beach bars and often feature a fruit liqueur, such as DeKuyper peachtree schnapps or Southern Comfort or tequila. These drinks often have names that are as wild as their formulas. Writer Joe Goulden brought back a copy of the *Beachcomber* free newspaper from the Delaware coast a few years ago that contained a "shooter survey" rating such libations as the Blood Clot, Midnight at the Oasis, 57 Chevy with Hawaiian Plates, Sex on the Beach, the Russian Quaalude, Deep Throat, the Chocolate Virgin, and Daphnie Divine's Deluxe Dixie Daiquiri. From the other coast comes the Bay Bridge Commuter

Shooter with vodka, gazpacho, horseradish, Tabasco, a prawn, and lime.

shopping list menu. Menu that not only tells you what is available, but what went into it, including the garnish ("garnished with a sprig of spring parsley," for instance).

short dog. (1) Single can of beer. (2) Small, cheap bottle of wine.

shot. A small, measured quantity of liquor—usually two ounces, give or take a half ounce.

shot glass. Small vessel for measuring liquor, usually one and a half or two ounces.

sinker. Heavy, dense version of dish, especially baked goods. (The term is likely to bring back the thought of a particularly bad example. In the author's case it was a heavier 'n lead stack of blueberry pancakes served to him in Maine, where they are called sinkas).

skinny. Latte made with 1 percent or nonfat milk.

skirt. Ring of ice cream sticking out around the edges of a scoop on a cone.

slab. Rib portion.

slider. Midwesternism for small burgers (such as one can get from the White Castle chain—which go down real easy).

smothered. Covered.

sparg. Asparagus.

splash. A small amount of water or soda, as in bourbon with a splash.

spritzer. White wine and soda water.

sproutsy. A vegetarian.

spud. Potato.

stack. A pile of pancakes or toast.

starters. 1990s menuese for appetizers.

sticks. Food sliced into long sticklike shapes—fried mozzarella sticks or batter-dipped zucchini sticks, for instance.

stinking rose. Garlic, among garlic lovers.

straight up. Without ice.

submarine. Sandwich served on Italian bread sliced longitudinally. Known also as a HERO, HOAGIE, ITALIAN, etc.

suds. Beer.

sunny-side up. Eggs that are fried with their yokes up and fully cooked on one side.

surf-n-turf. Generic name for meat and seafood on the same platter.

swill. Beer.

* T

Tabhead. Person on a diet, from Tab, the diet cola.

table from hell. Term used in the restaurant business for a table of people who are drunk and abusive.

T&T. Tanqueray and tonic.

tater. Potato.

teen/teenie. Martini.

Tex-Mex. Type of food that is influenced by innovations on either side of the Texas-Mexico border.

three-martini lunch. Code word for the excesses of expense-account dining. It has recently become emblematic for the kind of common business lunch that began to erode with growing health consciousness; however, such lunches are still fairly common.

thunder thigh. (coffeehouse) Quadruple grand whole-milk latte with chocolate syrup and extra whipped cream.

torpedo. Sandwich served on Italian bread sliced sideways. Known also as a HERO, HOAGIE, ITALIAN, etc.

trash fish. Cheap, unpopular whitefish.

tube steak. A hot dog.

twist. Twist of sliced lemon peel.

 U

Umbrella Room, the. A sidewalk food cart; "Let's grab a quick lunch at the Umbrella Room." This term was acquired in New York City by Joseph C. Goulden, who reports that it is popular there.

unleaded. (coffeehouse) Decaffeinated coffee.

 V

veggies. Vegetables.

veggy. (1) Vegetarian. (2) Sandwich made with vegetables and cheese.

vegucation. Education about vegetarianism.

vergus. Menuese for the juice of unripened grapes.

V's. Vegetables.

 W

waitstaff. Male and female waiters taken as a group.

wall box. Miniature jukeboxes on booth tables in a diner.

watering hole. A bar.

wedge. Sandwich served on Italian bread sliced sideways. Known also as a HERO, HOAGIE, ITALIAN, etc.

western. Omelet (or a sandwich containing an omelet) filled with ham, green pepper, and onions.

wet dog. Description used for a bad wine with a chemical smell.

whiskey. Short order call for rye bread—a play on the rye whiskey connections.

with wings. To go.

wolf down. To eat quickly.

works, the. Everything: all the extras in food. A pizza called the Works on sale at Foodee's in Concord, New Hampshire, offers all the classic accoutrements: tomato sauce, mushrooms, pepperoni, green pepper, onions, three cheeses, and hamburger or sausage.

wreck 'em. Scramble eggs in short-order-cook slang. "Wreck two" is an order to scramble two eggs.

Z

zapper. Microwave oven.

zip-code wine. A wine-trade term for a French wine from a shipper who has an impressive address but whose grapes do not come from that region.

zombie food. Unacceptable food that has been brought back to acceptability with the aid of irradiation or other sterilization techniques.

SOURCES

Phyllis Richman, *Washington Post* food critic, was most helpful, as was the food file in the Tamony Collection.

"Short-Order Musts" in the *New York Times* for September 24, 1991, is an invaluable source of short-order-cook slang, and Janey Milsead's *Los Angeles Times* piece on bartender slang in the April 23, 1993, issue of the Sunday magazine is especially good.

Food Arts: The Magazine for Professionals is a great source of inside food slang and terminology. Roberta B. Jacobson also contributed.

—— ✳ 14 ✳ ——

THE GREAT OUTDOORS

Slang on Ice, on the Rocks, on the Road, in the Snow, on (and Under) Water, in the Woods, on the Mountains, and From the Air

Fresh air, it would seem, has the ability to foster slang—especially as we find new sports and activities to pursue out of doors. What follows is a potpourri of outdoor slang mixing backpacking, biking, boarding (including bodyboarding, skateboarding, and snowboarding), climbing, cycling, fishing, gardening, hang gliding, hunting, ice fishing, in-line skating, lifeguarding, skating, skiing, snowmobiling, and surfing. For good measure there is also a smattering of the slang of park rangers, tree surgeons, meteorologists, and the racetrack.

✳ A

aerial bodyboarding. (surfing) Reentry in which the entire board extends above the crest of a wave.

aggro. (rock climbing) Aggressive; driven.

air. (snowboarding) How high the boarders get from the vertical wall of snow. "I caught a lot of air on the first hit."

alley-oop. (snowboarding) When the snowboarder goes straight up in the air, makes a turn, and comes back down. "Hey, that guy just did a front-sided alley-oop."

also-ran. (horse racing) Describing a horse that finishes out of the money—that is, comes in fourth or worse.

amped. (surfing) Overdoing it, overenergetic, making loud or sudden movements.

asphalt surfer. (surfing) Skateboarder.

auger. (ice fishing) A tool used to drill a fishing hole in the ice. Some augers are hand drills, and some are gasoline operated. Others are electric, but if you can't park nearby, carrying a heavy battery for the electric auger is no fun.

à vue. (rock climbing) French for "on sight." If a route is climbed with no falls and absolutely no prior information other than the grade, it is considered a true *à vue* ascent.

axel. (ice skating) The only jump that takes off from a forward position and therefore one of the more difficult. Takeoff is from the forward outside edge of the blade, landing on the back outside edge of the opposite foot. The turn comes in midair and the skater lands backward. Named for its inventor, Norwegian skater Axel Paulsen, who was dodging snowballs at the time.

* B

backdoor. (surfing) Going with your back facing the wave.

backhand surfing. (surfing) Riding with one's back to the wave (also GOOFY FOOT).

bacon-in-the-pan. (in-line skating) When you wipe out badly on a ramp and slide back down to the bottom.

bake. (surfing) Someone from Bakersfield in the Central Valley of California; e.g., "What a Bake!"

banana hammock. (lifeguard lingo) Men's bikini-style bathing suit.

barney. (surfing) A poor, clumsy surfer (from *The Flintstones* but certainly reinforced by the purple television dinosaur).

base-area stone grinder. (skiing) A novice who is unable to stop until he or she is sprawled out on the ski-area parking lot.

bat. (horse racing) A jockey's whip.

bathtub. (skiing) Mark left in snow from a fall on the seat of the pants; a *sitzmark*.

beach Betty. (lifeguard lingo) Bikini-clad bathing beauty.

beach break. (surfing) Waves breaking close to a beach on a sandbank.

beached. (surfing) Stuffed from eating.

belay. (rock climbing) Securing a climber by the use of a rope.

beta. (rock climbing) Information about a route, ranging from required gear to movement sequences.

BICO. (meteorological slang) Baby, it's cold outside.

biff a crash. (mountain biking) Synonym: *wipe out.* "I biffed and then wiped away the blood."

big mama. (surfing) The ocean.

birder. Affectionate name for bird-watching enthusiast.

blasted. (surfing) To wipe out. Normally getting blasted is the product of riding too deep in a tube or getting blown off your board by the spray coming out of a tube.

blind eye. (naturist/nudist) Describing a beach or other public place where nudity is allowed.

blitz. (lifeguard slang) A multivictim rescue.

blowdown. (backpacking) Large trees that have fallen across the trail.

boards. (skiing) Skis.

bobhouse. (ice fishing) A name used for ice-fishing shelters.

bog down. (surfing) Unable to accelerate because of equipment design, lack of skill, or poor wave quality.

bonk. (mountain biking) Total exhaustion caused by lack of sufficient food during a long race or ride.

bouldering. (rock climbing) Climbing on rocks that are small enough that ropes aren't necessary. It often serves as a means of practicing difficult climbing moves.

bowl. (surfing) Wave shaped by a section of reef that causes it to break with more than usual suddenness and force.

breakaway. (competitive cycling) Racers or a group that get ahead of the main pack.

breaking maiden. (horse racing) Jockey scoring his or her first career win.

bridge. (mountain biking) To leave one group of riders and join another group that is farther ahead.

buck pocket. (hunting) A spot where male deer gather, usually in high country.

buffasorus. (lifeguard) One who is in shape and looking good.

bugboy. (horse racing) Apprentice rider.

bulldog. (rodeo) To wrestle a steer to the ground by seizing its horns and twisting its neck until the animal falls.

bulletproof. (skiing) Icy surface so dense that it could bounce a bullet.

bumbly. (rock climbing) Any climber who isn't as good as you are.

bumping. (in-line skating) Skating down stairs; can be done forward, backward, even sideways. Synonym: *bashing.*

bunny-hop. (mountain biking) To jump the bike, without dismounting, over a log, rock, or other obstacle.

burly. (snowboarding) Impressive.

butt floss. (beach talk) Thong bikini.

✳ C

camel. (ice skating) One of the most popular spins, and it's upright. Starts on forward outside edge, spinning on toe, then dropping onto the flat of the blade. Variations include low camel, flying camel, back camel, and the Hamill camel.

camp robbers. (backpacking) Jays, crows, pigeons, and ravens that frequent camp and steal your food.

Casper. (surfing) A beachgoer with a pale complexion, from Casper the Friendly Ghost.

cement. (skiing) Heavy, wet snow.

chainsuck. (mountain biking) When the chain becomes caught between the chainstay and the rear wheel, whether due to mud buildup or poor frame design.

chalk horse. (horse racing) Favorite in a race.

chalk people. (surfing) People who live far from the beach; inlanders.

chasers. (competitive cycling) Racers who are trying to catch a group that has gotten ahead of the main pack.

chicken heads. (rock climbing) Small knobs of rock used to get a handhold.

cloon. (mountain biking, skiing, and snowboarding) Slamming into the ground, resulting in a ringing head or a delay in the action.

coming down. (surfing) Warning cry to anyone taking off in front of you on a wave.

conditional instability. (meteorological jargon) It may rain—or it may not rain.

crankling. (backpacking) Hiking at a fast pace.

crater. (rock climbing) A fall in which the climber hits the ground so hard he leaves a small crater. "Poor form and to be avoided," say climbers.

creamed. (surfing) To be caught by the curl of a wave and violently tossed off one's board.

critical section. (surfing) A section of wave that is difficult to ride—usually deep within the curl.

crossover. (ice skating) Primary method of gaining speed and rounding corners. Begins on a curve, passing free foot in circle in front of other foot. Forward (clockwise) crossovers begin on the left foot, backward or reverse (counterclockwise) crossovers begin on the right foot.

* D

death cookie. (skiing) Loose, icy lumps of snow/ice, often the result of grooming machines in humid, freezing conditions.

death spiral. (ice skating) Executed (not literally) only in pairs and a mandatory move. Male skater spins in a pivot position (toe pick in ice, circling around it), holding female partner's hand. She's parallel to the ice, spinning horizontally on one edge.

dialed in. (mountain biking) When a bike is set up nicely and everything works just right.

ding. (surfing) A damaged spot on a surfboard.

dog. (rock climbing) Short for *hangdog*. Climbing a route by hanging on to the rope, sometimes spending more time hanging than climbing. Not a good thing.

domestique. (competitive cycling) A racer who sacrificially works for the team leader to insure that he or she is in contention to win.

drafting. (mountain biking) Riding close behind another rider to save energy by using that racer as a windbreak.

drill and fill. (tree doc slang) To hollow out and fill part of a tree.

drilled. (surfing). To wipe out. Normally this involves hitting the bottom, looking like you are going to hit the bottom, or being tossed over rocks.

drop in. (surfing) Starting off on a wave by leaving the paddle late and then forcing the board over the crest of a wave. The result is a freefall, and the necessity for a hard, fast bottom turn.

drop knee bodyboarding. (surfing) Kneeling on a body board (usually with one knee) while moving on the wave face.

✳ E

earthy crunchy. (gardening) A hippie or organic gardener.

echelon. (competitive cycling) A staggered line of racers, taking orderly turns at the lead. The echelon is determined by the crosswinds.

Elvis syndrome. (rock climbing) When a climber stands on a small hold for too long and starts trembling and twitching from the waist down. Also called sewing-machine leg or Elvis leg (because it's all shook up).

end-to-ender. (backpacking) Someone who hikes from the start of a long trail to the finish.

epic. (surfing) Really good or large. "I had an epic session" or "Shoulda been here yesterday, the surf was epic!"

escrow. Birder term for sighting a bird that has not been made a distinct species in anticipation of its change in status. It can be added to one's life list at this point.

✳ F

face angel. (skiing) A takeoff on snow angels done by kids. How used: After a FACE PLANT (a sudden face-first fall) one flaps his/her arms and acts as if it were planned.

face plants. (skiing, biking, and anything else where you can fall forward) Landing on your face. Hitting the ground face first. "Joe hit a tree root and did a spectacular face plant." Synonyms: *auger, digger, soil sample, spring planting.*

face shots. (skiing) Splashes of powder in your face when the powder's so deep and light that it's flying everywhere as you ski down the fall line.

fat air. (hang gliding) Preferable flying conditions.

feeding. (competitive cycling) When the team manager hands up a bag containing food or liquids or both to a racer during a long race.

fetch. (surfing) The distance over which wind blows to create the swell. Waves may travel a great distance out of this wind before reaching the coast as a ground swell.

field. (competitive cycling) The main group of riders, also called the bunch, pack, or peloton.

fish stick. (ice fishing) An ice-fishing pole. It has a place where the line is wound (no reel), a point so that it can be jabbed into the ice above the fishing hole, and an eyelet on the other end for the line to go through.

fish storm. (meteorological slang) One that stays far out at sea.

flag. (ice fishing) Winter fishing gear equipped with some way of indicating when there is action involving a fish. This signaling device is called a flag. Being "flagged" is when the flag is sending its message to the fisherman who is watching his flag(s) from a distance.

flapper. (rock climbing) A large piece of torn skin; a skin flap. It is often reattached (or at least held in place) with Super Glue or tape.

flash. (rock climbing) To climb a route on the first try without ever physically touching it before. Less of an accomplishment than À VUE, but still good.

flip. (ice skating) A toe-assisted jump, taking off from the left foot going backward and landing on the right foot.

flip joint. (ice skating) Despite the name, no somersaulting is involved. Takeoff is from the back inside edge with a landing on the opposite back outside edge.

flyer. (mountain biking) A surprise attack, usually done alone.

forehand surfing. (surfing) Riding while facing the wave.

free climbing. (rock climbing) To climb using hands and feet only. The rope is only used to safeguard against injury, not for upward progress.

freshies. (skiing) The first tracks in fresh powder.

* G

gaper. (rock climbing) A non-climber who watches climbers.

geriatric ski school. (skiing) A group of older students.

gnarly. (surfing) Treacherous, dangerous, hairy.

goat boat. (surfing) A boat for goats. Otherwise known as a surf ski.

gobs. (skiing) Geeks on boards.

goby. (rock climbing) A flesh wound, usually from crack climbing.

goofy foot. (surfing and snowboarding) Surfing with one's right foot forward (also BACKHAND SURFING).

granny gear. (mountain biking) The third and smallest chainring on a mountain bike, combined with the biggest sprocket. This is the lowest gear, used for extremely steep climbs. Also called pixie gear or weenie gear.

grinding. (in-line skating) Jumping up onto a curb and sliding across it on your skates.

gripped. (rock climbing) Extremely scared, from white-knuckled to glassy.

grommet. (surfing) Adolescent or preadolescent surfer.

grovel. (surfing) To maintain speed on a broken wave in an attempt to find an area that has a face.

gumby. (skiing) A novice skier with no muscles. Also, a *wet noodle*.

gutter bunny. (mountain biking) A bicycling commuter.

✳ H

hack-and-whack. (gardening) A landscaper who massacres a garden that was in good shape.

hair. (surfing) Nerve or courage.

haken. (surfing) Pronounced *HAWK-in.* To go surfing.

halfpipe. (snowboarding) A U-shaped part of the slopes. "We're heading to the halfpipe to pull some tricks."

hammer. (mountain biking) Riding hard, going all out.

hammered. (mountain biking) Exhausted, beaten to a pulp, wiped out.

hammering. (competitive cycling) Strenuous pedaling.

hangers. (skiing) Novices who lose their skis while on the lift.

Hawaiian pullout. (surfing) A way of pulling out of a wave involving pushing the nose under the wave face in much the same manner as a duck dive.

hawg. (fishing) Big bass to a bass fisherman ("bassin' man").

headstand. In zoo lingo, what they call it when an elephant squashes its victim with its massive head. They can also do quite a bit of damage with their well-muscled, 180-pound trunks, and even their relatively tiny tails pack the punch of a baseball bat.

heat seekers. (park ranger slang) Rangers who specialize in fire fighting, law enforcement, and emergency medicine.

herbs. (skiing) Strange, nerdy people who take up skiing. (Derived from the guy named Herb who used to appear in Burger King commercials.)

hit. (snowboarding) A point on a vertical wall of the halfpipe where the snowboarder's board hits. "That first hit is awesome."

hitten. (surfing) Adjective describing something of extreme goodness.

home run. (in-line skating) A fall while grinding in which both feet slide out from under you, as if you were sliding into home plate.

hook. (competitive cycling) When one racer—either on purpose or accidentally—moves his back wheel against the front wheel of the racer behind him.

hot box. (meteorological slang) The area of land covered by a severe-storm warning.

hot camp. (hunting) One with running water.

hydrant lift. (ice skating) Pairs only. Male throws female partner over his head while skating backward and catches her. Includes a half-turn. If all goes well, she should be facing him when it ends.

✳ I

in lily whites. (horse racing) A horse with his legs wrapped in white bandages.

involuntary dismount. (mountain biking) A crash.

involved. (gardening) A bug-ridden plant. As in, "Don't touch that bush; it's involved."

jam. (snowboarding) A congregation of snowboarders, usually in the halfpipe. "Let's jam to see who can get the best hit."

Jams. (surfing) Brand of colorful swim trunks, almost knee-length and usually loose to the point of bagginess. Trunks that look like real Jams often share the name.

JDLRs. (park ranger slang) Park visitors who *just don't look right,* as in, "I've got a carload of JDLRs up here. I'm going to pull them over and check them out."

jingus. (rock climbing) Anything you don't like is automatically jingus—and probably heinous to boot.

Joe Baywatch. (lifeguard lingo) Overly earnest lifeguard who isn't any fun—from the television show *Baywatch.*

joey. (skiing) Obnoxious show-off typically wearing Day-Glo and bragging loudly in the lodge; known to flash money; doesn't own chains.

juice heads. (lifeguard lingo) Compulsive bodybuilders.

jump. (mountain biking) A quick acceleration usually developing into a sprint.

kelphead (surfing) A beginning surfer who spends most of the time with his or her head in the kelp.

kick. (competitive cycling) A final burst of speed that provides the main acceleration in a sprint.

latronic. (surfing) Pronounced *lay-TRON-ic.* See you later, as in, "Latronic, dude."

layback. (ice skating) Upright spin, usually performed by women, in which the head and shoulders are dropped backward. Not to be confused with laid-back.

lead-out. (competitive cycling) An intentional move where the designated contender for the win rides behind a "worker" until just before the finish and then speeds around his sacrificing teammate for the final sprint.

ledged out. (park ranger slang) When a tourist tries something really stupid like trying to retrieve a souvenir over the edge of, say, the Grand Canyon and needs to be rescued.

lethal projectile. (skiing) A student who is out of control but doesn't know it.

lid kid. (surfing) Usually young bodyboarder.

lip. (surfing) The crest of a wave—which pitches and falls out in front of the wave or spills forward down the face.

loop jump. (ice skating) Begins and ends on back outside edge of same foot. The directionally challenged applaud its simplistic design. In a toe loop, movement is the same but the toe pick strikes the ice when jumping and landing.

lull. (surfing) A period of time where waves are at their least intense. Occurs between sets.

lutz. (ice skating) This jump, which is similar to a flip, needs a wide curve because the skater starts in one direction and finishes in the other. Takeoff is from the back outside edge, with a landing on the opposite back outside edge.

M

manky. (rock climbing) Almost worthless, as in manky protection.

mashed potatoes. (skiing) Snow in warm weather.

max out. (surfing) To go over the limit.

mazurka. (ice skating) It's not a folk dance. Jump takes off from the back outside edge, the right foot crosses in front of the left, a half-turn, right toe pick hits the ice, onto left forward outside edge. Now do the hokeypokey and turn yourself around.

moist tongue. (meteorological slang) A ribbon of high humidity.

mountain bike/moto/beater/bomber/ clunker/cruiser/fat tire flyer. (mountain biking) Your bike.

mudder. (horse racing) A horse who runs his best on a muddy or soft racing surface.

mushy. (surfing) Poor-quality, small surf.

N

nailed. (surfing) Wiping out. Getting nailed normally involves some sort of impact, such as the crest of a wave falling on your head, your head hitting the bottom, or someone else hitting you.

neutercane. (meteorological slang) A tropical storm that has hurricane potential.

never ever. (skiing) A beginner.

never will be. (skiing) A student who is and always will be a beginner.

nuking. (gardening) Spraying plants with large amounts of pesticides.

nuts, tapers, and **camming devices.** Metal devices that are temporarily placed in cracks for protection. Such devices have virtually replaced pitons, which can damage the rock.

O

oatmeals. (surfing) Little, mushy waves.

off the lip. (surfing) Any move pulled by hitting the breaking crest of a wave.

off the Richter. (surfing) Very good, an allusion to the Richter scale for measuring the intensity of an earthquake.

Oral Roberts. (skiing) A student

who is hurt one moment, but fine the next. The term refers to the evangelist and healer.

 P

passmodious. (surfing) Really tired.

patch. (figure skating) A space on the ice rented by a skater or pair of skaters to practice figures.

pearling. (surfing) Burying the nose of the board in the water; comes from "diving for pearls."

petal pushers. (gardening) People who sell plants at garden shows, as in, "Get those petal pushers out of here."

pickup man (rodeo) Cowboy who assists saddle-bronc and bareback riders get out of harm's way.

pink. (foxhunting) Scarlet livery of the staff of the hunt, so called not because of the color but rather to honor a famous British tailor named Pink.

pishing. (birding) Scolding sound made by birders to keep intruders out of an area—such as keeping owls away from small birds. A newspaper description of pishing (*Washington Post,* December 31, 1995) looks like this: "pish, pish, pish; tchich, tchich, tchich."

platter lift. (ice skating) Move in which the man raises his partner over his head, hands on her hips, leaving her horizontal to the ice and backward to the man.

pogo. (mountain biking) (1) To bounce on a full-suspension bike like a pogo stick. (2) For a full-sus-

pension bike to bounce annoyingly and uncontrollably.

poodles. (skiing) Instructors who wear expensive ski clothes.

positive vorticity advective. (meteorological slang) It's going to rain.

potential. (lifeguard slang) Possible drowning, as in, "We've got a potential out there by the jetty."

pretzel/taco. (mountain biking) To wreck a wheel.

prime. (competitive cycling) See **SPRINT.**

pull. (competitive cycling) To take a turn at the front of an echelon breaking wind for the followers.

pull off. (competitive cycling) To move to one side so that the next racer can take a turn at the front.

 R

rads. (rock climbing) Sport climbers.

rail slide. (in-line skating) Sliding on your skates down a handrail.

rainbow jersey. (mountain biking) The coveted rainbow-striped jersey awarded to world champions in each of cycling's disciplines.

rank. (rodeo) Term applied to an animal who is suggesting by its history that "you're going to get your butt whipped." As in, "He is the rankest bull I've ever been on in my life."

rappel. (rock climbing) To descend a rope by means of mechanical brake devices.

rental rodents. (skiing) Kids on skis.

rev-head. (surfing) One who thinks cars are more important than surfboards.

'rhoid buffing. (mountain biking) Going down a hill so steep that your butt touches the rear wheel.

road rash. (in-line skating) Any wound associated with unintentional momentum reduction induced by contact with pavement.

rock. (lifeguard lingo) Swimmer without the bod for the beach. Also, *stone.*

rock dance. (surfing) Walk over sharp, moss-covered rocks to recover a surfboard.

rogue. (horse racing) A bad-tempered horse.

rooster tail. (1) (snowmobile) The snow thrown up behind a racing snowmobile. (2) (surfing) Spray thrown in an arc from the back of a surfer's board going into a good turn.

* S

sailing a bird. (hunting) When you hit a bird and it flies a hundred yards before falling.

salchow. (ice skating) Pronounced *sal-cow.* An easy single or double jump but one that requires height. Starts on back inside edge and finishes on opposite back outside edge. Named for its creator, Sweden's Ulrich Salchow, who won Olympic gold in 1908.

scitz (skitch). (in-line skating) To hold on to a moving automobile to get a free ride across part of town or up a hill. "I scitzed a ride on a Mercedes this morning."

scraping point. (horse racing) Running along the rail, which is the shortest distance around the track.

screamer. (rock climbing) A long fall.

scud. (meteorological slang) A low, fast-moving cloud.

scud missiles. (skiing) Tips of jagged rocks flush with the surface that tear up your bases.

set. (surfing) A group of waves that is sizably larger than most.

set an edge. (surfing) Dig the rail into the edge of a wave face.

shin-bang. (skiing) The pain caused by constant pressure of the boots on the shins.

shoulder. (surfing) Part of a wave to the side of the broken section that is steep enough to surf on.

shred. (snowboarding) To ski powerfully. "I'm going to go out and shred the slopes."

sinker. (lifeguard lingo) Drowner.

sit spin. (ice skating) The body is low to the ice with the skating (spinning) knee bent and the free leg extended beside it.

skinhead. (hunting) A young doe, which has no antlers.

skying out. (hang gliding) Flying so high the pilot could reach a ceiling of eighteen thousand feet, the highest permissible by the Federal

Aviation Administration in uncontrolled airspace.

slipstream. (competitive cycling) An area of reduced air pressure behind the leader that enables following racers to draft the leader and use less energy.

smokin' (all racing and downhill sports) Going fast.

snakebite. (mountain biking) Most common type of flat tire. Caused by hitting an obstacle so hard that the inner tube is pinched against the rim. Results in a double puncture that resembles two fan holes. Also called a pinch flat.

snow pigs. (skiing) The ski patrol.

specking out. (Hang gliding) Flying so high that you're a speck in the sky.

spike camp. (hunting) A bare-necessities hunting camp with no running water.

spinner bodyboard. (surfing) Three-sixty-degree turn that is achieved while still moving on a relatively straight course (i.e., the angle of entry is the same as the angle of exit).

spinning. (competitive cycling) Fluid, fast pedaling.

SPORE. (skiing) Stupid people on rental equipment.

sprint. A special bonus prize given to the first racer across the line on a designated lap of a criterium or specific point on a road race. Also known as prime, pronounced *preem*.

squirrel chasers. (skiing) Cross-country skiers.

squirrelly. (competitive cycling) A nervous or unstable racer.

squirrels. (tree doc slang) Workers who climb the tallest trees.

star lift. (ice skating) Pairs. Male raises partner into air by her hip, from his side. She is in the scissor position and can have one hand on his shoulder.

SAY WHAT?

That old myth about Eskimos having scores of names for snow has, alas, been disproven. But skiers are working on their own vocabulary of snow: (1) *champagne powder*. Light, small-flaked powder snow that has a low water content. (2) *corn*. Pellets that have frozen/thawed in the spring. (3) *mashed potatoes*. Heavy snow with high water content; typical of spring conditions; hard on the thighs. (4) *New England clam powder*. (5) *New England powder*. Aka bulletproof powder or solid ice. Icy pellets the size of small clams. (6) *Portland cement*. Northwest heavy snow, aka Cascade cement. (7) *Sierra cement*. Sierra tends to be very wet and after a freeze takes on the hardness of cement.

stoked. (surfing) Happy. This is pretty common in its use, but it originated in the surfing community.

suck milk. (surfing) To wipe out, drink white water.

suck-up. (surfing) A wave shape caused by a shallow object (relative to the wave height). This causes a lack of water flow and a nonsmooth spot on a wave. This can be caused by sandbars, rocks, or any submerged object.

surf hamburger. (lifeguard lingo) Swimmer who gets banged up in the undertow and comes out of the water with many red marks and bruises.

switchback. (mountain biking) A tight, zigzag turn on the face of a mountain.

* T

take a flier. (competitive cycling) To go off the front of the pack, usually alone and catching the other racers by surprise.

tea bagger. (surfing) Bodyboarder.

textile. (naturist/nudist) A clothed person.

through the boilermaker. (hunting) A shot to the heart—best because it kills quickly.

throw jump. (ice skating) Pairs. Male helps partner go airborne.

tip-up. (ice fishing) The pole that a fisherman sets up outside a fishing shelter. It's a self-contained fishing unit that signals the fisherman about possible action on the line. When a fish messes with the bait, a flag goes up.

tires. (in-line skating) Skate wheels.

toads. (surfing) Take off and die syndrome: when a late takeoff results in a heavy wipeout.

top roping. (rock climbing) A belay from above. It protects the climber from falling even a short distance.

tourons. (park ranger slang) Tourists who act like morons when they enter the park.

toxics/toxic socks. (backpacking) Hiker's socks after a few weeks on the trail.

trads. (rock climbing) Traditional climbers.

trash. (hang gliding) Turbulent air; to be done in by the same, as in, "I was trashed today."

tree injection. (skiing) Hitting a tree, as in, "That hot dog is just asking for a massive tree injection."

trumps. (gardening) Wealthy people who want instant gardens without having to work on them.

TTTC. (meteorological slang) Too tough to call.

twitching. (birding) Hard-nosed "combat" birding in which discomfort and danger do not deter. A line from *Sports Illustrated* on fanatical British birders contained this line: "In 1990 two twitchers were killed by Shining Path guerrillas who doubtless had their own interpretation about what non-

Latinos with binoculars were doing in backwoods Brazil."

* V

valley cowboys. (surfing) Inland surfers.

victory at sea. (lifeguard lingo) Choppy waters. No swimming.

* W

wack or **bonk.** (hang gliding) To drop the nose of the glider sharply when landing, causing a crash.

wang. (hang gliding) A "wingover" maneuver involving a sharp ninety-degree turn. Looks impressive.

wanker two-planker. (snowboarding) Derogatory term for a snow skier.

washy. (horse racing) A horse that becomes so nervous that he sweats profusely before a race.

wheelsucker. (competitive cycling) A cyclist who refuses to take a turn breaking the wind for the rest of his team at the front of the pack.

whipper. (rock climbing) A long or violent fall in which the climber hits the end of the rope and is snapped like a whip.

widow maker. (tree surgery) A large, dangling tree limb that could fall off and kill.

wipe out. (surfing) To fall off your board while riding on a wave. (See also DRILLED, NAILED, and BLASTED.)

woodpecker snack bar. (tree doc slang) An insect-infected tree.

worked. (surfing) Beaten up by a wave.

* Y

yahoo. (hang gliding) Glider version of paratroopers' "Geronimo!"—pilots yell this as they step off a precipice.

yard dogs. (gardening) Nursery employees, as in, "Make the yard dogs water the begonias."

yard sale. (skiing) What it looks like after you fall and spread assorted bits of equipment all over.

yogi-ing. (backpacking) Acting like Yogi Bear to persuade strangers to share their food with you.

SOURCES

Some of the jargon used by modern rock climbers came from an article by Will Gadd in *Rock & Ice* magazine, July/August 1993, and from an August 8, 1993, article by Hal Mattern in the *Arizona Republic* entitled "Arizona Climbers Rock! Scaling Vertical Walls Is Down-to-Earth."

Terms for mountain biking came from the Internet site provided by *Velo-News, the Journal of Competitive Cycling,* Boulder, Colorado.

Skiing terms are Internet derived. A particularly useful horse-racing glossary appeared in the *Shreveport* (La.) *Times* of April 26, 1991.

Trevor Cralle's *Surfin'ary: A Dictionary of Surfing Terms and Surfspeak* (Ten Speed Press, 1991) is the first and last work on the subject. A superb snowboarding glossary appeared in the *Hagerstown* (Md.) *Herald Mail* for February 17, 1992.

───── * 15 * ─────

MEDIA SLANG

Words From Those Who Fill the Pages and the Airwaves

Midway Sings Limey Prof to Dope Yank Talk
—Headline in the *Chicago Tribune,* October
18, 1924, on the occasion of the arrival of Sir
William Craigie in the United States to begin
work on *A Dictionary of American English*

The first journalist asked about the slang of her trade for this chapter insisted that there was no such thing. A few hours later she called back and said that she was wrong—and proceeded to reel off a bunch of terms. Seems that she had gone to lunch with a group of co-workers who had addressed the premise that there was no journalism slang and the terms had begun to come forth.

This underscores the unwritten first law of slang and jargon, which is that people in traditional occupations are seldom aware that their speech is just as quirky and slangy as most others.

To be sure, most teenagers and rock musicians are aware of their slang, but that is because it is ever-changing and brash. Journalistic slang is so ingrained in history and in the craft that it does not appear to exist.

* A

above the fold. (newspaper) Describing a story that is important enough to merit placement above the fold of a full-sized front page.

ACE. (newspaper) *Assistant city editor* for short.

Activity. TV weather word that means nothing, but sounds important. "We can expect some thun-derstorm activity in the next seventy-two hours." Newspapers still refer to them as plain old thunderstorms.

actualities. This is a reborn radio term for "what is actually happening," a snippet of on-the-scene reporting or a view of an event unfolding before the camera's eye, which the producer hopes will transcend verisimilitude and achieve verity.

ad jack. (newspaper) Small ad promoting a feature of the newspaper, used as a filler, placed under a paid ad to "jack" it up to fill a hole.

advancer. Story written in advance of an event, such as a play or state fair.

agate. (newspaper) Tiny type in newspapers—"Let's run the survivors' names in agate." *Agate* is actually a proper name for type 5.5 points in size, but has come to mean all small type including 6-point type, nonpareil.

a-matter. (newspaper) That which can be written in advance of a story or interview.

another pretty face. A derogation of local anchormen.

art. Any kind of picture.

astonisher. An exclamation point. Proofreader calls it bang, bing, yell, shout, hurrah, backbone.

✳ B

balloon. A story promoted on page one over the name of the paper.

banner. (newspaper only) Headline running across more than half of the page at the top.

bastard title. Title standing alone on a separate page preceding the text.

beat or **run.** When a reporter is detailed to cover a group of news sources, he is said to have a beat. "He covers the city hall beat."

bird feed. (electronic journalism) *Feed* is any transmission; the *bird* is a satellite, its name taken from the Early Bird designation of Telstar. A transmission via satellite is a bird feed.

bite or **snatch.** A short piece of film that comes inside a VOICE WRAP, as in, "Give us a bite of Carter."

bite a dog. Create a story.

blacksmith. Below-par reporter or writer, i.e., one who pounds out copy or news stories.

bleeding type. Type that has been trimmed so closely and mutilated that it will not print clearly.

BOM. Business office must. A story generated by the business side of the paper, often to please an advertiser.

break. (1) (newspaper) Division to a new paragraph. (2) When a news event occurs, as in a breaking story.

break page. The page on which a story is continued.

buckeye. Derogatory term for an ad visually unsophisticated or lacking in taste.

bull dog. The first morning edition of an evening newspaper and the first night edition of a morning newspaper. Also, advance edition of the Sunday paper, which in some cities can be bought late on Saturday.

burn. To give away or compromise a source.

* C

carry. What a story can support in terms of headline size, art, and sidebars.

cartouche. Decorative panel or border enclosing a legend or graphic; usually oval-shaped.

checkbook journalism. Controversial method of news gathering that pays news sources for telling their story to the press.

Chinese. Term describing the TV or motion-picture camera technique of "panning" while moving away from the subject.

churn rate. (newspaper) The number of readers you have to replace or resell as subscribers each year. The average churn rate for metropolitan dailies is about 70 percent—meaning that if you were to maintain a readership of 500,000, you have to get 350,000 back each year.

circle wipe. Video effect in which image first appears as a small dot in the center of the screen, then grows to full size while covering the preceding scene.

cold copy. In broadcasting, announcement read unrehearsed.

copy. Manuscript text to be set in type or broadcast.

cough button. Announcer's switch in broadcast studio allowing him or her to cut off the mike momentarily.

country-club journalism. Journalism viewed with sarcasm. Idea that real competition in the world of journalism is limited due to the many shared ideas, backgrounds, and associations of the owners.

crawl. In TV production, lettered titles and credits that move up or down, side to side, on the screen. Usually seen at the conclusion of a program. Also *title crawl, title roll, crawling title, creeper,* and *creeping title.*

crib. Plagiarize.

crick. Critic.

cub. Novice reporter.

* D

dead. Copy is called dead after it has been set and proofread. Type that has been used and is not to be used again is dead.

desk. (newspaper) Department in newspaperese—city, desk, sports desk, copy desk, etc.

deskman. The term loosely descriptive of both copyreaders and editors.

Dewey Beats Truman. Any wrongheaded news story is a Dewey Beats Truman, an allusion to the *Chicago Tribune* banner headline after election day, 1948, when the paper was sure that Thomas E. Dewey had beaten Truman. For instance, *USA Today,* Thursday, October 12, 1989 a day before the Dow fell 190.58 points in Wall Street's worst day since the October 1987 crash: "Despite superstition, stocks do well on Fridays the 13th."

dingbat. (1) In printing, any typographical ornamentation. Also, *flubdub.* (2) A printer's slang term for an ornament, or flourish, used to decorate the composition.

double truck. Two-page ad or spread/layout like one page with no gutter down the middle between the pages.

drooling. Unrehearsed talk to fill out allotted program time.

dummy type. Type randomly laid to show how a designed space will look. It is meant to be seen but not read.

✳ E

ear. In newspaper layout the little box appearing on either side of the page-one layout—weather, slogan, etc.

early fringe. Period before prime time.

eighty percenter. Another *USA Today* term, for a story done in advance and awaiting a news peg. Usage: "Let's do an eighty percenter on the Rolling Stones and put a top [beginning of story] on it when the tour opens."

etaoin shrdlu. An invention of Linotype operators, who used him as a temporary "slug"—the name of a story. His name was set in type by running a finger down the left two vertical rows of the Linotype keyboard (don't look for it on your typewriter—Linotypes have a special keyboard). Sometimes, however, etaoin wasn't so temporary, and his name inadvertently made its way into print.

exclusive. Overworked term that usually means nothing more than "we think we were there first and/or nobody else was interested."

eyewitness news. Term used in television for news operations that hardly ever have reports from eyewitnesses.

✳ F

feed. Network lingo for live or taped segments sent from one location to another, by phone lines if audio, by satellite if video.

fishback. Magazine term for a reference to an earlier article, as in, "First reported in the October 1996 issue, p. 22."

five W's and an H. Journalism's basic questions: who, what, when, where, why, and how.

flag. Newspaper term for nameplate or logotype appearing atop page one.

fluff. Soft, inconsequential material posing as news—for instance a local news story on a network entertainment show used by the station.

folo. A secondary article on the same subject as the main article.

friar. A spot of too little ink showing on an impression.

front matter. All material in a book or publication that precedes the actual start of the text.

✳ G

gawk shows. Daytime talk television featuring the bizarre—*Jenny Jones* is the perfect example.

gimper. A human-interest "sob" story about an incurable disease, loss of life, severe injury. Usage: "Let's do this gimper. It's got a wheelchair case in it."

go hunting. In TV, command to cameraman to use his judgment in finding a good camera shot.

gonzo. Form of journalism based on the notion that the best fiction is better than any nonfiction and that "with an expense account anything is possible."

graf. Paragraph in the newsroom.

grip. Studio stagehand—aka cable puller, dolly pusher, floor man, gofer.

gutter. In printing, two inner margins of facing pages of a publication. Aka back margins.

happy news. Television. Local news format that emphasizes the upbeat and features good-looking, personable, joking anchorpeople.

hard news. That which is newsworthy without embellishment or hyping—a midair collision or a presidential election.

harlequins. Heavyset decorative type elements.

hat trick. The feat in hockey of scoring three goals in one game. The media equivalent is appearing on *Meet the Press, Face the Nation,* and *This Week.*

head. Headline. The longer form is rarely used. The different head-

lines are identified by numbers. The term is used in SUBHEAD, which is universally used for subheadline. A good headline is called a great head.

hickey. Printer's slang for ornament.

honeymoon. Period of at least a few months after an election during which Congress and the press refrain from criticising the president, governor, mayor, or other elected officials.

horse. To read proof without the aid of a copyholder.

hot corner. A *USA Today*-ism for the lower right-hand corner of page one that carries a hot, often offbeat item with a color picture.

human interest/HI. That quality in a story that makes it good newspaper copy even though it contains no news. Such a story paints an interesting picture of life.

hype. Publicity that the reporter does not like. The double whammy comes when the term *so-called* is used with *hype.* "The so-called advantage of compact discs is hype," for example, is a line from a recent issue of *Forbes.*

inverted pyramid. Describing an article written with the most important information at the top and the least important information at the bottom, so that the bottom can be lopped off for space.

island position. (1) Ad surrounded entirely by editorial material. (2) Broadcasting: commercial with programming on either side.

∗ J

Jimmy Olson photo. A photo of great importance and moment, named for the photographer on the *Daily Planet,* Clark Kent/Superman's paper. From the *Washington Post* of January 13, 1991: "Almost 23 years ago, a *Jimmy Olson photo* from Vietnam played its own role in our history. It was a picture of the bleeding and dead Marines sprawled on a tank retreating from Hue in the Tet offensive of 1968. When then-senator Eugene McCarthy saw the photo, he said later, he knew that 'that was the turning point.' The opposition to the war that formed around McCarthy's presidential candidacy drove Lyndon Johnson from the White House."

journalese. The particular code in which journalists slant or peg a story.

J-school. Journalism school.

jump/jump-over/run-over. The part of a story that is continued on a later page. Also used as a verb. "Jump the yarn over onto page seven." Papers fret about the fact that it takes a lot of reader interest to turn to page C-22.

jump-head. The headline that appears above a jump.

∗ K

kotex. Derogatory term for giveaway weekly with little or no hard news.

∗ L

lead. The first line or paragraph of an article or broadcast news item intended to seduce the reader into reading the whole article. "The lead is to a newspaper writer what a home run is to a ballplayer—the sum total of his art, the feather in his cap, the pat on his back," Thomas Collins of Long Island, New York, *Newsday* once wrote.

lede. This is the way that all newspapers write the word "lead." The reason would appear to be not letting it become confused with *lead*—the metal—which in this day of electronic composition is still used in terms like *extra lead* for more space.

legman. Old-fashioned reporter who makes his/her living from calf muscles.

lobster shift. Late-night or early-morning working shift, used in both daily print and broadcast media. It is commonly from 11 P.M. to 7 A.M., 12 P.M. to 8 A.M., or 1 A.M. to 9 A.M. and, according to the lore of the press, comes from the fact that people on this shift live their lives backward, as lobsters sometimes move in reverse.

∗ M

man bites dog. Story that works because it is the reverse of the predictable dog biting a human.

masthead. Statement of the name of a paper, its ownership, place of publication, subscription rates, etc., usually on the editorial page.

*

ALLEGEDLY SAID WHAT?

A Decoder for Deciphering the News

An introductory lesson in the language of journalese:

activist. Not a bureaucrat.

adult. Dirty, as applied to bookstores, magazines, and movies.

alleged. Word used by people in the news business to prevent lawsuits and drive the rest of us crazy. "The alleged murder took place as the victim was shot in the back."

arguably. Impossible to substantiate, as in, "He is arguably the best National League left-handed pitcher ever from Connecticut with three consonants in his middle name."

brash. Said of those who can only talk about themselves; egocentric.

bureaucrat. Term used to describe a public servant when the story is about red tape, excessive regulation, or anything else negative. The same person becomes a *civil servant* in a positive story.

by all accounts. Term used when details are sketchy and no direct quote can be found.

cannot be independently confirmed. Said of rumor that is so juicy that it cannot be left out of the story.

cannot be ruled out. Term used with the highest grade of pure space-filling speculation.

caring. Not outwardly mean or rotten.

claimed responsibility. Confessed to a crime, often a heinous one involving more than one death. "A terrorist group today claimed responsibility for taking the lives of fifty-four innocent people."

coming of age. Term used when a newspaper has finally gotten around to writing on a subject but has no news lead for it save for the vague notion that it has come of age. "Woolen Mittens Come of Age," for instance.

craggy. Ugly: ET-like.

crusty. Obnoxious.

densely wooded area. Where most "badly decomposed" bodies are found; target for small planes in trouble.

ebullient. Crazy; off-the-wall.

emotional. Required adjective for *reunion* and *homecoming.*

execution-style. Shot at close range; hence, a nice way of saying that the reporter on the scene became nauseated.

freewheeling. Chaotic; confused. "In a freewheeling interview the candidate lashed out against the Kremlin, frequent-flier programs, diet colas, supermarket shopping carts with defective wheels, and the arms race."

golf ball. Unit of measurement for hailstones.

guru. Any authority who has not made an ass of himself in the last six months or, in the case of financial gurus, the last two weeks. Seldom, if ever, applied to Indian wise men anymore.

hard charger. Tooth-grinder; person you would not want to sit next to on an airplane.

hardworking. Plodding and dull.

ill-fated. Anything that has crashed and whose wreckage is now being "sifted through by federal investigators."

indefatigable. A real pest; someone who calls the reporter at home during the World Series to complain about something.

in recent memory. Everyone else has gone home, the library is locked, and this is the only thing I can think of that compares to the situation at hand.

irreverent. Swears and shouts a lot.

job action. Inaction.

labor of love. The province of eccentrics and borderline crazies. "His campaign to save old outhouses is strictly a labor of love."

little-known. Used when a reporter is showing off and saying, "Here is something I know, but you don't."

long-awaited. Recently announced.

message. Three or four ads, as in, "We now pause for this message."

mild-mannered. Deeply introverted; mousy.

militant. Fanatical.

modest. Term applied to most houses and many salaries. It has been observed that journalese has decreed that all houses are either modest or stately.

much-maligned. Seldom-maligned, often applied to lesser vegetables in newspaper food sections, for example, a *Washington Post* May 1986 food feature on "The Much-Maligned Artichoke." Such articles always go on to tell you that the artichoke, turnip, Brussels sprout, or whatever is actually "far more versatile than you have known until now."

myth. A notion we have been pushing for years, but we are now ready to drop.

no explanation was offered. We forgot to ask; there was nobody there but the cleaning crew.

noted authority. Said of anyone whose name appears on the reporter's Rolodex.

obscure. Anything not known to the reporter before working on the story. "She was charged under the provisions of an obscure law making it illegal to bury people alive."

observers. Cabbies, bartenders, bellhops, and camel-tenders to name a few. Not to be confused with "thoughtful observers" or "veteran observers."

once thought to be. This is what we were saying last Wednesday.

only time will tell. Sign-off line beloved of television reporters covering summit conferences or unresolved municipal issues: "Will the town dump continue to be open on Sundays? Only time will tell."

outgoing. A happy drunk.

outspoken. Noisy; abusive; a pain in the neck.

overcrowded. Crowded, in articles about schools, mental institutions, and prisons.

peppery. Short and overbearing; a real pest.

presumably. Code word telling the reader that the writer is about to take a wild-assed guess.

professional. Virtually anybody who works for a living.

reportedly. This means that we have no idea if this is so, but it sounds good.

reputed. Known to all living things, as in the phrases "reputed Mafia kingpin" or "reputed underworld chieftain."

riveting. Said of potboiler novels involving submarines, nuclear weapons, or terrorists.

Rubensian. Fat.

ruddy-faced. Drunk.

scandal-scarred. Term tied to Teamsters pension fund.

self-evident. I just figured this out myself. "The relationship between excessive dental flossing and anti-social behavior is self-evident."

so-called. Bogus and contemptible.

spry. Any senior citizen who is not in a wheelchair or coma. (So defined in John Leo's *Time* essay on "Journalese for the Lay Reader.")

struggle to come to terms with. What people do after a mishap.

summit. Any meeting attended by people above the clerical or secretarial level.

twisted wreckage. Place from which survivors emerge miraculously.

unexpected. We told you yesterday that this wouldn't happen.

unprecedented. That which has not happened recently; not in our files.

viable. Workable in the abstract. Applied to options and alternatives.

visibly moved. Crying or sobbing on the part of a public official or VIP. Regular people are still allowed to cry.

was unavailable for comment. Nobody was home when we called. Used when somebody is being accused of misconduct.

well-groomed. Vain with a touch too much aftershave lotion.

well-manicured lawns. Used to describe neighborhoods with high-priced houses and small-minded people.

without a scratch. Condition of race car drivers who are not hurt in spectacular crashes.

world-class. Puffed up term for someone or something that is good.

ME. Managing editor.

media circus. Event that, to the consternation of reporters with notepads, has drawn more than one television camera. For television people a media circus is any event that attracts Sam, Barbara, Tom, and Dan and features an open bar and free buffet.

mike stew. Background sound, unwanted and extraneous, picked up by the microphone.

morgue. The place or room where dead copy is kept, where cuts of pictures are filed, a collection of references, clippings, etc. Increasingly electronic.

MOS. Man on the street; target for quick interviews.

noodling. Background music played as the titles and credits come on.

obit. Obituary.

off its feet. Badly set type that is not standing up straight and thus makes only a partial impression.

off the record. An arrangement with the media not to use the information discussed—unless it is obtained elsewhere.

op ed. In newspapers, *opposite the editorial page.* This page features commentary, ideas, illustrations, etc.

pablum. Like the cereal, writing that is soft, bland, oversimplified.

pack journalism. The phenomenon of reporters chasing after the same stories, using the same or similar leads, and by consensus, deciding what shall be the news of the day.

paint it red. Write a story as sensationally as possible.

peewee. Short bit of news used to fill space in a newspaper; a filler.

photo opportunity. Also *photo op,* or, as the congressional-press-gallery monitors advise, *PO.* This generally means that a politician, often with diplomat or other bigwig in tow, will emerge—or briefly invite cameras in to an otherwise closed meeting—for photos and TV pictures only, not for comments. However, reporters often pose or shout questions anyway. Once restricted to the political arena, photo ops are now offered by athletes, actors, rock stars, and others.

pi. Jumbled type—obsolete in its original sense but still sometimes heard in reference to jumbled typesetting.

piece. An article.

piece of manpower. A network term for "star."

'plosives. Contraction of explosive sounds sometimes produced in a mike when letters such as *B* or *P* are overstressed during pronunciation.

printhead. Print journalist to TV journalists.

 R

reefer. (newspaper) A cover-page reference to inside contents. It is the word *refer* recast with emphasis on the first syllable.

rim. Outer edge of the copydesk, around which copyreaders sit, as opposed to the *slot* or inner edged presided over by the executive in charge of that desk.

river. Undesirable streak of white space running down through several lines of type because certain words in each line happen to end at the same point, making the space between words line up from line to line.

roser. *ROSR,* for *radio on-scene report.*

running story. One that goes on and on, such as the O. J. Simpson trial.

 S

scandal sheet. Newspaper specializing in trysts, love nests, people with their paws in cookie jars, gossip, weaknesses, and more.

scoop. Information obtained by or given to a single reporter, who thereby "scoops" his competitors.

screamer. (print) (1) Banner head-

line, often exceptionally bold and large. (2) An exclamation point.

second-coming head. (newspaper) The largest headline type that a given paper can use—alluding to the notion that this would be the type size used with the second coming of Christ.

second-day lede. (newspaper) Story running on the day after an event, such as an airline crash, that can no longer lead with "plane "crashes" but needs something like "pilot error suspected in yesterday's crash . . ."

see you in the aim. See you in the morning. *Aim* is a slurring of *A.M.*

Segue. TV term for a transition. Segues often mean going from the scene of a disastrous flood to a line like "Next, the new faces of *Melrose Place.*"

shout. (publishing/printing) Slang for exclamation point. Also called screamer or shriek.

silly season. Period when hard news is not easy to find, which is usually late in the summer when Congress is adjourned, the president is on vacation, and the financial markets are in low gear.

skinback. Story that makes up for a missed "truth." Real-life example: newspaper runs series saying that local schools are slipping, then the outcry is so great that it runs a story saying that other data suggest the schools are, in fact, improving.

skybox. (newspaper) Box at top of a front page.

slop. (newspaper) Anything set in

type that does not make it into the paper in a particular edition.

slot. (newspaper) The center of the various news departments (or desks) on a newspaper. The man or woman in charge of any of the desks is said to be in the slot.

slug. (1) The word placed at the beginning of a story and on each subsequent page to identify it. "Slug the yarn, Mayor." (2) Identifying mark or label for a story. May be the briefest possible statement of the nature of the news story, as "hotel fire"—also *catchline, slugline, guide,* and *guideline.*

snapper. (drama/comedy) Talent's exit line.

snipe. In outdoor advertising, strip of copy added (often at an angle across a corner) over poster ad, providing an additional message such as special process, names, or slogans.

sob sister or **slobby.** A reporter (usually a woman, but the term is not changed when it refers to a man) skilled in the art of painting a sympathetic picture of a figure prominent in sensational news. She ghosts the stories you read that carry the byline of the most recent murderess.

sound bite. A quotation or statement carried by the electronic media. It has become a valuable tool in election and reelection campaigns as a good sound bite can serve as an unfiltered, spot commercial. By contrast, statements that show up in the print media do not have the same effect

and may, in fact, end up in an editorial opposing the candidate.

spec. Working without guarantee that your story will be accepted and paid for.

spin. Partisan interpretation, such as that given by a press secretary to the press.

spot. Speakeasy originally, now any bar. "There's a new spot across the street."

spot buy. (advertising/broadcasting) Purchase of available commercial time; less than full-program sponsorship.

stand-upper. Television term for a report in which the correspondent stands, with microphone in hand, and delivers a segment of the news, with a prop like the U.S. Capitol in the background.

stet. Term used in print media that means "let it stand." For instance, a line is marked out in pencil, but it is then decided to restore it, which is done by writing *stet.* In electronic media the term *stet* is often spoken as a code for restoring something to the original.

stock footage. (television/film) Motion picture footage or television videotape retained on file that can be used in more than one production. Also called stock shot, library footage, library shot, library material, archive material, or file film.

stringer. Reporters or broadcaster who works on speculation for a newspaper, newsmagazine, wire service, or broadcast organization.

subhead. The small headlines that

appear in the body of the story and below the main headline.

swing-man. The copyreader who relieves the copy chief.

T

tab. A tabloid newspaper.

take. (print) A page, as in, "Give me a couple of takes on the judge's record with murder trials."

talking heads. Politicians or analysts talking on television—a sure channel-switcher for viewers, TV producers feel. President Bush on February 21, 1992, under fire for a slumping economy, said, "Let's not listen to the gloom and doom from all those intense talking heads who are happy only when they say something negative."

tally light. Red TV-camera light indicating when the camera is on. Also, camera cue light or cue light.

thirty. The end. This slang expression is rarely used in speaking.

thumbsucker. An article speculating on the significance of a news event.

TK. To come. In journalism, used for material not yet in place. "The piece is all done but his age is TK."

toy department. Media sports department.

trained seal. Magazine staff writers who work on salary and write stories for the magazine.

tube buster. (newspaper) A story so hot that it will burst the plastic tube wrapper that so many papers come in today.

U

update. Local TV news term for promotion: as in, "Find out at eleven—new hope for the dead" or "Verdict at ten."

V

visibility. What politicians need to get elected—speeches and positions that get them exposure in the media.

voice-over. Spoken commentary accompanying the film being shown.

voicer. Radio broadcast for a report read without embellishment.

voice wrap. The use of a newscaster's voice to introduce and to close a piece of film or tape.

W

walk-up. A story that runs the day before or the day of a major scheduled news event, for example, the opening ceremonies of the Olympic Games.

whiparound. (broadcasting) A news-show technique in which an anchorman introduces the three successive reporters in one long breath, as the cameras cut from one to the other without new introductions.

widow. (print) (1) Printers term for

a short word or part of a word standing alone on the last line of a body of type. (2) A short line, the last of a paragraph, that appears at the head of a paragraph or column. Only if it is a paragraph should a short line start a column or page.

wipe. (television) Transitional technique between shots using a boundary electronically created to separate images as one is replaced by another via a moving line, expanding or contracting circle, or another of several hundred geometric wipe patterns.

wire. (newspaper) That which comes in from a wire service such as the Associated Press or any other electronic source. The term is still very much in use although all the telegraph wire has been replaced by satellite, microwave, and phone lines.

wood. (newspaper) Filler material in early editions of a paper.

write around a hole. (newspaper) To write around a key piece of information in a story that is not yet available.

writethru. Wire service term for a story that has been completely rewritten and for which the original should be discarded.

SOURCES

Dave Metheny of the *Minneapolis Star-Tribune* provided the major boost for this chapter in a series of memos on the talk of the newsroom. Thanks also to Russell Ash, Hal Davis, Sam Freedenberg, Tom Gill, Joseph C. Goulden, Arnold R. Isaacs, Charles D. Poe, Dan Rapoport, Dorothy Repovich, Bob Skole, Anthony A. Spleen, David Streitfeld, Elaine Viets, and Tony Wynne-Jones for their help with this section.

There are few articles on this subject. Two that I consulted were *Newsweek,* September 4, 1989, and an article in the January 1932 *Writer's Digest* by Arthur C. Norris.

─── ✳ 16 ✳ ───

MEDICAL AND EMERGENCY ROOM SLANG

Words You Don't Want to Hear From Your Hospital Bed

> The range and number of these [slang] terms suggests the extensiveness of the verbal aggression towards patients among medical personnel. These terms are all used "backstage," never in the presence of a conscious patient.
>
> —From "Not Sticks and Stones, but Names,"
> by Lois Monteiro, in *Maledicta,* summer 1980

There are two medical languages. One is the highly technical, Latinate tongue that has been called medicant. In this tongue a headache is *cephalalgia,* sweating is *diaphoresis,* vomiting becomes *emesis,* and the inability to tell time is *horologagnosia.*

It is also stuffy and bureaucratic: measurements and characteristics become *parameters, centimeters* comes out as "sawntimeters," and doctors and nurses become the generic *providers* (turning patients into *consumers*). Former surgeon general C. Everett Koop has said, "I'm still old-fashioned enough to think of myself as a physician, not a provider. And I think of my patients as patients, not consumers." Some have abandoned *provider* for the even more distant *HCP*—health care provider(s).

We are confronted with something called *the health industry,* which one can only assume is a term that was imposed by the *insurance industry.* The folks who insure your health want you to cozy up to terms like *payer, vendor,* and *third-party providers.* These third-party folks only provide for that which is *covered,* making them less than full providers.

As one critic writing in the *New England Journal of Medicine* put it, the medical industry takes English and turns it into something that is "impressive, intimidating, and incomprehensible."

It poses those very questions that we as patients must grapple with: Would we, for instance, be better served if we were told we had leprosy or Hansen's disease? Unless we are hypochondriacs, wouldn't most of us prefer to hear that we "just have a simple rash" than hear it in Latin, which comes out as a case of *pityriasis rosea?* And what of the medical pronoun *we,* as in "we treat this with rest and aspirin"? Some see this as the mark of a partnership between patient and doctor ("we will beat this one"); others see it as the doctor's way of saying that the medical profession (the collective use) is of one mind on this matter.

But another level of communication is working here: blunt, irreverent, and not meant for public consumption. It is pure slang—the slang of doctors, nurses, and hospital technicians.

* A

albatross. Chronically ill patient who will remain with a doctor until one of them expires.

ALC. *A la casa*—send the patient home.

angel lust. Male cadaver with an erection.

ax. A surgeon.

Aztec two-step. Diarrhea acquired in Latin America.

* B

baby catcher. Obstetrician.

bag. To administer an oxygen mask.

banana. Patient with jaundice.

beached whale. Obese patient.

big C. Cancer.

blade. Surgeon.

blown mind. Gunshot wound to the head.

blue blower. Patient with severe lung disease.

blue pipe. Vein.

bobbing for apples. Using the finger to unclog a severely constipated patient.

boogie. A tumor.

bordeau. Urine with blood in it.

bounceback. Patient who keeps returning to the hospital.

box. To die.

BRAT diet. Common prescription for infant diarrhea: *b*ananas, *r*ice, *a*pple sauce, and *t*oast.

bronk. To undergo bronchoscopy.

buff up. To ready a patient for release.

bug juice. Antibiotics.

bugs in the rug. Pubic lice.

bull in the ring. A blocked large intestine.

bury the hatchet. Accidentally leaving a surgical instrument inside a patient.

* C

cabge. (Pronounced *cabbage*). A coronary artery bypass operation.

C&T Ward. Place where comatose patients are placed in a hospital. It is short for "cabbages and turnips."

Captain Kangaroo. Chairman of a pediatrics department.

cath. To catheterize.

circling the drain. Said of patients who are getting sicker and are close to death.

code azure. Message to other medical professionals to do nothing extraordinary to save a very ill patient who will die shortly no matter what is done. It is the opposite of the official Code Blue, which mobilizes the staff in an effort to save someone.

creepers. The elderly—a reference to walkers and wheelchairs.

crispy critter. A patient with severe burns.

crock. (1) Complainer. (2) Hypochondriac.

cut and paste. To open a patient, discover that there is no hope, and immediately sew him up. Well, almost immediately. Sometimes young surgeons practice surgical techniques for a while first.

 D

deep fry. Cobalt therapy.

Delhi belly. Intestinal upset acquired overseas.

dirtball. Patient who enters the emergency room filthy and smelling badly.

dishwasher. Sterilization machine.

DNR. Do not resuscitate: order on a patient's chart to tell medical staff that the patient is terminally ill and does not want anyone to try to bring him back to life if he dies. The British equivalent is *DNA*, for *do not attend*.

doc. Doctor to a doctor. For instance, firms that help MDs with the financial side of their practice are known as doc watchers.

doc-in-the-box. Small medical facility, usually in a shopping center, where one can go for treatment without an appointment.

domino transplant. A rare organ transplant in which a person is given a new heart and lungs.

doorhandle. British medical slang for a patient who recalls an additional symptom or malady as he is walking out the door.

DOW. See MI.

dowager's hump. Manifestation of osteoporosis.

Dr. Feelgood. A doctor who is indiscriminate about prescribing drugs.

drooler. A catatonic patient.

duck. Portable urinal for bedridden male hospital patients. Before these were made of plastic, they were known as glass or porcelain ducks.

dump. Patient that nobody seems to want.

dwelly belly. Slang for Hispanic patients with abdominal pain, from the Spanish word for grief, *duele*.

dwindles, the. Advancing old age.

✳

SAY WHAT?

In his excellent *Weekend Telegraph* "Wordplay" column for November 2, 1991, Fritz Spiegl lifted the curtain on the deepest secret of British medicine, the letter code:

BBA. Baby born in ambulance.

BUBAR. Buggered up beyond repair, an acronym reserved for victims of surgical incompetence.

GOK. Patient with "God only knows."

HSP. Heartsink patient—i.e., one who causes the doctor's heart to sink the moment the patient walks in the door.

NAD. No abnormality detected.

OAC. Patient with an " 'orrible 'acking cough."

PAFO. Pissed and fell over.

 E

eating in. Intravenous feeding.

eating the bill. Providing care for indigent patients who are not covered by insurance. Usage: "We ate the bill on that guy."

ER. Emergency room.

✳ F

fanger. Oral surgeon.

fascinoma. A "fascinating" tumor; any interesting or amusing malignancy.

finger wave. Rectal exam.

flatline. To die.

flea. Internists, so called because they are the last ones to leave a deceased person, the last ones to admit that a patient who has suf-

fered a cardiac arrest is actually dead; they keep trying when all hope for survival is long past.

FLK. Funny-looking kid. Used in the newborn nursery.

FLP. Parents of an FLK.

fluids and electrolytes. That which is consumed at happy hour.

four F-er. A gallbladder patient: fat, fortyish, flatulent female.

frequent flier. ER repeat customer.

full moon. Full ER or overcrowded waiting room.

 G

gasser/gas passer. Anesthetist.

gatekeeper. HMOese for an internist or family-practice doc whose role is to keep costs low by only allowing a certain number of patients to go to specialists.

GGF1. Short for granny or grandpa's got a fever and that a basic set (1) of tests should be done. This term was used in the first episode of the television show *ER* in 1994 in that immortal set of lines: "Give him D-5. NS cc's. Do a head CT. Noncontrast. Get Psych Services down here for a consult. Do a GGF1."

GLM. Good-looking mother. Used in pediatrics especially to describe a nice-looking parent.

gomer. A complaining, irksome patient. Medical lore holds that this began as an acronym for *get out of my emergency room*. However, William Safire has suggested that it may have come from the Scottish dialect word gomeral for simpleton.

gone camping. Describing a patient in an oxygen tent.

gone to ———. Hospital euphemism for a death; for instance, a member of the staff at a Virginia hospital reports that it is "gone to Chicago" where he works.

goober. Tumor.

gorked. Anesthetized.

grapes. Hemorrhoids.

 H

hammer. Local anesthetic.

head. A brain-injury patient. Usage: "I've got a head I've got to deal with."

head whack. Head injury.

hey docs. Alcoholics handcuffed to wheelchairs in big-city medical wards who, at the sight of a white coat, bleat out in chorus, "Hey, Doc!"

hit and run. Operating quickly so as not to be late for another engagement.

hole in one. A gunshot wound in the mouth or other bodily orifice.

hospitalitis. Malaise of patients who have been in the hospital too long.

 I

ivy pole. Rack from which intravenous equipment hangs.

 J

jungle rot. Fungus infection of the crotch area.

 K

knife-happy. Describing an overly enthusiastic surgeon.

 L

liver rounds. A staff party, so called because of liver-damaging alcohol.

lolfof. Little old lady found on floor; used in emergency medicine especially.

loop the loop. Flamboyant surgical rearrangement of the intestines.

loose change. A dangling limb in need of amputation.

lunger. Patient with obvious lung disease.

✳ M

Melody Hill anemia. Drunk on cheap wine. The name of any cheap wine can be inserted before the word *anemia*.

MI. Normally this stands for *myocardial infarction*, but a Florida MD explains that some acute MIs are not admitted to hospitals as "hospitals use MI to mean 'monetary insufficiency.'" An alternative initialism is *DOW*, which stands for *deficiency of wallet*.

molar masher. Dentist.

Montezuma's revenge. Diarrhea, especially when touched off by foreign food or a trip to a lesser-developed nation.

Mount Saint Elsewhere. Inferior hospital for welfare charges and the terminally ill.

✳ N

not even in the ball game. Confused, senile patient.

✳ O

oids/roids. Steroids.

old-timer's disease. Alzheimer's disease.

organ recital. A hypochondriac's medical history.

O sign. Comatose patient with mouth open wide. See also, Q SIGN.

✳ P

pan. To pass out bedpans.

pecker checker. Urologist.

pet arm. A useless appendage due to paralysis.

phlebitis. Flea bites.

pink cheater. Latex finger cover used in gynecological and proctological examinations.

pink puffer. Patient breathing rapidly due to lung disease.

pit, the. The emergency room.

player. Same as GOMER.

plumber. Urologist.

PMSB. Initialism for *poor miserable son of a bitch*. Explained by a neurologist in this sentence: "This PMSB comes in complaining of a thousand things, and rightfully so!"

PPPP. Diagnostic initialism for a patient in bad shape: particularly piss-poor protoplasm.

preemie. Premature infant.

psychoceramic. Same as a CROCK.

✳ Q

Q sign. An O SIGN with the patient's tongue hanging out—a worse prognosis.

quackpractor. Chiropractor.

quad. Quadraplegic.

R

rear admiral. Proctologist. (*Maledicta* editor Reinhold Aman has noted that this term was given a boost when President Carter was operated on for hemorrhoids by Dr. William Lukash, who held the rank of rear admiral.)

red dot. Slang for physicians from India, who may have a red dot on their forehead; frequently anesthesiologists.

red pipe. Artery.

reeker. Smelly patient.

road map. Injuries incurred by going through a car windshield face first.

roasted goober. A tumor after intensive cobalt treatment.

rooters. Indigents and hangers-on who gather in big-city emergency rooms to be entertained by legitimate cases.

 S

scope. To undergo endoscopy.

scratch and sniff. A gynecological examination.

shadow gazer. Radiologist.

short-order chefs. Morgue workers.

shrink. Therapist or psychologist.

SICU. (Pronounced *sick-U*) Short for *surgical intensive care unit.*

sieve. Intern or resident who will admit persons to his or her service for the most minor illnesses. Contrast with WALL.

silver goose/silver stallion. Proctoscope.

smilin' mighty Jesus. Spinal meningitis.

SOB. ER-speak for patient "short of breath."

soufflé. A patient who has jumped or fallen from a high place; e.g., a sidewalk soufflé.

speed bump. Hemorrhoid.

spots and dots. Traditional set of childhood diseases: measles, mumps, and chicken pox.

squash. Brain.

stamp. Skin graft.

stirrups. Apparatus used when women are given "internal" exams or are delivering a baby.

sturgeon. Surgeon.

T

TEC. Dead; short for *transfer to eternal care.*

tern. Intern.

Thorazine shuffle. The slow, lumbering gait of psychiatric patients who have been given large doses of phenothiazines.

3H enema. One that is "high, hot, and a hell of a lot." Given to selected patients who have given the staff a hard time.

three P's. Term some doctors use to refer to the pill, permissiveness, and promiscuity.

three-toed sloth. Patient with diminished capacities, usually from long-term alcoholism.

tough stick. A person whose veins are hard to find when drawing blood.

train wreck. A patient with several serious medical problems.

tube. Used as a verb, as in, "I'm going to tube the patient in 419." Means to insert a breathing tube into the patient's airway to help him or her breathe.

tubed. Died, as in going down the "tubes."

turf. To move a patient, as in, "Turf that woman in the ER to obstetrics."

TWA. Third world assassins. Slang for the allegedly poor medical care delivered by physicians who went to medical school in foreign countries.

twitch. Hypochondriac.

✳ V

vedgy. A patient requiring intensive care, incapable of movement.

vegetable garden. Ward for those in comas.

V-fib. Paramedic lingo for ventricular fibrillation. It means that the heart has stopped pumping and is merely quivering in what might be called death throes.

vitals. Pulse, blood pressure, and other vital signs.

✳ W

WADAO. Weak and dizzy all over.

wall. Intern or resident adept at not admitting patients to his or her service. Contrast with SIEVE.

wallet biopsy. Finding out how much care a paying patient can afford. If a patient fails a wallet biopsy in a private hospital, he gets transferred to a public hospital. Defined by David Olive, author of *Business Babble: A Cynic's Dictionary of Business Jargon,* as "a preoperative procedure performed in private hospitals to determine the likely duration of a patient's stay."

ward X. The morgue.

whale. Grossly obese patient.

wig picker. Same as SHRINK.

witch doctor. Specialist in internal medicine.

✳ Z

zap. To administer electroshock therapy.

zorro belly. Patient with many scars on stomach indicating earlier surgery.

✳

SOURCES

Thanks to Dr. P.B.P., Dr. F.M., Dr. Joseph Morales, Dr. Reinhold Aman, and Dr. Aman's journal, *Maledicta,* which contained the following: "Milwaukee

Medical Maledicta" by Sue Ture (*Maledicta* 8, 1984–85), "Not Sticks and Stones, but Names" by Lois Monteiro (*Maledicta* 4, no. 1, summer 1980), "Common Patient-Directed Pejoratives Used by Medical Personnel," by C. J. Scheiner, (*Maledicta* 2, 1978), and "More Common Patient-Directed Pejoratives Used by Medical Personnel (*Maledicta* 7, 1983). The *Newsweek* "Buzzwords" sections of February 19, 1990; May 28, 1990; July 9, 1990; and April 29, 1991, were most helpful.

17

MENTAL STATES

*Cutting With a Dull Tool, Too Much Cuckoo
in the Clock, and Other Fulldeckisms and
Marbles Metaphors*

But the first time I heard that idea, it was from the eminent prosecutor,
Mister Shanley, and when Richard Shanley says something, and it sounds
good to me, I start wondering if maybe all of a sudden I'm not traveling
with a full seabag anymore.

—From George V. Higgins's
The Judgment of Deke Hunter

I have frequently remarked that the Americans, who generally treat of business in clear, plain language, devoid of all ornament, and so extremely
simple as to be often coarse, are apt to become inflated as soon as they attempt a more poetical diction. They then vent their pomposity from one
end of a harangue to the other, and to hear them lavish imagery on every
occasion, one might fancy that they never spoke of anything with simplicity.

—Alexis de Tocqueville,
Democracy in America

S lang dotes on mental illness, oddness, and offness. There are scores
of slang synonyms for mental aberration and various states thereof.
Without leaving the *D*'s, we have *daffy, dippy, dotty, dingy,* and
dingaling, and the *B*'s include *bananas, beany, birdy, buggy, bugs, bug-
house,* and *bonkers.*

This lexicon is cruel, yet paradoxically kinder than the proper language of psychiatry. To be branded as loopy or wifty seems less dire than
being labeled neurotic or psychotic. In fact, the trend seems to be toward
metaphoric description as opposed to a single word. There is nothing
new about this. People have had bats in their belfries, snakes in their
heads, and bees in their bonnets for generations, but what is new is that
we seem to be in the midst of a bumper harvest of metaphors for being a
bit "off." It is by far the biggest and fastest-growing metaphoric harvest of
the century, and vast collections of them are floating around. A gigantic
collection on the Internet carries the name *fulldeckisms* (from the notion
of "not playing with a full deck").

If this started out as a means of folk expression, it has crept up the social scale to the point where a columnist in the British *Times Literary Supplement* reporting on eccentric behavior among executives at Harper-Collins publishers "made it sound as if the publishers of the Bible had gone one horseman short of an apocalypse." In his column in the *Toronto Globe and Mail,* Robert Fulford talks of "rococo" examples along the lines of "He's a flying buttress short of a cathedral." Fulford, by the way, calls them "marbles metaphors," from the classic "missing a few" or "lost his marbles."

These have certainly been influenced by what have been termed Westernisms or ruralisms—folksy, bucolic similes and metaphors along the lines of "steeper than a cow's face," "dumber than a barrel of hair," "as useless as tits on a boar hog," and "long as a Texas lie."

Here is a contemporary collection of slang expressions that all mean more or less the same thing. The trick here is to come up with a new metaphoric way of saying that same thing.

✳ A

Has an **apartment** to let.

Has an unfurnished **attic.**

✳ B

Only **baba** and no **lu.**

Got **beamed up** and forgot to come down.

No **beans** in his or her pod/No **beans** in his or her pot.

Doesn't know how many **beans** make five.

Belt doesn't go through all the loops.

Gone around the **bend.**

Too many **birds** on his/her antenna.

Swallowed the **bottle** instead of the pills.

Bow is unstrung.

Brain is stuck in first gear.

Brain cells never divided.

No room at the **Brain Inn.**

His/her **bread** ain't done.

Two **bricks** shy of a load.

A **bubble** off of plumb (or out of level).

She's/he's not the brightest **bulb** on the Christmas tree.

Out where the **buses** don't run.

Missing a few **buttons.**

✳ C

Not **cable** ready.

Car isn't hitting on all cylinders.

No **cheese** on the taco.

A few **chips** short of a bag of Wavy-Lays (used by Maureen Dowd in the *New York Times*).

No **comics** with the bubble gum.

Not **computing** with a full disc.

Her/his **corn bread** ain't cooked in the middle.

A few **croutons** short of a Caesar salad.

A **cup and saucer** short of a full place setting.

All the **cups** aren't stacked in the cupboard.

 ∗ D

The **date** on his/her carton has expired.

Dealing with a **dead battery.**

A **dial tone.**

Missing a few dots on his or her **dice.**

His/her **dipstick** doesn't quite touch the oil.

Temporarily **disconnected.**

All of his or her **dogs** aren't barking.

One **doughnut** shy of a dozen.

Dow Jones average is off a few points.

Left one's **dresser drawers** open.

Cutting with a **dull tool.**

 ∗ E

Over the **edge.**

Elevator doesn't run to the top floor.

Running on **empty.**

empty suit. Person of authority lacking authority and/or intelligence and/or conviction. From the *Washington Times* of November 13, 1990: "If President Bush doesn't identify himself with something, he'll be written off as an empty suit." Writing in the *Washington Post,* Mark Shields wrote on the eve of the 1994 election: "To call Rep. Michael Huffington, the Republican state nominee [California], an empty suit is to libel the nation's garment industry."

Enchiladas have lost their chili.

Coming in on three **engines.**

∗ F

Too much **fee-fye** and not enough **fo-fum.**

About due for a **fill-up.**

No **fish** on the hook.

Fishing without bait.

No batteries in the **flashlight.**

All **foam** and no beer.

A few **fries** short of a Happy Meal.

Ready to join the **frogs** on the lily pad.

Not playing with a **full deck.**

∗ G

Missed the last **gas station** on the highway of life.

From the shallow end of the **gene pool.**

No **grain** in the silo.

Has a **guest** in the attic.

* H

Her/his **hard drive** is full.

Hat is on too tight.

Has had his/her **hat** blocked with him/her still in it.

Driving with one **headlight.**

Has lived too long at the **high-tension-wire café.**

Off his/her **hinges.**

Playing **hockey** with a warped puck.

No one **home** in the dome.

Nice **house,** nobody home.

One **hush puppy** short of a barbe-cue platter.

* I

Two **ice cubes** short of a full tray.

* J

No **juice** in the cable.

* K

He's a few **kilocycles** short of his assigned frequency.

Not **knitting** with both needles.

Has a **knot** in his/her kite string.

* L

No **lead** in the pencil.

A **leak** in the think tank.

No **leaves** in the tea.

No **lemon** in his lemonade.

A few **loons** in the bin.

Member of the **loony** book club.

A **low-watt bulb.**

Lunch box. (Presumably a play on "out to lunch").

* M

Missing a few **marbles.**

Too much **motor** for his/her axle.

Hangin' out with **Mr. Peanut.**

Too much **multi** in the personality.

Puts **mustard** on his/her Froot Loops.

* N

Nuttier than a squirrel's breakfast.

Nutty as a fruitcake.

* O

Has only one **oar** in the water.

He/she has both **oars** in the water

but they're on the same side of the boat.

Overdrawn at the memory bank.

 P

No **paint** on the canvas.

Cuts out **paper dolls.**

A mind like **Paul Revere's** ride—a little light in the belfry.

A few **peas** short of a casserole.

Plays **piano** in a marching band.

Half the **pickets** are missing from his/her fence.

A few **pickles** short of a jar.

Somebody blew out his/her **pilot light.**

Somebody pulled his/her **plug.**

A dim **porch** light.

A thruppence short of a **pound.**

Puppies not woofin'.

 Q

Running two **quarts** low.

 R

Serves the **racquet** instead of the ball.

Driving in **reverse.**

Rice Krispies don't snap, crackle, and pop.

Off his/her **rocker.**

Not present at **roll call.**

Has a **room** for rent.

 S

He/she forgot to put his/her **sail** up.

Two **sandwiches** short of a picnic.

A **screw** loose.

In one too many **scrimmages** without a helmet.

Ain't traveling with a full **seabag.**

Few **shingles** missing from his roof.

Has all of his/her **shit** in one sock.

His/her **skylight** leaks a bit.

One **slice** short of a loaf.

Living in an incompatible **solar system.**

Abducted once too often by **space aliens.**

Splinters in the windmills of his/her mind.

On the highway of life, he/she is a **stalled vehicle.**

No **strings** in the racquet.

No **students** in the class.

He/she fell out of the **stupid** tree and hit every branch on the way down.

 T

One **taco** short of a combination platter.

On his/her **team,** they're one player short.

A few **termites** in the attic.

He/she has a few loose **tiles.**

Driving with his/her **top** down.

Is out of his/her **tree.**

On a **trip** with no luggage.

No **turning ballerina** in the jewelry box.

Runs a **typewriter** without a ribbon.

 U

Off in the **upper story.**

Born **upstairs** over a vacant lot.

His/her **upstairs** ain't fully furnished.

 V

Volunteers as a bowling ball.

 W

Running with one **wheel** in the sand.

The **wheel** is running but the hamster is dead.

No **wheels** on the golf cart.

No **wick** in the candle.

No **wind** in the windmill.

Not **wrapped** too tightly.

 Y

No **yoke** in the egg.

SOURCES

Robert D. Specht, Bob Skole, Roberta B. Jacobson (who sent along not one, but two, compilations), Joseph C. Goulden, Robert C. Norris, James W. Darling, the late Charles D. Poe, and Joseph E. Badger all helped with the compilation of this list. The best list of Westernisms that the author has seen was compiled by David McQuay and appeared in the *Denver Post* of August 25, 1985, and the best article on the subject to come to my attention is Robert Fulford's "Never at a Loss for Marbles Metaphors" in the *Toronto Globe and Mail* of November 30, 1994.

— * 18 * —

NAUTICAL SLANG

At Sea With the Language

Every seaman, whether naval, Merchant Marine, or yachtsman, knows that when he steps aboard a vessel he is stepping into another existence and wishes it to remain that way.

—Gershom Bradford, author of *The Mariner's Dictionary*, quoted in the *St. Petersburg Times*, December 9, 1984

What distinguishes nautical slang from other slang is that so much of what was once specialized slang and jargon is now standard English. From *stem* to *stern*, from *port* to *starboard*, dozens of terms are now—and have long been—found in conventional dictionaries along with the notation *naut.*

Much of this slang and terminology came ashore long ago. The author spent three years in the U.S. Navy in the early 1960s, where he was well indoctrinated in the slang of the sea. Imagine my surprise when I came out of the Navy and found nautical images in a brokerage house where I went to work for a year. There people routinely *jumped ship,* produced *boilerplate,* and went *full speed ahead* . . . trying, of course, not to go *overboard* in the process.

This is not to say that this traditional slang is safe from the onslaughts of verbal reform and political correctness. During the 1970s the U.S. Navy attempted to purge itself of its traditional slang. The shipboard *mess* was officially renamed "enlisted dining facilities," the *galley* of yore became a "kitchen," and the *brig* became a "correctional facility." In deference to the genderless society, the Department of Defense ruled in 1979 that a ship would be an "it" and not a "her," and that it would be "crewed" and not "manned."

In 1984, a good year to lash out against such things, then–secretary of the navy John F. Lehman Jr. condemned "the bureaucratization of naval language" and ordered all naval facilities to return to traditional use by January 1, 1985. Halls were once again *passageways* and toilets became *heads.*

Without replaying all of the traditional terms, here is a selection of to-day's un-"reformed" nautical slang, whether it be from the USN or the World Cup or the works of Tom Clancy.

* A

air boss. Head of the aviation department on an aircraft carrier.

airdale. Any person in the air (aviation) department aboard an aircraft carrier. If this was once derogatory—an Airedale is a dog, after all—it is used with some pride by those in the air wing of a carrier.

all hands. The entire crew of a ship.

anchor. Lowest-ranking man or woman in the class at the U.S. Naval Academy.

ash can. Depth charge.

* B

basement. Hangar deck of an aircraft carrier where the aircraft are kept when not in service.

battlewagon. Battleship.

beach, the. Ashore, whether it be Cannes or Norfolk.

belay that. Stop that.

bellhop. Sailor's term for a marine, especially one in dress uniform. Sometimes stated as "seagoing bellhop."

big chow. Meal served before a big day in the Navy; for instance, before a major aircraft carrier attack.

bilge. The proper meaning of this term is that portion of a ship below the waterline. The slang use of this term refers to (1) bad food and (2) bad information. At the

U.S. Naval Academy it means (3) to flunk out. Annapolitan Bill O'Neill reports that a gate at the Naval Academy is known as the bilge gate, which is "one small gate that lads being bounced out of the academy pass through; hence no middle will walk out that gate, though civilians use it. A middle will step into the roadway and stroll out the big gate, instead."

bilge rat. Boiler technician or other belowdecks sailor.

bilge water. Soup.

bird farm. Aircraft carrier.

bird hatching. Fathering more than one child; term coined by Adm. Hyman Rickover.

black shoe. A member of the regular seagoing navy, as opposed to naval aviators, who are allowed to wear brown shoes.

bluejacket. Sailor.

blue shirt. Aircraft handler on an aircraft carrier.

blue thunder. Expensive speedboats used by government drug agents to intercept drug smugglers' boats.

blue-water ops. Aircraft carrier flight operations beyond the reach of land.

blue-water sailor. Boater who heads for the open seas, as opposed to those who stay close to the coast.

boat pox. Gel-coat blisters on fiberglass boats.

boomer. (1) Submarine with nuclear missiles. (2) Member of the nuclear-powered Navy.

boondocker. Basic U.S. Navy boot

for some forty years up to their phasing out in 1997. They were tough, unforgiving, and by the Navy's own admission the service was losing people from foot problems created by the boots.

boot. Sailor fresh from boot camp.

brightwork. Brass that must be polished.

brig rat. Prisoner serving time in the brig, a naval prison.

bunk. A sailor's bed.

 C

cag. Commander of the air group, the chief pilot on an aircraft carrier.

can. Destroyer; short for tin can.

captain of the head. Sailor in charge of cleaning toilets.

cat. The catapult used to launch planes on an aircraft carrier.

Charlie Noble. Smokestack of a ship's galley.

Cigarette boat. Fast, cigarette-shaped speedboat popular in south Florida and the vessel of choice for dealers in illegal drugs.

Cinderella liberty. A Navy or Marine Corps pass that expires at midnight.

coasties. Members of the Coast Guard.

coffee grinder. Winch for controlling yacht sails. Also simply known as GRINDER.

conn. Control of the ship. An offi-

cer of the deck on a Navy vessel will "take the conn" when taking responsibility for the ship's course and speed.

Crabtown. Annapolis, Maryland.

Crotch, the. The U.S. Marine Corps.

crow. The sleeve insignia eagle that marks petty officers in the U.S. Navy. To get one's crow is to get a promotion to petty officer.

cryppies. Cryptologists.

cumshaw. That which is obtained by bribery or other illegal means.

 D

dead horse. A debt, to a Navy man.

deck ape. (1) Enlisted sailor assigned to deck or gunnery duties. (2) In pleasure and sport boating, it is a crew member who does the hard work with ropes and sails.

deep-six. To throw away or kill, as in "deep-sixing a project." Its traditional meaning is to drown, alluding to a person who is six fathoms deep.

Dilbert dunker. Contraption of the modern U.S. Navy used in training to simulate the action of an airman ditching at sea.

dolphins. The U.S. Navy submariner's badge.

Dutchman. A plate covering a crack or other imperfection.

 E

easy. Carefully.

ego alley. Part of the water where

the wave-blasting powerboats go to show off.

end on. Head-on.

Event 1000. The code word for any incident in which men are trapped in a submarine stranded on the bottom, and search and rescue operations are to be initiated.

fender belly. Term for a fat, potbellied sailor, usually a "lifer," such as an old Navy chief petty officer.

field day. Day, or portion thereof, set aside for cleaning up a Navy vessel or base.

fish. Torpedo.

flag plot. Navy term for a command center. It comes from the fact that a naval officer above the rank of captain is allowed to fly a flag showing his or her rank: a flag officer.

flattop. Aircraft carrier.

floating coffin. An unsafe ship.

floating palace. A large and comfortable ship.

fouled. Jammed or obstructed.

four-oh/four-point-oh. Outstanding; used to express the highest degree of admiration. It comes from the highest rating—4.0—that one can achieve on a Navy fitness report.

four-oh sailor. Human perfection. In John Barron's *Breaking the Ring,* a character defines a 4.0 sailor as "a guy who can walk on water without getting his shoes wet."

four-striper. Navy captain.

Freshwater Navy. The Coast Guard.

galley yarn. A rumor in the Navy; one that originates—metaphorically or actually—in the ship's kitchen or galley.

geedunk. Navy/marine term for ice cream, candy, junk food, etc.

gertrude. Underwater telephone, used for communication between submarines. The term shows up, among other places, in Tom Clancy's *Hunt for Red October.*

ghosts. Imperfect sonar images.

Gitmo. Guantánamo Bay, Cuba; specifically, the U.S. Navy base there.

glory hole. Quarters for chief petty officers aboard Navy ships.

gouge. (1) To cheat. (2) The answer or solution. (3) The latest inside information—the *skinny*.

grinder. (1) Large winch for raising and lowering sails. (2) Person positioned just behind the mast who controls such winches. A 1984 article on the crew of America's Cup entry *Liberty* in *USA Today* termed this the "most brutal physical position" on a twelve-meter yacht. (3) A Marine Corps parade ground.

gummer's mate. Dental technician.

H

hash mark. Stripes worn on the sleeves of Navy enlisted men, representing years of service. Each stripe signifies an enlistment.

head. (1) Toilet. (2) Compass heading. This sets up a basis for confusion, as in, "Quartermaster, where is your head?"

heavier metal. A larger, more powerful warship—a cruiser is heavier metal to a destroyer crew.

holiday. An imperfection; a spot left unfinished or uncleaned.

Hollywood shower. Full-length shower; a rarity on most Navy vessels, where freshwater conservation measures are normally in effect and the procedure is to lather up, shut off the water, wash, and then turn the water on to rinse off. A line from Tom Clancy's *Hunt for Red October:* "A Hollywood shower is something a sailor starts thinking about after a few days at sea."

hook. The anchor.

hooligan. Not seamanlike; something that has been sloppily slapped together.

hot bunk. The use of the same bed by more than one sailor, who move in and out of that bunk as their watches (shifts) change.

huff duff. High-frequency direction finder (HFDF).

hydraulic sandwich. Liquid lunch.

I

Irish pennant. Loose rope or loose thread on a sailor's uniform.

* J

jarhead. Member of the Marine Corps to a sailor—who is likely to be called SWABBIE in return.

---

*

SAY WHERE?

A recent book, *Those Vulgar Tubes* by Joe J. Simmons III (Texas A&M University Press), which is a scholarly study of the disposal of human waste at sea aboard European ships of the fifteenth through seventeenth centuries, contains a list of some of the names given to shipboard facilities over the years—including *vulgar tubes.* The list:

Beak head/Roundhouse
Forestage/Sanitary
Garderobe/Seat-of-ease
Head/Steep-tub
Pissdale/Stern-turret
Quarter Gallery/Toilet box

joe. Coffee.

Julie. The system that activates the Navy's sonar buoys. As James W. Canan was doubtlessly pleased to report in his book *The Superwarriors,* it was named Julie "after a Philadelphia stripteaser who had a reputation for turning passive boys into active boys."

jump. To leave; to jump ship is to leave without permission.

jury-rig. To repair or put together in an emergency; to slap together.

 K

keelhaul. To punish. It is an allusion to the long-outlawed practice of punishing a sailor by dragging him by rope under the keep of the ship.

 L

lay day. A day off from racing, such as can be requested by either boat during the America's Cup competition.

liberty. Overnight leave, save for CINDERELLA LIBERTY.

liberty hound. One who finagles extra time off; one who takes all the time off allowable.

lights out. Radar is off in the USN.

 M

mast. Ship captain's hearings before which sailors are brought and punished for minor infractions.

mat. The main deck of an aircraft carrier.

mating dance of the lead-bottomed money-gobblers. Phrase used to describe the positioning of boats for the start of the America's Cup and other major races.

Med, the. The Mediterranean Sea, in the parlance of the Navy's Sixth Fleet.

Mickey Mouse rules. Petty rules and regulations. In his marvelous book on nautical terminology, *Salty Words,* Robert Hendrickson writes, "One theory holds that World War II U.S. Navy Military Indoctrination Centers, or MIC's, where undisciplined sailors were restrained, gave their initials to this expression for petty rules."

monkey fist. Knot put at the end of a heaving line, often with a small piece of lead or other weight in the middle of the knot to allow it to be thrown easier.

mosquito boat. Motor torpedo boat or PT boat.

mothballs. In reserve.

mother/mom. The aircraft carrier to those pilots who were launched from it.

mousing. Lashing across a hook to keep it from slipping.

mule. Handler on the flight deck of an aircraft carrier.

 N

navy shower. Water-conserving practice in which a sailor wets down for a few seconds, turns off the water and lathers up, and then enjoys a few more seconds of freshwater to rinse off. It is preferable to have a HOLLYWOOD SHOWER.

nuc. Sailor in the U.S. Navy who serves aboard a nuclear sub or other nuclear-powered vessel.

 O

OD. Officer of the deck in the Navy. The OD is in charge of the ship and is the representative of the captain.

old man, the. The captain.

 P

padre. Chaplain in the Navy.

paint. Scanned by radar.

painter. A rope in the bow of a boat used to tie it to a dock or another vessel.

pepper report. Navy ammunition report.

pipes. Boatswain—bos'n.

pitman. Same as SEWERMAN.

plank owner. Traditional name for a member of a ship's original crew—i.e., one who trod its deck timbers, or planks, when still new—that still applies in the plankless nuclear age.

pointy end. Name used by aircraft carrier pilots to describe the front end of the boat.

porkchop. Navy supply officer. Ac-

cording to *The Random House Dictionary of the English Language, porkchop* is a traditional metaphor for a "livelihood, especially one acquired with little effort."

purple shirt. Member of an aircraft-carrier flight-deck fueling crew.

 Q

quarters. Living spaces on a ship.

 R

racer tracers. Groupies who follow sailboat racers around the world.

rail meat. Crew in competitive sailing used for ballast only.

rates. Deserves, USN.

razor blades. A scrapped ship that has presumably been converted to razor blades.

red lead. Ketchup.

red shirt. Emergency-crew member on the deck of an aircraft carrier.

reefer ship. Supply ship with refrigeration facilities.

rock stars. Pro sailors; egomaniacs to weekend boaters.

romper. A ship that has moved more than ten nautical miles ahead of its convoy—to have romped ahead—and is unable to rejoin it.

roof. The flight deck of an aircraft carrier.

rubber duckie. Inflatable rubber

boats that are towed behind ships to confuse radar-guided missiles; a decoy.

S

screw. The propeller.

scuttlebutt. (1) Drinking fountain. (2) Gossip and rumor.

seagull. (1) Navy term for one who follows the ship or fleet—applied to spouses and prostitutes alike. (2) Chicken served on a Navy vessel.

seaweed. Spinach.

secure. To put away or tie down.

sewerman. Crew member on a large sailboat who is in charge of sails belowdecks—or the sewer—where new sails must be unpacked and repacked during a race.

shellback. Sailor who has crossed the equator; hence one with some experience.

Sherwood Forest. Missile room on a U.S. submarine.

ship over. To reenlist in the Navy.

ship's husband. The yacht-basin antonym for the golf widow.

shooter. The catapult officer on an aircraft carrier.

sick bay. Medical area on a Navy ship.

Silent Service. Sobriquet of the modern submarine force.

SINS. Situational Inertial Navigation System. Navy.

six-pack license. License that allows a civilian to commercially captain a boat with no more than six passengers on inland waters.

skins. Waterproof oilskin clothing.

skunk. To a submariner, an unidentified surface contact.

skylarking. Goofing off, Navy style.

slop chute. (1) A ship's garbage chute. (2) Canteen where beer is sold.

snipe. Navy seaman working belowdecks in the engineering department.

soup. Fog.

splice the mainbrace. To have a drink; head off for happy hour. Although this term dates back to the British Navy and the era of wind and sail to indicate a ration of grog, it is used playfully today by people conscious of its anachronistic quality.

spud locker. Place where food, including potatoes, is kept. Aircraft carrier pilots refer to crashing into the back end of a ship as "hitting the spud locker."

squid. Sailor.

stamps. Mail clerk on a Navy ship.

straphanger. Boat owner's guest who knows nothing of sailing.

stray dogs. Married male powerboaters who prowl about the waterways looking for women.

striker. Sailor training in specific area; trainee.

stripes. An officer in the Navy, because of the gold stripes worn on their dress uniforms.

swab/swabbie/swab jockey. Common seaman.

✳ T

tadpole. Frogman not yet fully qualified, such as one still in training.

tin can. Navy destroyer.

tin fish. Torpedo.

two-foot-itis. The mock disease that infects recreational-boat owners who are always looking for a vessel that is two feet longer than the one they have.

✳ U

under the gun. Under armed guard.

✳ V

vice boats. Big, powerful muscle boats of the type first made popular on the *Miami Vice* television show.

vulture's row. The island area of an aircraft carrier where mechanics, plane pushers, and others concerned with flight operations congregate during deck landings.

✳ W

weasels. Men with great boats, but whose personality is such that no woman would ride with them.

WET. Weekend training, in the Naval Reserves.

white-blue-white. Marine summer dress uniform: white cap, blue tunic, and white trousers.

✳ X

XO. The executive officer, or second-in-command, on a naval vessel.

✳ Y

yellow sheet. An aircraft spotter on an aircraft carrier. They control BLUE SHIRTS.

yeoman. A Navy petty officer with clerical duties.

✳ Z

Z-gram. The terse, direct style of memos and orders pioneered by Adm. Elmo Zumwalt during his tenure as chief of naval operations.

SOURCES

Bill O'Neill, Dick Dana, James Darling, Charles D. Poe, and the Tamony Collection were all of help in compiling this glossary. An article on "seafaring terms you won't find in the dictionary" from the June 21, 1990, *Washington Times* by Don Kowet was of use, as were several nautical Internet sites.

──── ✳ 19 ✳ ────

PENTAGONESE

Fort Fumble Speaks

Pentagonese. (World War II to Modern; all Services). n. A peculiar artificial language developed by the aborigines of the Puzzle Palace for the express purpose of confusing the troops. It is extremely difficult to translate into English.

—From *A Dictionary of Soldier Talk*
by Col. John R. Elting, Sgt. Maj. Dan Cragg,
and Sgt. Ernest Deal

Perhaps no institution has twisted the mother tongue more systematically . . . than the Defense Department. Not only do Defense officials tend towards a particularly leaden bureaucratic patois, often called "Pentagonese," but military secrecy requirements also generate a dense thicket of evasive phrasing and arcane code words.

—David C. Morrison, *National Journal*

Today is ArmForDay, the culmination of HawMilWeek, when civvies say thanks to all the pork chops, bubble heads, zoomies, and gun bunnies who protect our butts all year long.

—Portion of an editorial from the *Honolulu Star-Bulletin* of May 21, 1994

I t was born of three unholy influences: (1) the bureaucracy, which it is at one with, (2) secrecy, which is its lifeblood, and (3) the need to obfuscate, especially useful in dealing with the Congress. The fact that its business is killing people tends to produce euphemisms for much military activity, as George Orwell noted in his classic essay, "Politics and the English Language."

In a time of emergency, Pentagonese can be useful in making a war sound like anything but, or, as the late Charles McCabe of the *San Francisco Chronicle* once defined it, "a non-lingo in which murder can be made to mean salvation."

During the darker days of the Vietnam War, the Pentagon created terms to make the adventure sound like a Boy Scout hike. The $34 given to families of South Vietnamese civilians killed by mistake was officially called a *condolence award,* and gross bombing errors were seldom termed anything more incriminating than *navigation errors, misdirections,* or *technical errors.* Defoliants that could kill plants fifteen miles from where they were dropped were termed *weed killers* ("the same as you buy in the hardware store at home,'' said an American official in 1966). Terms like *routine improvement of visibility in jungle areas* and *resources control* gave it the sound of a 4-H conservation effort.

Here is a sampling of what it sounds like today and how it translates into plain English. To get the full effect, read it in conjunction with the chapter on bureaucratese and think of it as a bureaucracy with enough nuclear firepower to knock the earth off its axis.

＊ A

ABC. The Pentagon's 1988 acronym list gives three translations: (1) American-British-Canadian. (2) Argentina-Brazil-Columbia (the ABC countries), and (3) atomic, biological, and chemical.

(This underscores the extent to which Pentagonese is dependent on acronyms. The aforementioned 1988 volume is, as the *Washington Post* termed it, "449 jam-packed pages of Pentagonisms.")

across the river. Washington, D.C., especially the White House and Congress.

air-breathing. Describing a missile or other airborne delivery system that requires air for fuel combustion and therefore must remain in the earth's environment. The term is used to distinguish these systems from those that are rocket propelled.

air support. Bombing.

alice/ALICE/ALCE. Medium-issue backpack with frame, an acronym from *all-purpose lightweight individual carrying equipment.*

angels. Air-intercept and close-air-support code word meaning aircraft altitude (in thousands of feet).

antipersonnel. Killer, in the sense that an antipersonnel weapon is meant to destroy people rather than equipment.

apportioning the poverty. 1990s term for the shrinkage that each branch of the armed forces will see during the decade.

attrit. To weaken or reduce by wearing or grinding down, but mostly used in the specific sense of losing troops by attrition, as from enemy hostilities. In use for many years, this bit of Pentagonese came into play during the Gulf War.

＊ B

backpack nuke. A nuclear device that can be carried by a single person.

balloon goes up, the. A major war starts.

Beltway bandit. High-priced consultant or consulting firm. The name contains an allusion to the Beltway, an interstate highway that goes around the city of Washington. (See also chapter 21.)

black list. As described in the December 1, 1991, edition of the *Department of Defense Dictionary:* "An official counterintelligence listing of actual or potential enemy collaborators, sympathizers, intelligence suspects, and other persons whose presence menaces the security of friendly forces."

blue top. Press release, from the traditional DOD press-release forms, which have blue tops. To "blue top it" is to put out a press release.

bogey. An air contact that is unidentified but assumed to be enemy, according to official DOD documents.

bogsaat. Acronym from *bunch of guys sitting around a table*—a particular form of decision making.

boilerplate. Standard verbiage (e.g., descriptions of budget program elements) used to describe fixed and unchanging items.

bootleg copy. Unofficial advance working copy of an official document.

brilliant pebbles. A defensive technology that would employ thousands of small satellites floating in space to home in on incoming enemy missiles and destroy them.

broken arrow. Mishap involving nuclear weapons, used in 1996 for the title of a movie about a nuclear accident.

bubblehead. Submariner.

burn me a copy. Make a photocopy.

 C

C-cubed. Communications, command, and control.

chairman, the. Chairman of the Joint Chiefs of Staff.

CINC. Commander in chief. It is pronounced *sink.*

CINCENT. *C*ommander *in* chief *Cent*ral Command.

Code 3. As explained by former assistant secretary of defense John G. Kester in his article on Pentagonese in the *Washingtonian:* "A high-ranking official—used in messages to designate rank of an expected visitor, as in, 'I have a Code 3 on board.' Code 1 is the President; Code 6's are too common to mention."

code word. Extra-secret; more secret than top secret.

collateral damage. Civilian casualties, in euphemistic Pentagonese. This term, which had been in use for many years in discussion of nuclear war, came into its own during daily press briefings in Riyadh, Saudi Arabia, to describe the overkill of conventional warfare. The term was a clear marker of the gulf between the military and the five hundred journalists who had been assigned to cover the war.

Here is how R. W. Apple Jr. of the *New York Times* treated the matter in a column of February 4, 1991: "There are obvious cultural differences . . . between the highly disciplined military men, with their odd words and phrases like *attrit* for 'wear down' and *collat-*

eral damage for 'civilian casualties,' and the reporters, who make their living by questioning authority and doubting official pronouncements. To them, Pentagonese is a laughable language."

country buster. Nickname for an extra-lethal nuclear warhead, and a clear play on the *blockbuster* of World War II and larger than a *city buster* of the early nuclear age.

crank. To start; to get going. The term applies to both machines and humans.

cubed out. Bona fide Pentagon slang for "filled to capacity."

* D

dampen down. To slow or minimize—as in the "dampening down of expectations" heard in briefings. The term is from firefighting and refers to the wetting (or dampening) of material so that it does not catch fire.

decapitation. Name for the contingency plan to use nuclear weapons to kill political leadership.

dense pack. A cluster of intercontinental missiles in hard silos.

dirty battlefield. Combat zone obscured by smoke and dust. Automated "smart" weapons may not work as well in such an environment.

DOE reaction. (acronym) Death of earth; Armageddon; doomsday.

dog and pony show. Formal presentation aimed at gathering support for a system or issue. Visuals (usu-

ally projected on a screen), handouts, and large graphs are essential to a true dog and pony show.

doolie. (Air Force) Air Force Academy cadet.

* E

Early Bird. Name for a compilation of military-related news clippings distributed early each morning for the edification of those who work at the Pentagon.

ejecta. Debris thrown up by the explosion of a missile.

escalate. Since the 1960s, to intensify, to wage a wider war. In 1966 the national commander of the Veterans of Foreign Wars, Andy Borg, called for a "big and fast step-up of the U.S. war effort in Vietnam." The UPI's Dick West termed it a "horrible blunder" because, as every hawk and dove knew, you don't step up a war, you escalate it.

event. Nuclear explosion or accident.

* F

faces and spaces. The joint consideration of positions and the personnel to fill them.

feasless. Without feasibility.

first strike. A nuclear surprise.

footprint. The area of destruction left by a nuclear weapon.

Fort Fumble. The Pentagon.

fourth medium. War in space—after the first three martial media: land, sea, and air.

fratricide. The putative tendency of one incoming warhead to destroy its companions on detonation. See DENSE PACK.

 G

GCD. General and complete disarmament, a term that first emerged from arms control talks in the 1960s.

gigaton. A measure of nuclear destructive power, the equivalent to a billion tons of TNT.

go-go. Acronym from *government-owned, government-operated.* A facility not in the hands or ownership of an outside contractor.

go-juice. Jet fuel.

Gold Room. Room 2E294 in the Pentagon, where the Joint Chiefs of Staff meet, so called because of the color of its drapes and carpets.

ground zero. (1) The point at which a thermonuclear weapon makes its impact. (2) Snack bar in the center of the courtyard in the middle of the Pentagon. It is of course an allusion to meaning (1) in that the center of the Pentagon would be a prime target in a missile exchange.

gun bunny. Artilleryman.

 H

hard. Protected—a hard target is one that has been covered with earth and concrete.

he/him. (1) The enemy. This is one of the surest ways in which one distinguishes the military mind from the public mind. The public says *they;* the Pentagon says *he.* An example in the Tamony Collection culled from reports on the Vietnam War: "I don't believe the enemy has any great capability to assume any general offensive in the near future. He has been hurt and hurt badly. He is tired." (2) The president of the United States.

heavy bead. The biggest of the big-ticket items in the annual Pentagon budget from the self-mocking notion that the budget is loaded with beads and trinkets.

horror stories. Term for public disclosure of parts rip-offs, such as paying $9,609 for a simple wrench and $900 for a plastic cup.

horseholder. A person who serves as an aide or in some other capacity (e.g., military assistant) in direct support of a general officer or senior civilian in the same sense that a gentleman would have his horse held during mounting and dismounting.

hot biscuit. A promising research program in the Pentagon.

hot line. The open telex line between the White House and the Kremlin—and not a telephone as often depicted.

human remains pouch. The term that the Pentagon used during the war in the Persian Gulf to replace the *body bag* of Vietnam infamy.

humint. *Hum*an *int*elligence, as opposed to that which is gathered elec-

Say What?

One of the hardest things for the Pentagon to get right is the name for the package in which you bring home the dead. *Body bag* was direct and unsettling, so the *human remains pouch* came into play during the Gulf War. This term was upsetting to some, including Oregon Republican senator Mark O. Hatfield, who felt that the Pentagon was trying to put the war into a tidy little linguistic package. His reaction to the new term was quoted in the *Boston Globe* of January 24, 1991: "That *[body bags]* is too messy. That conjures up all the wrong images, of blood and pain and suffering. Now body bags are called human remains pouches. There, America, does that make you feel any better?"

tronically, or *sigint* for *sig*nals *int*elligence.

hummer. (1) (nuclear) One of the names that those who man missile silos use for missiles; a humdinger. (2) The Hawkeye E-2 early-warning aircraft.

idiot blocks. Option lines at the end of a staff paper that allow the decision maker to indicate his decision or desires by using a check mark (e.g., approved _____, see me _____, brief me _____).

igloo space. Area in an earth-covered structure of concrete and/or steel designed for the storage of ammunition and explosives.

indians. Staff members.

in the loop. Afforded top information. In what Hedrick Smith calls the "national security power fraternity," you are in the loop if you are on "the

short list" to receive daily intelligence documents.

jam. To interfere with. Electronic jamming is the purposeful impairing of the enemy's electronic systems.

Jo. Female soldier, as in "GI Jo."

judy. In the clipped air-intercept code, the name for "I have contact and am taking over the interception." In other words, "I've got this one."

kill-jamming. To impair the ability of an aircraft's electronics and communications while a second plane comes in for the kill.

kneecap. The NEACP (National Emergency Airborne Command Post) jet plane that sits in waiting to get the president out of Washington when enemy missiles are headed toward the city.

L

Langley. The CIA, which is based in Langley, Virginia.

leather personnel carriers. Mock-Pentagonese term for boots. In tune with the Pentagon's penchant for three-letter acronyms, they are often called LPCs.

leprosy effect. An ill-fated program or weapon that taints everything associated with it.

life support areas. Military bases to those in charge. The troops did not buy this absurd example of Pentagonese.

loose nuke. Nuclear warhead that is on the black market, not in the hands of the United States or Russia.

M

MAD. Mutual assured destruction; the theory that neither superpower will attack the other because retaliation would be fatal.

Mark 1 Mod 1. The earliest version of something; usually a weapon and almost always a dud.

megadeath. A million dead.

MFR. Memorandum for record; a written memo recalling what went on at a given meeting.

milicrat. Blend of *mili*tary and bureau*crat*.

mushroom treatment. Pentagonese

for keeping congressmen in the dark and "feeding them crap."

N

narrow yellow. OCSA Form 159, Referral Slip, used in passing routine actions to others; it is a narrow yellow form that may have been named after the pop song "Mellow Yellow."

NOFUN. No first use of nuclear.

NUTS. Nuclear utilization targeting strategy; a theory/strategy based on the idea that military targets, and not cities, will be targeted in a nuclear exchange.

O

off-load. Unload.

on-load. Load.

overkill. More destructive ability than plausibly required.

P

Peacekeeper. The MX missile.

Pentagoose Noose. Nickname for the *Pentagram News,* distributed within the building.

physics package. Thermonuclear bombs named kindly.

piffy-ab. The President's Foreign Intelligence Advisory Board or PFIAB.

program. Almost anything. More than thirty years ago Sen. Stephen Young defined a Pentagon program as any assignment that took more than one phone call to complete.

Puzzle Palace, the. The Pentagon; FORT FUMBLE.

retool. To do it over—usually in an expensive and laborious manner.

the revolving door. The practice that allows military officials to leave the Pentagon for corporate jobs with defense contractors.

rotor head. Helicopter pilot.

rug rank. Higher ranking; an officer who rates a rug on his or her floor.

RV. Reentry vehicle; the cone-shaped package that carries a nuclear warhead to its target.

SANE. Survival and national existence: U.S. name for the doctrine of the former Soviet Union that one had to fight a nuclear war to win the conflict.

sanitize. To edit out; to censor.

scare book, the. Nickname for the periodic report once issued by the secretary of defense that was entitled *Soviet Military Power.* So called because of its tendency to focus on Soviet military strength. Scare books were usually released to coincide with the Pentagon budget request.

scenario-dependent. Dependent on a chain of events.

search and destroy. Pure Pentagonese for destroy and search.

Secdef. The secretary of defense, for short. The *Washington Post* reported in 1988 that a sign in the top man's military airplane on his private cabin read "Secdef and Mrs. Carlucci."

second strike. An attack following a retaliatory strike.

selected. Promoted.

selected out. To be let go or fired.

sigint. *Sig*nals *int*elligence, or that which is gathered electronically rather than by spies (HUMINT).

sign off on. To sign or initial; to pass along, but more specifically to approve something without assuming responsibility for it.

SIOP. The plan for nuclear war; the initials stand for Single Integrated Operational Plan. Peace has been described as a "benign pre-SIOP environment."

soft. Vulnerable, not protected from nuclear attack; a city, for instance. People are "soft targets."

southside basing. The idea that U.S. missiles could be nestled against the southern side of high Western mesas to protect the missiles from incoming missiles.

stand down. To relax or take time off from normal duties for reflection.

stovepipe. An organization that is aligned vertically and specializes in one area, such as logistics, finance and accounting, personnel training, etc. It also applies to informal vertical communications for tasking, coordination, etc., direct from one action officer to another action officer.

straphanger. Person who tags along to a briefing or on a trip even though his presence is not required.

straw man. A concept or other document prepared as a basis for discussion or coordination. Sometimes referred to as a think piece, a straw man is usually the forerunner of a later document and is often nothing more than something set up to be knocked down to get at a more important matter.

sweet. Weapons-speak for workable.

* T

tank, the. The Joint Chiefs of Staff Conference Room, also known as the Gold Room, after its decor.

thermal radiation. Name for nuclear heat moving along the ground at the speed of light. At the source the temperatures are equivalent to those at the center of the sun.

threat tube. The path of an incoming missile.

three-humped camel. That which results when the three services work jointly on a project.

ticket puncher. (1) Military bureaucrat. (2) Someone who undertakes an assignment (e.g., combat) because it looks good on a résumé, or because its absence will look bad. See SE-LECTED and SELECTED OUT on page 286.

tooth-to-tail ratio. Combat power in comparison to support (noncombat) base.

top gun. Nickname for the U.S. Navy's Fighter Weapons School located at the Naval Air Station in Miramar, California.

top line. The maximum dollar amount that the Department of Defense, service branch, or other military unit has to spend. This is, of course, the opposite end of the spectrum from the well-known bottom line.

triad. Mystico-cant name for U.S. nuclear response—submarines, land-based missiles, and long-range bombers.

tube. Same as THREAT TUBE.

* U

unk-unks. Unknown unknowns, factors considered—or not considered—in deciding on new weapons systems. "Things we not only don't know about, but don't even know we don't know about," is how John G. Kester defined them in his article "How to Speak Pentagonese" (*Washingtonian*, February 1982).

* W

walks on water. Miraculous; perfect—officers talk of gaining walks-on-water fitness reports.

weapons system. Weapon. At some point it became unfashionable to call a weapon a weapon, and even the simplest tool of combat became a system.

whiz kid. Derogatory term for a systems analyst or senior Department of

Defense staffer, a term that came into being with the civilian "brain trust" brought in by Secretary of Defense Robert Strange McNamara.

window. Gap or opening. A "window of vulnerability" is a defensive gap that would allow an enemy a first strike.

wiring diagram. An organizational chart.

WTO. Washington theater of operations; ironic self-deprecating reference to the Pentagon.

yellow cake. (nuclear) Uranium concentrates used in nuclear weapons.

yellow stuff. Small tractors, earth movers, etc., used in military operations.

zoomie. Pilot.

SOURCES

Among the many attempts to decode the language of the Pentagon, the best was John G. Kester's February 1982 *Washingtonian* article. The Tamony Collection provided many examples, as did the *Washington Star* files at the Washingtonian Room in the Martin Luther King Library in Washington. Joseph C. Goulden and Charles D. Poe and the late James Thorpe III provided much help. Books of special value:

Eiler, Mark M., *Language of Defense: A Handbook of Acronyms and Terminology,* 1990.

Joint Chiefs of Staff, *Department of Defense Dictionary of Military and Associated Terms* (Joint Pub 1-02), Department of Defense, December 1, 1989.

Lambdin, William, *Doublespeak Dictionary,* Pinnacle Books, 1979.

Shafritz, Jay M., *Words on War,* Prentice Hall, 1990.

Tsouras, Peter, Bruce W. Watson, and Susan W. Watson, *The United States Army: A Dictionary,* Garland Publishing, 1991.

——— ❋ 20 ❋ ———

PERFORMING SLANG

Terms From out of the Mosh Pit and the Greenroom

There is a Gresham's law in language as in economics. Bad currency once admitted will tend to drive the good out of circulation. The bilge of Hollywood will sink the language of Churchill and Lincoln.

—Lord Conesford, "You Americans Are
Murdering the Language," *Saturday Evening
Post,* July 13, 1957

The newspaper that transmogrified American slang . . .

—*Variety* described in the *New York Times,*
November 10, 1987

Show business slang is influenced by special forces. For starters, there are these two:

1. *Yinglish* (a term coined by Leo Rosten for the combination of Yiddish and English), which has long been the argot of many in show business.

2. The trade weekly *Variety* has not only influenced show business talk, but the total body of American slang. Many *Variety*isms have lost their currency, such as *passion pit* (for a drive-in movie lot) and *gams* (female legs), but others are still very much with us.

However, other influences pale in comparison to the overall impact of television, which has taught us its own internal lingo as well. What's more, television lets us in on the slang of the rest of show business. Legitimate theaters have had a greenroom for generations, but not until the goings-on in the greenroom became a topic of conversation on the *Tonight Show* did we all become aware of it.

What helps distinguish television from the rest of show business and other fields of endeavor is its compulsion to air its internal business. For this reason, terms such as these routinely pop up in television conversation: *segues, ratings periods, lavalier mikes, booms, wipes, fills, rim shots, pans, Minicams, voice-overs, feeds, simulcasts, laugh tracks, promos, overnights, outtakes, remotes, spin-offs, residuals, teleprompters,* and so much more. Most of us know, for example, that if we ever got a call out of the blue from 30 Rock or Century City for a guest-host shot, the thing to do would be to immediately call AFTRA and the William Morris Agency.

We are, in fact, treated as if we were all part of "the business" (as opposed to the movies, which is "the industry") and addressed as if we really cared if the station we're watching is an *indy,* an *affiliate,* or an *O&O* (owned and operated by the network), or that some executive has decided that it sounds better if a *repeat* is called an *encore presentation.* Newspapers don't tell us what went on in the composing room, magazines don't report their *front of the book* meetings; but television revels in the off-camera. "As I was telling Johnny during the break . . . ," says one guest, and another tells us for the 110th time that he's never been in a greenroom that was actually green. There is so much on-camera chat about the greenroom that it has entered American mythology, with many of us believing that it is the place where all the really funny lines are spoken and all the really good gossip is traded.

A glossary:

✳ A

above the line. The cost of a movie before the camera begins to roll. Compare with BELOW THE LINE.

actcom. Action comedy, in televisionland. The actcom has been defined as a sitcom that starts with a disruption of the status quo and then follows the central character's action as he or she tries to bring things back to normal. By this definition, *I Love Lucy* was the prototypical actcom.

AFTRA. Pronounced *af-tra,* it stands for the American Federation of Television and Radio Artists.

Allen Smithee. Name used by directors who are unhappy with the films they have created and choose to remain anonymous.

alternative. Short for *alternative rock* and generally connoting any pop style too uncompromising, ar- cane, or intense for mainstream consumption.

ankle. To quit or depart. A term from *Variety.*

apple box. Wooden device used in filming to make a person or object appear taller.

arcs. TV scriptwriter's term for a villain who stays on for a string of episodes rather than one show.

auspices. Television-programmer talk for writers and producers. A show, such as *Homicide,* may have outstanding auspices but less than leading ratings.

ax. Horn or woodwind, but most commonly applied to the saxophone.

✳ B

B. Second-rate, as in B material or the B western of yore.

back end/back-end money. Reference to the final profits in a film after all expenses have been met.

backer. Investor.

bankable. Describing a star whose presence in a film virtually guarantees investors and audiences.

barn. Name for old-fashioned movie theater in the era of multiplex boxes no larger than big family rooms.

below the line. Describing the actual costs of producing a movie.

best boy. The gaffer's first assistant in the motion picture business.

bester. Name for BEST BOY if she is female.

big planet. Television-programmer talk for a huge show around which SATELLITE HITS may cluster.

billing. Order in which actors' names appear in ads, on marquees, and in film credits.

bimodal appeal. In television programming this term describes a show that appeals to both children and older viewers.

Black Rock. CBS corporate headquarters in Manhattan, from the dark gray color of the building.

bloom. A sudden flash of light on television from light reflecting off objects.

blue material. Comedy-club slang for dirty jokes.

blunting. In television, competing with a show on another network by programming a *similar* show on your network, say, running a movie musical against a music special. Compare with COUNTERPROGRAMMING.

boffo. Box office hit. A term from *Variety.*

bofs. In the record business, albums that feature "the best of."

bookers. In talk radio and television the people who arrange for guests. The term is a misnomer in the case of the major television news shows, which do more than book guests but rather chase daily for the powerful and provocative.

bootleg. Record industry term for a recording that is unofficially and illegally released—such as Bob Dylan's *Great White Wonder* title.

box bible. *TV Guide.*

break. Moment at which a motion-picture distributor breaks even and starts to amass profits.

buck. In Hollywood, $100,000. William Safire may have been the first to report that when a movie mogul says "ten bucks," he is talking about a million dollars.

bucket of blood. Comedy-club slang for dives complete with hecklers and the smell of stale beer.

bumper. Prerecorded radio or television station identification with something extra—music, a jingle, or sound effects.

burnt. Term used by disc jockeys to describe a tune that has been played once too often.

business, the. Television; as contrasted with motion pictures, which are termed the INDUSTRY.

bye-bye. Broadcasting term for phrases beginning with words like "We now take you to . . ."

✳ C

cart. Radio talk for a cartridge—usually an eight-track containing the prerecorded.

chop socky movie. Karate and kung fu movies as a genre. A term from *Variety.*

clapper. Person who holds the hinged, black-and-white-striped device that is used to "slate" each movie shot.

comeallye. Folk music term for the scores of songs beginning with the words "Come all ye . . ."

confrontainment. Staple of TRASH TV in which people are pitted against one another for high ratings; blend of *confront*ation plus enter*ainment.*

contest pig. Disc jockey term for listener using a speed dialer to win giveaways.

continuity. Movie name for person in charge of making sure that all actors and crew have scripts, that there is continuity from scene to scene, and that all changes are made. Previously known as script girl.

counterprogramming. Offering different television programming in an effort to attract a different audience—for instance, programming a comedy against a news special.

cradle to grave. Television-programmer talk for a show or event that appeals to everyone from teenagers

to their grandparents. Rare, but applicable to the Olympics, NCAA basketball Final Four, and the World Series.

crash and burn. Comedy-club slang for a bad set with zero laughs.

crash TV. Quasi sports shows emphasizing sex and violence. The pioneer examples of the genre, which *Newsweek* has typified as "rough, tough, and rotten": *RollerGames* and *American Gladiators.*

crawl. The rolling of credits at the beginning and/or end of a television show.

creep. Same as CRAWL.

crossover artist/crossover star. Performer who can move from one realm to another, such as from country-and-western recording to pop music or the movies.

crushed the crowds. Comedy-club slang for made them laugh.

✳ D

dead air. Broadcast silence—the great anathema of radio.

Die Hard on a _____. Any of the many cinematic clones of the high-adventure *Die Hard* series. *Under Siege,* for example, was known in Hollywood as *Die Hard* on a ship.

dish. Ground terminal that receives satellite signals.

docudrama. Fictionalized depiction of a personality and/or event.

dolly grip. In movies the person in charge of the camera dolly, the four-wheel platform on which the camera rests.

DOR. In the music business: dance-oriented rock.

downtown set. A cheap television game-show set.

dramedy. Dramatic comedy in television—*M*A*S*H* and *All in the Family* are classics of this genre.

drive time. Radio broadcast periods during which commuters are in their cars. Compare with HOUSEWIFE TIME.

drooling. Unrehearsed conversation used to fill time in radio and television.

✳ E

ear candy. Light, syrupy music billed as "easy listening."

ECU. Hollywoodese for "extreme close-up," an image so close to the viewer's eye that it often stirs unsettling, even painful emotions.

elevator music. The same thing as EAR CANDY.

✳ F

fade. To raise or lower the volume of sound slowly.

fannies. Ardent fans of television personalities who send in nude photos of themselves.

favored nations. Agent's term for getting a stipulation in a contract that no other performer will get a better deal. An agent for a big star might say, "This contract has got to be favored nations."

flagging. The diagonal shift of the top portion of a television picture, causing the picture to bend to the right or the left.

flash and trash. Derogatory name for local news specials during ratings periods, which tend to feature especially sexy or violent topics.

flop sweat. Nervous reaction to failure or impending theatrical doom.

fluffer. In the X-rated film business the name for the woman who keeps the male talent enthused between scenes.

flyover people. Television term for the people who live in between New York and L.A., the two cities in which the vast majority of television shows are produced.

four-walling. Renting a theater for the showing of a movie. Under such an arrangement the renter pays all expenses but takes all the box-office receipts.

Freddy Krueger room from hell. Comedy-club slang for a horrible audience.

front end. Money made before or during the production of a movie, as opposed to money from profits determined later, the BACK END.

✳ G

gaffer. The chief electrician on a movie set responsible for everything that has "juice" running through it. This term and GRIP are slang that has long appeared in movie credits.

golden gater. In Hollywood, a script that is so bad that it is suicidal; akin to jumping off the Golden Gate Bridge.

gorilla. An enormous hit (movie, play, record); a blockbuster.

greenroom. Place in which actors, actresses, television-show guests, etc., wait to go on.

grip. Technician/handyman on a movie set. Hollywood's version of the Broadway stagehand.

gross player. Movie actor who is a big enough star to demand a percentage of a film's gross income for acting in it.

grunge. Rock style generally associated with alternative metal bands from the Seattle, Washington, area. It is similar in feel to hard rock but different in attitude, drawing more from punk-rock ennui than heavy-metal anger.

 H

hammer. A handyman on a movie set.

hammock. To program a weak television show between two strong ones.

hammock hit. Television show that has good numbers but only because it is hammocked between two hits.

hardcore. J. D. Considine, music critic of the *Baltimore Sun* defines it as "the purest and most de-

manding music in any pop style; that which appeals only to the most knowledgeable and devoted fans; e.g., 'Eschewing pop, he only listened to hardcore rap.' " Considine adds it is also a "hyperfast and determinedly inaccessible form of punk rock, originally referring to early-eighties punk-rock scenes in Los Angeles and Washington, D.C."

heat. In Hollywoodese it is either (1) box office power or (2) word of mouth.

hell gig. Comedy-club slang for an engagement sans crowd.

HINT. Happy idiot news team or happy idiot news talk, both inside references to the encouragement of banter and chitchat between segments of the local TV news.

hitting the post. Disc jockey term for talking over the musical introduction to a song and ending just as the lyrics begin.

hoofer. Dancer.

house. Name for a funkier, electronically advanced version of disco that came on the scene in the early 1990s.

house nut. The operating and overhead expenses of one who shows a movie. It must be paid before a profit can be posted.

housewife time. Name for the period from 10 A.M. to 3 P.M. in radio. Compare with DRIVE TIME.

HUTs and PUTs. Television-programmer talk for "homes using television" and "people using television." In a *New York Times* article of June 6, 1993, on the talk of programmers, we find this example: "There was snow all over the East, so the HUTs and PUTs were up."

* I

idiot cards. Cue cards, or sheets of cardboard on which a performer's lines are written.

if it bleeds its leads. Motto of local television news—especially during SWEEPS.

industry, the. The motion-picture business; Hollywood. Compare with the BUSINESS.

indy. Independent, in show business, whether it be an independent television station or moviemaker.

indyprod. Hollywoodese for "independent producer."

in the can. A movie that has been shot but is still not ready for distribution.

* J

Jacuzzi jazz. Derogatory term used by musicians to describe the commercial, pop jazz of artists like Kenny G.

* K

key grip. The head of the grip department, which on a motion-picture set is in charge of setting camera equipment and devices that control shadows—all the equipment that does not have a plug (things with plugs are controlled by the GAFFER).

kidvid. Television or home video for children.

* L

lavalier. (1) A small microphone used in television that fits around the person's neck or can be clipped to the person's lapel or dress. (2) To attach a microphone: "Lavalier the lady for the cooking demo."

legs. Strength and longevity at the box office.

letterboxed. Videotaped movie with dark bands to preserve the film's wide-screen proportions.

liner. A broadcasting term for the statement that identifies a station, its place on the dial, and its format. "You're listening to 101.7 WKIX, Middletown, the best in contemporary country."

linguine in clam sauce. Hitting a bad note in jazz, according to an article in *USA Today,* June 19, 1992, on a New York jazz festival.

loop. The central rhythmic phrase on a rap recording.

lunar rotation. Disc jockey term for a record that is played infrequently, as in "once in a blue moon."

* M

maggot. Call-in radio host/producer name for a caller who is always on the line with a boring or repeat message.

major. One of the top distributors of

movies (Universal, Columbia, Paramount, etc.).

market. Broadcasters way of saying where you are from or are currently working. "He is a credit to this market" are the words of a radio producer talking about an on-air personality.

megadoc. Big multipart documentary, such as Ken Burns's *Civil War* and *Baseball.*

mersh. Recording industry slang for commercial. The *Boston Globe* for August 15, 1991: "Well, here it is, finally. On their long-awaited fifth album Metallica, reigning kings of smart thrash metal, goes mersh—that's industry slang for commercial."

mike sock. Foam rubber sleeve that fits over the business end of a microphone. It helps cut down on the extraneous sounds created by wind, heavy breathing, and the like.

mix. To combine sound from different sources.

MOR. Middle of the road. That which appeals to middle-class, middle-aged Americans; light rock, for instance.

mosh. Dance favored by THRASH fans, who hurtle against one another while flailing arms and bobbing in time; usually includes stage diving, in which audience members leap onto the crowd from the stage, and crowd surfing, where the stage diver is passed over the heads of moshers in apparent gratitude for not having killed anyone.

mosh pit. Area of crowd in which moshing takes place.

nix. To refuse, ban, overrule. A term from *Variety.*

nonpro. Person outside the movie industry.

no quote. In the film industry this term is used to describe an artist willing to work below his or her normal fee (quote).

nostril shot. Unflattering camera angle on television.

numbers. Receipts in Hollywood. A movie that is grossing a lot is said to have "good numbers."

O&O. A station that is owned and operated by the network, as opposed to an affiliate.

oater. Movie western, from the oats that horses eat. A vintage term from *Variety* that still comes into play when someone plans to film a western.

open mike. Entertainment in which people perform without auditions or other qualifications. Comedy clubs and places featuring acoustic music often have open-mike nights.

out of the box. Disc jockeyese for playing a new recording the day it is released.

overnights. The overnight ratings in television.

pasadena. A pass in many show business realms. For example, a person being rejected for a television game show will be labeled "pasadena," which is a play on the word *pass*.

payola. A term from *Variety* for an illegal cash payoff made to get airtime for a record.

people meter. Device for registering in-home response to television.

Pepsi skating. Movie-theater-staff term for people moving across soft-drink-covered floor.

personality. One who plays himself on radio or television. A man who does a music and talk show for commuters on their way to work is known as a morning personality.

phoner. (1) Radio talk-show interview conducted by telephone. (2) A false—or phony—plot device, whether it be in Hollywood or on Broadway.

picnickers. Movie-theater-staff name for people who bring their own snacks to the theater.

piggybacking. Video retailing term for the special displays and packaging linking other products to just-released videos. The hit movie *Dances With Wolves* was first sold at McDonald's for example.

plugola. Noncash gifts given to radio disc jockeys for playing songs. A free trip to Hollywood or Vegas is a common bit of plugola. It is distinguished from PAYOLA, which is a monetary gift.

points. Percentage of ownership in a movie or play.

PPV window. In video retailing the guaranteed period when video has exclusive rights to a film before it can be shown on pay-per-view and cable TV.

prequel. Movie slang for film whose story line comes before rather than after that of a hit—the opposite of a sequel. Or, as one wag put it, "If we'd known the first picture was going to gross $289 million, we wouldn't have killed off the stars."

PSA. Public service announcement on radio and television.

✳ Q

Q. Recognition. It comes from TV-Q, a system that rates actors by their recognition by television viewers. One gets more money if one has a high Q.

quote. In Hollywood, the amount of money that an actor made on their last contract, as in, "What was Whoopie's quote?" See also NO QUOTE.

✳ R

rave. All-night dance party featuring oddly dressed, energetically undulating ravers, brutally loud techno music, and hypnotic lighting.

riggers and juicers. Crew of electrical assistants who work on a movie set to set up and control lights.

rim shot. Comic punctuation from a drummer, it comes immediately after the punch line of a joke.

riot grrrls. J. D. Considine, music critic of the *Baltimore Sun*, wrote that this is a "postfeminist pop movement drawing from bands like Bikini Kill and Babes in Toyland, focusing on aggressive feminine pride and flouting of sexual stereotypes; generally easier to find in newspaper or magazine trend stories than in nightclubs or concert halls.

rip and grin. Describing the usher who takes tickets at movie theaters.

roboanchor. Inside the business term for a TV anchor who reads but does not understand the news.

rockumentary. Documentary film about rock 'n' roll or rock musicians.

running W. Trip wire used to make horses fall at critical moments in the making of a motion picture. The cruel device—responsible for the death of many animals—has been outlawed.

 S

satellite hit. Television-programmer talk for a show that is secondary to a big hit or BIG PLANET.

scrambler. Device used to keep cable-television subscribers from getting pay stations and events without paying for them. A decoder is required to unscramble a scrambler.

scrim. (1) To soften the intensity of a light. (2) A screen or curtain used to create the effect of mistiness onstage or on the screen.

second unit work. Film work that involves no principal actors—such as shooting exteriors of buildings.

segue. (1) To move from one thing to another. (2) Transition, as in, "That was a nice segue." Pronounced *segway,* the word is Spanish.

shark club. Club that charges young musicians and groups to play. For instance, a shark club may require a group to buy one hundred tickets to their own performance.

shock jock. Radio disc jockey whose specialty is off-color material and general irreverence and rudeness.

sitcom. Situation comedy. A term from *Variety.*

ska. A precursor to reggae; essentially it's a faster version of the same sound.

skitcom. Skit-based comedy show.

slasher movie. As defined by film critic Roger Ebert: "Movies starring a mad-dog killer who runs amok, slashing all of the other characters."

sleaze TV. Talk shows featuring sex, gore, and sensationalism. The same thing as trash TV.

slot. Time period in television programming.

slugline. The slogan line that goes along with motion picture advertising.

SNL. *Saturday Night Live* for short.

soca. *Soca* is short for a blending of *so*ul plus *ca*lypso in the music business.

sound bite. A quotation recorded on location that is used in a later radio or television newscast as part of a larger report.

special. Anything not in the normal television schedule of programs. Television commonly puts its mistakes and visual typos into prime-time "bloopers" packages and calls them specials.

SPEDs. Stupid, pretentious English directors.

splatter movie. One with a lot of blood and gore.

spot. Prerecorded broadcast announcement.

staffer. Radio or television staff announcer.

stepping on it. Term used by disc jockeys to describe the gaff that occurs when their introduction to a song runs into the first words of the lyrics.

street date. A video industry term for the day designated by studios and distributors on which stores can begin to rent a title.

stretch. An actor reading or working hard to fit into a part, as opposed to a natural fit. This term has become part of a common talk-show question: "Was that a stretch for you or did it come easy?"

stunting. Television tricks used to hook an audience at the beginning of the year or during a rating period. The tricks include special two-hour episodes, guest appearances, and tie-ins with other shows.

superstation. A local television station that has been distributed to cable systems nationwide via satellite.

sweeps. Periods during the year when the nation's fifteen hundred local television stations are rated for audience share. TV news often uses its sleaziest and most salacious items for sweeps weeks or sweeps months.

* T

talent. Performer, as in, "Do we need limos for the talent?"

tejano. (music) Literally, "Texan." The Spanish word is believed to be derived from an Indian word for allies or friends—now used to refer to a movement of young Texans of Mexican descent, typically bringing modern pop instrumentation and presentation to a mixture of traditional tunes and new songs sung in Spanish.

tent pole. Television-programmer talk for a show, usually a comedy, that stands in the middle of the prime-time lineup—usually at 9:00 EST—that holds up everything around it. *Cheers* was the classic tent-pole show.

Tex-Mex. (music) The music played for social dancing along the Texas-Mexico border. The accordion-led music sounds like a cross between the polka, brought to Texas by Eastern European settlers, and mariachi and other Mexican musics.

30 Rock. Headquarters of the National Broadcasting Company, which is at 30 Rockefeller Plaza.

thrash. J. D. Considine, music critic of the *Baltimore Sun,* wrote that this is a form of heavy-metal rock favoring jackhammer instrumental lines and brutally fast tempos, with lyrics generally devoted to death, doom, and destruction; bands include Metallica, Megadeth, Anthrax, Nuclear Assault, Biohazard.

thrashcore. Thrash with hardcore punk, making the music more politically informed but less listenable than regular thrash.

three-sheet. Bragging; excessive promotion in show business from the old 41-by-81-inch movie posters. The most common-size movie poster—originally 28 by 42 inches, now 27 by 41 inches—is a one-sheet.

toilet. A second-rate or small-time nightclub or comedy club, in the parlance of stand-up comics.

topline. To get top billing in a play or movie.

topspin. Momentum in Hollywood.

traction. Television-programmer talk for a show that attracts the same faithful viewers week after week.

trades, the. The magazines and newspapers that serve the entertainment industry.

trash TV. Talk shows featuring sex, gore, and sensationalism. The same as sleaze TV.

turnaround. In Hollywood, the dropping of a project by one studio thereby making it available to another.

tweeny. Brief element of dialogue between the sex scenes in a porno film.

 U

up-front exposure. Money put up to get a film started, regardless of whether it is actually made.

uptown set. Glitzy television game show set with lots of lights and good carpeting.

 V

V-chip. An electronic lock that prevents young eyes from viewing sex and violence on their television screen.

VOC. Television talk for "voice over credits."

voice-over or VO. Describing a commercial or other television item on which the voice of an announcer is heard but the person is not seen.

 W

wackies. Term coined by David Letterman's staff for skits that employ elaborate props and sight gags, like a volcano spewing creamed corn.

weeper. Sad movie.

weight. Clout that an agent or artist has in Hollywood, as opposed to HEAT, which is a star's clout at the box office.

went up in flames. Comedy-club slang for really bombed.

wide/wide break. Exposure for a movie. A film that opens "wide" is likely to debut on close to two thousand screens.

wipe. (1) To bring one scene in on top of another on film or television. (2) To fire a person.

wrangler. In Hollywood, a person

Say What?
Sein and Dave

TV has brought us lingoes within lingoes—for example Trekkie talk from *Star Trek* (including Klingon)—which create their own lexicons. Here are a few examples from two of the most popular shows of the 1990s: the *Late Show with David Letterman* and *Seinfeld*.

Double Crunch. (Sein) Cereal Jerry consumes in vast quantities. Fictional.

double dipping. (Sein) Sticking a chip back in the dip for a second time. George did this at a funeral.

home base. (Dave-ism) Dave's desk.

my boys. (Sein) Jerry's name for his genitals; George's name for his sperm.

nostril penetration. (Sein) The criteria for determining a true nose picker.

on the bus. (Dave-ism) Describing guests who get bumped when the show goes on too long.

snappies. (Dave-ism) One-liners.

who is in charge of animals that will appear in a film.

* Y

yawner. Boring show. A term from *Variety.*

* Z

zit-com. Comedy for the young.

SOURCES

The Tamony Collection provided special help in preparing this collection, as did several columns by William Safire that originally appeared in the *New York Times*. The late Charles D. Poe made major contributions.

A number of articles were of special use, including "A Lesson in Radio Lingo" in the *Christian Science Monitor* for April 20, 1993, and "HUTs, PUTs and Traction: Television-Programmer Talk" in the *New York Times* for June 6, 1993. A number of *Newsweek* "Buzzword" columns were used in preparing this chapter, including the ones for November 13, 1989 (agents), May 7, 1990 (TV news), August 27, 1990 (talk radio), and June 28, 1993 (Letterman slang). The first and best "Sein" lexicon appeared in the April 9, 1993, *Entertainment Weekly*. The writing of J. D. Considine, music critic of the *Baltimore Sun,* was a valuable assist on pop music terminology.

——— * 21 * ———

POLITICAL SLANG—
CONGRESSIONAL VERSION

The Lingo of the Hill People

Most of what is said in Congress sounds like a foreign language and requires an interpreter. . . . Congress becomes so entangled in vocabulary
that people often have to work past midnight to figure out what they're
doing.
—Susan Trausch, writing in the *Washington
Post,* March 16, 1986

What language do they speak around here?
—*A Congressional Intern Handbook*
by Sue Grabowski

W ashington, D.C., is a city of odd slangs, dialects, and jargons (bureaucratese, Pentagonese, legalese, diplomatese, etc.). At this lati-
tude and longitude *Fort Fumble* is the Pentagon, the *sound of
the city* is a reference to paper shuffling, *reprogramming* is moving money
from one place to another, and getting *riffed* is short for "reduction in
force" and is the same thing as losing your job. It is peopled, among others, with *insiders, Beltway bandits, GS-11s, influence peddlers, superlaw-
yers, LAs, death-squad Democrats,* and *supply-siders.*

One also has to keep one's bearings. *The other end of Pennsylvania
Avenue* means something different depending on where one stands—or
sits—and if you are in the Pentagon, *across the river* is a reference to the
White House or Congress, but if you are on north side, the same term alludes to the Pentagon.

Of all of these discernible jargons, the most fascinating may be that
time-honored tongue spoken on Capitol Hill. Some of the words, names,
and phrases peculiar to Congress are as old or older than the republic,
while others are as recent as coinages of the 105th Congress and the en-
actment of the 1997 Tax Reform Act. What they all have in common is
that they are actually used in the day-to-day working of the national legislature.

∗ A

AA. Administrative assistant. The top staff aide in a congressional office. Few people on the Hill actually ever call someone by their full title, tending to refer to Congressman Smith's AA or the senator's LA.

affair. Fund-raising event. Congressional affairs range from bull roasts to fancy dinners, and the cost of admission can range from $10 to $1,000.

ahead of the curve. This is where astute players and politicians would like to be—in the position of anticipating problems before they surface. In what Hedrick Smith in *The Power Game* called "one of Washington's most telltale phrases," Reagan budget director David Stockman sought to be "ahead of the power curve."

are they in/are they out? Questions asked to determine if Congress has reconvened (in session) or adjourned (out of session).

Atari Democrat. Those who foresee a bright future in high technology and electronics. The term was coined by Elizabeth Drew of the *New Yorker,* who alluded to the electronic game and computer company. It lost some of its appeal in 1983 when Atari cut its U.S. workforce and moved those jobs to Taiwan.

attack dog. Term that came into prominence during the Clarence Thomas Supreme Court nomination hearings, meaning a senator on the Judiciary Committee who attacked the credibility of University of Oklahoma law professor Anita Hill, Thomas's accuser. The *Washington Post* reported (December 18, 1991) that New York governor Mario Cuomo had branded Sen. Alfonse D'Amato (R-N.Y.) an "attack dog" and refused to apologize.

∗ B

back flip. A change in position, often sudden. A vote switch.

back-loading/front-loading. Delaying tax cuts—and therefore revenue losses—until the future, or letting them take place quickly. Former Office of Management and Budget director David Stockman used this lingo in describing the debate over when to put the Reagan tax cuts into effect. Congress, he said in his book, *The Triumph of Politics,* phased in revenue losses, thereby back-loading them "into the foggy future two or three elections down the road."

beauty contest. A nonbinding primary election; a vote that does nothing more than measure popularity. For instance, the Vermont presidential primary is a beauty contest.

bells and whistles. Puff and hyperbole of the type that is sometimes employed by an agency to "sell" a program on the Hill. A common characteristic of a bells-and-whistles program is that it offers "something for everyone."

big casino. The center ring, grand

prize. Ronald Reagan in 1974 referred to the presidential election as "the big casino," according to William Safire in *Safire's Political Dictionary*.

big ticket. High-priced item in an appropriations bill, often military hardware such as the B-2 Stealth bomber, costing $860 million apiece.

blue smoke and mirrors. Verbal sleight of hand used to sell a program to Congress or a candidate to the public. Independent presidential candidate John Anderson quipped that Ronald Reagan's economic policies would need "blue smoke and mirrors" to work. Journalists Jack Germond and Jules Witcover used the phrase as title for their book on the 1980 presidential election.

body slam. A devastating political comment. Vice presidential candidate Lloyd Bentsen's "Senator, you're no Jack Kennedy," during his debate with then-senator Dan Quayle, still holds the body slam prize.

bogeys. Spending targets given to the armed services by the secretary of defense.

boll weevil. Nickname for conservative Southern Democrats—pests who keep the pressure on the Democratic membership.

bombthrower. Anyone who will not compromise.

bork. To block the confirmation of a Supreme Court nominee. This eponymous verb comes from Robert Bork, who was nominated to the Supreme Court in 1987 by President Reagan but was rejected by the Senate by a vote of 58–42.

bread-and-butter liberal. One who believes in the basics of jobs, housing, education, and health care.

bringing home the bacon. Obtaining federal projects or dollars for one's state or district.

bubba factor. The potential impact of Southern conservatives in an election, those plainspoken, rural folks who won't abide city ways and have little tolerance for social programs or liberal candidates.

bulldog. Like the animal breed, a politician known for his or her stubborn, unrelenting grip or stance.

bundling. The practice of a PAC (or political action committee) giving an elected representative a bundle of smaller checks as opposed to one large one.

bunk. (1) Meaningless oratory designed to impress one's constituency. (2) Politics viewed with a cynical eye.

 C

casework. Dealing with the problems of constituents. It is a constant in the workings of a congressional office and commands a major portion of staff time.

caseworker. Staff member whose prime responsibility is constituent problems.

caucus. (1) A meeting of party

members in either house to elect leaders and set the legislative agenda. (2) Any informal gathering of lawmakers working on a legislative action. (3) A group that meets regularly to monitor and advance the interests of a specific group.

Christmas express. The surge of congressional junkets just after Congress adjourns and just before Christmas.

Christmas-tree bill. A bill that has been adorned with extra, often unrelated, pieces of legislation. Can also be used as a verb, as it is in this quote from Alan Otten writing in the *Wall Street Journal:* "On Capitol Hill, the practice of tagging a host of special-interest amendments to a popular bill is known as 'Christmas-treeing' that bill."

clean bill. A new version of a bill, replete with a new number, prepared after a committee has reworked the original. It allows the bill to move on its own rather than having each revision voted on individually.

clinker. An amendment or rider to a bill that is so out of place that it stands out like a misplaced musical note. From the Dutch *klincard,* a vitrified brick that clinks when struck. President Nixon in November 1973 complained about "a couple of clinkers" in the Alaska pipeline bill with which business groups were unhappy.

cloakroom. A large room just off the floor of either chamber.

closure. The same as CLOTURE.

cloture. Process by which debate can be limited in the Senate without unanimous consent. When invoked by roll call vote, it limits each senator to one hour of debate.

coattail. The ability of a presidential candidate to help win seats in Congress for members of his party.

dark side of the moon. The House of Representatives in contemporary Hill slang.

Dear Colleague. Traditional salutation used in letters in which one member asks another for support or cosponsorship of a bill. Defined deftly in Sue Grabowski's *Congressional Intern Handbook* as a "hustle" in the form of a letter.

death-squad Democrat. Late-eighties label for Democrats who support right-wing leaders in Latin America, such as those who support aid to El Salvador.

demagogue it. To take a dramatic, grandstanding position on an issue without necessarily supporting or believing in the position; to mislead with spirit.

Dirty Dozen. List of members with the worst environmental records.

dirty laundry. That which is sometimes aired at confirmation hearings.

dirty tricks. Political shenanigans employed by one party or candidate against another.

district work period. Congressional recess.

doorkeeper. Person who has various duties ranging from announcing the president's arrival in Congress to the control of gallery passes.

dove. Legislator who is specifically against military intervention by the United States and generally against increased military spending of any kind. Their opposite number is the hawk, and a well-known congressional watering hole is the Hawk & Dove.

duck. A pest or nuisance, such as a lobbyist.

* E

Eagles. Centrist/Wall Street Republican contributors.

elevator phenomenon. The predictable inflating of senators' and representatives' egos when they realize that they have, among other perquisites, private elevators at their disposal. Noted by Mark Green and Michael Waldman in *Who Runs Congress*, 1984.

Everest committee. Any congressional team organized to investigate something just because, like Mount Everest, it's there. "I hear tell," Will Rogers once wrote, "Congress is a mite concerned with its members' tendency to form a committee at the drop of a hat. But everything's all right now. Congress has just announced it's forming a committee to investigate."

executive session. A meeting closed to the public and the press.

* F

fat cat. A big giver.

filibuster. To delay or stop action on a bill in the Senate through constant talking. It is a time-honored technique that is almost always employed by a minority to try to defeat a measure favored by the majority.

floor. The working area of the Senate or House chamber.

freshman. A newly elected member serving his first term. In the House, freshmen regard themselves as a class, as in the freshman class of the 105th Congress, and elect class officers.

* G

gag rule. Any special rule that limits the debate on a bill.

-gate. The common congressional suffix for scandals since Watergate, as in Koreagate and Irangate. The original scandal was named for the Watergate apartment complex where the incident that first announced the problem took place. Also popular is the *-scam* suffix, as found in ABSCAM, Contrascam, and Debatescam. The original name was the FBI code name for its foray into the realm of congressional ethics. ABSCAM stood for *Ara*b *scam,* a reference to the front group for the operation, the bogus Abdul Enterprises.

gavel-to-gavel. The period from the

moment either house convenes until the moment it adjourns.

gerrymander. To design or redesign a congressional district to unfairly favor the party in power by taking advantage of traditional voting patterns.

ghost senator. Sometimes slang for a strong administrative assistant.

ghost speech. A speech that is never delivered but appears in the *Congressional Record* or the printed record of a committee.

goat. Derogatory slang for a constituent.

goat food. Shameless political posturing.

goo-goos. Forces of and for *good government*. The League of Women Voters is a perennial source of goo-gooism. Although the term sounds intensely defamatory, it is often used with some affection.

grassroots. The folks back home; people who are not in the business of politics.

gray ghost. A senator's or representative's chief staffer.

Greenies. Environmentalists. Derived from West Germany's environmental Green political party and the international Greenpeace movement.

Gucci Gulch. Polished marble hallway outside House Ways and Means Committee room in the Longworth House Office Building where well-tailored lobbyists who specialize in engineering tax breaks and loopholes for their clients gather, especially while committee members are meeting in secret to deal with tax reform matters.

gypsy moth. Republican moderate. According to William Safire in his *New York Times* magazine column on language, the term was created by Rep. Lawrence DeNardis (R-Conn.), who said that the gypsy moth was as much of a nuisance in New England and the Great Lakes as the BOLL WEEVIL is down South.

✳ H

hawk. One who tends to favor military intervention and increased military appropriations. Compare with DOVE.

head count. The supposed lineup of votes for a bill, amendment, or confirmation.

heavy hitter. A congressman or lobbyist who swings a big bat, a powerful individual.

Hill, the. (1) Congress. (2) The neighborhood surrounding the U.S. Congress.

hit list. A group that has been targeted for removal whether they be members of Congress or federal employees. The group may be legislators whom the White House would like to see defeated in the next election or a group of government officials the administration would like to get rid of.

hopper. The box on the House clerk's desk where bills are placed on introduction. In the Senate, bills are introduced by verbal announcement.

horse and jockey. A common truism in politics is that one cannot be both candidate and campaign manager.

horse trading. Swapping political favors.

hot air. Inflated, insincere speech.

hot-button. Describing that which is value-intense and controversial.

hustings. Where election speeches are made.

 I

idiot sheets. Questions to be asked of witnesses, prepared for not-always-knowledgeable lawmakers by their staffs.

influence peddler. Lawyer, lobbyist, or anyone else who seeks special privileges from Congress for his clients. The term, which entered American political slang in the early 1950s, is reserved for those who are paid for their skills.

 J

junket. Derogatory term for an expenses-paid trip made by a member of Congress. A trip is a junket if paid for by public funds or by a special-interest group.

 K

kicker. A hidden, unsuspected section of a bill.

 L

LA. Legislative assistant, the person in a congressional office who is in charge of legislation.

lame duck. (1) Name for an incumbent member who has lost an election but whose term has still not run out. (2) Adjective applied to Congress after the November elections and before the convening of a new Congress in January.

lawyer's bill. Any bill that, if enacted, would create a lot of confusion and litigation.

leadership, the. How Congress refers to its officers and ranking committee members.

leaning. Status of a legislator who is still uncommitted on a major upcoming vote but tending—or leaning—toward one side.

leg counsel. Short for legislative counsel.

limousine liberal. A wealthy political liberal.

logrolling. Horse-trading votes to get important, or pet, bills passed.

love fest. Label slapped on any overt display of bipartisan cooperation.

 M

mangy dog. Description of legislation that has more flaws than a dog has fleas.

McGovern Democrat. Term that has

come to mean a liberal whose beliefs are so far to the left that the person is out of the mainstream of American politics. It is a reference to Sen. George McGovern and his 1972 candidacy, in which he strongly opposed U.S. policy in Southeast Asia.

meat ax. Popular—and graphic—congressional metaphor for across-the-board budget cutting; it is often used in the context of the Gramm-Rudman-Hollins budget-reduction act, which can bring the meat ax down evenly on domestic and defense expenditures. The opposite of meat-ax cuts would be selective or "scalpel" cutting.

MEGO. My eyes glaze over; bored. Common Washington response that has become a fond bit of Hill shorthand.

must list. Legislation that must be passed during a session. For example, the Senate majority leader might have two items on his must list at a given moment.

Newtspeak. Direct way of speaking used by Speaker Newt Gingrich.

nonpaper. A briefing paper that is circulated around the Hill but does not carry the author's name.

oilies. Nickname for oil industry lobbyists.

old guard. Originally applied to the conservative element in the Republican Party, it is now used for any long-established group—for instance, old-guard Southern Democrats.

omnibus bill. Any piece of proposed legislation that deals with a variety of subjects.

one-minute. A speech lasting no more than sixty seconds, which a member of the House can make on any topic before the official start of business.

orange pouch. Marked mail sack for expedited delivery to member's home district or state. Also known as a gold bag.

other end of Pennsylvania Avenue, the. One of the ways that Congress refers to the White House, and vice versa.

over on the floor. Reference to the chambers where the two houses meet.

PAC. Political action committee.

pigeonhole. To kill a bill by keeping it in committee and not reporting it to the larger body. The term comes from the cubicles—or pigeonholes—in the old congressional desks.

platform. The principles that a political party stands for during an election.

player. One who operates effectively in Congress.

SAY WHAT?

Newtspeak for Neophytes

Newt Gingrich has created his own method of verbal attack based on a partisan choice of words. In 1990, a GOP committee called GOPAC distributed a brochure filled with choice Gingrich buzzwords for describing one's campaign and that of one's opponents.

YOU:	YOUR RIVAL:
pristine	sick
tough	pathetic
pioneer	traitor
workfare	welfare
crusade	crisis
common sense	ideological
hard work	cheat, steal
confident	insecure
unique	bizarre
moral	permissive
pro-(issue)	anti-(issue)
activist	radical

point man. Member who is moving a piece of legislation through Congress.

porcupine power. The prickly power of blocking and obstructing.

pork. Funds from the PORK BARREL.

pork barrel. Nickname for the federal treasury, into which legislators "dip" to finance projects for their home districts. The lining up of locally popular projects, such as special highway extensions, is known as pork barrel politics.

pork panic. Term applied to quick legislative activity that ensues when pork is threatened.

postcard pressure. Collective impact of constituent mail, with special reference to the printed postcards that are often in the arsenal of special interest groups.

posture. (1) To make an obvious bid for attention on an issue without really doing anything. For instance, to make an abstract attack on government corruption. (2) Military preparedness.

public trough. The federal money supply—from which consultants, corporations, and other members' constituents feed greedily.

pump priming. Using federal funds to stimulate the economy, whether it be the national economy or a local one.

* R

railroad. To push or jam a bill through Congress.

rainmaker. (1) Anyone with an ability to get things done legislatively. (2) A lobbyist capable of causing big dollars to flow into campaign chests and other important matters.

revenue enhancement. Hill talk for taxes when one does not want to mention taxes. Another euphemism cropped up in 1982 when a tax increase was proposed and was described as "updating the revenue mechanism." Still another: "closing loopholes."

rich man's club. The Senate, at times.

robo. (1) A form letter members use to answer some of their constituent mail. These letters are generated by a robotype machine, which also provides a facsimile signature. (2) The robotype machine itself.

root canal politics. The politics of pain, of austerity budgets and deep program cuts.

Rosemary's baby. Any monstrous piece of legislation. The name was given, for instance, to the monster 1989 budget and the unwieldly 1,376-page budget-reduction act by disgruntled legislators. The nickname comes from the book by Ira Levin and the subsequent Roman Polanski movie in which a woman unknowingly bears the devil's baby.

* S

safe seat. Incumbency that attracts no more than token opposition.

safety net. Level of established financial support for individuals through Social Security, Medicare, welfare programs, and Veteran's Assistance.

sagebrush rebels. Informal but cohesive band of Western legislators whose major concern since the late 1960s has been local control over the millions of acres of federal land that lie west of the Rockies.

seatwarmer. A senator or representative who has been appointed by a governor to fill a vacancy, with the understanding that he or she will *not* run in the next election.

showhorse. Member who is known for the ability to garner attention and publicity; a showboat.

six-pack Republican. (Sometimes known as Joe Six-Pack Republican.) Populist GOP member or candidate.

slash and burn. Tactics used without consideration of the possible harm to others.

sleaze factor. That component of an administration, political party, etc., that is corrupt, unethical, controversial, scandal-ridden, or otherwise under a cloud.

slippery slope. What nominees find themselves on when a committee finds, and perhaps leaks, damaging information and support begins to erode.

slop-over. Term that has been used

pejoratively to describe the items found in the back of the *Congressional Record.*

slush fund. Any covert, suspect, or otherwise tainted source of campaign money.

smoking gun. Metaphor used at either end of Pennsylvania Avenue for unequivocal guilt, as if one has walked in on a man with a smoking gun in his hand standing over a bullet-ridden body. Just before the Senate report on the Iran-contra affair was released in 1987, Sen. David Boren (D-Okla.) was quoted as saying, "There's no smoking gun."

softball. An easy question, which an experienced politician can easily hit out of the ballpark.

spin doctors. The practitioners of "spin control," which is applied at either end of Pennsylvania Avenue and is endemic during election campaigns.

According to the *Economist,* the term was coined in the Reagan White House during his first term and became important after the first 1984 Reagan-Mondale presidential debate in Louisville. By the time of the 1988 Bush-Dukakis debate at Wake Forest University, so many "spinners" were working for each candidate that the *Washington Post* declared a postdebate state of "spinlock."

squish. Nickname for an uncommitted conservative.

stem-winder. A speech that commands attention; a genuine, old-fashioned oration that galvanizes a crowd.

sticker shock. Term borrowed from the auto showroom that has been facetiously used on Capitol Hill to describe the reaction to the unit cost of new weapons.

stump. To travel around giving political speeches. It derives from the speech from the stump of a tree, one given on the road, usually in a small town.

* T

tap dance. Briefing or testimony that is slick and pleasant but says little.

three I's. Three countries with large natural constituencies among the American population: Ireland, Israel, and Italy.

tie the president's hands. Words commonly summoned when a legislator decides not to challenge the administration, as in, "I won't tie the president's hands on this one." It is most commonly invoked during foreign policy debates.

towered. Drunk. This term showed up in the weeks following the rejection of John Tower as defense secretary, as in, "Let's go out and get towered."

tree huggers. Environmentalists who come to Congress to lobby for their cause.

* U

up or down. Yes or no; not a test vote, not a substitute or amendment, but the real thing.

* W

war chest. Campaign kitty; funds held in reserve by an incumbent to fend off future challengers.

whip. (1) Member of each party in each house who is charged with rallying the party to pass or defeat a piece of legislation. The position amounts to that of assistant party leader. (2) To act as a whip, such as "whipping the Ohio delegation."

winger. A person of the far right or left.

workhorse. Member known for effectiveness and getting the job done; compare with SHOWHORSE, for one who is adept at getting publicity and putting on a good show.

working the crowd. Currying political goodwill at a gathering. For instance, a politician worthy of the title will work the crowd at a county fair, funeral, or Memorial Day parade.

world's greatest deliberative body, the. Description sometimes applied to the U.S. Senate.

* Y

yellow dog Democrat. A Southern expression for a Democrat who will vote for whoever the party's candidate is, even a yellow dog.

SOURCES

A number of sources contributed to this glossary including years of reading about Congress in the *Washington Post,* the *Congressional Record,* and *Roll Call.* The author also relied on research conducted with Paul Clancy for their book *The Congress Dictionary* (Wiley, 1995).

22

REAL ESTATE

Vocabulary to Go With a CNTRY KIT, FDR, 3BR, 2BA, W/DD, ALRM, C/V, GRDN & RFDK, for $495,000

I n his novel *Independence Day*, Richard Ford makes poetry out of real estate terminology doting on descriptors like "three-bedroom, two-bath, expandable, no fplc."

It does have its own melody, tuned to and fueled by contracts, liens, easements, and the like—legal paperwork. This guarantees that much real estate jargon sounds identical to legal jargon. On the other hand, there is the fancy-smancy real estate sales talk that turns a covered parking space into a *porte cochere,* a covered patio into a *lanai,* and can turn any corner with a sink and a stove into a *kitchenette.*

This slang glossary can help in bridging the communication gap, but if you are in the market for a home, it is more important to know the particular brand of *adspeak* used to sell houses, which tends to be highly euphemistic.

Somewhere in between legalese and the bloated language of the sales brochure lies real estate slang. It sounds like this:

✳ A

accordion ARM. Adjustable rate mortgage (ARM) in which the length of the loan expands when rates go up and compresses when rates go down.

alligator. Investment property whose income does not cover insurance, mortgage, and taxes. The presumption here is that an alligator "eats" capital.

anchor. Major element around which a shopping center or mall is built. Depending on the size of the development, an anchor might be one or more major department stores, a supermarket, or a large discount store.

ARM. Adjustable rate mortgage. These mortgages have interest rates that change every year. The rate is usually tied to one-year Treasury bills. The loan usually starts with a low interest rate, then it increases annually between one and two points. The loan usually can't rise more than two points a year

✳ B

balloon. A final payment on a loan or mortgage that calls for an unusually large amount of money. It is one that has ballooned at the end.

banana council. British do-nothing housing council. *Banana* is an acronym for "building absolutely nothing anywhere near anyone."

Bart Simpson house. House with a castlelike architecture, complete with turrets. So called because they look like the cartoon character's hairstyle.

binder. Payment that keeps a property from being sold for a specified time.

birdbath. Paved area that holds water (even though it was not meant to).

biz 'burbs. Former bedroom communities that have been transformed into job centers through massive commercial development. Once suburbs, they are now industrialized and are also referred to as edge cities.

boilerplate. Time-tested language in deeds, leases, and other agreements.

bottom feeder/bottom fisher. One who tries to purchase a home for the lowest possible price in a weak market. Defined in a *Washington Post* real estate article of early 1991: "The bottom fishers are out in force in the Washington area these days, hoping to snare the weak or financially faltering home seller or builder by offering a rock-bottom price and the chance to get out from under a crippling financial obligation."

bridge loan. One that lets the borrower settle on a new home before the old house is sold.

'burbs. Suburbs.

buydown/buydown mortgage. Arrangement under which a buyer is allowed discounted, below-market interest rates for the first few years of a long-term, fixed-rate mortgage.

buyer from the East. West Coast term for naive purchaser; what car salespeople call a barefoot pilgrim.

buyer's broker. Person hired by the buyer to represent his or her interests and negotiate for the buyer in a real estate transaction.

✳ C

CAC. Real estate ad abbreviation for *central air-conditioning*.

CACH. Central air/central heat.

carriage house. A single-family house plan with a second unit on the garage.

catslide. Term used in parts of the South for a house style called saltbox colonial or saltbox in the rest of the country.

CC&Rs. Covenants, conditions, and restrictions—the limitations placed on deeds.

charming. (adspeak) Old.

charm of yesteryear. (adspeak) Lead pipes, no air conditioner, frayed wiring, no insulation, etc.

chef's kitchen. The trendy way to describe a kitchen that may offer little more than a gas range.

choke point. Point at which mortgage interest rates prompt strong resistance by potential home buyers. The choke point for most consumers is about 13 percent.

clear title. Ownership without an encumbrance.

close to nature. (adspeak) Squirrels in the attic.

cloud. An outstanding encumbrance, such as an unpaid tax lien. It comes from the concept of something that has a cloud over it.

combo condo. A building that has a combination of condominium units and town houses.

condo. Condominium.

convenient to everything. (adspeak) Next to the interstate and abutting train tracks.

country living. (adspeak) In the middle of nowhere.

cozy. Small.

cramdown. The reduction of mortgage debt by a judge in a bankruptcy proceeding.

crank. Refinancing an existing mortgage obligation.

creative financing. Nonconventional loan.

curb appeal. Describing a property that because of such things as fresh paint and a manicured lawn appeals to potential buyers who are still in a car.

 D

DG. Realtors' sly way of saying that a house is not a good one: a dog.

dirt value. The value of a property if the existing house is torn down to make way for a new and larger one.

DLR. Double living room.

dockominium. A marina that is run like a condominium, with each member owning his or her own slip.

dog. Inferior or unsellable house to Realtors and lenders.

dollhouse. (adspeak) Cramped.

downstroke. Seed money for an investment.

 E

earnest money. Cash used to bind a sale.

ego pricing. (1) Extravagant price set by seller that seems to be tied to self-esteem. (2) A seller's demanding too high a price for a property because of the value he or she places on improvements and decor.

empty-nesters. Couples with grown children who no longer live at home.

∗ F

Fannie Mae. Federal National Mortgage Association (FNMA).

farming. Real estate lingo for cultivating customers in a particular neighborhood. Many agents who farm choose an area with about two hundred homes. The idea is that neighbors will call that agent when they decide to sell.

FDR. Formal dining room.

first. A first mortgage, used to distinguish it from a SECOND.

fixer-upper. Property that requires a lot of work.

fizzbo. Realtor's pejorative term for "for sale by owner."

flex room. In small, entry-level houses, an optional room that can be used for a den, office at home, guest bedroom, or dining room.

flip. A series of real estate sales among partners in which the purchase price is inflated to unrealistic levels. The partners then sell the property to someone who obtains a mortgage for an amount greatly exceeding its true value. It is illegal and fraudulent, as underscored by this *Boston Globe* headline of 1991: "10 Charged in Fraud for Brockton-Area Real Estate 'Flips.' "

flipper. One who buys a house strictly to make a quick profit.

front foot. The property line that joins the street, body of water, public way, etc.

front money. Down payment.

fsbo. See FIZZBO.

∗ G

garbage fees. Legal fees charged by lenders at settlement, such as messenger and document charges, that are often viewed as excessive. When an article appeared in 1993 in the *Los Angeles Times* on real estate terminology, one reader wrote to the paper to comment: "The term *garbage fee* was invented by the first cheapskate who demanded first-class service but was too sleazy to pay for it."

garden carpet. Floor covering that is so dirty that it could support a vegetable garden.

garden level. Basement.

gazump. Raising the price of a property after a deal has been struck (but no contract has been signed). This term originated in England, where the practice has been a major factor in the real estate market. The Sunday *Telegraph* for April 5, 1987, cited "gazumping as a major cause of one in three buyers' purchases falling through after an offer has been accepted."

GEMS. Growing equity markets; fixed-rate loans with payments that increase at regular intervals.

GI loan. In the new meaning for this term, *GI* stands for generous in-laws.

Ginnie Mae. Government National Mortgage Association (GNMA).

ginnies. Bond funds that invest in mortgage securities backed by GNMA.

grandfather. To allow a flaw or violation to remain. It comes from the *grandfather clause,* a provision in a new law or a regulation that exempts those in existing property.

granny flat. Small apartment above a home or garage.

grant gnats. People who earn their living securing federal and state housing funds.

✳ H

handyman special. In need of repair. This term has been applied to houses in such dire and dilapidated condition that it is now something of a joke.

hard money. Money put into improved ownership or equity. Compare with SOFT MONEY.

haver. Person who owns, has, a property that will satisfy a buyer's needs.

holy shit area. Describing an area of houses one more expensive than the other. It comes from the comments of sightseers touring the area in question.

house on steroids. Small home transformed into a big one after major remodeling work.

✳ I

inside lot. Lot that is not on a corner.

✳ J

jumbo loan. Mortgage loans over $202,300.

junior/junior lien. Claim against property that can only be exercised after a prior claim has been settled.

✳ K

kennel. Substandard house; a dog.

kicker. Loan surcharges.

kiddy condo. Condominium that is bought by parents for a child to live in while in college.

knockdown. (1) Structure built from preassembled components. (2) House bought to be leveled to make way for a bigger house.

✳ L

liars' loan. House loans in which lenders require little documentation as long as the borrower puts down a sizable down payment of more than 25 percent. These mortgages are common among those who say they earn a certain amount of money but whose income tax returns show their earnings are much lower.

lonely Charlie. Business transferee with too much time on his hands to look for a new home awaiting the move of the rest of his family.

lookie-lookies. People who look and look but never seem prepared to buy.

low-doc loan. Mortgage given to people who find it difficult to document their income.

low-doc mortgage. Loans made with little or no paperwork (documentation) usually granted to repeat buyers with built-up equity.

lower level. The basement. In 1996 a Realtor told a *Boston Globe* writer why ads contain phrases like "lower-level in-law's apartment": "When you think of a basement, you think of something that's dirty."

LULU. Locally unwanted land use.

lvl. Adspeak for level lot.

✳

Maggie Mae. Mortgage Guaranty Insurance Corporation.

mall. To build a large regional shopping center. The development of many of these malls over the last twenty years has been referred to as the "malling" of America.

meeting of the minds. Mutual agreement at the time of contract.

mingling. Term for those who share properties—apartments, condos, house—to help pay for the cost of housing.

monkey. Mortgage, sometimes phrased as "monkey on the house" or "monkey with a long tail."

move downs. Nervous about lean economic times, these folks move into smaller houses to lower their housing costs.

must-see. Code for dwelling that

looks better on the inside than outside: a property that does not have CURB APPEAL.

✳

neutron-bomb loan. A low, teaser-rate adjustable mortgage that can kill the borrower but save the lender.

new price. (adspeak) A 1990s replacement for *reduced.*

new security system. (adspeak) Located in high-crime area.

NIMBY. Not in my backyard. Rallying cry of those who oppose halfway houses and nuclear-waste dumps. The antonym for this are the BANYS, for builders against NIMBYs.

nouveau-prairie style. An architectural style of tract house that has a Frank Lloyd Wright look.

✳

old-world charm. (adspeak) House needs work.

OP. Realtor's term for overpriced.

open house. Period when a property can be viewed without an appointment.

OPNG. Realtor's term for overpriced and no good.

✳ P

pedestrian pockets. A mixed-use community that stresses walking and bicycling instead of parking lots and the automobile.

penthouse. A favored term of brokers because it sounds so much more swank than *top floor,* however bland the unit there may be.

pink house syndrome. Term for the tendency of some people to do something to their house to make it more salable, but that actually makes it harder to sell—such as painting it pink.

pioneer buyers. Buyers willing to trade mega-commutes for a shot at affordable housing.

PITI. Principal, interest, taxes, and insurance; used to express the monthly payments on a property. Pronounced *pity.*

podmall. Small convenience-oriented shopping center serving a neighborhood; a strip center.

points. Fee charged by a lender for making a loan. Points are over and above the cost of interest, and one point is equal to 1 percent of the mortgage amount.

puffing. "Misleading but not wholly untrue statements that are sometimes made to sell real estate," according to Thomas and Charles F. Hemphill in their *Essential Dictionary of Real Estate Terminology.*

 Q

qualifying. Process by which real estate agents eliminate nonbuyers and concentrate on those eager and able to buy.

 R

railroad flat. Apartment set up with one room after another so that you have to pass through one room to get to the rest.

ranchplex. Two-story units with no basement.

real estate grass. Annual rye, which quickly sprouts to a lush, dark green. It sells houses but is only good for one season.

red-light words. Terms that advertisers are avoiding in the 1990s for fear of being charged with fair-housing violations. A *Washington Post* article of May 29, 1994, by Dale Russakoff told of Realtors avoiding such terms as *executive* (could be construed as racist), *master bedroom* (suggesting slavery), and *sports enthusiasts take note* (could discourage the disabled).

redlining. Lending policy that prevents loans in certain areas. It is an illegal tactic used to thwart racial integration in housing.

rehab. Rehabilitate.

rehabber. One who rehabs dwellings.

 S

sandwich/sandwich lease. Three-party rental agreement between landlord, the original tenant, and a tenant who is subletting the property.

sausage house. One built on zero

lot lines with only one or no side yard.

second. A second mortgage on a property that already has a mortgage, known as a FIRST.

sleeper. Nice, well-priced house that attracts little attention.

smart streets. A planning scheme for new towns where technology such as fiber optics is built into the infrastructure just as are water, sewer, and storm drains.

soft-money. Money put into interest. Compare with HARD MONEY.

spacious. Average in size.

starter home. Cheap, low-end home. It is one of the most common examples of the coded vocabulary of real estate advertising. In truth, in too many cases the term *starter home* actually means dilapidated.

strip. To build a small community shopping center; a convenience mall. "Stripping" is "malling" on a smaller scale.

sweat equity. Hard work invested in a property.

✳ T

teaser rate. A first-year mortgage rate that is below the going rate, also known as a starter rate. They are offered to make adjustable-rate mortgages more attractive.

thirty-year fixed. Thirty-year mortgage based on a fixed rate of interest for the life of the loan. First-timers usually feel more comfortable

knowing the interest rate will not change. Fixed-rate mortgages can also be taken out for ten, fifteen, or twenty years.

TND. Traditional neighborhood development, with conventional main street and a small-town atmosphere.

TOD. Transit-oriented development—one built around bus or rail lines.

two-steps/two-step mortgages. Also called 5/25s or 7/23s, these mortgages offer two interest rates—a fixed rate for five years or seven years, then it switches to an annual adjustable rate or another fixed rate for the balance of the loan.

✳ U

Uncle Louie. Any relative of the buyer who is going to "help" inspect the house.

upgrades. Improvements.

upside-down. Said when prices drop so much that a loan against a house exceeds its value.

✳ W

WBFP. Wood-burning fireplace.

wide-body lots. Wide but shallow building lots that save land and permit builders to pack more houses onto smaller sites.

W-2ers. Lender term for the preferred kind of home buyer, who gets yearly statements of income

SY WHT?

W BFP is one of many common real estate abbreviations that create a language. Most are easy, but some are puzzlers for the uninitiated: ROW, RHFP, BBHA, and FHW respectively stand for right of way, raised hearth fireplace, baseboard hot air, and forced hot water.

As a service to readers, the *Boston Globe* real estate section recently translated this ad:

"13 Bond St. Beauty. Unique & Wonderful. Immac. Cond. DLR w/ WBF (Vict. mirror). Cntry kit., FDR, 3 BR, 2½ BA, W/D, Alrm, C/V, Grdn & Rfdk. $495,000. Excl."

Translated: The ad was for a clean South End home with a double living room, a wood-burning fireplace with a Victorian mirror hanging above it, a large kitchen, formal dining room, three bedrooms, two and a half bathrooms, washer-dryer, alarm, central vacuum, garden, roofdeck, listed exclusively with the advertiser.

on W-2 forms. Self-employed individuals who don't get W-2 forms have a much tougher time getting loans.

ww. Wall-to-wall, as in ww crpt.

 Y

yield. To surrender or give up a property.

 Z

zero lot line. Describing a portion of a property where there is no yard; where the edge of the building is the edge of the property.

zipper lots. A version of the wide-and-shallow lot with the garage on the side that lines up with the backyard of another lot in the rear.

SOURCES

Gina Cressey, Roberta Jacobson, and Norman Stevens helped with this chapter. Work by Bradley Inman in the *Sacramento Bee* and Warron Boroson in the *Bergen County Record* provided the latest list of popular real estate lexicon used by architects, lenders, planners, and builders.

23

SEX, THE BODY, AND BODILY FUNCTIONS

R-Rated Terms You Probably Won't Find in Your Junior Dictionary

> You can hardly assert that their inclusion would ruin the morals of the multitude?
>
> —Eric Partridge asking one of the editors of
> the *Oxford English Dictionary* in 1947 or
> 1948 why the words *cunt* and *fuck* were
> excluded. They have since been installed.
> From the *London Times Literary Section,*
> November 28, 1975.

First came sexual euphemism. There was a time when Dr. Thomas Bowdler brought us a cleaned-up edition of Shakespeare's works in which a "gipsy's lust" became a "gipsy's will." And there were the writers of the last century who could not bring themselves to write words like *trousers* and *breeches* and settled for terms like *inexpressibles* and *unmentionables.*

Slang of the most forthright kind came forward to replace all of this. It was there all the time, but this was center-stage stuff. Linguistically, we let it all hang out, and modern speakers and writers held nothing back—"today an asterisk in a book is as rare as a virgin in life," said one startled critic not that long ago. When the smoke cleared, all the old dirty words and their hyphenated variations were in standard dictionaries, and Hollywood started vetting scripts by making sure these words were included, not excluded. (Is it my imagination or is there a law that requires all movies made after 1965 to have the word *asshole* in the dialogue?) Small-town theaters offered X-rated movies with titles like the redundant *Sluts in Heat,* and couples went shopping for sexual toys as if they were out to buy a Cuisinart.

Of late, however, it has become apparent that the words that the Federal Communications Commission used to call the "big six" (those that could not be used on the radio: *piss, fart, shit, fuck, cock,* and *cunt*) will always be with us and for all intents and purposes are no longer slang, but part of standard dictionary English. Many others have little or nothing to do with sex or elimination but are what kids used to call "curse words."

Modern sexual slang, on the other hand, does not make the dictionary and tends to be more of a throwback to euphemism than four-letter-word directness. We hung on to some of the Victorian urge to euphemize. In 1990 it is still common to ask a woman visitor "Would you like to powder your nose?" and some call a graveyard a "garden of remembrance." Euphemism has made the universe a little less perilous and harsh. Without a little euphemism, strikes would be harder to avert, fights would be harder to avoid, and parents would be dumbstruck when it came to explaining "the birds and the bees."

Here are a number of the terms—old and new—that are part of today's slang. By its nature it is a sampling. One could make a list of several hundred nicknames for the penis and twice as many for breasts—from *angel cakes* to *zingers*.

✳ A

adult. Dirty; sexually explicit.

ass bandit. Homosexual male.

aural sex. Phone sex.

✳ B

bag. Condom.

ball. A copulative verb: to have sex with.

balls. Testicles, from the much older Anglo-Saxon *ballocks.*

baster baby. Reproduction by artificial insemination, sometimes achieved with the aid of a turkey baster.

bazongas. Breasts.

BC. Birth control.

bearded clam. The female genitalia.

beast with two backs. A couple during intercourse.

beauty spot. The female genitalia.

beaver. The female genitalia.

bed hop. To sleep around.

belly ride. Copulation.

bi/bicycle. Bisexual.

big brown eyes. The breasts.

big daddy. Penis.

bikini stuffers. Breasts.

blow your top. Achieve sexual climax.

blue steeler. A particularly virile erection.

bobbitt. To cut off a penis, from what Lorena Bobbitt did to her husband. An early use of this verb occurred in the *Washington Post* for January 28, 1994, in a movie review by Rita Kempley in which a character in the film "picks up a carving knife and threatens to Bobbitt Sebastian."

body-rub shops. A term used more commonly in Canada than the

United States meaning massage parlors.

boinng. The sound and act of having an erection. In 1981 the *New England Journal of Medicine* carried an article on the subject entitled "Falling in Boinng Again." A letter to the editor in the May 20, 1982, issue objected: "Boinng is not an affliction. On the contrary, boinng, like love and watermelon, is one of life's genuine pleasures."

boner. As always, an erection.

boobiferous. Busty.

boobs. Breasts.

bouncers. Breasts.

bouncy-bouncy. Sexual act.

box tonsils. (collegiate) To kiss passionately.

breeder. Homosexual term for a heterosexual, derogatory.

brush the beaver. To masturbate (female).

buckets. Breasts.

buff the helmut. To masturbate (male).

bugger. (1) To practice anal sex. (2) One who practices anal sex.

buns. The buttocks. An ad for a Cleveland health club is headlined, "All rolls and buns drastically reduced."

burping the worm. To masturbate (male).

butch. Lesbian who wears suits, motorcycle jackets, and other male clothing.

* C

cadet. Condom.

cakes. The buttocks.

camel toes. The vagina.

carpet munching. To give oral sex to a female.

catcher's mitt. A diaphragm.

choking the chicken. To masturbate (male).

circle jerk. Group masturbation.

closeted. Not revealing one's sexual orientation to the general public.

Coney Island whitefish. Condom.

cork. Tampon.

crack of heaven. The female genitalia.

cream sauce. Semen.

cum. (1) Semen. (2) To ejaculate.

cut. Circumsized.

cybersex. That conducted over the Internet.

cyberslut. Woman who offers sex on the Internet; cyberspace nymphomaniac.

* D

daisy chain. Three or more people linked sexually at the same time. The term has been applied nonsexually to a business arrangement in which three or more companies gratify each other while ripping off the public.

dating. Increasingly, having sex

with. Here is a line from the *Houston Chronicle* of November 23, 1994: "[Richard Gere] confronted Sylvester Stallone at a recent London party thrown by Elton John and asked if he were dating [Cindy] Crawford only he didn't say *date*." Traditionally this term was, and in many quarters still is, in the words of lexicographer Charles D. Poe, "used in such a way as to conjure up an Archie-and-Veronica, movie-and-maltshop kind of vision."

diddle. (1) Play with. (2) Copulate with.

DOM. Dirty old man.

down there. One's genitalia.

drag. Dressed in a way associated with the opposite sex from one's own.

drag queen. Man who dresses like a woman.

dry run. To bring to climax without undressing.

 E

ear sex. Phone sex; aural sex.

eleventh finger. The penis.

enema bandit. Homosexual.

exhaust pipe. The anus.

 F

fag hag. Heterosexual woman who socializes with and dates gay men.

family jewels. Male genitalia.

fart knocker. Braggart.

faygeleh. Yiddish slang for gay derived from the word for bird.

femme. Lesbian or gay man who dresses and acts effeminately.

fern. Female genitalia.

fish skin. Condom.

flesh session. Copulation.

44s. Breasts.

French embassy. Place where gay sex is available.

French letter. Condom.

French tickler. Condom.

friend of Dorothy's. Gay. A direct allusion to Judy Garland's character in the *Wizard of Oz*. Garland has long been popular with gay audiences.

frig. Sex between women involving the rubbing of the genitals with the fingers.

fun bags. Breasts.

fur pie. The vagina.

fuzzy taco. Female genitals.

F-word. Widely used euphemism for the word *fuck*.

 G

Garden of Eden. The female genitalia.

gay. Homosexual. In his *New Dictionary of American Slang*, Robert Chapman notes that use of the word in that sense may date from seventeenth-century England when *gay* was used as an adjective to describe people addicted to "dissipations and social pleasures." The *Oxford English Dictionary* cites its use in the same sense in James Shirley's 1637 play, *Lady of Pleasure.*

getting your plumbing snaked. Having sexual intercourse.

glove. Condom.

golden mound. Female genitals.

go over the mountain. Achieve sexual climax.

group grope. An orgy.

G spot. An erotic zone or point of passion. Originally a specific spot on the vaginal wall and named for its finder, German gynecologist Ernst Grafenberg, the term is now used generically. The *G* now seems to stand for something closer to "gee whiz" than Grafenberg.

 ✱ H

hard-off. Woman arousing no male sexual interest.

hard-on. Male erection.

hee-haws. Breasts.

helmet. Circumsized penis.

herotica. Female erotica.

hide the salami. Copulate.

hobble. To have sex.

hobbler. Slut.

hogans. Breasts.

honeypot. Female genitals.

hooters. Breasts.

horizontal bop. (collegiate) The sex act.

horse. Condom, specifically a Trojan (from Trojan horse).

hot beef injection. Coitus.

hot box. Female genitals.

Hudson River whitefish. Condom.

huevos. Testicles, Spanish for eggs.

hump. To engage in sexual intercourse.

hung. (1) Describing a well-endowed male; big. Often stated in simile form as "hung like a bull," "hung like a rabbit," etc. (2) More generally: how endowed, as in "hung like a mouse" or "hung like a cricket."

SAY WHAT?

*G*etting your plumbing snaked is just one of a number of terms for sexual intercourse in the "getting your" genre: *getting your drain cleaned, getting your rocks off, getting your ashes hauled, getting some mud for your turtle.*

A step removed are phrases like *shaking the dew off your lily* and *doing the horizontal bop.*

* I

in the life. Gay. In the Internet glossary "Queer Slang in the Gay 90s" it is stated that this term is most common in the black community.

Irish dowry. The female genitalia.

* J

jack off. To masturbate (male).

jill off. To masturbate (female).

Jimbo. Penis, allegedly the term of preference of Pres. Lyndon Johnson.

jo-bag/jolly bag. Condom.

Johnnie. Penis.

joy hole. The female genitalia.

jugs. Breasts.

* K

kazoo. Anus or vagina.

knob. The meatus.

knocking boots. Coitus.

kosher. Circumcised.

* L

labonza. Buttocks.

lap dancing. For a naked stripper to rub her body against the crotch of a male customer, usually to orgasm and for a fee.

lay your cane in a dusty corner. To have sexual intercourse. This metaphor acknowledges that the participants may be old.

lech. Lecher.

les. Lesbian.

Little Elvis. The name Elvis Presley gave to his member.

load. Semen.

love glove. Condom.

love juice. Semen.

love purse. Female genitals.

lubie. Lubricated condom.

* M

magnum. Oversize condom or penis.

main vein. Penis.

Manhattan eel. Condom.

maracas. Breasts.

marital aid. Sexual toy such as a vibrator or dildo.

mattress mambo. To have sexual intercourse.

maypole. Sizable penis.

McQ. Quickie, from the *Mc* of *McDonald's* of fast-food fame.

meat rack. Gay-male cruising area.

mooning. Displaying one's butt for shock value.

morner. Sex in the morning—before a NOONER.

mount joy. The female genitalia.

mouse. Vagina.

Mr. Happy. Penis; a term given added

currency because it has been used by Robin Williams in comedy routines.

muff diving. To give oral sex to a female.

mustache ride. Oral sex. In this regard, sideburns are "thigh ticklers."

 N

napkin ring. Penile ring.

nookie. Sexual intercourse.

nooner. Sex at noon. (It would be irresponsible not to point out that the sentence "Sex at noon taxes" is a palindrome, meaning it reads the same forward and backward.)

 O

O. Orgasm.

one-eyed wonder. Penis.

one-night stand. One-time sexual encounter.

OTR. On the rag; menstruating.

outing. Uncloseting gays without their permission.

over the shoulder bolder holder. Bra.

 P

paddling the pink canoe. To masturbate (female).

parallel parking. (collegiate) The sex act.

parsley patch. Pubic hair. By extension, to make love is to take a trip around the parsley patch.

parting the Red Sea. To masturbate (female).

personals. Classified ads to attract others.

Peter, Paul, and Mary. Ménage à trois.

pink palace in the Black Forest. The vagina.

pitch a tent. Get an erection.

play pocket pool. To masturbate (male).

plug. Tampon.

pluke. Have sexual intercourse.

pocket pal. Condom.

pood. (Rhymes with *wood*.) Penis.

pop one's cookies. Ejaculate.

popsicle. Penis.

porking. Copulation.

Port Said garter. Condom.

propho. Condom.

prunes. Testicles. This term creates some strange comparisons. In Joseph Wambaugh's 1984 novel, *Lines and Shadows,* we read these lines: "Manny's prunes were big as honeydews. Manny Lopez had balls to the walls."

pud. Penis.

punchboard. Promiscuous female.

 Q

quickie. A fast sexual interlude.

quief. Air escaping vagina after intercourse.

*

SAY WHAT?

Roberta B. Jacobson, Ph.D., kindly created and offered a decryption of the codes and phrases that appear in personals.

after my release. I'm in prison.
animal lover. I have four large dogs who all sleep with me in the bed.
A-NS (or A-ns). Absolutely nonsmoker.
BIF. Bisexual female.
BIM. Bisexual male.
Call my work number. I'm married.
CBB. Currently behind bars.
Confused about love. Not sure of my sexual preference.
DF. Divorced female.
DM. Divorced male.
first-time try at this. All my previous personals were published in other cities.
GF. Gay female.
GM. Gay male.
into jeans scene. Informal type of person.
into leather scene. Into S&M.
let's meet for a drink. I'm too cheap to buy you dinner.
mysterious. Nutty as a fruitcake.
neg. Tested negative for HIV.
NK! No kids.
no financial considerations/not interested in financial considerations. I want sex but am not willing to pay for it.
no home phone. I'm married.
no responses to letters without photos. My prime consideration is what you look like.
NS. Nonsmoker.
PA. Party animal.
personable. Will talk your ear off.
pleasant. Ugly as sin.
plump. Fat.
pos. Tested positive for HIV.
s (or s). Smoker.
seeking companion. I am impotent.
seeking good times. Am only interested in sex, not a relationship.
seeking someone who loves children. I've got five (or more) kids.
seeking well-established . . . You must be rich.
SF. Single female.
SM. Single male.
(to) turn my life around. I'm a compulsive gambler, alcoholic, etc.
video fan. Couch potato.

✳ R

racks. Breasts.

raincoat. Condom.

Roman. A person with a proclivity for orgies, used in personal classified ads.

roto-rooter. Penis.

rough rider. Ribbed condom.

rubber duckie. Condom.

✳ S

safe. A condom. This is an old term given new meaning in the context of "safe sex."

schwanz. Penis.

sex worker. Gender-free term for prostitute.

she-inal. Urinal for women allowing them to urinate while standing.

shoot your wad. Achieve sexual climax.

shower cap. Condom.

shtup. To copulate with.

size queen. Gay male especially interested in partners with large penises.

skin. Condom.

slam. (1) Sexual intercourse. (2) Female genitalia.

slap the salami. To masturbate (male).

snatch. The female genitalia.

spank the monkey. To masturbate (male).

stern-wheeler. Homosexual.

strange. Sex with a stranger or out-of-towner, as in, "Got me some strange."

switch-hitter. Bisexual.

✳ T

T&A. Tits and ass.

tatas. Breasts.

threesome. Sex with three people.

tickle the tack. To masturbate (female).

tink. Penis.

titskis. Breasts.

titty shake. Topless bar.

tongue wrestling. Deep kissing.

tonsil hockey. (collegiate) Deep kissing.

toys. Sexual aids and pleasure enhancers.

trouser trout. Penis. By extension, masturbation is fishing for trouser trout.

TS. Transsexual.

tube steak. Penis.

turtleneck. Uncircumsized penis.

TV. Transvestite.

twig. Vibrator with a slender business end.

✳ U

udders. Breasts.

umbrella. Condom.

unit. Penis.

V

vanilla. Describing conventional sex.

Vatican roulette. The rhythm method of birth control, which attempts to avoid conception through timing, named for the Vatican's opposition to mechanical means of contraception.

Venus mound. The female genitalia.

W

wake and bake. Sex on awakening in the morning.

wall job. Stand-up sex.

W/E. Well-endowed, in the code of the personal classifieds.

well hung. Describing a male with full-size genitals.

wet deck. Describing an aroused woman.

whisker biscuit. Female genitals.

wide on. Female version of HARD-ON; aroused.

wiener wrap. Condom.

woodie. An erection.

X

XXX. Particularly graphic and explicit depiction of sex.

Y

Y, the. The crotch. Oral sex is sometimes described as having "lunch at the Y."

Z

zipless fuck. Quick sexual encounter with someone you have never seen before, a term made popular in Erica Jong's *Fear of Flying*.

∗

SOURCES

This collection was aided by material found in the journal *Maledicta,* the *Journal of Verbal Aggression, Playboy,* the Tamony Collection, and *Modern English* by the pseudonymous Jennifer Blowdryer (Last Gasp Press, 1985). Important help came from the late Robert T. West, Leonard Ashley, the modest JBW, Norman D. Stevens, and the late Charles D. Poe. Scott Callis also contributed. The Internet site "Queer Slang in the Gay 90s" (copyright 1986 Gay-MART Enterprises, Vancouver) was most helpful as were a number of other on-line glossaries.

24

SPORTS SLANG

Introductory Jockese: Of Sports, Games, and the Mother Tongue

What am I supposed to believe when some TV announcer talks about a noseguard making a key tackle? Come on. A noseguard is a piece of equipment.

And what is this nickel defense? I used to know a guy named Floyd Nickel. Pretty good athlete. You don't suppose? No, no. He went into auto insurance.

—Michael Kernan in the *Washington Post,*
September 11, 1982

The influence of sports on the American language is stunningly strong and—at the end of the 1990s—appears to be at an all-time real and metaphoric high.

Senators throw "softball questions" (i.e., easy) at confirmation hearings, and everyone seems to be willing to settle for a rough "ballpark figure," while the president reckons his legislative "box score" with Congress. We "play for keeps" (marbles), get "faked out" (football), and sometimes "get the benefit of a doubt" (fencing). "Inside baseball" has gained popularity outside baseball as a way of describing inner-sanctum goings-on, and just about everybody seems to be playing "hardball" (which, as it turns out, appears to be from handball, not baseball). When all else fails, we "fall back and punt."

This creeping sports-ese began its encroachment years ago. In fact, the transfer has not always been welcomed. *Hit and run* is a baseball term that upset many when in the 1930s it first became a term for an automotive felony. Other terms are so much a part of our daily language that we are largely unaware of their sports origins. *Charley horse* was a baseball term that has become so standard for the ailment it describes that even medical doctors don't call it by its medical name *(quadriceps famoris)* anymore.

Sports slang is in a class by itself. It is so vast and extensive that its terminology is counted in the thousands. I authored a baseball dictionary in 1989; it contained more than five thousand terms, of which the vast majority were slang. But that is baseball. What about a pastime as humble as marbles? (About the only thing that the author excelled at as a kid.) I have begun a collection of marble terms because they are fast becoming archaic and will soon be "lost," and I have already come up with more than three hundred. There are more.

Given this state of affairs, a compromise has been struck and a sampling of slang from various sports has been compiled. Each term has been labeled for the sport it comes from. Those terms that apply to a number of sports are labeled "basic jock talk."

* A

ace. (1) (tennis) A serve that one's opponent fails to return. (2) (golf) A hole in one.

ad. (basketball) You've got the ad, or advantage.

air ball. (basketball) Shot that misses the rim of the basket.

aircraft carrier. (basketball) The big man; a driver whose dominance can make a team a winner.

air pass. (basketball) When the dribbler throws or taps the ball in the air and then touches it before it reaches the floor.

alibi-itis. (basic jock talk) The ailment of players who offer an excuse or alibi whenever they do not make the correct play.

alley-oop. (basketball) A high lobbed shot/pass that is tipped in by a player near the basket.

all net. (basketball) Nothing but bottom. Also *bic, scoop, string music, swish.*

alphabet string. (health club talk) Appliance suggested for women too large for the traditional G-string.

also-ran. (basic jock talk) A competitor who is defeated in a race.

anchor. (1) (basketball) A shot likely to go "clang." Also known as a brick. (2) (basic jock talk) A member of a team, heavily depended upon, who is the last to perform in a relay race, as in track or swimming. The anchorman in bowling is the last to perform for his team.

apple. (basic jock talk) The ball, especially basketball and baseball.

arbiter. (baseball and softball) An umpire.

armchair quarterback. Fan of televised sports who thinks he has most of the answers; not restricted to football, or even sports (one can, for example, be a political armchair quarterback).

around the world. (basketball) A schoolyard shooting game in which players try to match each other shot for shot along an arc.

audible. (football) Play that is called verbally by the offensive team after it has positioned itself over the ball.

* B

back-bounce pass. (basketball) A bounce pass made in a backward direction toward a teammate. It may be a blind pass or the passer may peer over his shoulder at the receiver.

backdoor. (basketball) Describing a cut toward the basket by an offensive player when he or she is being overplayed.

backdoor play. (basketball) A play directly under the basket and behind the backs of the defenders. An offensive player sneaks in behind the backs of the defenders and takes a pass under the basket from a teammate for a backdoor play.

back nine. (golf) The last nine holes on an eighteen-hole course.

bag. (baseball and softball) A base. Also called sack, hassock, pillow, canvas, etc.

bail out. (baseball and softball) To draw back from the plate to avoid being hit by a pitched ball.

ball hawk. (basketball) Player who specializes in recovering loose balls; An aggressive defensive player who dives for and recovers loose balls, blocks passes and shots, and makes steals and interceptions.

ball hog. (basketball) One not popular because he or she doesn't like to pass the ball.

Baltimore chop. (baseball) A batted ball that strikes home plate or the ground near home plate and rebounds high into the air. The batter can often beat out a Baltimore chop for a base hit.

bang. (basketball) To hit the boards hard.

bangboard. (basketball) The glass, metal, or wood surface above and to the sides of the basket, used for carom shots taken from an angle, particularly layups.

banger. (pool and billiards) A clumsy, ineffective player.

bank board/bankboard. (basketball) See BANGBOARD. Another term for backboard, so called because many players use the backboard to "bank" their shots toward the basket.

bank's open, the. (basketball) An interjection uttered while releasing a shot off the backboard.

barn burner. (basic jock talk) An exciting contest.

baseball pass. (basketball) A long, one-handed pass to a receiver up court. Used for distance and speed or both mainly by centers starting fast breaks.

bases drunk. (baseball) Bases loaded.

basketball Jones. (basketball) Playground-basketball addict. On the street, a "jones" is an addictive habit.

basket catch. (baseball and softball) A catch of a fly ball at waist level, the glove and the bare hand cradling the ball.

basket-hanging. (basketball) Staying in the offensive area of the court when the rest of the players have moved to the other end. The basket hanger hopes to receive a long pass and take an uncontested shot. Also called cherry picking.

batboy shot. (baseball) A term attributed to the Yankee's Oscar Gamble for a home run that is hit so hard that the batter simply hands his bat to the batboy. Similarly, last August broadcaster Tom Marr, in attempting to describe the magnitude of a John Lowenstein home run, simply noted, "They show movies on a flight like that." These big homers have also been called moon shots.

battery. (baseball and softball) The pitcher and the catcher.

bean. (baseball) To hit the batter on the head with a pitch.

beanball. (baseball) Pitch aimed at a batter's head.

bedposts. (bowling) The 7-10 split.

bell lap. (track, cycling) The last lap of a race.

bench jockey. A player who rides (heckles) opposition players from the bench or dugout.

bench warmer. (basic jock talk) Player who is seldom brought into the game: a substitute.

bic. (basketball) This term for a successful shot that touches no iron is popular in the D.C.-Baltimore area.

big ball. (softball) One of a number of names for softball.

Big Dance, the. (basketball) The NCAA tournament, when the Big Player can hit the Big Shot and later sign a sneaker deal for the Big Bucks.

big man. The center on a basketball team.

bird cage. (basic jock talk) Protective face mask.

biscuit. (hockey) The puck. The object of hockey is to put more biscuits (pucks) in the net than the opposition.

blackout. (spectator) To prohibit the telecasting of a sports event in a specific area.

bleeder. (baseball and softball) A batted ball that just trickles past the defensive players for a "weak" base hit.

blind pass. (basketball) A pass in which the passer does not see his receiver but expects him to be there.

blind side. (basic jock talk) The side away from which a player is looking.

blitz. (1) (basketball) To win a pickup game in straight baskets, usually by 9–0. Also *skunk.* (2) (football) A massive attempt by the defense to penetrate the offensive line and ground (tackle) the quarterback.

block, on the. (basketball) Where a player sets up to receive the ball near the basket.

blocker. (hockey) Used by the stick hand, this glove generally has a foam-padded shield attached.

blooper. (baseball and softball) A batted ball that arches over the heads of the infielders and drops in front of the outfielders for a base hit.

blue. (baseball and softball) Any umpire, from the color of his or her uniform. It is used in lines like "Oh, come on, blue" after a dubious call.

board 'n' cord. (basketball) A shot banked off the backboard.

boards. (basketball) Backboards.

bob and weave. (boxing) To move one's upper body from side to side and forward and back in an effort to avoid an opponent's punches.

bobble. (baseball and softball) Juggling the ball while attempting a catch, or dropping the ball for an error.

bogart. (basketball) A strong move inside.

bogey. (golf) A score of one stroke over par on a hole.

bomb. (football) An extremely long pass.

boo bird. (basic jock talk and spectator) Disruptive fan who boos frequently at sporting events.

boogie. (basketball) To drive fast.

book. (basic jock talk) (1) To run fast; to BOOGIE. (2) Data on an opponent.

bootleg. (football) Any play in which a man carrying the ball pretends to give it to a teammate, then hides the ball on his hip and takes off.

bow. (basketball) Shorthand for elbow; to bow is to elbow an opponent.

bowling pass. (basketball) A one-hand pass thrown with an underhand motion similar to that used by a bowler. It is an air pass.

box out. (basketball) To keep an opposing player behind you so he cannot rebound the ball; a screening tactic used by the defense to gain control of the ball.

break the ice. (basketball) The custom, common on some playgrounds, of not keeping score until at least one basket has been made.

brick. (basketball) A misfired shot with little chance of going in. Also *anchor.*

brush back. (baseball and softball) To attempt to move a batter away from the plate by pitching the ball high and inside.

brush block. (basketball) A combination of a block and a screen in which an offensive player rubs against a defensive player while on the move.

bucket. (1) (basketball) Two-point field goal. (2) (hockey) Helmet. (3) (bowling) A spare in which the 2, 4, 5, and 8 pins are left standing.

bulk up. (basic jock talk) To add to muscle size by exercise and weight lifting.

bump and run. (football) For a pass defender to bump into a potential receiver (which is legal) to upset his balance and then run alongside him.

burn. (1) (basketball) To make a move that takes advantage of an opponent's defense. (2) (basic jock talk) To win convincingly.

burner. (1) (basic jock talk) Pinched nerve. (2) (football) Speedy wide receiver, who can "burn" the opposition.

bush. (basic jock talk) Short for

bush league, as in dishonorable, gutless, or without class.

bus stop. (basketball) A jump shot. Also *J, joint.*

bust. (basketball) An explosive drive to the hoop.

butcher. (basketball) (1) A physically abusive defensive player. (2) To inflict physical punishment on another player.

butterfly. (hockey) The method by which a goalie becomes active—diving, flopping, and falling to his knees to make saves.

buttonhook. (1) (football) Forward-pass play in which the receiver runs downfield and then stops to turn evasively (hook) toward the passer. (2) (basketball) To go in one direction and then turn sharply and double back.

buzzer shot. (basketball) A shot made in an attempt to score as the buzzer sounds.

* C

cabbageball. (softball) One more name for Chicago sixteen-inch softball.

cage. (hockey) A one-piece helmet with mask. Many goalies have pictures painted on it.

cager. (basketball) A player—slang derived from original playing area, the "cage." In the early days, basketball games were played with a cloth or wire netting around the floor to prevent the ball from going into the crowd. It also prevented

unruly spectators from harming players and officials.

cagey. (basketball) Describing a smart, experienced player who has basketball savvy. (This term probably originated in the days when basketball was played in a cage.)

camel toe. (volleyball) Ball struck with knurled fingers.

camp. (basketball) To establish position in the low post for an extended time.

can the shot. (basketball) To score a basket.

card. (basic jock talk) Scorecard.

cellar. (basic jock talk) Last place.

chalk talk. (basic jock talk) A lecture or discussion conducted by the coach, often with the use of a blackboard.

charity stripe. (basketball) The foul line, where one goes to take a free—or charity—shot.

chaser. (basketball) Normally the man nearest midcourt in a zone defense. His job is to harass or chase the man with the ball.

chatter. (baseball and softball) The continual encouragement (to your team) and the discouragement to the other team that goes on during a game. For instance, you offer your pitcher ritual lines like "No batter here" and "They're scared of you out there."

cheap shot. (basic jock talk) An act of deliberate violence against an opponent, and one that is committed when the opponent is not expecting it and is not able to defend himself: unsportsmanlike conduct.

check. (1) (hockey) To impede the progress of an opponent by use of the body (body check) or the stick (poke check or stick check). (2) (basketball) A blocked shot.

check up. (basketball) To play defense.

cheese. (pool and billiards) Luck.

cherry pick. (basketball) To remain near the basket while play is at the other end of the court in hopes of getting a long pass and an undefended basket.

chippie. (basketball) An easy shot.

choke. (basic jock talk) To misplay, usually in a crucial moment in the game, because of anxiety, apprehension, or tension.

chopped ball. (baseball and softball) A swing of the bat in which the batter strikes downward with a chopping motion so that the ball bounces high into the air. The purpose of a chopped ball is to allow the runner to reach first base by beating the throw.

chops. (boxing) The jaw.

Cinderella team. (basic jock talk) A team with little hope at the beginning of a season or tournament that goes on to unexpected success. Among the most notable college basketball Cinderella teams were Utah's 1944 NCAA champions, CCNY's 1950 NCAA and NIT champions, and Texas Western's 1965 NCAA champions.

circus catch. (baseball) Any catch with a sensational element, such as diving and rolling on the ground.

cliff-hanger. (basic jock talk) A game or other event that is so closely contested that its outcome is uncertain until the very end.

clinch. (1) (basic jock talk) To win a championship before the end of the season by building a lead so great that it cannot be overcome by an opponent. (2) (boxing) To hold an opponent with one or both arms so as to prevent or hinder his punches.

clothesline. (football) To strike an opponent, often a pass receiver breaking downfield, across the face or neck with an extended forearm. Clotheslining is illegal.

coast to coast. (basketball) Taking a rebound and single-handedly taking it to the other end of the court for a basket. Going baseline to baseline.

cobra. (1) (health-club/gym talk) Person with a big, muscular back that dwindles down to a narrow waist. (2) (volleyball) A ball struck with straight, locked fingertips.

coffee. (golf) The tee, what else?

cold hand. (basketball) A player who has trouble making shots is said to have a cold hand.

combination. (boxing) A series of punches delivered in rapid succession.

combo coverage. (football) Defensive football in which man-to-man and zone defenses are combined.

cookie monster. (bowling) A 5-7-10 split.

cords. (basketball) The net below the rim of the basket. A quotation by Dave DeBusschere displayed at the Basketball Hall of Fame in Springfield, Massachusetts, says, "It's kind of nice to get out there and make a couple of shots and hear the cords sort of talk back to you when you make a good jump shot."

counter. (football) A play that goes in the opposite direction of its original movement.

counterfeit. (basketball) A shot with a dubious chance of going in.

cousin. (baseball) A pitcher whom a batter usually finds he can hit well.

crackback. (football) Blocking maneuver by a pass receiver who runs downfield and then turns around to clear out the man covering him.

crawling. (football) An attempt by a ball carrier to advance the ball after he has hit the ground.

crease. (hockey) Also known as the goalmouth. The protected area in front of the net. Goalies can use its markings for positioning and to help with the angles. No other player is permitted in the crease before the puck arrives.

cross training. (basic jock talk) Using one sport to practice the techniques of another; for example, using in-line skating to improve skiing skills.

cup. (basic jock talk) A hard, cup-shaped device for protecting the male genitals.

cut. (basic jock talk) (1) In basketball, football, and other team sports, to make a quick change of direction in an effort to elude an opponent. (2) To drop a prospective player from a roster or team.

D

day. (basketball) Caucasian or white, as in, "The dude's game is strictly day, man."

dead. (basketball) Having completed a dribble and being forced either to shoot or pass.

deadwood. (bowling) Pins that have been knocked down but remain on the alley or in the gutter. In tenpin bowling, deadwood must be removed before the ball can be rolled. In candlepins, deadwood remains on the alley and is in play.

death valley. (basketball) The foul lane.

deef. (tennis) Default.

deke. (hockey) A fake by the puck carrier that enables him to stick-handle around an opponent.

deuce. (basic jock talk) Two, as in, "You've got to win by a deuce."

dinger. (baseball) A home run.

dink. In tennis, volleyball, and other net games, a softly hit ball that goes just beyond the net.

dish. (1) (basketball) To pass off neatly; to make a deft pass, usually for an assist. (2) (baseball) Home plate.

ditchers. (basketball) The back men in a zone defense.

divot. (golf) A piece of sod cut and lifted out of the ground by the clubhead.

doctor. (basketball) A player who operates well and makes house calls—to score from the inside in a showy manner.

does windows. (basketball) Can dunk the ball.

dog. (1) (football) To rush the passer, the same as RED DOG. (2) (pool and billiards) To blow a shot; one who blows shots.

dog it. (basic jock talk) To play lackadaisically; to goof off.

dogleg. (golf) A sharp turn on the fairway.

double pump. (basketball) Bringing the ball up and down after leaving your feet, yet still shooting it before traveling. Also *double clutch.*

double-team. (basic jock talk) To guard one offensive player with two defensive players, to prevent a shot, pass, or dribble.

downtown. (basketball) Deep. A three-point shot will come from downtown.

drill. (basketball) Nail a field goal.

drive in. (baseball and softball) To bat in a run with a hit ball.

ducats/ducks. (basic jock talk) Tickets.

duffer. (golf) A player who lacks skill and experience.

dunk/dunk shot. (basketball) A shot blasted into the basket with the re-lease coming after it has entered the cylinder.

Dutch 200. (bowling) Rolling a 200 game with alternative strikes and spares.

∗ E

eagle. (golf) Two strokes under par.

eat the ball. (football) For a potential player to hold on to the ball and be tackled (for a loss of yardage) rather than throw it.

elbow. (basketball) Corner of the painted area under the basket. A player may shoot from the elbow.

empty-net goal. (hockey) A goal scored when the goaltender has been pulled.

enduro. (basic jock talk) Endurance race.

enforcer. (hockey) Player whose forte is intimidating the opposition. Frank Luksa of the *Dallas Morning News* defined the term this way in 1993: "Player with an IQ equivalent to temperature of ice. His only forte is fouling to intimidate. He plays eighty games, scores two goals, spends 2,500 minutes in the penalty box. Don't invite him home. He will spear your house pet."

∗ F

face. (basketball) (1) Respect and honor—that intangible at stake in any man-to-man playground encounter that makes even single plays memorable. When it's at stake, one can do only one of two things: save it or lose it. (2) An emphatic dunk or shot right in the face of an opposing player. Also used to urge a fellow player to stop his man, as in, "Get in his face."

face job. (basketball) An individual offensive or defensive move so captivating that it wins for one moment the karma of face.

fade. (football) To gradually move backward or laterally.

fake. (basic jock talk) To indicate intention to go in one direction without actually doing so.

faker. (basketball) A player who feints or fakes.

farm out. (basic jock talk) To send a player to a farm or feeder team.

favorite. (basic jock talk, but also common to horse racing) Team or entry in a contest who seems to be most likely to win.

Faye Dunaway. (basketball) A fadeaway shot.

feeder. (basketball) The player "feeding" the ball to his teammate, who will try to drive in and score a basket.

finger roll. (basketball) A basket that is made as the ball rolls off the tips of the shooter's fingers.

firehorse basketball. (basketball) Slang from 1960s, early 1970s, for game action that employs fast breaks, long passes, and one-handed shooting from angles.

five-hole. (hockey) The sometimes-open area between a goalie's legs; it is the most common term among several of similar nature. The others are one-hole (over the left shoulder), two-hole (over the right shoulder), three-hole (left side), four-hole (right side).

flake. (basic jock talk) A player known for his eccentric conduct.

flanker. (football) An offensive player set into a position beyond the end before the ball is put into play.

flash cut. (basketball) A sudden cut into the lane for a possible pass in and easy score; then, if the ball is not passed, jumping back out on the side from which entry was made.

flats. (football) The areas on either extremity of the line of scrimmage and extending about five yards into defensive territory. A "flat pass" is one thrown into this area for short yardage.

floater. (baseball and softball) A ball that stays in the air for a long time, appearing to float.

flopper. (hockey) A goalkeeper who frequently falls to the ice to smother the puck.

flow. (football) The direction in which the players are moving after the play has begun.

flush. (basketball) To score.

fly hack. (rugby football) The wanton kicking of a loose ball by a panicky player.

footer. (basketball) Big, slower player.

forkball. (baseball) A pitch delivered with the index and middle fingers that drops as it nears the plate.

freelance. (basic jock talk) Originated on the playgrounds. It means that each of the five players has an individual style rather than a team game with a one-for-all attitude.

freelance play. (basic jock talk) An offense allowing individual choices, as opposed to a set play.

free trip. (baseball) Base on balls.

freeze. (basic jock talk) To attempt to retain possession of the ball or puck for an extended time without making an effort to score.

frontliners. (basketball) Collective term for the two forwards and center.

frostie. (softball) Slow-pitch pitch that arcs above twelve feet. It alludes facetiously to the frost that appears at higher altitudes.

fungo. (baseball) A practice fly hit to a fielder by tossing the ball in the air and hitting it as it falls.

funk dunk. (basketball) Any sort of dunk that showcases flair or leaping ability.

furniture. (tennis) Racket frame.

* G

game face. (basic jock talk) Looking mean and determined. The term may have been created to describe former New York Knick Bernard King.

game full of leather. (baseball and softball) One characterized by good fielding.

game point. (basketball) The juncture in a game where one score can win it.

garbage. (basketball) A loose ball or rebound that results in a layup or short jumper.

garbage time. (basketball) When the players play individual basketball rather than a team game and try to fatten their statistics.

gift of grab. (basic jock talk) The skill of a pickpocket in being able to steal the ball.

Ginny. (tennis) The Virginia Slims tennis tour, for short.

give-and-take. (hockey) A technique in which the goalie gives the shooter an open target, then quickly closes (or takes away) the hole when the opponent shoots.

golf widow. A woman whose husband spends a great amount of time on the golf course.

good cheese. (baseball) Blurring fastball. Fastballs are, or have been, called breezers, aspirins, smokers, sizzlers, soakers, rivets, and steamers.

good hands. (basic jock talk) The ability to catch a ball.

good wood. (baseball and softball) What one says when one makes solid contact with the ball, despite the fact that hardly anyone bats with wooden bats anymore.

googan. (pool and billiards) A recreational pool player.

gopher ball. (baseball and softball) A pitch that is hit for a home run.

gorilla juice. (basic jock talk) Steroids.

grand slam. (baseball and softball) A home run with the bases filled.

granny shot. (basketball) An underhand free throw.

grass cutter. (baseball and softball) A hard-hit ball that skims along the green.

graveyard. (bowling) Low-scoring lane.

grease it. (basketball) A cry heard from shooters whose shots are hanging on the rim.

gridiron. (football) The field itself, from the appearance of its horizontal lines, which are spaced five yards apart.

grips. Shoes. Everything from blinking L.A. Gears to K Mart specials and Doc Martens. It ain't the shoes, contrary to Spike Lee's ad pitch, it's the player in the shoes.

groove. (baseball and softball) To pitch the ball right in the middle of the strike zone.

gunner. (basketball) Someone who shoots a lot. Also *chucker, heaver, pump.*

gun-shy. (basic jock talk) Overly cautious, especially after an injury, such as a baseball player who has been hit by a ball.

gusjohnson. (basketball) To dunk so ferociously that the rim is separated from the backboard. (Ex-pro Gus Johnson did it once.)

gutter ball. (bowling) A ball that rolls off the alley and into the gutter, or trough. A gutter ball is a dead ball and counts as a turn.

gym rat. (basic jock talk) A regular.

* H

hack. (basketball) Hitting a player across the hands or arms as he tries to dribble or pass the ball.

Hail Mary. (football) A pass thrown into the end zone into a crowd of receivers and defenders. This is a desperation play commonly attempted in the last few minutes of a game by a team that is losing.

handle. (basketball) A player with good ball-handling skills is said to have a good handle.

hang. (baseball and softball) Said of a pitch that fails to break.

hang time. (1) (basketball) The period of time a player hovers in the air—or hangs—while driving to the basket. (2) (football) The amount of time a punted ball remains in the air.

harrigan. (pool and billiards) A lucky shot.

hat trick. Three goals by one player in one game. The term is common to ice hockey and soccer.

headhunter. (baseball) Pitcher using fastball to settle grievances, real or imagined.

heady. (basketball) Adjective applied by announcers to short, slow players who can't shoot.

heave. (basketball) A "hope" or desperation shot where the player does not take the time or have the room to aim the ball properly.

hipping. To hit an opponent with your hip.

hit the dirt. (baseball and softball) To slide.

hold court. (basketball) To remain in successive pickup games by virtue of consecutive victories.

hole. (basketball) The basket.

hole high. (basketball) Ball position parallel to the circle, wheel, arc, or area surrounding the free-throw line.

homebrew. (basic jock talk) Locally bred player.

hoop. (basketball) The metal rim of the basket, eighteen inches in diameter. Also called the cage or the bucket.

HORSE. (basketball) That most basic of playground diversions, in which each player must match the successful shot of any previous player. If your predecessor misses, you're free to shoot from anywhere. Anyone who misses after someone else's make is assessed a letter; spell H-O-R-S-E and you are one. If life's hectic, just play P-I-G.

hospital pass. (rugby football) Dangerous pass that could, as they say in Britain, "put you in hospital."

host. (basic jock talk) To be the home team.

hot corner. (baseball and softball) Third base.

hot dog. (basic jock talk) (1) One who shows off. (2) To show off.

hot hand. (basketball) The player who is having a good night with his shooting and "can't miss" from the field.

house ball. (bowling) A ball that is provided by the bowling center.

house call. (basketball) A showy move.

hung him out to dry. (basketball) A player driving around his defender for an easy two points. It usually suggests that the offensive man had no trouble in getting by his opponent.

hustler. An individual who seeks to induce persons less skilled than himself to gamble at pool or billiards.

 I

iceman. Hockey player.

ice time. (hockey) The amount of playing time accumulated by a player during a game or season.

in-and-out. (basketball) A shot that appears to be ready to drop through the rim but is just a fraction off-line and bounces or spins out.

inside. (football) The interior line; between the tackles.

in the refrigerator. (basketball) The term applied to a game so far out of reach that the team ahead will win the game. It's "in the refrigerator."

in-your-face. (basketball) Describing a disrespectful or disdainful style of play.

iron man/woman. (basic jock talk) One who chooses to play though injured.

 J

J, the. (basketball) The jump shot. Also *bus stop, joint.*

jab. (boxing) A quick, straight blow,

usually delivered to the opponent's head with the lead hand (the left hand in the case of a right-handed boxer).

jack. (lawn bowling) The small white ball, two and a half inches in diameter, that serves as the bowler's target.

jam. (1) (baseball and softball) To pitch inside to a batter, usually close to his hands, to prevent him from hitting the ball solidly. (2) (basketball) To DUNK.

jam up. (basketball) When a defensive team clogs up the middle of the court. (A zone or floating defense may do this.)

jock. (basic jock talk) (1) An athletic supporter or jockstrap, for short. (2) An athlete. (3) Describing that which is athletic in nature, such as a "jock school" or "jock [fraternity] house."

juice. (basic jock talk) Steroids.

juice monkey. (basic jock talk) One bloated or otherwise affected by steroids.

juke. (1) (basketball) An awkward or unusual shot. (2) (football) To fake an opponent, especially a potential tackler, out of position.

jumper. (basketball) A jump shot.

junk. (1) (basketball) A sudden move used by either an offensive or defensive player, usually as a decoy. (2) (baseball) Pitches that are regarded as being of inferior quality, usually slow curveballs. (3) (volleyball) Off-speed shots.

 K

K. (baseball and softball) A strikeout. The symbol *K* is used in scoring a game to indicate a strike.

keeper. (football) Offensive play in which the quarterback holds on to and runs with the ball rather than passing it or handing it off.

kegler. (bowling) A bowler.

key. (basic jock talk) To watch and take one's cue from a player on the other team.

key, keyhole. (basketball) The entire free-throw area. It includes the free-throw lane and the free-throw circle.

keystone sack. (baseball and softball) Second base.

killing the clock. Another way of saying "freezing the ball."

kill shot. (1) (football) Extremely aggressive tackle of a severity that means the man tackled will have to be aided from the field. Lawrence Taylor of the New York Giants defined the term on the eve of Super Bowl XXI in 1987: "A kill shot is when snot's coming from his nose and he's quivering on the ground." (2) (tennis) In tennis and other racket games, a shot hit with such force that it is virtually unreturnable. Sometimes called a smash.

kill the clock. (basketball) Sneakers.

kip. (gymnastics) In swinging from a horizontal bar, a movement at the end of the swing in which the performer snaps the legs back and straightens them, then raises the body to an arm-support position.

kiss. (1) (basketball) Banking the ball off the backboard into the basket. (2) (billiards, pocket billiards) A shot in which the cue ball rebounds from one object to another.

kitchen. (shuffleboard) Space in

which player loses ten points. Players work hard to put their opponents in the kitchen.

kitten ball. (softball) (1) One of a number of historical names for softball. (2) The term still has application as sixteen-inch players talk disparagingly about folks who play with a twelve-inch ball. A line from a 1976 issue of the periodical *Windy City Softball* tells of a "kitten ball team from Indiana" being introduced to Chicago-style ball (and being whomped).

knock-hockey player. (basketball) A bank-shot artist.

✳ L

lane. (basketball) The area between the free-throw boundaries and from the end line to the free-throw line. Also, *alley, crease, well, hole.*

last bullet. (softball) Slang term for the upcoming third out in the last inning for the losing team.

laugher. (basic jock talk) Lopsided victory; a blowout—so easy that the winning team has fun. One big laugh.

laxman/laxwoman. (lacrosse) Lacrosse player.

layup. (basketball) A shot made close to the basket in which the ball is played off the backboard.

leader board. (golf) Scoreboard on which the rankings of golfers in a tournament are listed.

leatherman. (baseball) A good fielder; one who uses the leather in his glove to advantage.

lemonade. (pool and billiards) To deliberately play below your true level of ability—as one might do at the beginning of a hustle.

like money in the bank. (basketball) Safe. A sure shot such as a slam dunk by Michael Jordan.

li'l' help. (basketball) The playground SOS. If your ball rolls away toward a neighboring game or gets stuck in a tangled chain net, this alerts others that you'd like them to retrieve it or offer their ball so you can jar yours free.

line-drive shot. (basketball) Some players favor hard, low-trajectory shots at the basket. But often this is a hard shot to make unless the player is extremely proficient. The shot also has a lot of velocity.

links. A golf course.

lock. (basic jock talk) A certainty.

look. (basketball) A pass, usually inside, that leads to a basket. Also *dish, find.*

lose the handle. (basketball) To lose control of the ball and turn it over to the other team.

✳ M

magic number. In baseball, football, and other sports in which league championships are decided on a won-lost basis, the magic number is the combined total of wins for the league-leading team and losses for the second-place team that will mathematically assure the league leader of the championship. For example, if team A leads the league by seven games over team B with ten games remaining on the schedule, Team A's magic number is four.

maiden. (horse racing) A racehorse that has never won a race.

Meminger's law. (basketball) An edict promulgated by former pro and New York–playground habitué Dean Meminger. It holds that, if you don't play ball, you can't hang out.

mitts. (hockey) The special gloves players wear.

mixer. (bowling) A ball that causes the pins to bounce around.

moguls. (skiing) Washboard ridges created by other skiers' skiing at an angle.

mombo. (basketball) A series of head, shoulder, or ball fakes.

Monday-morning quarterback. (basic jock talk) Sports fan with all of the answers the day after the game.

money player. A player who comes through in key situations, when money is at stake, such as in the play-offs and championship games. Also used to describe rookies who signed pro contracts for many millions of dollars.

move the ball. (softball) Hitting the ball. It is used in the fast-pitch game.

Mr. Kodak. (pro sports) A vain player, one who poses for press photographers.

mulligan. (golf) A free shot given a player after a poor one.

mush ball. (softball) (1) The sixteen-inch softball to distinguish it from the smaller twelve-inch version. (2) The sixteen-inch game. (3) One of a number of names for softball.

mustard came off the hot dog. Used to describe a player's action when he tries a fancy play. "The mustard came off the hot dog on that pass."

my bad. (basketball) My mistake. An expression of contrition, uttered after an air ball or an air pass goes out of bounds.

my house. (basketball) My territory; the free-throw lane, as in, "Don't bring that weak [stuff] into my house!" (*Phoenix Gazette,* August 14, 1994, Peter Corbett)

next level, the. (basic jock talk) Where college players want to go after they leave school, e.g., the NBA.

nickel defense. (football) Strategy in which an extra defensive back is put in the backfield to defend against a pass. The term alludes to the fact that there are five (a nickel) defenders rather than four.

no harm, no foul. (basketball) One of the original Chick Hearn phrases. A play involving physical contact— but not enough to warrant a foul being whistled.

no-man's-land. In tennis and other net games, a midcourt area between the baseline and the service line from which it is difficult to make an effective return. The player is too far from the net to volley properly, and not back far enough to execute solid baseline strokes.

nosebleed country. (spectator) Seats high above the action.

nosebleeder. (basketball) Player who can go high in the air for rebounds.

noseguard/nose tackle. (football) A guard or a tackle who stands in front of—or nose to nose with—the opposing center during certain plays.

nothing but net. (basketball) Describing a basket in which the ball does not hit the rim.

nurse. (billiards) A playing technique in which the shooter keeps the balls in position for consecutive shots by striking them softly.

nutmeg. (soccer) To push the ball between the defender's legs, run around him or her, control the loose ball, and continue dribbling. It is very embarrassing to a defender to be nutmegged.

office pool. A gambling exercise in which you try to pick the winner of every game in the tournament. Called a pool because you get soaked for whatever fee is needed, and you never win.

Invariably, the winner is someone's twelve-year-old kid who picked the winners according to the most popular college jackets in middle school. The biggest entertainment value comes in seeing the office basketball expert lose his national champion in the first round to an upset by the Sally Struthers School of Career Advancement. (*Baltimore Sun,* Ray Frager, March 17, 1995, NCAA preview)

ohfer. (baseball and softball) A batter who is hitless in a game, as in he was 0-for-4.

old boys. (rugby football) Players who are thirty-five years old or older.

on deck. (baseball and softball) Scheduled to bat after the present batter.

110 percent. (basic jock talk) Extra effort.

paint. (basketball) The free-throw lane, usually painted a different color from the rest of the court floor.

paint, in the. (basketball) A phrase indicating that a player is in the lane area near each basket. So named because the lane is often a different color from the rest of the floor. And, yes, we know that the entire court is painted. It's a basketball thing, you wouldn't understand. (*Baltimore Sun,* Ray Frager, March 17, 1995, NCAA preview)

paint the corners. (baseball and softball) Pitch that crosses the inside or outside part of home plate for a strike.

palm. (basketball) (1) To hold the ball in one hand, usually for show. Obligatory for most varieties of FUNK DUNK. (2) The illegal dribble on which there's no prohibition in the speakeasies of the schoolyard.

palming. (basketball) Losing control of a dribble and—for a split second—carrying the ball in the palm of the hand. If a referee spots it, the other team gets the ball. Also called carrying.

pancake. (football) Throwing a block that plants an opponent on his back.

paste. (basic jock talk) Defeat.

pepper. (baseball) Played with one batter and one or more fielders. The batter either bunts at or takes a half swing at the ball tossed by the fielder immediately after he or she fields the ball. The ball is continuously thrown, batted, and fielded in rapid succession.

physical. (football) Rough or dirty. A team that is "very physical" is nasty.

pick. (basketball) Stationing oneself so that the defensive man guarding the ball handler will be unable to stay with him, having run into the picker.

pick and roll. (basketball) (1) An offensive play where one man sets a pick, then moves or rolls around the defender and heads toward the basket to receive a pass. (Zander Hollander's *Encyclopedia of Sports Talk*) (2) A play in which the player setting a screen for a teammate with the ball suddenly cuts toward the basket for a pass.

pickup. Unorganized ball. Pickup game, pickup team. Also *drop-in, free play, ratball.*

pigskin. (football) (1) The football. (2) Relating to football, as in "pigskin preview."

pillow ball. (softball) The sixteen-inch softball to distinguish it from the smaller twelve-inch version.

pillows. (hockey) Overside leg pads to provide not only protection but defense. Once stuffed with horse-hair, they now contain synthetic material. There are no metal parts.

pipes. (hockey) The posts to both sides of the goalie that support the net. The pipes are six feet apart.

pit. (football) The area along the line of scrimmage where the two lines clash.

playing the angles. (hockey) The goaltender's position in the net in relation to the puck. When playing back in the net, goalies have to move farther to make a save. Playing out front cuts down on the area to cover. See FIVE-HOLE.

pluggers. (football) Linebackers.

poach. In doubles play in tennis and other court games, to cross into one's partner's court to cut off a shot and volley.

poodle. (bowling) To roll the ball into the gutter.

pork chop. One who is overweight.

post. (basketball) Another term for the pivot man's spot on the court. It is "high" when he plays near the free-throw line, and "low" when he plays near the basket. (Zander Hollander's *Encyclopedia of Sports Talk*)

prayer. (basketball) A shot let go in such desperation that it seems only divine intervention will put it in the basket.

pressure cooker. A close, important game—which goes down to the final minutes of play where everything is on the line. (Term from "Chick's Lexicon"—i.e., one from Chick Hearn)

PT. Playing time.

pulling the goaltender. (hockey) This usually happens late in games with one-goal differences in the score to allow the team trailing to add an extra skater. See EMPTY-NET GOAL.

pumpkin. (hockey) Your head.

pump shot. (basketball) An overhead, two-hand shot taken in midair. The shooter lifts the ball over his head, then cocks (pumps) his arm and shoots the ball before hitting the floor. (William T. "Buck" Lai's *Winning Basketball*)

punch on. (basketball) To score on a defender.

punk dunk. (basketball) A dunk in which the dunker attempts to humiliate the dunkee.

puppy. (health-club talk) Beginner at the health club.

quarterback. The player who generally supervises his team's tactics and gives signals.

rabbit dunk. (baseball) A baseball that is livelier than normal, and thus one capable of being hit a long distance.

rack, the. (basketball) The basket. Also, *cup, dog, hole.*

radio pitch. (softball) As described in *Softball Player's Magazine*: "Batters can hear it, but can't see it." It has been used to describe the fastball of Debbie Doom of El Monte, California.

rainbow shot. (basketball) A high-arcing shot, usually from the outside over the heads of tall defenders.

rat race. (basketball) A high-scoring game.

rattle. (basketball) A successful shot in which the ball hits the inside of the rim several times before dropping through.

red dog. (football) Defensive play in which the linebacker crashes through the line to kill the offensive play before it begins. In an earlier time this was known as rushing the passer.

redshirt. (football) A college player who has been withheld from competition for a year so as to extend his eligibility to play.

ref. (basic jock talk) Referee.

rep. (basketball) Reputation.

ribbie. (baseball and softball) Improved way of saying RBI, for run batted in, as in, "He's got fifty-seven ribbies and it's still June."

ringer. (basic jock talk) Illegal player: a contestant entered dishonestly into a race or contest. Also, in horseshoe pitching, a horseshoe that is thrown to encircle the stake and is worth three points.

ring his bell. (football) To hit someone hard in a contact sport.

rip. (basketball) A successful shot, usually a swish.

ripped to the bone. (health-club talk) Describing one who is all muscle—also, *roped* and *inside out.*

roid. (basic jock talk) One on steroids; a juice monkey.

rookie. (basic jock talk) A first-year player; a novice (an apparent corruption of *recruit*).

round-tripper. (baseball) A home run.

rugger. (rugby football) (1) The game of rugby. (2) One who plays the game.

rugger hugger. (rugby football) A rugger's date or spouse.

run a clinic. (basketball) (1) To execute a play crisply. (2) To win convincingly.

run-and-gun. (basketball) Describing an open style of play in which direct assaults are made on the basket.

run it back. (basketball) The request of a pickup team that has just been beaten for an immediate rematch.

running game. (basketball) Teams that have perfected the fast break play a running game. It features a quick pass from the rebounder to an outlet man, usually on the side of the court. The objective is to have as many players as possible breaking for the basket with the defense out of position.

* S

sack. (1) (football) A tackle of the quarterback behind the offensive line, usually as the result of a BLITZ. (2) (football) To tackle the quarterback. (3) (baseball) A base.

sandbagger. (bowling) An individual who purposely keeps down his average in order to receive a higher handicap than he deserves.

sandwich. (football) To trap an offensive player between two defenders.

school. (basketball) To take advantage of someone by pulling a deft offensive move—from the notion that the person is being taught how to make the move.

scissors cut. (basketball) When two or more players crisscross each other's path.

scrambler. (football) A quarterback with a reputation for moving around to avoid being tackled.

scratch hit. (baseball and softball) A ball, usually weakly hit, that none of the fielders can reach in time to retire the batter.

scrimmage. (basic jock talk) Game-like practicing with two sides and scores, but sometimes fewer than normal number on a side.

second effort. (basic jock talk) Sudden display of power and determination by an individual or team following a setback.

second wind. (basic jock talk) A renewal of energy after a period of exhaustion.

sewer. (basketball) A basket so loose that anything going near it goes down it.

shag. (baseball and softball) Chasing down and catching batted fly balls during batting or fielding practice.

shagger. (softball) Name for the youngsters who are hired to retrieve over-the-fence home runs in slow-pitch softball tournaments and bring them back for reuse. A major tournament like the Smoky Mountain Classic or the Twitty City will witness as many as one thousand balls going over the wall.

shake. (basketball) To elude an opponent, usually by duping him with a stutter step or juke, and then breaking away.

shake and bake. (basketball) To feint, fake, and ultimately score with a graceful move.

shirts vs. skins/shirts 'n' skins. (basic jock talk) Means of distinguishing one team from another in pickup games: one team wears shirts while the other is bare-chested.

shoestring. (basic jock talk) At or near ground level. Catching any ball just as it is about to hit the ground is a "shoestring catch," and a "shoestring tackle" in football is one made just above the knees.

shoot for it. The shooting of fingers, or the shooting of a shot, to decide who'll get possession when a jump ball or another quandary arises.

shoot the boot. (rugby football) To fumble the lyrics of a rugby song at the postmatch bash.

shovel/shovel pass. (football) A forward pass tossed underhand.

showboat. A player who shows off; a hot dog.

shuffle cut. (basketball) After the player has made a pass, he then moves away from the pass by cutting around a teammate who has set a pick for him.

sin bin. (hockey) The penalty box.

sixth man. (basketball) The player who is regularly used as the team's first substitute.

skate save. (hockey) To stop the puck with a skate.

skinned. (softball) The proper condition and description of a softball infield that is devoid—or skinned—of grass.

skull practice. Practice involving the mental rather than the physical nature of the game in question.

skunk. (basketball) To win a pickup game in straight baskets, usually by 9–0.

skunk rule. (softball) Proviso encounters in which a game is ended if a team is ahead by a certain number of runs at the end of an inning.

sky. (basketball) Not merely to jump, but to sail—in pursuit of hoops, bounds, rejections, or just a whiff of rarer air. Also, *rise, talk to God.*

skyhook. (basketball) A high hook shot taken from an altitude above the level of the basket.

skywalk. (basketball) An aerial stroll.

slab. (baseball) The pitcher's rubber.

slam dunk. (basketball) A dunk shot of unusual force and spectator appeal.

slants. (softball) Pitched balls, especially in fastball parlance.

slap shot. (hockey) A hard shot made by bringing the stick into a high backswing, then forward, hitting the ice and puck simultaneously, causing the puck to be lifted from the ice.

slashing. (hockey) Frank Luksa of the *Daily Morning News* defined it this way in 1993: "Not to be confused with tripping, hooking, holding, or cross-checking. Slashing employs the stick as a scythe in a hacking motion to cause a rival to fall down. When prone, he is easier to skate over and leave blade tracks across the chest."

sledgehammer. (pool and billiards) A heavy stroke, especially on the break.

sleeper. (basketball) An easy basket. Normally the offensive player is all alone under the basket. Also called an easy bunny.

slingshot. (softball) Fast-pitch delivery in which the arm gripping the ball leaves its position at the waist, is whipped backward to the stretching point, then moved forward with as much speed and force as possible.

slump. (basic jock talk) Time in which a player or team lacks effectiveness.

smile. (golf) Golfer's lingo for the crescent-shaped scar left on a ball's surface by a badly aimed swing.

snakebit. (basic jock talk) A team or individual athlete that seems to attract an inordinate amount of bad luck.

southpaw. (basic jock talk) Left-hander, originally a baseball term but now used in all sports.

span. (bowling) The distance between the thumb hole and finger holes over the surface of a bowling ball.

spar. (boxing) To box, usually in a practice session.

spearing. (hockey) The illegal use of a stick to poke another player.

spears reverse dribble. (basketball) Bringing the ball back toward oneself prior to switching hands on the dribble, thus protecting it before taking it across the body in front of the defender.

spike. (1) (baseball) To slide with one's baseball shoes, or spikes, high so as to hurt the man covering the base. (2) (football) To celebrate a touchdown by slamming the ball into the ground of the end zone.

split the post. (basketball) Two players crisscross around a post player and into the lane.

sportoons. Name given by Joseph P. Kahn of the *Boston Globe* to *Roller-Games, American Gladiators,* and other shows "masquerading as a sporting event."

spotter. (1) A person who assists a television or radio broadcaster by identifying the players on the field. (2) (gymnastics) An instructor who assists by supporting, lifting, or catching the gymnasts as a stunt is being performed during a practice session.

spread, the. (basic jock talk) The number of points by which one team is believed to be better than another for the purpose of wagering. If the spread is five, it means that the stronger team is favored by five points.

squad. (basketball) A total of twelve men in pro basketball. Of the five on the floor, one is a center, two are forwards, and two are guards.

stand-up. (hockey) The style in

which a goalie remains in an upright position, using his stick and skates to make saves below the waist.

starting five. (basketball) The five regulars on a basketball team who are in the starting lineup.

stick save. (hockey) To stop the puck with a stick.

stick-um. (football) Sticky substance that a pass receiver puts on his hands to hold on to the ball.

string music. (basketball) Sportscaster Joe Dean's term for a shot that bottoms out.

stroke. (basketball) Shot or shooting motion. Larry Bird has a stroke of genius.

studfish. (basketball) Someone who can play.

stuff. (basketball) Dunk; also to block someone's shot.

stuff shot. (basketball) Stuffing the ball into the basket from above after a leap high toward the basket. See DUNK.

stunting. (basketball) Sometimes referred to as multiple defenses. The strategy of changing defenses to confuse opponents.

stutter step. (football) Shuffle or quick step that is used to deceive a defender by giving the illusion that the runner is about to stop or turn. It is also used by pass receivers trying to stay in bounds as they catch sideline passes.

sucker pitch. (softball) Short pitch that a player throws with exaggerated motion hoping that the batter will mistime his or her swing.

sudden death. An overtime period in which the team that scores first wins the game.

suit up. (basic jock talk) To dress to play.

Sweatlanta. (Olympics) Name for Atlanta created by the athletes during the 1996 games.

sweep. (football) An attempt to carry the ball around the defensive end.

sweet spot. The spot toward the end of the baseball bat, on the face of a golf club, or at the center of a paddle or racquet on which the ball is best hit.

swingman. (basketball) A versatile player who can play two different positions.

swivel hips. (football) Attribute of a player who is particularly hard to catch and tackle.

swisher. (basketball) A successful field-goal attempt (usually from long range) that apparently does not touch the basket rim.

 ✳ T

tailor. (basketball) Someone not only deft at blocking shots, but at altering them, too.

take the train. (basketball) A less-than-diplomatic suggestion that someone has traveled.

taste that. (basketball) After blocking an opponent's shot, say this to remind him of what he can do with it.

taxi squad. (football) Reserves who can be activated on short notice to replace players who are injured.

tenant. (basketball) Player who tends to stay too long in the shooting lane—where one is allowed only three seconds.

tending. (basketball) Goaltending.

Texas leaguer. (baseball and softball) A fly ball that drops between an infielder and an outfielder for a hit.

thin. (basic jock talk) Said of a team without reserve players.

throwbacks. (professional sports) Term for old-fashioned facsimile uniforms worn for a game to commemorate an anniversary or special event.

tick. (basketball) Shot.

tight. (basketball) Tied.

toilet seater. (basketball) A shot that rolls around the rim several times before dropping through or spinning out.

tomahawk. (volleyball) Hitting the ball with the back of one's forearm; a reverse bump.

tools of ignorance. (baseball) The catcher's paraphernalia.

top shelf. (hockey) The area where a puck enters the net just below the crossbar. See FIVE-HOLE and PLAYING THE ANGLES.

touch. (football) Game in which tackling is forbidden and a player is considered ''down'' when he or she is touched below the waist.

touches. (football) Measure of how many times a player touches the ball during a game.

trailer. A player in ice hockey, basketball, and other goal games who follows behind the player who is in possession of the puck or ball to be in a position to receive a pass.

transcon. (basketball) See COAST TO COAST.

trapper. (hockey) Used by the open hand, this glove is used mostly to catch the puck.

trash talk. (basic jock talk) Aggressive talk on the court or playing field.

traveling. (basketball) Walking with the ball or taking too many steps without dribbling. Results in loss of possession.

tree. (basketball) A tall player.

trim. (basketball) To make a shot.

triple double. (basketball) Single-game performance in which a player gets double figures (ten or more) in points, rebounds, and assists.

tude. (basketball) Attitude.

turkey. (bowling) Three consecutive strikes.

turnaround. (basketball) A play with several options that is used by a pivotman.

turnover. (football, basketball, etc.) The loss of possession.

twig. (hockey) Hockey stick.

twine. (basketball) Net. Root for the expressions *twine time* and *twine twinkler.*

two-bagger. (baseball and softball) A double.

 U

ump. (baseball) Umpire.

Uncle Charlie. (baseball) A fine

curveball, also called a yakker and occasionally the yellow hammer.

undercutting. (basketball) A dangerous and, when intentional, unsportsmanlike practice consisting of running under another player when he is already in the air attempting a shot.

uprights. (football) The vertical posts that support the crossbar in a goalpost.

✳ V

V-ball. (volleyball) The game of volleyball.

✳ W

waffle. (hockey) Blocker pad on player's stick hand.

waggle. (golf) To move the clubhead back and forth with short, quick motions when addressing the ball.

walking. (basketball) Traveling with the ball.

walk-on. (basic jock talk) A player who has not been recruited who shows up for a tryout on a college team. A walk-on is drawn to the school by academics and does not have an athletic scholarship.

walkover. (basic jock talk) An easy victory.

wallyball. Volleyball played on squash court.

wave, the. (spectator sports) The visual effect of a human wave or surge created as fans rise quickly to their feet as the swell passes through their section of the grandstand.

weak hand. (basketball) The off hand.

weak side. (basketball) The side of the lane away from where the ball was when a play or pattern was initiated; usually a minority of the offensive players are stationed on this side. (Jim Pruitt's *Play Better Basketball*)

Western Union. (basketball) The telegraphing of a pass or a shot so that a steal or block results.

wet ones. (baseball) The latest name for illegal spitballs from the name of the commercial moist towelette.

wheel. (basketball) Ankle.

wheels. (basic jock talk) Legs. A player with exceptional running speed is said to have them.

white knuckler. (basic jock talk) A close game; one that goes down to the wire.

white man's disease. (basketball) An inability to jump. Sometimes referred to as "the dread disease."

whitewash. To hold an opponent scoreless; to shut out an opponent.

wiff. (golf) To miss the ball entirely.

wig-wag. (football) Hand signals, as opposed to instructions brought into the huddle by a player.

wild-card team. In professional football, basketball, and soccer, a team that qualifies for play-off competition by virtue of having the best record of all the teams within the conference that did not automatically qualify.

Wimby. (tennis) Wimbleton.

windmill. (softball) The name for a fast delivery that begins with a full circle.

wind sprint. (basic jock talk) A short run.

wipeout. (basketball) To win by a big margin.

wood. (basketball) The court. Short for hardwood, but applies to all surfaces.

woof. (basketball) To address an opponent in an intimidating fashion.

X-games. Nickname for TV and cable extreme games including sky surfing and street lugeing.

yips. (golf) Pressure that affects a player; usually referred to as "the yips." To choke.

yolked. (health-club talk) Person with low body fat and plenty of muscles.

your world. (basketball) You're all alone, take your shot.

yo-yoing/yo-yoing up and down. (basketball) When a guard dribbles the ball up court, it's as if the ball is on a yo-yo string. Consequently, the guard is yo-yoing the ball up and down.

Zamboni. The four-wheeled vehicle that is used before a contest is played to vacuum excess water from a field with an artificial surface; also the vehicle that is used in resurfacing an ice-hockey rink. The Zamboni lays down a thin film of water that freezes to become the new surface.

zebra. (basic jock talk) Referee in any sport in which that person is distinguished by a striped shirt.

zip. (basic jock talk) A score of zero.

zone. (basketball) A style of team defense in which each player is assigned to guard a designated floor area, rather than a specific player.

zoning. (tennis) Excellent play.

zoom. (basketball) To defend.

SOURCES

Webster's Sports Dictionary (Merriam-Webster), Tim Considine's *The Language of Sport* (Facts on File, 1982), and Harvey Frommer's *Sports Lingo* (Atheneum, 1979) are just a few of the many sources of more sports slang. The Tamony Collection pays particular attention to sports. "Asphalt Argot" from *The Back-in-Your-Face Guide to Pickup Basketball* and William T. "Buck" Lai's *Winning Basketball* were also important.

——— ✳ *25* ✳ ———

TEEN AND HIGH SCHOOL SLANG

A Dialect of Many Subcultures

One cannot keep up with slang, especially the slang of the young, which is designed to be unintelligible to adults, and, once decoded, since today's young reject history, has turned into vapour or unspeak.
—Anthony Burgess writing in the London
Times Literary Supplement,
December 5, 1986

I can take a phrase that's rarely heard. Flip it, now it's a daily word.
—Rap musician Rakim, quoted in the
Los Angeles Times, August 29, 1988

In this the age of Beavis and Butt-head, hip-hop, and a multitude of cliquish cultures, teenage slang is probably no more subversive than it ever was.

However, it is more diverse: hip-hoppers, industrial-music fans, grunge-ophiles, gangsters, metal-heads, ravers, surfers, skaters, skiers, and snowboarders have their own slang. Other slang varies from one ethnic group to the next: Hispanic teens use some Spanish-language terms, while African-American teens throw around words such as *kickin'* (hanging out) or *gerpin'* (trying to find a date).

While each subgroup and culture comes with its own set of words, some youth slang is spread wide; it comes from movies or song lyrics and catches on nationwide. But some is geographical; kids on the western or southern side of Santa Clara Valley, California, have words and phrases that are exclusive to their cliques or peer groups. And you may catch surfer teens in Santa Cruz, California, calling girls "birds" or referring to great waves as "epic."

Despite all of this, there is a middle ground, a general teen argot, that we can at least try to capture.

What links the generations is that much teen slang tends to be about the same things. Today there are a host of words for cool—including *cool* and *phat*—and another batch for geeks and dorks—including *geeks, dorks*—just as there was for the class of '57. Other terms, including *groovy* and *funk,* which today mean stodgy or out of it, now mean the opposite of what they did to the flower children of the sixties.

What was once barfing or losing one's lunch has emerged into a rich vocabulary of vomit synonyms. When *USA Today* wrote about teenage slang in 1988, a fourteen-year-old reader wrote to say that she knew fifty-three different terms for blowing rainbows. Some terms that were once reserved for the young have now slipped into quasi-standard English—for instance, *hassle* (as in, "That is too much of a hassle for me"), *put-down*, and *uptight*.

What all of this proves is that the slang of the young is mercurial, unpredictable, and somewhat allergic to print. If a noted linguist is quoted in the papers as saying that *bad* no longer means good, the term seems to come back with a vengeance. If teachers start using a term, it is likely either to die or to have its meaning change radically. "Teenspeak—the language of youth—is as fickle as fashion," wrote Leslie Rubinkowski of the *Pittsburg* (Calif.) *Press* in late 1992. "Just when you latch onto enough words to communicate, the entire vocabulary changes. And tomorrow, this entire primer on teenage slang will be history. In fact, among some teens it already is dust."

In other words, if you are a teenager and need this list, you're in deep trouble.

* A

abusak. Elevator music, a blend of *abuse* and Muz*ak*.

ace-high. The best.

acid. Steroids.

aggresso. To act assertively; an act of aggression.

aggro. Great; good.

agro. Mad; pissed off.

air guitar. Imaginary guitar played along with real music or without.

airhead. (1) One who is empty-headed, dumb. (2) Someone who is out of it. This term dates from a time when many of today's teenagers were infants, but it still hangs on.

air mail. Garbage thrown out the window.

all-nighter. A party or study session that lasts all night.

Andy. The person in a band who is such a zero that no one gives a care about him. Origin: Andy Taylor of Duran Duran. Usage: "Danny Wood is the Andy of New Kids on the Block. Adam Clayton is the Andy of U2. Mick Mars is the Andy of Mötley Crüe."

arbuckle. Dingbat.

as if! (1) To the contrary. (2) No way.

ass out. In trouble.

attitude adjustment. High on drugs or booze.

atwood. Canadian synonym for

wedgie. Usage: "This worn-out, old pair of underwear is giving me an atwood."

audi (1) Good-bye, I'm leaving. (2) I'm out of here. "I'm audi." (3) To run. All of these are from the name of the imported luxury car. Variation on all of this is "I'm Audi 5000."

awesome. (Pronounced *aah-some*.) Great; good; okay. This term is passé in some circles, current in others. Can be elevated to "totally awesome" or "mega-awesome" for emphasis.

* B

B. Frisbee. "Let's play some B."

bad. Good. People keep saying that this term is verging on the edge of the archaic, but it just keeps hanging on.

bag. Kill; stop.

bag some rays. Same as "to catch some rays," to get some sunshine.

bail. (1) *v.* To cut a class; bail out: to leave, thereby blowing off some distasteful task or event. (2) To put something down—"Bail that!" is used like "Screw that!"

bail out. To leave.

bake. To smoke marijuana.

baked. Really stoned.

bald. Bad; terrible.

Baldwin. (1) attractive guy. (2) A male Betty.

ballin'. Going fast, as in, "I was really ballin' down the highway."

B&B. Beavis and Butt-head.

banjaxed. Demolished, ruined (as a car).

bank. Cash; money itself. This term is common in rap music lyrics.

Barney. (1) Unattractive guy. (2) Not a Baldwin.

bat caver. Person in black.

b-boy/b-girl. Rap music devotee. The *b-* in these terms stands for *beat.*

B-boys. Beavis and Butt-head.

b-boy stance. Defiant pose typically taken by crossing both arms across the chest. This is a term and posture common to rap music.

beach whistle. A tampon tube washed up on the beach.

beat. That's terrible.

beauteous maximus. A good deal; a good job.

beef. A butt fall in skateboarding.

being styling. Being dressed up; in high style.

bencher. An old person, such as is found on benches in shopping malls.

Betty. An attractive female, as in Betty Rubble of the television show *The Flintstones.* Synonyms: *fly houchy, freak mama.*

biftad. A preppy. A 1988 article in the *San Francisco Chronicle* on local high school slang reports that it is from quintessential preppy names, as in, "Say, Biff!" "Yes, Tad?"

biggums. Overweight.

biscuit. Easy.

bitchen-twitchen. Excellent; great; classy.

bizotic. *Biz*arre plus ex*otic* equal weird.

Black & Decker. A real grind; a power tool (to which it is a punning reference).

blaze. To leave—as in, "Let's blaze."

bliss ninny. A silly, disoriented person.

blow it out. Forget it; let's move on.

boarder. Skateboarder.

boarding. Riding a skateboard.

bogue. (1) Smoke a cigarette. (2) To be stood up—as in, "I was bogued last night."

bogus. Phony; bad.

bomb. Cool. Michelle Guido of the *San Jose Mercury News* wrote on September 5, 1995, "If you have a cool bone in your body, you already knew that when it comes to teen slang, "bad" is good. But nowadays, "bad" is not as good as "dope," and neither is as good as "bomb." As if to confuse adults, when teenagers today call a movie a "bomb," it's not a complaint, it's a compliment.

bonzai. Large or massive.

boogerhead. Nickname for a friend—affectionate.

book/book it. To move fast; to run like crazy, as in, "He's really book'n round the bases."

boom. A stereo, especially a car stereo.

boot. To vomit.

bowhead. A Texas teen defines this one as a bouncy cheerleader type who "ignores her intelligence, is superficial, and wears bows in her hair."

box. (1) Large, portable stereo tape/radio combination. (2) Large woman.

boxie. Bleached blonde. See LOXIE.

Brady. Not cool, as in *The Brady Bunch.*

brainiac. Intelligent student.

brick. To be scared, as in, "We saw their front line and bricked." Probably from the expression "to shit a brick" as an indication of fear.

buff. Muscular; tough.

buggin'. (1) Being upset. (2) State of relaxation.

bummer. A bad break; a nasty experience. This term has been in use since the days when it was used to describe a "bad trip."

bump'n. (Pronounced *BUM-pun.*) Of the highest quality, such as clothes or music. Sometimes extended to "bump'n like a mug" for emphasis.

bum-rush. To come in; to break down the doors—a common rap term.

bunk. Uncool.

burly. A hard thing to accomplish.

burn. (1) To be put down. (2) A put-down, as in, "What a burn dad."

burnout. One who abuses drugs or alcohol.

burnt. Terrible; tough; strict.

bush. One's real boyfriend or girlfriend; one with roots. Compare to SCOPE.

bus head. What one looks like after a long school field trip or away game.

bust. (1) *v.* To be in trouble, such as getting busted by one's parents over homework. (2) *v.* A rude insult, commonly stated as, "Bust you out." (3) *n.* A good shot, especially in basketball.

bust this. Watch this.

buttons. Remote control device for TV.

buzza. What's up?

buzz crusher. A killjoy.

 C

caj/cas. Casual.

calendar. One month.

camel toe. This is what you get when your jeans are too tight in the crotch area. Usage: "Buffy, perhaps you shouldn't wear those size-four jeans. They give you camel toe."

cameo. A type of haircut popular among young black males. The hair is trimmed short on the side and flat or angular on top.

cap. To put down; to insult.

cashed. Used up; finished.

catch one. To get drunk on beer.

checking. Pulling down another's outerwear boxer shorts from behind as a surprise.

check you later. Bye.

cheesehead/cheese meister. A jerk.

cheesy. (1) Phony. (2) Tacky. Mostly passé.

cherry. Something good; cool.

chick with a stick. Girl jock, presumably a reference to softball and field hockey.

chief. Form of address applied to virtually anyone.

chill/chillin'. (1) *v.* To calm down; to become cool; to relax. (2) *adj.* Calm, cool, or laid-back. (3) *v.* To stand up for a date. This is a term common in rap music lyrics.

chill out. To settle down; to quiet down; to get cool.

chill with you later. See you later.

chilly. With it; in tune with the times.

chilly most. Someone who is very cool; a paragon of chill.

chog. Someone from New England.

chomp. Verb meaning to copy.

chopped. (hip-hop) Physically unattractive or obnoxious.

chuborian. Fatty.

circle of death. A bad pizza.

click. A clique.

clockin'. Bringing in; acquiring.

clueless. Describing someone who doesn't know what is going on, who doesn't have a clue.

Clydesdale. A stud; good-lookin' guy.

cob. Not cool; stupid.

cold-blooded. Very cool.

cook. Cool.

cool. Fine; first-rate; copacetic. The term has displayed remarkable staying power.

SAY WHAT?

Clueless?

The movie *Clueless,* which roared out of the box-office gate in July 1995 with a $16-million gross in its first five days, was Hollywood's attempt to package teenage slang. Press releases were actually sent out with a guide to some of the movie's jargon. As Cher (played by Alicia Silverstone) explained in the release, "Just follow this simple glossary, and a world of chilling Baldwins and Bettys will open before you." Although many of these appear elsewhere in the text, here in one place is the *Clueless* vocabulary:

As if! To the contrary. No way.

Audi. Good-bye, I'm leaving. I'm out of here. "I'm audi."

Baldwin. Attractive guy. (As in the acting Baldwin brothers.)

Barney. Unattractive guy. (As in the big purple dinosaur.) Not a Baldwin.

Betty. Attractive woman. (As in Archie's friend.) A female Baldwin.

Big time. Totally. Very.

Buggin'. Irritated, perturbed. Flipping out. "I'm buggin'."

Clueless. Lost, stupid. Mental state of people who aren't your friends; uncool.

Furiously. Very, extremely, majorly.

Hang. Get tight with. Ally with.

Majorly. Very, totally, furiously.

Mentally challenged. Stupid. Clueless.

Monet. Looks fine from a distance, but a mess up close.

Monster. Much too big and loud. Very good.

Postal. A state of irritation, psychotic anger, and disorientation.

TB. True blue. Loyal, faithful.

Toast. In trouble, doomed, exhausted, towed up, history.

Towed up. Tore up, in bad condition. Trashed, toast.

Wass up? See ZUP?

Wig, wiggin', or *wigged.* Become irrational, freak out. Go postal.

Zup? Is anything new? What's up?

---

costing. Expensive, as in shoes that look "costing."

coyote-ugly. Extremely ugly.

cozy. Dull or lacking in interest. This same definition fits for the adjectives *precious*, *special*, and *quaint*.

crankin'. Excellent, especially in music.

crazy. Good; hip.

creepers. Thick-soled black shoes.

crew. One's circle of friends.

crewby. Crew; that is, rowing, jock.

crib. Home.

critical/crit. Cool.

cruising. Searching for a date.

crunchy. It's an adjective for someone who is overly earth-loving, probably from the characterization "crunchy granola."

crush'n. That which looks good, especially clothes.

cujette. Female version of CUJINE or cousin.

cujine. Cousin; same as HOMEBOY but in an Italian neighborhood.

curbie. Smoker who must go out where the cars are parked to light up.

cut down on/cut on. Insult.

 D

d. Bad.

daddylac. An expensive car that has been given to a young driver by his or her parents.

daddy mac. An attractive male. Synonyms: *mac daddy, freak daddy.*

dag. To slow down, especially on a skateboard.

dap. Well-dressed.

Dead-head. Grateful Dead fan.

dead presidents. Money. Synonyms: *inns, ducats, duckets.*

death. To be very appealing; to die for.

decent. Excellent.

decorate your shoes. To vomit.

def. Outstanding; terrific. This is a common term in rap music lyrics. An article in the *New York Times* ("Words to Rap By," August 22, 1988) quotes Robert Farris Thompson, a professor of African and Afro-American art at Yale University: "The rappers are saying 'def' derived from 'death' meaning terrific . . . when in the forties boppers said: You kill me, you send me to heaven."

deffest. The best; the coolest.

demoto. Someone who is unmotivated and not doing well in school. The opposite of MOTO.

dexter. Nerd.

dibs. (hip-hop) Residence.

digit head. One who studies too much, or more specifically, works too long in front of a computer.

digits. Telephone.

dippin'. To listen in on somebody else's conversations to obtain gossip.

dipstick. Idiot; jerk; loser.

dis/diss. To show disrespect; to harass. This term is common in rap music lyrics. It is commonly believed to have been clipped from *disrespect,* although some teenagers insist that it is short for *dismiss.*

dissin'. To treat a person with disrespect.

ditz. Female airhead.

ditzy. Silly or goofy.

do. Hairstyle, from *hairdo.*

doable. (1) Sexually attractive. (2) Has mate potential.

doe. Cool.

dog. (1) To intentionally ignore. (2) To criticize or bother. (3) To work hard, as in "dog it." (4) To crumble under pressure, in skateboard talk. (5) To have sexual intercourse. (6) To beat up.

dogess. Bitch.

donnez-moi un break. Give me a break. Explained by a sixteen-year-old from Connecticut: "It's a French-class thing. Anyone with a minimal French background will recognize 'give me a,' and they assume that *break* means break. *Break* is French for station wagon, however; it makes a cute joke expression."

dooky. Excrement, as in, "He smells like dooky."

dope. Great; superb—a common rap term. Synonym: *fresh.*

dopey. Hip.

dorky. Stupid. Old, totally passé slang given new life by Beavis and Butt-head of MTV fame, whose vocabulary is limited to "That sucks," "This is cool," and dork-related remarks like "Look at this dork."

do the do. Have sex.

double bagger. Person so ugly he or she needs two bags over his or her head instead of just one.

drain a pain/drain the main vein. For a male to urinate.

drive the porcelain bus. To throw up into a toilet.

drop science. Verb, rap origin. To give important information, say something people should listen to. "I went to Yankee Stadium to see Nelson Mandela drop science on why it's not cool to do business with South Africa."

drop some iron. To spend some money.

dual. Good.

ducats. Money.

dude. (1) Originally a guy, but now genderless. This term is tricky because a dude can be applied to someone who is especially well-dressed or, cynically, to one who is a mess. (2) A form of address, as in, "Hey, dude." (3) A friend.

Many people believe the term *dude* originated with surfers, as in, "Yo, dude, what's up?" In fact, says Albert Lewin of Los Angeles, coauthor with his wife, Esther, of the *Random House Thesaurus of Slang,* the term, spelled *dudde,* dates from Shakespearean days. It eventually came to mean an overdressed Easterner who went West (hence the term *dude ranch*).

duggy. (hip-hop) Stylishly dressed. "I'll be lookin' duggy on the first day of school."

duker. Massive bowl movement.

dust. Verb meaning to get rid of, dump. Usage: "My boyfriend was treating me like dirt, so I dusted that old troll at the prom."

dustup. A fight.

dweeb. Loser; nerd; person one would not want to have to share a locker with.

 E

ear duster. A gossipy person.

eat chain. Drop dead; short for "eat a chain saw."

SAY WHAT?

The term *dude* has its extensions:

The dude on the dollar bill = George Washington.
The frood dude = Sigmund Freud.
The fugue dude = J. S. Bach.
The salad dude = Caesar.
The short, dead dude = Napoleon.

eating in hell. Dining at Taco Bell.

egg. To smash raw eggs on a car, house, or other large object. The practice is called egging.

ends. Money.

express. In the mood to party.

✳ F

faced. Put-down; having lost face.

face-paint. To fall off a skateboard onto one's face.

fan (it). Forget it; let's not do it; pass. One father, Walt Gianchini, says that his daughters are likely to say "Let's fan on that" after he has suggested something like a Sunday picnic.

fat. Nice; good.

fetus. A real loser.

fierce. Terrific.

file. Dangerous.

filthy. Hip.

fine. Describing a cute person of the opposite sex.

fired up. Excited.

fire on (someone). To hit or punch.

five-o. Police—from the old *Hawaii Five-O* television show, presumably recaptured in reruns.

flail. To do poorly on or fail a test; to mess up.

flake. To miss an appointment or not show for a date.

flamin'. To become infuriated, mad.

flex. To leave.

floppy disk. One who studies too much.

flu. Fine; good, the same as FRESH.

fly. In the know; street-smart.

fly-boy/fly-girl. Attractive young man/woman.

fork the lawn. To vandalize a property by sticking hundreds of plastic forks in the lawn on a cold night, which will be frozen in place by dawn.

for real even? Are you serious?

Fred. An unattractive or unintelligent male, as in Fred Flintstone of the TV show *The Flintstones*. Synonym: Barney, as in Barney Rubble of the same show.

Fred Smith. The imaginary perfect boyfriend, the one who does everything right. Usage, for when the flesh-and-blood boyfriend seems inadequate: "Oh, yeah? Well, Fred Smith would never say such an unsupportive thing."

fresh. Fine; very good. When a writer for the *Detroit News* discussed this term in a 1985 article on teenage slang, he said, "Possibly the most d'fficult new slang term to define, *fresh* can encompass an individual's attitude, a state of mind, a mode of dress, or an enlivening influence or situation." It is a term of approval in rap music lyrics.

front. Confront.

frontin'. (hip-hop) Lying, a phony person.

full hank. Nerd.

full of acid. Describing a well-built guy who looks to be on steroids.

fully-on/fully. Perfect; the best possible.

funk. Someone who thinks he or she is cool but definitely is not.

* G

gaffle up. To confuse, mess up, hurt.

gag. A valley girl, from "Gag me with a spoon."

gangsta. A person in a gang.

gank. Flirt.

gapo. (acronym) A giant *a*rm*p*it *o*dor; gorilla.

gaucho. To expose one's buttocks at someone, usually through a window (also known as mooning).

gay. Not cool; totally stupid.

gaydar. The ability to tell at a glance if someone is gay. Presumably a blend of *gay* plus ra*dar*.

geed. Looking good.

geek. Loser, nerd. A rare perennial in usually ephemeral teenage slang. *Geekoid* is used in some circles.

gel. To relax.

generic. Dull; out of it.

gerbil. To spill. "I just gerbilled my diet Pepsi all over my desk."

get a life. Get your act together: stop bothering me.

get horizontal. To lie down (alone or with someone else).

get naked. Not what it seems, but rather, a way to say let's go.

getting off with your bad self. Obviously feeling good about something that you have done.

get up! Good job!

get yours. Defined in a collection of teenage slang in the June 19, 1988, *Newsday* (Long Island) Sunday magazine as "a friendly greeting used when you see a guy and girl together and you know one of them; then you yell 'Get yours,' meaning go for it."

gimp. A loser.

girly-mon. Effete or weak man, from the *Saturday Night Live* bodybuilders Hans and Franz, who say "girly man" in a German accent.

glitterbag. Flashy female given to

shiny clothes, hair piled high with Aqua Net, and gum chewing.

gnarly. Largely passé in the late 1990s: disgusting; gross. But in some circles and in some situations, it also means good, cool, hip.

god box. Remote control for TV.

godly. Cool.

goob/goober. Nerd, loser. But "to goober" is to spit through one's two front teeth.

good answer! Cool, good—from the *Family Feud* television quiz show.

gooey. Girlfriend.

gorpoblorcho. Imaginary chemical used by chemistry teachers.

GQ or **Q.** Nice clothes, from the fashionable men's magazine *Gentlemen's Quarterly.*

granola. One who dresses and shares the preferences of the 1960s. This term has gotten a significant boost from the *Bloom County* bohemian character Lola Granola.

grill. Face, from the grill of a car. "How'd you get that scrape on your grill?"

grindage. Food, a term popularized by comic Pauly Shore.

grip. Money.

gritch. To complain (combination of *grip*e and b*itch*).

groovy. Stodgy, old-fashioned; 1960ish. But also sometimes used in its original sixties context.

ground. To punish by keeping at home, as in, "I'm grounded for the week because of my report card."

guidette. Female GUIDO, who is likely to use much hairspray to keep her hair piled high and poufy. See also GLITTERBAG.

guido. Male characterized by slick hair, gold jewelry, a hairy chest (exposed), acid-washed jeans, and a fondness for Bon Jovi music. A sixteen-year-old from the Bronx says that although this started out as a stereotype of "cool" Italian-American guys, it now includes any group or nationality—for example, Greek and Jewish guidos.

gumby. An unintelligible person.

guns. Muscles.

gutter wear. Hip, punky clothing.

* H

hack. To get rid of undesirable people quickly.

ham. Any alcoholic beverage.

hane. Heinous, or gross.

hang. Relax; hang out.

happy camper. Someone having fun, although this is often phrased in the negative, as "not a happy camper."

hard. Tough; authentic—a common rap term.

hardcores. Tough courses.

hard way to go. Sympathetic response to somebody's sad story.

harsh. (1) Strict; bad. (2) *v.* To abuse someone, give them a hard time. Usage: "Readers were really mad at Mike when he harshed on Nelson."

hawking. Searching for a date.

WHO DAT?

Pauly Shore is an acquired taste—harder to acquire as one gets older. He is, however, a walking embodiment of slang. In a 1995 interview with Al Brumley, staff writer of the *Dallas Morning News,* Shore described his movie/MTV persona as the weasel character who is "basically southern-California slang, but in my own way." He said in the interview, "It's very childlike. The whole 'Hey, bu . . . ddy' thing and all that stuff, you know? I've always been like a weaselly kind of guy, and I think that's why people relate to it, because they can picture me trying to meet girls or get in clubs and getting thrown out by the big bouncer and winding up at Burger King late at night."

The weasel made its first movie appearance in *Encino Man,* in which Mr. Shore and a bud dig up a caveman after an earthquake, and zaniness ensues.

headbanger. Heavy-metal fan.

hein. Person who is ugly and/or possessed of a rotten personality.

hella-. Prefix meaning "very," as in "hellacool" for very cool.

hellified. Super.

hellish. Horrible.

hello. I heard that.

high postage. A conceited woman.

hi-jack. To take something trivial, almost borrowing.

hip-hop. Catchall for rap music, rapping, break dancing, graffiti, and playing records. The language heard in rap lyrics has been called hip-hop slang.

hippy witch. Girls who dress in black and wear sixties-style clothing.

hittin'/hit'n. That which tastes good.

hit up. To ask someone where they are from.

ho/hoe. A slut, and an obvious play on the word *whore.*

ho! Great; good-looking; "Look out world!" A seventeen-year-old informant says that this term got a boost from the movie *Biloxi Blues.*

holler at/hollerat. Talk to.

holmes/homes/homie. Derivations of HOMEBOY/HOMEGIRL that mean the same thing; a common rap term.

homeboy/homegirl. Friendly term of address for someone from the same neighborhood or school; a neighborhood friend.

homiez. Friends; preferred spelling for *homies,* short for homeboys or homegirls.

hood. Neighborhood.

hook. Catch on.

hook up. To begin a relationship.

hoopty. (hip-hop) Car.

horn. Telephone.

hosebag. Slut.

hot. Extremely appealing or good-looking; very cool.

hottie. Cute person of the opposite sex: a hot one.

house. (1) To have a major success; to bring down the house—a common rap term. (2) To steal.

house ape. Small child.

hubba. Stupid.

hype. Great.

hyped. Full of energy.

 I

I heard that. I agree.

illin'. Stupid; unchillin'. This term is common in rap music lyrics.

I'm sideways. Good-bye.

iron pimp. School bus.

it ain't all that. You're overstating; don't exaggerate.

it rules. It is awesome.

Izod. Preppy guy or girl.

 J

jacked. Happy.

jack shit. Nothing, as in, "I'm doing jack shit."

jack up. To kick in the rear end.

jag. A loner, a nerd.

jam. (1) In the world of rap, a con-cert, party, record, good time, etc. (2) To leave quickly.

jammin'. Music that sounds good.

jeepin'. (1) Having sex in the backseat. (2) Socializing in a Jeep.

jingus. Bogus.

joanin'. To insult publicly, as in, "They were joanin' me about my car." When this term was reported by the *Washington Post* in 1987, it was suggested that it might be derived from Joan Rivers, but a number of readers wrote to point out that the term was an old one that was common in the black community when Rivers was waiting for her first break.

jockin'. For a girl to hang on a guy.

johnny. Cop.

joint. (1) Marijuana. (2) Jail. (3) A fight.

joints. (hip-hop) Any popular brand of sneakers.

juco. Junior college.

juice. (hip-hop) Power, influence, respect.

juicer. Steroid user.

juke. (1) Elude. (2) To make a direct hit.

jump his/her bones. To have sex with. Almost always phrased conditionally, as in, "I'd like to . . ."

junks. Basketball shoes, especially expensive ones.

 K

kegger. Party with beer, from the notion that these parties often feature kegs of brew.

keystone. Describing the police.

kick back. To relax.

kickers. Sneakers.

kickin' it. Doing something even if it's just hanging out.

kick it. To relax. Synonym: *to chill out.*

kill. Really good.

killer. (1) Good, like killer shoes. (2) A tough course, especially in college.

knob. A loser.

kooky. With it, circa 1996.

* L

lame. (1) State of boredom. (2) Stupid or nerdy. A lame time would be a dull party.

lame-out. Really dumb or boring, as in a total lame-out.

lampin'. Hanging out, as one does when standing around a lamppost.

lardo. Fat person.

later. So long; good-bye.

law, law. I don't believe it.

left hanging. Stood up.

let's cruise. Let's go.

like. To say. This linguistic development was enough to net an article in the *New York Times* ("For 'Teenspeak,' Like Another Meaning for the Multipurposeful 'Like,'" August 25, 1988).

living large. Doing well, in rap talk. A ghetto kid who gets rich.

load. Car.

loadies. (1) Drug abusers. (2) Acquaintances whom you might party with but wouldn't want to be one of.

loaf. A fat person.

loft. Skateboard hang time.

loose. A senseless, daring act.

lop. A nerd or dork.

lost between the bells. Late for class.

lost in the sauce. Out of it.

loxie. A natural blonde, like Goldilocks, but unlike a BOXIE, who gets it out of a bottle.

L-12. Stupid times twelve.

lunchin'. Characteristic of one who is out to lunch.

* M

macking. Searching for a date.

mad. Thumbs-up.

magnet. (1) A DWEEB who won't even move from his/her seat; a "gluebottom." (2) A school or school program created to attract students so that racial or enrollment imbalances can be corrected voluntarily.

major. Extremely important.

majorly. (1) Very. (2) Totally, furiously.

mall crawler. Teenage girl who spends almost all of her spare time at the mall.

maw. To kiss; to pet.

maxin'. Relaxing.

mega-. Prefix of emphasis, along with MUNDO-.

melba. Odd or unusual.

mellow up. Calm down.

mental. Describing any strange person.

mersh. Abbreviation of *commercial.* Kind of an old word, deriving from the 1985 Minutemen record *Project: Mersh,* "but I don't care. If I define a word that's too cutting-edge, readers complain I'm co-opting their culture. If the word's old, they complain about that. Well, I have two words for you: Bite me."

mesoza. A group of small, wormlike, parasitic animals. Usage: "The mesoza hanging on the street corner harassed Karen when she walked by in her miniskirt."

mess 'em up. Good luck; the equivalent of "break a leg."

mess up. To screw up; to fail.

metal mouth. Teenager with braces.

Mickey D's. McDonald's. The company now uses this name in some of its ads, which are obviously aimed at the young consumer. There are other slang fast-food names, including the "BC lounge" for Burger Chef, and the perennial "DQ" for Dairy Queen.

mint. Good; great, same as KILLER.

mobile. Attractive.

modeiant. Of or pertaining to the rock group Depeche Mode; something worthy of them.

molded. Embarrassed.

momaflage. To conceal an item from mother in a suitcase.

Monet. (1) looks fine from a distance but really a mess up close. (2) Not a babe, really.

money. Friend.

mother's nightmare. Describing a punky look and a feel.

moto. Someone who is motivated and doing well in school.

Muffie and Biff. Charactronyms for preppies by high schoolers.

muffin head. Term reserved for really nice-looking guys. Origin: a crazed, chameleon-headed friend of mine who enjoys baked goods almost as much as she enjoys a good man. Use it like so: "Henry Rollins is such the muffin head. Pity that he's twice my age." Any pastry-type item available at the bakery will work just as well. *Croissant* and *crumpet* are two of my favorites.

mug. Guy.

munchie. A cut or scrape gotten from falling off one's skateboard. Inspired by the feeling that the pavement is "munching" on one's skin.

munch on. To treat unfairly; to come down on.

mundo-. Prefix of emphasis along with MEGA-. Something that is very strange, for example, is "mundo-bizarro."

my bad. My mistake.

my peeps. My parents.

 N

narc. Loser; nerd. Once a term for a narcotics agent or someone giving them information.

neat whistle. Person wearing odd or weird clothing.

nectar. A good-looking girl.

ned. Marijuana.

nice do. Slur aimed at a bad or odd hairstyle.

9.5 fling. As defined by a seventeen-year-old female: "When a snobby girl suddenly flings her hair as an act of drawing attention."

nitro. Very good; better than DOPE—a term associated with rap.

no duh. No kidding.

nog. To come into contact with.

nooks. Pain, especially to a high school jock.

not! Interjection used to show disapproval or label as stupid. "You may use NOT! but only in a highly ironic sense, aware that you are making fun of *Wayne's World* and all it represents," Leslie Rubinkowski wrote in the *Pittsburg* (Calif.) *Press* in 1992. "If you took such a concept seriously, you would be nothing but a follower. You would be, in the world of Wayne, a sphincter boy." Wayne, of course, was Wayne Campbell, the Excellent Host of his own cable-TV show, who starred in this movie with his dorky sidekick, Garth Algar. The term could only be used ironically because it was quickly adopted by the likes of columnist George Will and television personality Jane Pauley.

not hard. Thumbs-down; bad (as in the bad sense of *bad*).

nuke. (1) To destroy; "I was nuked by that chemistry exam."

 O

old boy. Father.

old girl. Mother.

ollie grab. To kick a skateboard up, catch it, and then jump back on it.

omigod! General exclamation that is "Oh my god!" compressed into a single word.

143. Teen beeper notation for *I* (one letter) *love* (four letters) *you* (three letters). There is beeper speak out there.

on hit. Good, exciting. Synonyms: *cool, funky, dope, kickin'.*

on the strength. Really great, in the rap lexicon.

organ recital. Sex education class.

 P

party hats. Noun. You get these when you're cold. Usage: "Margie, I would advise you to throw a sweater on over that thin little T-shirt, as your party hats are on full display."

perpetrators. The source of an action—any action, not just crime.

petunia. Man or boy who pays a great deal of attention to his appearance.

phat. (pronounced *fat*) Good, cool. " 'Cool,' " wrote Michelle Guido of the *San Jose Mercury News* on September 5, 1995, "still means cool, but it's not as cool as 'phat'—which is really, really cool." Another newspaper advised: "*phat* doesn't mean your kid is overdosing on junk food,

SAY WHAT?

Not!/Nul!

How do you take Wayne worldwide?

In Britain, two hundred thousand little slang dictionaries were handed out explaining that the Wayneism *sshhyearhhhhrrrrighttt* actually means "Unlikely, I believe."

The German and Italian promoters did their best with the terms. *Schwing!* became "Sboing" in Italy but was left alone in German. The immortal bit of Waynespeak "And monkeys might fly out of my butt" became, according to an article in the *Los Angeles Times* by Rone Tempest, *Come le scimmie potrebbero volarami fouri dai culo* in Italian and *Und ehe ich mich versehe fliegen mir Affen aud dem Hintern* in German.

The toughest challenge was French. To make the French go for *Wayne's World,* full of its distinctively American slang, the film's distributors turned to a pair of young Frenchmen who call themselves Les Nuls (the Nothings). So when the film hit the French cinemas in 1992, the boys from Illinois had a whole new vocabulary checking out the bombes and the zarb dudes who look like they're about to gerber. Les Nuls, arguably the hottest comedy team in France, are the duo Alain Chabat and Dominique Farrugia. They turned to French teenage street slang and a kind of pig-latin argot called verlan, in which syllables of words are reversed. Voilà, a lesson in Waynespeak *à la française* from an October 21, 1992, report from Terril Jones of the Associated Press Paris bureau:

- "Party on" becomes *megateuf* (*teuf* being the reverse of *fête,* or party).
- "Weird" is *zarb,* or verlan for bizarre.
- "A babe" is *une bombe,* while a big-time babe is called Bombraham Lincoln. A dude's schwing, a healthy man's reaction to a bombe, is spelled *cha-wingue.*
- "Hurl," or vomit, is *gerber.*
- "Not!" at the end of a sentence is simply *Nul!*

According to the AP's Terril Jones, the trick to the translation was to rework some of the allusions to American pop culture. When, for example, Wayne drives alongside a limousine, leans over, and says, "Pardon me, do you have any Grey Poupon?" the line comes out as, *Je vous verrais bien dans un Fiat Uno,* or "You'd look great in a Fiat Uno," taken from a TV commercial for the car at the low end of Italian automaker Fiat's line.

O7734?

This report appeared in the August 9, 1996, *Virginian-Pilot:*
    "So not only do twentieth-century teens have their own dialect,
but their beepers do, too. Don't freak. It's not a 911 situation. Here's the
411 on the digits to comprehend the communication. 143—I love you.
411—Need information or want to give information. 911—Emergency
call now. 07734—Turn the pager upside down and it reads 'hello.'
617173—Good (6) nite (17173) *—a space. *The pager alphabet:* 8—A,
8—B, 6—C, 0—D, 3—E, 94—F (because of the "ph" sound), 6—G,
4—H, 1—I, 7—J 15—K, 1—L, 177—M, 17—N, 0—O, 9—P, 9—Q,
12—R, 5—S, 7—T, 11—U, 11—V, 111—W, 25—X, 4—Y, 2—Z. Note:
Some people have an identification code. Some use their name using the
beeper alphabet; others use their birth date or little numeric idioms like
'007.' "

either. It's just another adjective of exaltation, believe it or not?"

How quickly does a term like this get devoured by the larger culture? This from the *New York Times* of April 10, 1993: "Queen Latifah bought a $135 canvas jacket from the Phat Farm on its first day of business recently. But the SoHo boutique hardly needed hip-hop credentials. This New York store of steel trees and street wear was created by Russell Simmons, the rap emperor-millionaire from Queens who began selling clothes, he said, because he dates a lot of models."

phat flavor. Good music.

pick no squares. Don't fight.

pick up your face. Response to somebody who has just done something stupid or embarrassing.

piece. Junk. Probably from "What a piece of shit!"

pimp. A cool guy who's popular with girls.

played out. Tiresome, boring.

player. (1) Person who two-times or flirts, as in, "Look out, she's nothing but a player." (2) Promiscuous person.

pond skum. Grease on hair.

poser. Someone who tries to act and dress like people in another group but is considered a phony by that group. In punk circles: punkster wanna-be.

posse. A group of good friends.

postal. (1) A state of irrational psychotic anger and disorientation. (2) Wacko, flipped. Gained notoriety in the 1995 film *Clueless.* At the time the movie was released, eleven disgruntled postal workers had killed thirty-five supervisors and coworkers in the prior twelve years.

pseudo. (1) Person you think little of, often paired by hyphen with a pseudo type—psuedo-hippie, pseudo-jock, etc. (2) Anything that is suspect.

psych. To exaggerate wildly; to put somebody on momentarily.

psychotic. Really great; good.

∗ Q

quality. Lousy; bad—the opposite of the real meaning of *quality.*

queef. Fart.

queer. Stupid or odd; it has nothing to do with sexual orientation.

queeve. To run out of energy, in the parlance of skateboarding.

∗ R

rack. (1) Sleep. (2) To sleep.

rack monster. A bed.

rack up. To kick somebody in the rear end.

rad/radical. Cool.

radical to the fifth dimension. Terrific.

raggin'. (1) Well-dressed. (2) Beating up on somebody. (3) Beating someone or winning ("He ragged on him in the race"). (4) For a girl to be having her period. (5) Make fun of.

raging. A good time; a lot of fun.

rags. Clothes; but most likely, concert T-shirts.

ralph. To vomit. It has been pointed out that the name Ralph mimics the sound of regurgitation.

ranker/rank out. One who backs out; to back out.

rat. One who habituates or does—a "gym rat" hangs out in gymnasiums, while a "rink rat" spends spare hours at a skating rink, and a kid who caddies is a "bag rat." Anyone who hangs around shopping centers is a "mall rat." Ancient in terms of this kind of slang, "rats" seem to be a constant.

raw. Great; very good; good-looking.

real slice, a. A bad day.

reeks. To smell.

remo. DWEEB.

rents. Parents (from which the word was clipped).

rickety-raw. Good-looking.

ride. A car, as in, "My ride is outside."

ride/ridin'. (1) To make fun of; verbal jockeying. (2) To flatter, such as praising a teacher to get a better grade.

rider. Negative term for someone who tags along when unwanted; a copycat. It is probably short for *ball rider.*

ride the slow train. To not want to party.

rip. (1) *v.* A rip-off; a bad deal. (2) *n.* To be cheated or robbed.

ripe. It means you smell.

rita. A girl, as in señorita. Usage (as seen in *Thrasher,* June 1991): "They mowed lawns, warshed windas, ran errands and panhandled to accrue the necessary dough to buy the hippest new skate threads, so they could flow with the ritas and honk the bettoid material." P.S. "Bettoid material" is a derivative of *Betty* (see *Sassy* glossary: definition #20, November 1989), and we're not sure about "honk," but think it means scam.

road dog. Best friend.

roasted. Drunk. Also, *baked, burnt, fried, ripped, toasted, tripped, wasted,* and *zoaded* (rhymes with *loaded*).

rock and roll. To do something rowdy or noisy.

rocker. Anybody who is into heavy metal.

rock your world. Phrase meaning both to beat you up but also to delight.

roll. A fat person.

rouge. To steal.

rude. Out of sight; cool—the same as *rad* or *radical;* totally good.

ruff. Neat, cool.

rush. To confront someone in a hostile or violent mood.

Ruth. Girls' bathroom, perhaps from the "House of Ruth" as a female sanctuary.

 S

salty. Angered: "My dad was totally salty on the phone."

sappnin'? What's happening?

scam. To lie, as in, "I had to scam my way out of it."

scamming. Flirting.

scarf. To consume quickly; for example, to scarf up a pepperoni pizza.

schwing. It requires a pelvic swing. This term got major play in the film *Wayne's World.* As the *Dallas Morning News* put it in 1992: "Teens by the tens of thousands flocked to the film this spring not only for fun, but also for the proper execution of 'schwing!' (Hint: It requires a pelvic tilt.)"

scoop. To kiss someone.

scope. (1) To hunt for something: "Let's see if we can scope a party." (2) To ogle. "Why you scopin'?" translates into "What are you looking at me for?" (3) Possible boyfriend—or girlfriend; one that one is scoping out. Compare to BUSH.

In an article on prep school slang (which is remarkably similar to public school slang), teacher and linguist Richard Lederer suggests that this is a clipping of *telescope.*

scrappin'. Fornicating.

scribe. Writing utensil.

scurb. Suburban skateboarder; one who skates on streets and curbs.

seven digits. Telephone number.

sev's. 7-Eleven store.

shady. Someone who's lying.

shagging. Picking somebody up by their underpants.

shemp. A young male, alienated from society, who detests trendiness yet follows the independent music scene religiously. Despite not wanting to be stereotyped, the shemp is very recognizable. His antifashion look consists of plain black Converse high-tops, black jeans, stupid band T-shirts, the ubiquitous flannel shirt, and prescription glasses. The shemp does zines, watches violent horror movies and dumb sitcoms, reads comic books, and is often an aficionado of pro wrestling. He subsists on American cheese and canned soup.

she reads Seventeen. Said of a trendy teenage girl.

ship to shore. Cordless telephone.

shot who? What? Pardon me?

shout at one's shoes. To throw up.

shun it. To go with it.

sick. Good; awesome, as in, "It was a sick party."

skanky. Rank or gross. Sometimes used specifically to describe a teenage girl who is so skinny that she is "gross looking." One sixteen-year-old definer adds, "Would be pretty if she gained weight."

skater. Skateboarder.

skate rat. Skateboarder. See RAT.

sketch. To mess up on a skateboard.

skidder. Backwoods teen in New England; after the name of a piece of logging equipment. "A skidder," says a western-Maine teen, "has a mean dog and a broken snowmobile in his yard."

skin it. Slap hands; new way of saying "Gimme five!"

skinz. A well-built woman.

slacking. Not keeping up with one's duties.

slam. To cut down verbally.

slap-down. (1) *v.* To embarrass. (2) *n.* An embarrassment.

slaps. Rubber-thonged sandals.

slice up. To criticize or cut down. Sometimes extended to "slice up like lunch meat" or the like.

slick. You could mean something is good or you could be sarcastic, as in, "Oh, real slick."

slider. An easy course in college—known as a gut or a breeze to the parents of those who take sliders.

sloshy, loopy. Drunk.

slutty. Adjective used to describe sloppy inanimate objects. Usage: 'Mmmm, I can't wait to eat a big, slutty burrito when I get to Benny's.'

smit. To skip.

smokin'. (1) Looking great. (2) Adjective meaning crazy or severely misguided. Usage: "If you think Warrant is a good band, you must be smokin'."

smokin' up. Smoking marijuana.

snake. To steal.

snap. To break a promise. A *snapper* is one who breaks promises.

sounds. Music.

spacin'. Not paying attention; being off in space. Spacin' usually occurs in class.

spack. Stupid, dense, spacey.

spazz. To become overly excited.

spent. Cash.

sping. Verb. Rock vocalizing that sounds more like speaking than singing. A spinger is different from a rapper, in that he is not doing rhythmic rhyming, just spinging. Example: Lou Reed.

splockenin'. Egging a car or house.

spoink. An indefinite unit of measure. "It was, oh, three spoinks high. I don't know."

spud. A jerk.

squash that/squash that melon. Forget it.

squid. Nerd, someone with tape on their glasses. Sometimes used as a joke with friends. By extension, a computer room or center is a *squid tank.*

step off. Leave.

stick. Skateboard.

sticks. Needles used to inject steroids.

stoked. Excited; psyched.

stole. To punch out; "I stole him" is to hit him with a knockout punch.

stud. Once a sexy male, increasingly a male who thinks he is cool/hot/fresh but is not. Loser; person who is strong and athletic but still a loser.

stud-muffin. An immodest good-looking guy.

stuffies. Stuffed animals.

stupid. Cool.

stupid fresh. Outstanding or spectacular—more than plain FRESH—in rap terminology.

stylin'. someone who dresses well.

sucky. Not good; that which sucks.

From the cover of the August 1991 *Sassy* is this question: "Long-Distance Romance: Sucky or Not?"

s'up/'sup. Greeting. It is short for "Whassup?"—a condensed version of "What's up?"

sure you're right. Said of someone not telling the truth.

sweat. (1) To trash; to break something. (2) To give someone a bad time.

sweet. Good; cool. Just as *sweet* means good, as in, "That's sweet." In a typical show of ingenuity, it can also mean just the opposite.

sweet hookup. A good deal.

swillmobile. Car full of empty beer bottles or cans.

swivel neck. Nerd.

syke. Same as PSYCH.

syndicate. Group of friends. Synonyms: *posse, houser.*

 T

take a chill pill. Calm down.

take the L train. To lose at something.

talking. Going out. If you're talking, you're not really together, though. You're getting to know each other.

talk out of the side of your neck. To bullshit.

talk the talk. Sound authentic. Now history in school hallways: embraced by twentysomethings.

tamale time. Embarrassment.

tard. Someone who is moving or acting slowly.

TBF. A goofy guy. It stands for "top button flag" because one so described is likely to wear his top shirt button buttoned.

teepee. To cover a house, tree, car, or other large object with toilet paper, from the initials TP.

that bites! That stinks.

that's a plan. Confirmation or agreement of a suggested action.

that's casual. A statement of acceptance.

thrash. (1) To spin a skateboard in midair; to make any good move on a skateboard. (2) To be really good at something.

thrashed. The state of being exhausted or otherwise depleted mentally and/or physically.

thrasher. (1) Skateboarder. (2) Skateboarder who doesn't give a damn.

thrashin'. Dancing.

three-ring circus. A fashion disaster, such as one's father in Bermuda shorts covered with some unspeakable plaid, black sneakers, and white tube socks with three rings encircling his leg just below the knee.

tight. Good.

tin grin/tinsel teeth. Braces.

tool. One who studies; a grind.

toss chow. To eat quickly.

totally. Fully. MTV's brain-dead dude Pauly Shore, whose film *Encino Man* introduced the nondude population to words such as *buff* (translation: cool), once predicted that someday the written part of driver's exams may replace "true" and "false" with "totally" and "not even."

to the curb. Dumped by one's girlfriend or boyfriend.

touron. Annoying tourist; formed, it seems, from blending *tou*rist and mo*ron*.

tow up. (1) Tore up, in bad condition. (2) Trashed, toast.

toxic. Astonishing.

toy cop. School or mall security officer.

trashed. Drunk.

trife. The wrong way. Living trife is living the wrong way; said of a bad person. "This may come from the Yiddish word trayf meaning not kosher," says Robert S. Greenman of Brooklyn, who picked up the term from his students.

trip. An experience on or off of drugs—same as the sixties.

trip-out. One who is out of it; a space cadet.

trippy. Neat; weird; far-out.

'tsup. Catsup. See 'ZA for a similar case of clipping.

tubaruba. TV.

tube/tube out. To watch TV.

tweaked/tweaked out. Spaced-out.

tweet. Teacher.

twillie. A fool.

twink. Loser; nerd.

 U

uh. Bad, ugly. "That shirt Todd is wearing is so uh.

units. Parents.

unruly. Gruesome, a term beloved of skateboarders, who talk of unruly spills.

upper story/upstairs. The mind; the brain.

up the ying-yang. A ridiculous amount; for instance, "I have homework up the ying-yang."

 V

vamp do. Slur aimed at a bad or odd hairstyle. Also NICE DO.

veg/veg out. To do nothing; to vegetate.

vid. A hassle or a bother.

 W

wack. Bad; lousy.

wail. To beat somebody up.

wakilana. Adjective meaning crazy, wacky, nutty, zany, madcap. Usage: "We had to reshoot the fashion photos because they weren't wakilana enough."

waldo. Out of it.

wanna-be/wannabe. An emulator; one on the periphery. The term is sometimes applied to a white who seems to be emulating blacks or a black who is emulating whites.

wasted. Drunk or high on drugs.

wastoid. Person throwing it away on drugs or booze.

waver. New Wave teen who goes to clubs, wears black, and "evolution-ized" from punk.

way. Plenty; accentuated, as in "way dumb" for very dumb.

weak. Not good; poor.

wedge. Food.

wench. Girlfriend.

whassup? What's up?

whistle. The whistle that only dogs hear: a girl who guys worship and adore for reasons that are not apparent to the female eye. She has lots and lots of boyfriends and many, many friends who are male, yet is not outrageously pretty or smart. What she does is kiss boy butt. She makes them feel special and wonderful. The whistle that only dogs hear has almost no female friends, nor does she care; in fact, she ignores everyone of her gender.

wicked. Cool.

wiggy man. A cop.

wig out. State of agitation.

wild. Cool.

Wilma. Unattractive female, as in Wilma Flintstone of the television series *The Flintstones.*

wilson. A really bad fall from a skateboard.

winner. Loser; a put-down when you have done something stupid.

wit. What you say when a bad joke has been told; delivered as if it were "nit."

woebetide. Bad news.

woodsy. Outdoor party.

woof. To brag.

woofie. Wimp.

wooshie. Soft; fuzzy.

word. (1) That which one cannot think of; a word for all words. It comes from rap music, where *word* is used when no rhyming word has been thought of. It can be found in lines like "That girl is fine. Word." (2) I agree; agreement.

wreck. To fight.

wuss. Wimp or coward.

X

X-ing. Tripping on the drug ecstasy or X.

Y

yawn in Technicolor. Vomit.

yea/yeay. Imprecise unit of measurement, as in, "He's yeay tall."

yen. Money of any kind.

yesterday. Out-of-date; outmoded. "Don't call someone a *babe* because that is, like, so totally yesterday."

Z

'za. Pizza. This is a major clipping in which only the last two letters remain.

zappening? What's happening?

zit. Pimple.

zoiks. An expletive employed when there is nothing else to say. It is without meaning.

zun. Pimple; possible reaction to the co-opting of *zits* by the sellers of commercial skin preparations.

zup? What's up?

SOURCES

Walt Giachini, guidance counselor at Wallenberg High School in San Francisco, obtained contributions from his four daughters—Julia, Brooke, Gina, and Kate. Teacher and writer Richard Lederer, writer Geof Huth, and researcher Charles D. Poe helped, as did Willy Risser and Andrew Dickson.

Robert S. Greenman, teacher and journalist, was kind enough to query students at the Columbia Scholastic Press Association summer workshop in June 1989.

In addition, a number of recent newspaper articles on teen and college slang were consulted, including ones from the *Los Angeles Times, New York Times, Washington Post, Detroit Free Press, Newsday, Concord* (N.H.) *Monitor, USA Today,* and *San Francisco Chronicle.* Also consulted were articles by Deborah Work in the *Fort Lauderdale Sun-Sentinel* (October 1993), entitled "Kids These Days It's Like They Have a Language All Their Own," and by Carol Cott Gross in *Newsday* (August 1995), entitled "Rents Want to Know: Whassup With Teen Slang?"

— ✳ 26 ✳ —

UNIVERSITY AND COLLEGE SLANG

A-OK, but Not Always PC

C ollege and university slang is a vibrant species, but not quite as ephemeral and ever-changing as is commonly assumed. Some of it is long-accepted ritual talk, and students will still be "pulling all-nighters" for generations to come. Even when the terms themselves change, they still sound like college slang—albeit dated. Go back to the 1930s and one finds that *wolfing* was snaking another's date, *hanging the hardware* was getting pinned, and *quilling* was kidding a professor along, which was known as *apple waxing* a generation earlier.

Back in 1937 an erstwhile professor at the University of Washington uncovered a host of student terms that are—at the same time—quaint and not all that far off the mark. His terms for a kiss or kissing included *gab goober, honey cooler, lollygagging, mug muzzle, parksology, paw, pitch-honey, rottenlogging, smooch,* and *tonsil swabbing. Tonsil swabbing* indeed! The 1989 UCLA collection offers *tonsil hockey,* while the 1991 UNC list features *suck tonsils.*

An earlier look at Johns Hopkins University slang reported in the *Baltimore Sun* in 1932 included *oiled, phutz around,* and *bozo,* which mean the same thing as they do today. Your homely coed circa 1938 was a *muddy plow,* and one of a number of terms used for an easy course was a *letter-writing course,* and to go to a movie was to *hit a flick.*

If there is a national expert on all of this it is Connie Eble, associate professor of English at the University of North Carolina and the author of *College Slang 101.* She has been collecting slang from her English students since 1972 and has put out annual lists of that which is current and in season.

Eble believes that campus slang is predominantly national with a lot of local variation, especially when places and local customs are alluded to. A *cradle hag* at UNC, for instance, is a female who spends vast amounts of time at a place called the Cat's Cradle. At Brown University, a certain piece of school-issue furniture is called a *chastity bed* because of its narrowness. A De Paul girl who is too trendy is called a *troll.* At Delaware, a girl from New Jersey with teased black hair is known as a *fluff monster,* and unappealing guys at the University of Alaska are known as *groovers. Emeroids* is what students at Emory call themselves, while *Reedie* works at Reed and *Mawters* at Bryn Mawr.

Meanwhile, alumni magazines and college newspapers are showing glossaries of slang indigenous to a given campus, and at Dartmouth new students are given their own book of campus slang called *Dartspeak.* With such help you can determine the local term for the person who studies too much. For instance, a recent article on slang in the *Tufts Criterion* says that the term of choice on that Massachusetts campus is still *throat,* which is short for *cutthroat* and refers to any grind or person out for grades.

By all accounts, all of this interest in college slang is not all that remarkable and may simply parallel a general national interest in various slangs, jargons, and dialects. College slang has been around for generations and seems to have been a constant for most of this century.

What *is* remarkable about it is that it seems to be ever-changing and subject to different influences, yet always seems to retain the same goofy, irreverent tone.

The following entries were collected over the last five years, and terms are tagged as to the locale at which they were collected. It is understood that they may exist on many campuses and may have originated elsewhere. Those entries marked as *Merriam-Webster* were collected in a 1993 survey by that company of the most popular slang by region.

* A

ABD. (University of Massachusetts) All but dissertation. Ph.D. students who have finished all graduate work except their dissertation.

aced. (North Dakota State) Did well on a test.

all that. (Hampshire College) Beyond good—something that's "all that and even more."

apes. (Carnegie Melon University) Fraternity brothers.

artsy-fartsy. (Rochester Institute of Technology) Describing an arts and crafts major.

* B

bag. (1) (Muhlenberg College) To sleep with. (2) (Princeton) To cut, to blow off.

bagger. (University of North Carolina) Stereotypical fraternity member, aka *fratty bagger.*

baggers. (Carnegie Melon University) Prospective freshman (visiting on "sleeping bag" weekend).

baggy. (Carnegie Melon University) When campus dining facilities are filled with baggers.

bail. (UCSB) Leave somewhere or skip a class.

baked. As has been the case for many years, collegiate for drunk or stoned.

beans. (Allegheny College) Townspeople.

beast, the. (University of Richmond) Milwaukee's best beer.

beauteous maximus. (Merriam-Webster, East) A good deal, a good job.

beaver or **beav.** (Smith College) As an adjective—not used as a derogatory description—means you're looking "hot."

be a Wendy. (Wellesley) To be like the stereotypically Waspy Wellesley woman.

beer bong. (University of Richmond) A tube in which beer rushes down into the mouth.

bifftad. New England preppyschool type.

bitchin'. Now, as for decades, college slang for good. A Californianism, this term swept the Eastern campuses in the early 1960s as mock-Californian.

black. (Colorado School of Mines) Incomprehensible course material.

blitzed. (Purdue) Became intoxicated.

blizz. (Merriam-Webster, West) A crazy or unrestrained action.

blow off. (1) (Princeton) To cut, to not go. (2) (Purdue) To ignore an otherwise important thing. (3) (Carnegie Melon University) Easy, simple, requiring little work. (4) (University of Pittsburgh) Slack off, quit, break off a relationship.

blow shit. (Purdue) To tease someone.

blunted. (University of Massachusetts) Stoned, high.

bogel. (University of North Carolina) To pass time without having a plan or destination.

bogus. (UCSB) Not as bad as HANUS.

bombed. (North Dakota State) Did badly on a test.

bone. (USC) To sleep with.

book. Also *bookin'.* (Carnegie Melon University) Used sarcastically to say you are definitely going to do something.

boot. (Merriam-Webster, East) Get sick from drinking.

boxing. (NYU) Engaging in sexual activity.

brutal. (UCSB) Difficult, as in a test or assignment.

buff. (Merriam-Webster, South) Muscular.

bump. (1) (Santa Monica College) Throw out (as in kill). "I bumped the class." (2) (Merriam-Webster, West) To skip or drop ("kill," from "bump off"). "I bumped the class."

bungee. (University of North Carolina) Very. "Joe has a bungee awesome smile."

buttloads. (University of North Carolina) Large amounts. "I can't stay out too late—I have buttloads of work to do."

* C

cabbage. As has been the case for many years, collegiate for money.

cack. (University of North Carolina) To play a joke or prank on somebody.

call the cops. (University of Colorado) Something wrong has been done to me.

cancer stick. Now, as always, slang for cigarette.

cheese. (Carnegie Melon University) Software.

cheesebox. (Carnegie Melon University) A computer.

cheezy. (Merriam-Webster, South) Corny, stupid.

chip head. (Merriam-Webster, East) A person who is familiar with computers.

chog (Merriam-Webster, Midwest) Someone from New England.

cholo. (Merriam-Webster, West) Macho. This term used to be used for a Mexican gang member. Now it is used as a description of anyone who is macho.

chug. Now, as for decades, college slang for drink beer quickly.

circle of death. (University of Massachusetts) (Merriam-Webster, East) Bad pizza.

clicky-windy. (Rochester Institute of Technology) A photography major.

clue. Someone not aware of what's going on. "She really is a clue."

clueful. (Carnegie Melon University) To have a clue: be aware of what's going on.

clueless. (UCSB) Not know anything about something.

college Communists. (University of North Carolina) Young Republicans, a term used derogatorily by campus liberals.

cool beans. (Merriam-Webster, Midwest) Great, very pleasing.

cool deal. (University of North Carolina) As has been the case for many years, collegiate for great, outstanding.

corporate fascist. (MIT) Person in interview mode, especially when dressed for an interview.

cows. (Carnegie Melon University) Sorority sisters.

cracker jack. (Baylor) Prejudice.

crash. (1) (Berkeley) To enroll in an overenrolled class. (2) (University of Kansas) To sleep.

crash and burn. (North Dakota State) To fail in a pickup attempt.

crib. (Merriam-Webster, East) Someone's home or abode.

crumbsnatcher. (University of North Carolina) Dependent woman or child. "My name is John. I'm thirty-two, single, and don't have any crumbsnatchers following me around."

cut. In the 1990s, as for decades, college slang for skip intentionally. It is so well entrenched that the only alternative to it is to "consciously avoid."

cutty-pasty. (Rochester Institute of Technology) A fine arts major.

* D

daddy, the. (University of North Carolina) The best.

DDFMG. (University of North Carolina) Attractive member of the opposite sex. From "drop dead fuck me gorgeous."

deal. (University of North Carolina) Cope. "She said she couldn't do the paper as well as the visuals, but I told her to deal."

dickweed. (University of Rochester) Jerk.

dig. In the 1990s, as for decades, college slang for understand.

digithead. (Rochester Institute of Technology) Computer sciences major.

dog. (1) (University of North Carolina) A male who treats females poorly, particularly by being unfaithful. (2) (Merriam-Webster, South) A friend, buddy.

do the (noun) thing. Yuppie way of turning a noun into an adjective. "Give me a call sometime—we'll do the lunch thing."

double. (MIT) Two all-nighters in a row.

down with that. (Washington University) I understand or that is cool.

dramats. (Carnegie Melon University) Drama majors, in general. Also known as the "ones wearing black."

drinking B's. (Smith College) Consuming cans of beer.

duck. (Allegheny College) Easy course.

* E

earth biscuit or **earth muffin.** (University of North Carolina) Environmentalist; one who clings to the styles and causes of the sixties. Also known as granola, green, hippie, flower child, and Woodstock wanna-be.

ease. (University of North Carolina) Become less aggressive, less tense, less nervous.

erg. (Columbia) A training exercise done by members of the crew team (male and female).

* F

fabulous. (University of North Carolina) Cool; good. Said in three stressed syllables, accompanied by finger snapping.

fade. (University of North Carolina) Take advantage of; to use for one's money.

fake bake. (University of North Carolina) An artificial tan acquired from the use of a tanning booth or bed. "The fake-bake business is always good right before spring break."

fattie. (NYU) Marijuana cigarette.

fine speci-men. (University of North Carolina) Good-looking males. "The bar is filled with fine speci-men tonight."

flailed. (UCSB) Blew it in a big way.

fly. (Merriam-Webster, East) Cool.

forclempt. (Merriam-Webster, Midwest) All choked up. This comes directly from a Mike Myers character, Linda Richman, on *Saturday Night Live.*

forty, a. (University of Colorado) Any forty-ounce alcoholic beverage.

foton. (NYU) A word meaning really flashy, almost neon. To describe a guy or girl that deserves the spotlight.

freshling. (Swarthmore) First-year students.

frick. (University of North Carolina) Exclamation of anger, frustration, condemnation. "Frick! I've got a paper, a project, and other homework to do over our fricking spring break."

from the ninth circle. (University of North Carolina) Tough or exacting; it alludes to Dante's *Inferno* and the various circles of hell. One of Eble's students provided this example: "My prof assigned a paper that's due the same day as her midterm. She's from the ninth circle." It does the same job as the *from hell*—as in, "midterm from hell"—expression of the late 1980s.

frosh. (Wesleyan University) First-year student.

fruits. (Carnegie Melon University) Students in the College of Fine Arts.

fugly. (NYU) Extremely ugly, presumably a blend of *fuckin' ugly.*

funneling (to funnel). (University of Massachusetts) Drinking one to six (avg.) beer(s) through a funnel.

∗ G

garden tool. (University of North Carolina) Sexually promiscuous female from the dialect pronunciation of *whore,* which is the same as the garden tool *hoe.*

gaungy. (University of North Carolina) Very big.

GDI. (Widely used) Goddamned independent.

gear. (University of North Carolina) Clothes.

geek box. (Purdue) A box (usually a tackle box) carried by electrical engineering managers. Contains millions of electronic components needed in lab.

geeking out. (Swarthmore) Expression of sympathy.

get shafted. (Georgia Tech) To be required to write an extremely difficult paper.

go grungy. (Kansas State) Go out without showering.

gone. (Purdue) Became intoxicated.

got reamed. (Purdue) Did poorly on an exam.

granny panties. (University of North Carolina) Big, cotton underpants.

grubbin'. (Hampshire College) Eating good food quickly. "That was really grubbin', man!"

grunt. (Rochester Institute of Technology) Army ROTC cadet.

gucci girl. (NYU) Gold digger.

gunslinger. (University of North Carolina) Female who rudely rejects a man. "Man, that girl just dissed me—she's a gunslinger."

gut. (Wesleyan University) On many campuses, an easy course. One of many such terms.

 H

hack. (MIT) (1) *n.* A prank. (2) *v.* To "explore" (i.e., going places where students aren't supposed to be).

haint. (University of North Carolina) Country, backward, ignorant person.

hammered. As has been the case for many years, collegiate for extremely intoxicated.

hangtime. (University of North Carolina) Time spent waiting before something happens. "I'm ready but I have thirty minutes hangtime."

hanus. (UCSB) Really, really bad (alternative spelling: *heinous*).

hating it. (University of North Carolina) Expression of commiseration. First student: "My professor really dicked me on that grade." Second student: "Hatin' it."

SAY WHAT?

G enerically, dozens of well-established terms cover snap courses, starting with the traditional *snaps, guts,* and *cakes.* They are also widely known as *mick* courses (from Mickey Mouse) and *slides* (by extension, a professor known for easy classes is likely to be known as Dr. Slide). Depending on the campus you are on, they are also variously known as crip courses or crips, loan-savers, blow-offs, easy A's, sleep courses, cruise courses, fluffs, bluffs, punts, puds, and skates. Rare but in use are the terms *sop* and *bunny.*

According to *Lisa Birnbach's New and Improved College Book,* each school tends to opt for its own name, so what is a *cakewalk* at Pepperdine is a *cake* at George Washington University. Some places have constructed their own easy-course vocabulary. The journal *American Speech* carried an article in 1980 on the *boat* courses at landlocked Gettysburg College, which were the ones you could "sail through." A *yacht* was a super*boat,* and a professor who taught a boat was known as an admiral. One prof, aware of his status as an admiral, greeted his class with a hearty "Welcome aboard" and word that the course was about to set sail. A final extension of the metaphor terms a pop quiz or a tough exam that sinks the boat a *jap.*

heater. (Merriam-Webster, East) A cigarette.

heinous. (Merriam-Webster, Midwest) Ugly, repulsive.

helmet. (Penn State) Women.

herb. (Merriam-Webster, East) A geek, loser.

herbalistic. (Hampshire College) Really stoned.

here's bread in your face. (Boston University) Forget it!

high postage. (Merriam-Webster, East) A conceited female.

hit the slot machine. (North Dakota State) Obtained money from the ATM machine.

homeskillet (Merriam-Webster, South) A good friend.

hook up/hook up with. (Merriam-Webster, West) To be with someone as in a romance, or to have sex with someone.

hose. (Carnegie Melon University) Description of a test/exam that is going to be/was impossible.

hosed. (Princeton) Failed to achieve something; rejected.

* I

in the house. (Merriam-Webster, West) Present, here. "So-and-so is in the house, so let's say hi."

* J

jet. (Merriam-Webster, South) To leave.

jimmy/jimmie. (Merriam-Webster, South) Condom.

jock. (UCSB) For a female to seek out a male athlete for sexual pleasure. "That girl is always jockin' someone."

jock'n. (Baylor) Nagging.

* K

keggin'. (UCSB) Good.

keg is kicked, the. (Allegheny College) The keg is empty.

ken. (University of Colorado) Guy that cooks a lot!

key, the. Important, current.

kickin' dancing. (Baylor) Country western dancing.

kicks. (Merriam-Webster, South) Shoes.

kind, the. (Merriam-Webster, West) Drug slang used to refer to whatever type of marijuana or other drug one is into. "Do you have any of the kind for me today?"

* L

lame. Now, as for decades, college slang for less than top quality: pitiful.

lesbigay. (University of Massachusetts) *n.* or *a.* Lesbian-bisexual-gay. Not derogatory.

long nose. (Merriam-Webster, East) A liar.

* M

make a run for the border. (North Dakota State) Head to Minnesota where the drinking age was nineteen (now obsolete).

mash. (University of Illinois at Urbana-Champaign) To kiss, neck, make out, etc., or (University of Nebraska at Lincoln) some sort of sexual activity.

meat market. Fraternity row—where boys pick up girls.

mint. (Carnegie Melon University) Really cool.

momaflage. (Merriam-Webster, East) To hide an item in your suitcase or knapsack that you don't want your mom to see (combination of *mom* and camou*flage*).

moneygrip. (University of North Carolina) Person who has money and flaunts it.

mouley. (University of North Carolina) Derogatory yet Endearing term of address used among males.

mutant. (MIT) Math major, especially theoretical math. Sometimes applied to theoretical physicists as well.

* N

nappy. Unhappy, disgusting.

narfs. (Carnegie Melon University) Stupid freshmen, or Republicans.

nasty. Sexual intercourse, as in, "So you two been doin' the big nasty."

nerd. (MIT) Same as TOOLING, but especially when one is turning down an opportunity to PUNT.

nerd kit. (MIT) A breadboard with power supply and a small set of integrated circuits for the digital lab courses.

nerd whomper. (Washington University) Dork.

new school. (University of Colorado) New trends, new phases.

nipply. (Baylor) Cold weather.

no can do. (CCNY) I'm sorry, I can't help you.

no way. (University of Pittsburgh) I don't believe it.

nuke. (Rochester Institute of Technology) (1) To destroy or delete. (2) To pull a prank on someone.

* O

occifer. In the 1990s, as for decades, college slang for policeman, as spoken under the influence.

o'river. Good-bye; mock pronunciation of the French *au revoir*.

ozone. (North Adams State College) Out of it, hungover, wasted totally.

* P

peachy. (Carnegie Melon University) Fine. For example: "How are you?" "Just peachy!"

penis. (University of North Carolina) Derogatory name by a male to a male. A pseudo-scientific way to call someone a dick or dickhead.

perv. (University of Rochester) To get women.

phat. (1) (Merriam-Webster, East) Good, special (also seen as *fat*). (2) (Merriam-Webster, Midwest) Very cool, very nice.

plasma. (MIT) Caffeine, in any of its forms.

pound a beer. (North Adams State College) Drink the beer quickly.

power sludge. (Carnegie Melon University) Strong coffee.

powertool. (MIT) To cram or study intensely.

psych! (Carnegie Melon University) Just kidding.

pull an all-nighter. College slang for pull an all-nighter.

punt. (MIT) To cut class, skip a problem set, or otherwise avoid doing academic work.

✳ R

rack. (University of Oklahoma) To sleep.

rage. (UCSB) To party to excess.

random. (1) (MIT) A non-MIT person who hangs out at MIT anyway. (2) (Merriam-Webster, West) Strange, weird, unexpected.

reality impaired. (Merriam-Webster, Midwest) Unintelligent (describes an airhead).

rent-a-cop. (Rochester Institute of Technology) Campus Safety.

rip, to. (USC) To do well in.

rocked. (Purdue) Did well on an exam.

Rocks for Jocks. Geology 101 for nonmajors—an easy course favored by those who spend much of their time on the athletic practice field.

roll. (Oklahoma State) To cut class.

✳ S

salt sucker (Merriam-Webster, Midwest) An individual from the Midwest who forgets to close his/her mouth when he/she swims in the ocean.

sauce. (Merriam-Webster, South) Beer.

scam (Merriam-Webster, South) To go looking for guys or girls: cruise.

scoping. (Princeton) looking for possible members of the other sex to date, etc.

scrod. (MIT) To have been screwed over, the past tense of screwed not to be confused with a young cod, also scrod.

scrump. (Rochester Institute of Technology) To have sex with someone.

seppo. (Hampshire College) Really bad. (Short form of *septic*.)

sexile. (Swarthmore) The state of banishment from one's room while one's roommate is with his significant other, a blend of *sex* plus ex*ile*.

shack. (University of Illinois at Urbana-Champaign) To stay at the apartment/dorm/frat/sorority of

✳

SAY WHAT 101?

Tradition dictates that easy courses get their own nicknames, which they are likely to hold on to for decades. Some of the more common examples include *Nudes for Dudes* (art), *Gods for Clods* (comparative religion), *Nuts and Sluts* (abnormal psychology), *Monday Night at the Movies* (film), *Baby Shakes* (introduction to Shakespeare), *Monkeys to Junkies* (anthropology), *Betty Crocker* (home economics), *Clapping for Credit* (music appreciation), *Chem for Cro-Magnons* (general chemistry, also *Kinder Chemistry*), *Art in the Dark* (introduction to art), and *Math for Trees* (mathematical studies). Even the places with the toughest academic reputations have their *Heroes for Zeroes* (Harvard's "Concept of the Greek Hero"), *Breathing for Credit* (Dartmouth's "Breathing Voice for the Stage,"), and *Moons for Goons* (Oberlin's "Planets, Moons, and Meteorites"). These easy-course names follow an old tradition of giving all sorts of nicknames to courses, including the ever-popular rhyming formation: *cut 'em and gut 'em* for anatomy courses, *bag 'em and tag 'em* for field anatomy, *hicks and sticks* for local rural history, and so forth. A few other real-world examples:

Princeton—Architecture 204 = "Architorture"
Purdue—Engineering 100 = "Sleep 100"
Berkeley—Astronomy 10: Self-Paced General Astro = "Astro Without Stars"
Carnegie Mellon—Statistics = Sadistics
Rochester Institute of Technology—Anatomy and Physiology = A and P
Georgetown—Modern Foreign Government = Mo-Fo Go; Problem of God: An Introductory Theology Course = God's Problems

your significant or not so significant other overnight.

shooting the shabookie. (Carnegie Melon University) 1. Taking it all in the card game hearts. 2. Anything particularly destructive.

slip 'er the Woodrow, to. (USC) To sleep with.

slore. (Bryn Mawr College) *Slut* plus wh*ore*—woman you dislike.

slort. (Carnegie Melon University)

To go to class with the express purpose of sleeping through it.

sog. (University of North Carolina) Spend a lot of time with a woman, implying that the male is slightly pussy-whipped.

spoink. (Merriam-Webster, East) An indefinite unit of measure. "It was, oh, three spoinks high; I don't know."

squid. (1) (Rochester Institute of

Technology) Navy ROTC cadet. (2) (Wesleyan University) Someone who always studies, especially on Friday nights. The local etymology of this claims it comes from the the glass-sided Wesleyan Science Center library where students studying late at night look like squid in an aquarium.

step. (Merriam-Webster, East) To back off (used as a warning).

step off. (Merriam-Webster, Midwest) To get away (used mostly as a warning).

stoked. (UCSB) Happy, elated, etc. (Merriam-Webster, Midwest) Excited, pumped up.

stopped by the Union. (North Dakota State) Had sex, because condom machines are located in the bathrooms of the Union.

superslamonic. (University of Colorado) The girl gets around!

suzie. Stereotypical sorority member. "My business class is full of suzies."

SWAG. (Purdue) Answer to homework or exam question usually written down minutes before it is due (originally, scientific wild-ass guess).

Swarthmore swivel. (Swarthmore) The college having only one dining hall, if you wish to talk about someone at a meal, you should first look left, look right, and look behind you to make sure that person isn't in earshot.

sweet. Good, fine, superb. This is a term with staying power on campus.

* T

tag. (Merriam-Webster, West) To mark (as with graffiti). "Look, they're tagging that wall."

taking the L train. (Allegheny College) To lose at something; get rejected by the opposite sex.

tea bagger. (North Adams State College) One who is left hangin', or looking stupid.

that's sweet. (Carnegie Melon University) That's really, really nice, awesome, terrific.

thes. (MIT) To work on one's thesis.

they're buzzin'. (University of Massachusetts) They're clueless—as when drunk.

throat. (University of Rochester) Someone who lives in the library, a study-geek.

tighty-whities. (University of North Carolina) Men's brief-type underwear.

toast. (MIT) What you are if you do badly on a test.

toasted. (Purdue) Became intoxicated

tomatoes. (1) (Carnegie Melon University) Engineering/science students who dress/behave like CFA students or vice versa. (2) (North Dakota State) Used in reference to a strange or stupid act by someone.

tool. (1) (MIT) To study. (2) (Princeton) Someone with political or business ambitions, usually a Woodrow Wilson school major. (3)

SAY WHAT?

The Top Forty

Connie Eble annual survey of slang terms at the University of North Carolina at Chapel Hill came up with this ranking of the most popular terms on campus from 1972 through 1993:

sweet. Excellent, superb.
chill/chill out. Relax.
slide. Easy course.
blow off. Neglect, not attend.
bag. Neglect, not attend.
killer. Excellent, exciting.
jam. Play music, dance, party.
scope. Look for partner for sex or romance.
wasted. Drunk.
clueless. Unaware.
diss. Belittle, criticize.
pig out. Eat voraciously.
bad. Good, excellent.
crash. Go to sleep.
cheezy. Unattractive, out of favor.
hook/hook up. Locate a partner for sex or romance.
trip/trip out. Have a bizarre experience.
dweeb. Socially inept person.
buzz/catch a buzz. Experience slight intoxication.
cool. Completely acceptable.
grub. Kiss passionately.
geek. Socially inept person.
granola. One who follows the lifestyle of the sixties.
homeboy/homegirl/homey. Friend, person from home.
not! No, sentence negation.
ace. Perform well, make an A.
dude. Male, any person.
the pits. The worst.
bagger. Fraternity member.
flag. Fail.
hot. Attractive, sexy.
slack. Below standard, lazy.
trashed. Drunk.
veg/veg out. Do nothing.

> *word/word up.* I agree.
> *awesome.* Excellent, superb.
> *book.* Leave, hurry.
> *turkey.* Socially inept person.
> *fox/foxy.* Beautiful, sexy.
> *sorority Sue/sue/suzi.* Sorority member.

(Purdue) Someone who is used and abused. (4) (SUNY at Stony Brook) Someone you pick up, use, and put back when you're done.

torque. (Purdue) To hit on someone.

trashed. (Carnegie Melon University) Overworked, tired, drunk. More often the former.

triple. (MIT) Three all-nighters in a row.

tuna. (Also *fish*) (Bryn Mawr College) A heterosexual woman who keeps company mainly with young gay men, as in, "Steve, Shane, and their tuna are going clubbing on Saturday."

24/7. (Many sources) All the time. From twenty-four hours, seven days a week. "He's with her 24/7." Also *365* for the same thing from the days in a year: "I could go out with this guy 365."

 U

un. (Various) An undesirable or unlikable person.

Undue Perversity. (Purdue) Purdue University.

 V

vegetables. (Carnegie Melon University) Science/engineering students.

virtual. (Merriam-Webster, West) Almost but not quite real (from *virtual reality*). "He has a virtual job."

 W

walk. (University of Texas at Austin) When a professor decides not to have class; sometimes used to describe cutting.

wank. (Columbia) (1) A person who is logged on for a huge amount of time. (2) To log on, to stay logged on, and to hack your brains out while drinking lots of Jolt or Mountain Dew (3) *adj.* Having the properties of a wank.

wasted. (Carnegie Melon University) Overworked, tired, drunk. More often the former.

wat up. (Merriam-Webster, South) How are you doing?

wigging. (Washington University) Stressing, going crazy.

woody. (University of North Carolina) An erection.

word. (Georgia Tech) Any hint on what might be asked on an exam by a professor.

 X

X-kegger. (Purdue) Party at which a specific number of kegs of beer were consumed. An eight-kegger, for example.

zone. (UCSB) Lose contact with the world (e.g., daydream in class).

zone out. (Merriam-Webster, East) To lose concentration.

zoomie. (Rochester Institute of Technology) Air Force ROTC cadet.

* * *

SOURCES

Campus talk is getting a lot of attention these days and has become something of a commodity. For years little attention was paid to this subspecies of American slang, but then in 1989 two important books were published, *College Slang 101* by Connie Eble and *UCLA Slang: A Dictionary of Slang Words and Expressions Used at UCLA,* edited by Pamela Munro. The UCLA book re-emerged earlier this year as the highly publicized *Slang U* from Crown Books. Then there was last year's *Unofficial College Dictionary,* which let us know that a party where no girls show up is properly called a *male-bonding event.*

Meanwhile, *Lisa Birnbach's New and Improved College Book* provided a new feature for a college guide, which was the slang indigenous to each college. Birnbach and her staff even let you know where blow-off courses are called *skates, guts,* and any of a number of other variations.

The official USENET dictionary of college slang, created by Jennifer Doyle, Princeton '91, was most useful, and many of the entries sent her from colleges around the country appear in this glossary. The Merriam-Webster hot words on campus 1993 survey was also a major source.

27

WAR SLANG

Out of the Jungles of Southeast Asia and the Great Sandbox of the Persian Gulf

Grains of "Sandspeak" from the War That Was on Every Channel . . . Some of it is new. Some of it is old. But an ofttimes bewildering wartime vocabulary is evolving in the desert of Saudi Arabia. . . . Even veterans of military service just twenty or thirty years ago find they are woefully out-of-date on terminology and slang.

—Jeffrey Ulbrich, Associated Press, from a
Dhahran dispatch appearing in the *Columbia
Missourian*, January 21, 1991

The patois of the Vietnam experience infiltrated the American conscious-ness slowly, for more than a decade, on a Ho Chi Minh trail of the mind.

—Martin F. Nolan, *Boston Globe*,
July 18, 1982

During the war in Vietnam, especially during the early days, it was not unusual for soldiers to use terms the army had acquired else-where at another time. Early in the conflict an Associated Press re-porter noted, for instance, that the troops were using such terms as *ichi-ban* (Japanese) for number one or very good, *idiwash* (Korean) for come here, and *bierstube* (German) for beer hall.

This is how it has always been. Soldiers bring the terminology of one fight or period of occupation to the next and then embellish it with new terms, until it takes on the flavor of that war. "The war in South Vietnam is producing its own vocabulary," wrote Jack Langguth in the *New York Times* for September 20, 1964. "Among the Americans stationed here, World War II's argot has long since faded away. Even Korea's glossary sounds dated."

Generally speaking, it will take a new war to update the slang of com-bat, and today's war slang is the slang of Vietnam and earlier wars up-dated with the slang of the Gulf War and more recent incursions, such as the one into Somalia.

* A

across the fence. Across a border, as if it were a fence. In Vietnam it referred to missions into North Vietnam, Cambodia, and Laos.

acting jack. Acting noncommissioned officer.

adopt-a-pilot. Ground forces' name for the urge to cheer aviators who would presumably soften up the resistance to a ground invasion.

agency. The CIA.

a-gunner. Assistant gunner.

airborne copulation. Euphemism for "I don't give a flying fuck."

airwing Alpo. A variety of field rations including corned-beef hash and meatballs with barbecue sauce, from the name of the popular brand of dog food.

AMF. Good-bye; it is short for "adios [or aloha], motherfucker." A popular and long-running television ad for the "Greaseman," a Washington, D.C., radio personality, ends with the "Grease" waving and yelling, "AMF."

ammo humper. Artilleryman.

angel. False radar image.

ape. Air Force Air Police, from the AP initials.

apple-sauce enema. Mild criticism. Defined in *A Dictionary of Soldier Talk:* "To give a chewing out (the enema) to a subordinate, but to do it so tactfully and gently that he goes away feeling better for the experience."

army brat. Long-standing name for the son or daughter in a regular-Army family.

artichoke suit. The brown and green "woodland" BDU (battle-dress utility) of the Gulf War.

artie/arty. Artillery.

ashtray. The desert; because institutional ashtrays (hotels, military institutions, etc.) feature sand.

auger in. To crash a plane, but especially apropos of jet planes, which resemble an auger or boring tool as they drill into the earth.

AWOL. Absent without official leave. An "AWOL bag" is a small piece of luggage.

* B

baby shit. Mustard.

bad paper. Discharge other than honorable.

banana clip. A curved ammunition clip designed to hold thirty rounds.

Band-Aid. Medical corpsman.

bandit. Hostile aircraft.

bang out. To eject oneself from an aircraft; to literally blow yourself out of the plane.

bare-ass. Barracks.

basic. Basic training; boot camp.

BCD. As in earlier wars, bad conduct discharge; but now after the Gulf War the facetious "big chicken dinner."

BCDs. Birth control devices. Refers

to military-issue spectacles that are so ugly that they act as an inhibition to conception. They are also known as *BCGs,* for birth control glasses.

beach. (1) The desert; fighting terrain. (2) Also, as reported by Harry Levins in the *St. Louis Post-Dispatch* of January 27, 1991, "a new way of saying *boondocks,* the old GI term for anyplace excessively rural or uncivilized."

big blue 82. The BLU-82 or daisy cutter, a 12,540-pound bomb creating tremendous blast overpressure.

big chicken dinner. New nickname for the BCD or bad conduct discharge.

big red. The brutal desert sun, as in, "Me and big red don't get along real well."

Big Red One. Nickname for the First Infantry Division.

big twenty. Army career of twenty years.

bird. Aircraft, but usually used for helicopters.

bird colonel. Full colonel, whose insignia are eagles.

birdfarm. Aircraft carrier.

birdland. Quarters for senior officers.

blade time. The time a helicopter is in the air.

bloods. Black troops.

blood stripe. Rank achieved at the expense of others.

blooper. The 40 mm grenade launcher and—less often—the soldier detailed to fire it, from the distinctive sound of the weapon when fired.

blow away. Kill.

blow smoke. To confuse; to cover up.

blue. A body of water, from its color on the map.

blue max. The Medal of Honor, from its blue field.

blue on blue. Friendly fire or shooting at one's own soldiers by mistake. This term stems from NATO exercises where the two forces were blue and red.

blues. An airmobile company.

bogey/bogie. Aircraft suspected to be hostile.

bolo. A soldier who flunks his rifle qualifications. A first-person witness, writer Joseph C. Goulden, reports, "As punishment at Fort Chaffee, Arkansas, circa May–July 1956, such a cluck was given a 'bolo,' a crude Southern scythe, and put to work cutting grass on the entire firing range."

bolo badge. A Purple Heart, the long-established medal awarded to soldiers wounded in combat. The term *bolo badge* was most likely to be applied when the wound was, in the words used by a *New York Times* dispatch, "foolishly acquired."

boloed. Destroyed; killed.

bone domes. The high-tech Kevlar helmets that became standard equipment during the war in the Persian Gulf.

boobies. Bobby traps.

boogie out of Dodge. To get out, beginning with the Gulf War—as in this quote from a marine captain that appeared in the *Boston Globe:* "We move in quick, hit hard, and then boogie out of Dodge. By the time he hits back, we ain't there." The Dodge in the construction is the Dodge City of the Wild West and alludes to any-place where there is the potential for gunfire.

boonie rat. Soldier who has spent a lot of time in the field.

boonies. Backwoods; the jungle.

boot. (1) Soldier just out of boot camp. (2) Adjective for that which is new and untested. At one point in *Rumor of War,* Philip Caputo wrote, "I was alliteratively known as the 'boot brown-bar,' slang for second lieutenant."

bottle-cap colonel. Lieutenant colonel, from the insignia that looks like the tinfoil on a bottle cap.

bought the farm. To have been killed. In *Soldier Talk* (1982), 1st Sgt. Frank A. Hailey, a veteran of World War II, Korea, and Vietnam, says that this term was coined by Americans during the Korean War and had the same meaning as *bought it,* a term borrowed from the British during World War II, did during the Vietnam War.

bouncing betty. A land mine that, when triggered, pops up waist high and sprays shrapnel.

brace. An exaggeration position of attention that recruits and cadets are sometimes required to adopt.

In *The Boo,* a novel about the Citadel, a military school, Pat Conroy describes plebes bracing: "Their chins are tucked in, their shoulders thrown back, and their backs are rigidly straight."

brew. (1) Coffee. (2) Beer.

bring smoke. To attack or punish.

broken down. Disassembled.

brown bar. Second lieutenant, who wears a single gold bar.

buckle. To fight.

BUFF. Nickname for the B-52 bomber, which stands for Big Ugly Fat Fucker. A number of war glossaries in family newspapers during the Gulf War reported that this stood for "Big Ugly Fat Fellow."

Bumfuck, Egypt. Remote site of hardship assignments; also known as East Overshoe.

bunker buster. A satchel charge composed of C-4 explosives and a short-fuse detonation cord, developed in Korea and used extensively in Vietnam.

burp. A marine, especially to an infantryman.

bush. (1) The field or the boonies. (2) *Ambush* for short.

bust. To reduce in rank or grade.

bust caps. To fire rapidly. In *Nam,* Mark Baker says that it is "probably derived from the paper percussion caps used in toy guns." See also CAPPING.

butter bar. (1) Second lieutenant, from the brass bar indicating that rank. (2) The bar itself.

buy it/buy the farm. To die.

* C

cammies. Camouflaged clothing.

cank. Pronunciation of CNX, the military letter code for cancel. There was much talk of the war in the Gulf being "canked" in the period before it began.

canker mechanic. A medic.

cannon cockers. Soldiers whose area of specialty is artillery. A character in Philip Caputo's *Rumor of War* is described as a "cannon-cockin' Texas shitkicker."

capping. Shooting at.

care package. Goodies (candy, cookies, etc.) from home.

cav. Air cavalry.

chair borne. Describing a military bureaucrat or paper pusher—a play on the term *airborne.*

Charlie. Short for Victor Charlie; the Viet Cong in the Vietnamese War. Also, variants along the lines of Mr. Charles and Mr. Charlie.

charlie tango. Control tower.

cheap charlie. Skinflint.

cheese. To suck up to a superior; brownnosing.

cheese dick. A person who sucks up to a superior; a "cheeser."

cherry. New man in unit.

chicken/chickenshit. Petty.

chicken cach. Packaged chicken cacciatore, served to the troops day after day. "The Spam of the 1990s."

chicken guts. Looped braid on officers' dress uniforms.

chicken plate. Personal armor, such as the kind that helicopter pilots wear across their chest and groin.

chopper. Helicopter.

chow. Food.

chuck. "A term applied by black marines to identify white individuals," according to James Webb in *Fields of Fire,* who adds that it was often used derogatorily.

Cinderella liberty. Period of freedom that ends at midnight.

civil serpent. Civil servant, especially one who works with the uniformed military.

clerks 'n' jerks. Support staff.

click. Kilometer, also klick.

clobber. (1) To attack a ground target from the air. (2) To defeat decisively.

cluster fuck. A totally screwed-up situation.

clutch belt. Cartridge belt worn by marines.

CO. Commanding officer.

cold, cold, smoked the bitch. Pilot's terse report on shooting down an enemy plane.

column. A battalion.

COMMFU. Completely monumental military fuckup.

commo. Communications in general, but often specifically used for radio.

connex. Large metal box for shipping and storage.

contact. Firing or being fired upon; engaging in combat.

copter. Helicopter.

cots. Apricots. During the Vietnam War a superstition developed among marine tankers that held that apricots—contained in some rations—brought bad luck. The word was "No cots."

crapper. Latrine.

C-rats/C's. C rations, which the military began phasing out in 1978. The new rations are called MREs, for *meal, ready to eat.*

crease. To wound; as in, "We just creased him and all it did was make him mad."

crispy critters. Enemy personnel killed by napalm.

Crotch, the. The U.S. Marine Corps.

crunchies. Ground infantrymen.

cuff 'em and stuff 'em. Policy of quick detention and transport taken toward noncombatants who might get in the way of military operations.

cunt cap. Green, narrow Army cap.

CYA. Cover your ass.

D

daisy cutter. The BLU-82 or BIG BLUE 82, an extremely powerful bomb creating a tremendous blast. Used in Southeast Asia to clear instant landing zones in the jungle.

day the eagle shits. Payday. The eagle is the federal government.

Dear John/Dear John letter. Letter from a girlfriend announcing that she has found another and it's all over.

deep kimchi (kimshi), to be in. To be in serious trouble, synonymous with "to be in deep shit." The term for the traditional cabbage dish survives from the Korean War to the present day and is found in many novels about the military, as in, "We'll be in deep kimshi with Sundown if we lose another bird" (from *The Warbirds* by Richard Herman Jr.). Herman adds in a 1992 letter, "Being in 'Deep Kimshi' is indeed 'Bad Juju (Black Magic).' "

deros. Acronym for *d*ate *e*ligible to *r*eturn from *o*verseas and/or *d*ate of *e*xpected *r*eturn from *o*verseas. In his *Everything We Had,* Al Santoli called *deros* "the sweetest word in the military language."

deuce and a half. A two-and-a-half-ton truck; a medium cargo truck.

dich. (Pronounced *dick.*) Vietnamese for dead and one of the terms used for enemy killed: "We got twenty-nine dead dichs up here and another seventeen hurtin'."

diddy-bopping. Walking carelessly.

di di. To run, from the Vietnamese.

dink. Derogatory term for an Asian.

dirty officer. Duty officer.

dog him out. To criticize; to chide.

dogs. Feet.

dog tags. Identification jewelry.

do-rag. Bandanna or scarf worn

over the head and tied at the back in lieu of regular headgear.

DOW. Died of wounds.

dream sheet. Official forms on which officers and enlisted members indicate their preference for their next location and job.

dry hole. Any target where you don't find anything and nothing finds you.

Du Pont lure. A grenade or C-4 plastic explosive, used for fishing.

dust-off. (1) Medevac helicopter. (2) To be lifted out by chopper.

∗ E

echelons beyond reality. Higher command; the source of orders and directives. This term implies that those at this high level of command are out of touch with reality—"beyond reality." It first showed up during the Gulf War.

eight. A master sergeant who is in pay grade E-8.

E-nothing. One at the bottom; an imaginary pay grade below E-1, a recruit.

evak'd. Evacuated.

∗ F

face-shot. Air-to-air missile fired on an enemy aircraft. Also known as *in the lips.*

fangs out. Excited, about to make a kill on the ground or in the air, as would a serpent.

fart sack. Bedroll.

fast movers. Primarily high-performance jet aircraft but also M-1 Abrams tanks and M2 Bradley fighting vehicles.

fat. Describing a unit that is over its authorized strength. In *A Rumor of War* Philip Caputo talks of a fat battalion.

fatty-gews. Fatigues.

field first. An NCO rank that does not exist in any regulations; the field first is the sergeant who runs the company while the first sergeant is in a rear area.

.50-cal. Fifty-caliber machine gun.

.51-cal. Machine gun used by the enemy.

figmo. Fuck it, got my orders.

fire base. Remote artillery base.

fire in the hole. Explosives about to be detonated deliberately, such as a satchel charge being dropped into a suspected enemy HIDEY-HOLE.

flapjacks. Looters, a term from the American operation in Somalia.

flying butterknife. Winged bayonet patch worn by paratroopers.

FNG. Fucking new guy.

four-deuce. A 4.2-inch mortar.

fox. To fire, from the old phonetic alphabet. To report "fox one" is to say that a pilot has fired his first missile.

frag. (1) Fragmentation grenade. (2) *v.* To grenade; to wound or kill with a hand grenade.

freak. Short for radio frequency.

---

*

SAY WHAT?

Where There Is a War There Is a Slang

Soon after American troops had landed in Somalia, reports were coming back of a new slang related to that operation (Operation Restore Hope for those with short memories). An article in the September 1993 *Soldier of Fortune* magazine contained a number of terms including these:

Bermuda triangle. Bandit-infested area where people "just disappear."

'Dish, the. The capital of Somalia, Mogadishu.

klingons. The twenty to thirty Somalis who would hang on to the side of decrepit Toyota taxis.

Ray-Ban bandits. Street urchins, sunglasses thieves, and feral children who would prey on American troops.

Sammies. Somalies.

Tar Baby, the. Operation Restore Hope.

---

freedom bird. Airplane returning soldiers to the United States.

friendlies. Allies, both military and civilian.

frog hair. Mythical unit of measure denoting a small distance, such as, "Lay that two frog hairs to the right." Same as RED CUNT HAIR.

fruit salad. Two or more rows of campaign ribbons.

FTA. Fuck the Army.

full bird. A colonel, from the eagle insignia.

funny money. Military payment script, called this because it looked like Monopoly money. This is traditional military slang as common to World War II as Vietnam.

funny papers. Maps.

fur ball/furball. (1) The frenzy of air combat; the hectic tangle of the dogfight. (2) The dogfight, or close air battle, itself.

* G

garritrooper. Term invented during World War II by cartoonist and writer Bill Mauldin to describe a soldier who was "too far forward to wear ties and too far back to get shot." The term survived, and Charles D. Poe has noted, "On Barry Sadler's album of Vietnam songs [*Ballads of the Green Berets*] there is one entitled 'Garet Trooper,' and the song's lyrics suggest that Sadler had in mind pretty much the same kind of soldier that Mauldin was describing."

get some. Kill.

getting short. Coming up on the end of one's tour of duty.

get your gut right. To eat; also to *take it in the face.*

ghosting. Special Forces term for hiding out so you wouldn't get put on a shit detail.

GI. An Army enlisted man, from the World War II initialism for "government issue." That this term, which came into being about 1940, is still used illustrates the power of slang over officialdom. In 1951 the Pentagon actually issued an edict prohibiting further use of *GI* within the military, stipulating that the proper term was *soldier.*

glad bag. Body bag.

goat rope. A confused situation, as one would experience trying to rope goats.

golden BB. American name for the Soviet antiaircraft doctrine that says that when you put enough ordnance in the air (see term and alternative definition in chapter 9), an enemy plane or two will be hit. Not a new term, it was used in the Gulf War as a derisive description of the Iraqis' emulation of Soviet antiaircraft defenses. The term *golden bullet* had limited use as a synonym for *golden BB.*

gone Elvis. Lost; missing in action.

good to go. Fit, competent, and ready to perform.

gook. Derogatory term for an Asian, from Korean slang for person.

GOYA. Get off your ass.

grease. To kill. "Brother or not," says a character in Alfred Coppel's *Apocalypse Brigade,* "you come out now or we grease you on the spot."

greased. Killed in action. These gruesome lines appear in John Skipp and Craig Spector's *The Scream:* "The A-gunner's brains blew all over him. His squad was getting greased."

greenbacks. American money.

green bait. Reenlistment bonus.

green beanies. U.S. Army Special Forces (from the Green Berets). To call a member of the Special Forces a green beanie is to risk personal injury.

green machine. The U.S. Army.

green pounders. The infantry.

grunt. Infantryman.

gun bunny. Artilleryman.

gung ho. Overzealous; driven.

gunny/guns. Marine gunnery sergeant.

gunship. Armed helicopter.

gut ripper. Antipersonnel mines and grenades used by either side.

gyrene. Marine.

hack it. To stand it.

hard rice. Munitions given to

friendly tribesmen during the Vietnam conflict.

hash mark. Diagonal uniform bars, each signifying four years of military service.

headquarters pukes. Administrative personnel removed from combat areas.

heart. A Purple Heart, the medal that signifies a combat wound. In *Fields of Fire,* James Webb reported on the "Three Heart Rule," which was in effect in Vietnam. It stated that any marine wounded three times within one combat tour was immediately removed from the combat zone.

heavy metal. Loosely applied term alluding to heavy artillery, naval arms, etc., and a clear reapplication of a term from a form of rock 'n' roll with considerable popularity among the soldiers in the Gulf War.

helitrooper. Soldier who jumps from a helicopter.

hero gear. Battle souvenirs.

hidey-hole. Any hole scratched into the ground or into the brow of a hill where a soldier can take refuge.

Hilton. Name of hotel chain invoked ironically for places totally unlike Hiltons. When Bob Hope returned from Vietnam in 1967, he noted, "Every broken-down hut, hooch, or Quonset hut is called the Chu Lai Hilton or the Hilton East or the Hilton something." The most famous Vietnam Hilton was the infamous Hanoi Hilton, a prison in which many American POWs were held.

hitch. A period of enlistment or reenlistment.

hog. (1) The A-10 or Thunderbolt II aircraft, sometimes called the warthog. (2) Helicopter gunship of the UH-Huey series.

hog-60. The M-60 machine gun.

homesteader. Soldier who manages to stay in one assignment for a long time.

honcho. A leader, boss, or man in charge. This common Korean War slang term soon entered general American slang. It's from the Japanese *han* (squad) plus *cho* (leader), reports Stuart Berg Flexner in *I Hear America Talking,* literally "squad leader," a corporal or sergeant. A common definition given during the war—number one man—suggested this Japanese lineage.

hooah/hoo-ah. An upbeat word that can be used to describe any military situation where the speaker is alive and well. For instance, it was almost invariably used to greet mail call. This has also been written as *urah* and *ooh rah* and was called "the signature call of the American forces" by the *Houston Post.* Also, *yeehah.*

hooch. Hut or simple dwelling.

hose down. To shoot with automatic fire.

hot LZ. Landing zone under fire.

hots. Hot meals.

hot skinny. Information.

Howard Johnson. Firebase built with future occupancy in mind.

HQ. Headquarters.

Huey. Nickname for the UH-1 series of utility helicopters, which one reporter described as a combination of "shuttle bus, supply truck, ambulance, and weapon of war." It comes from the official term *helicopter, utility* or *HU.*

humma. Et cetera; whatever.

hummer. (1) The successor to the jeep and the most common military vehicle in the Gulf; same as HUMVEE, this term really came into its own in the Gulf. Listen to a few lines from Don Kirkman of Scripps-Howard News Service on the vehicle: "President Bush's Thanksgiving dinner was served on the hood of a Hummer. Bob Hope and his troupe of entertainers bounced from base to base in Hummers. The humble Hummer seems to be in the background of every news clip about troops in the field." (2) Much less commonly used as a nickname for the Navy's Hawkeye early-warning aircraft.

humvee. Popular name for the military's High-Mobility Multipurpose Wheeled Vehicle (or HMMWV), which is the new version of the jeep—bigger, faster, diesel-powered.

hundred and worst. The 101st Airborne.

hurtin'. Injured or dead.

 I

I&I. Intercourse and intoxication; a clear play off the initialism R&R.

illum. An illumination flare.

incoming/incoming mail. Hostile artillery fire.

in-country. Country outside the United States to which one is assigned. During the Vietnam War it meant being in Vietnam: "After R and R in Bangkok, I was back in-country."

Indian country. Unsecured territory.

ink blot. A fortified enclave for supplies and weapons.

intel puke. Person in intelligence, especially one working far from the front.

in the lips. Air-to-air missile shot taken directly at an enemy aircraft. Same as *face-shot.*

Irish pennant. A loose thread, strap, etc.

 J

jacket. One's official service record; the military equivalent of one's permanent record.

jack-off flare. Handheld flare, tube shaped, about a foot long, that is fired by striking the bottom. The projectile comes shooting out trailing a bunch of sparks.

Jesus nut. The bolt that holds the rotor blade to a helicopter.

Joe. Any U.S. enlisted soldier. Contraction of World War II's GI Joe.

john. Lieutenant; hence "first john" and "second john" for first and second lieutenant.

John Wayne. (1) To act heroically. (2) Soldier who "acts it up" for the media, especially the camera.

John Wayne High School. The U.S. Army Special Warfare School at Fort Bragg.

Jolly Green Giant. The CH-47 double-rotor helicopter. Also, *log.*

junk on the bunk. Inspection in which one's field equipment is laid out and displayed on one's bunk.

K

kaserne. German for "barracks," this is now used to describe a military base anywhere in the world.

K-bar. A military knife.

khaki tit. The Army as provider. A regular Army person is said to suck the khaki tit.

KIA. Killed in action.

kick. Dishonorable discharge.

kill. A downed enemy aircraft. This term has been in use since World War II, replacing the equivalent *victory* of World War I.

kill box. Rectangle on aircraft radar screen on which target is seen blowing up.

killer bees. Attack aircraft; from the name of a species of Africanized bee much discussed in the United States at the time of the Gulf War.

kill-fire. A burst of gunfire that is so effective it leaves nobody to return fire.

klick. Kilometer. Also, *click.*

KP. Kitchen police; mess hall duty.

K-pot. The current-issue Army Kevlar helmet and a parallel term to the *steel pot* of the Vietnam era, which referred to the then-standard Army helmet that consisted of a fiber helmet liner and an outer steel helmet.

KYPIYP. Keep your pecker in your pants; long-established VD control motto.

L

lanyard puller. Artilleryman, a reference to the time when cannons were fired by pulling a lanyard.

lay chilly. To freeze.

LCs. Line-crossers; enemy who defect.

leaflet drop. Spending money on girls and booze with reckless abandon.

legos/legs. Unit that is neither airborne nor mechanized; ground soldiers to airborne rangers.

lick. A mistake.

lifer. Career military person.

lifer juice. Coffee.

liquid cork. Diarrhea medicine.

log. The CH-47 double-rotor helicopter. Also, *Jolly Green Giant.*

long tom. Long-range .155 mm artillery.

louie. Lieutenant.

love Scud. The penis, as a guided missile.

lower than whaleshit. In terms of rank and status, at the bottom of the ocean.

LP. (1) Listening post. (2) Landing platform.

lum. Illumination flares.

lurp. Special ration of food packaged for those on long-range patrol.

lurps. Rangers engaging in long-range reconnaissance patrols.

LZ. Landing zone.

* M

Maggie's drawers. (1) Red flag displayed from the target pit on the rifle range when a shot has completely missed the target. (2) A miss.

meals refusing to exit. Reinterpretation of the initials MRE, which really stands for "meals ready to eat."

mechanical. Ambush weaponry triggered by the enemy; mines, flares, etc.

mess/mess hall. Dining facility.

mess kit repair battalion. Mythical unit to which goofs and BOLOS are sent.

mike-mike. Millimeter.

million-dollar wound/million-dollar zap. A noncrippling wound that is serious enough to warrant return to the United States; a ticket home.

missing link. Second lieutenant.

MLR. Main line of resistance, or front line. Often used in the bravado sense of "I've got more time on the MLR than the REMF has in-country."

MRE. Meal, ready to eat; the field ration replacing the C and E rations.

Mr. No-shoulders. A snake, starting in Vietnam, where they were common.

Mr. Zippo. GI operating a flame-thrower.

mule. Small, motorized platform used to carry arms, but sometimes also supplies and troops. Sometimes called a mechanical mule. In Philip Caputo's *A Rumor of War,* one is described as "a heavy-weapons carrier that looked nothing like a mule, but rather resembled an oversized toy wagon."

mummy sack. Rubber body bag.

mustang. Officer who has come up through noncom ranks; also, one who has been given a battlefield promotion.

mystery meat. Mess hall meat lacking clear identity.

* N

Nam. Vietnam.

newby/newfer. Replacement person.

Nintendo effect/Nintendo war. Term used to describe the videotapes of exploding buildings that made the Gulf War bombing seem as if it were a Nintendo video game.

no-clap medal. Good conduct medal, from the belief that one will be given the medal if one avoids VD.

no days like that! Not likely to happen.

no-hope pope. Name for reserves and a parallel to the name for active-duty forces: "people with no lives."

no sweat. No trouble; I can handle it.

not a problem. Standard response of troops to their officers in the Gulf and a far cry from lines like "Sounds like a personal problem to me" of the Vietnam War era.

November foxtrot whiskey. Another way of saying "no fuckin' way." From the phonetic alphabet.

nuclear coffee. Drink prepared by taking the instant coffee, cocoa, creamer, and sugar contained in an MRE (meals ready to eat) accessory package and mixing them in a canteen half filled with water.

number one. The best.

number ten. The worst.

nylon. Parachute.

O

O-club. Officers' club.

o-dark-thirty. Very early in the morning.

officer material. Not officer material; a goof-off.

OP. Outpost.

ossifer. Officer.

outgoing/outgoing mail. Friendly artillery fire.

outside, the. Civilian life.

outstanding. Term of mock enthusiasm for anything from the excellent to the barely passable.

over-two. More than two-thirds of the way through a normal enlistment, which is three years long.

P

palm. Napalm.

patch guys. Highly experienced fighter pilots recognizable by the many patches signifying awards, special schools, and experiences.

PBI. Poor bloody infantry.

pencil. Reporter without a camera crew; print journalist.

penguins. Air Force ground crews, because they are wingless birds.

PI. Political influence or a political interest. For instance, a private whose father is a member of Congress would find the initials PI on his service jacket.

pick up brass. To leave; to move out. It comes from the rifle range where soldiers are required to pick up their brass shell casings when they are done.

ping. To criticize.

pocket leave. To take one's leave without leaving the post or base. It is probably called this because the leave papers never leave the leave-taker's pocket.

pogues. Rear-echelon military personnel. Derogatory.

point. Forward man on a combat mission.

police. To clean up.

pop. To kill; to *waste;* a term that first saw use in Vietnam.

pop smoke. To ignite a smoke grenade to signal an aircraft.

pos. Position.

prang. To land a helicopter roughly.

prick-77. The standard battlefield radio whose official name is the AN/PRC-77.

psywar. Psychological warfare.

PT. Physical training.

ptomaine domain/ptomaine palace. Mess hall.

Puff the Magic Dragon. A C-47 transport plane armed with 7.62 mm machine guns, which was used in support of ground troops.

pull rank. To exercise the power of one's position or rank.

pull the pin. To leave, from the rapid exit one makes after pulling the ring on a hand grenade.

Purple Hurt. Purple Heart.

purple vision. Night vision.

PX. Post exchange; military store.

 Q

quartermaster property. Dead, because burial is a job of the Quartermaster Corps.

 R

rack. Cot or bed.

rack time. Sleep.

rail. First lieutenant, from the single silver-bar insignia signifying that rank.

Rambo. According to a March 20, 1989, *Houston Chronicle* article, this is a term "used derisively by soldiers for someone who is braver than he is intelligent."

Ranch Hand. Allusion to defoliation in Vietnam. A Ranch Hand plane was a C-123 outfitted with gigantic defoliant-filled tanks.

R&R. Rest and relaxation, or rest and recuperation. In Vietnam, R&R was a three-to-seven-day vacation from combat zones. "Rape and ruin" is just one of a number of unofficial interpretations of R&R.

rat fuck. Mission or operation that is doomed from the beginning.

ration drawer. Person who collects food, pay, and benefits without working for them.

ration of shit. A hard time.

read. To hear or understand.

real estate. Territory lost or gained.

reckless rifle. Recoilless rifle.

recon. Reconnaissance.

red cunt hair. Bawdy unit of measure denoting a small distance, such as, "That is one red cunt hair out of alignment." Same as FROG HAIR.

red phone. Emergency telephone reserved for the direst of emergencies.

reefer. Refrigerator or refrigerated vehicle.

REMF. Rear-echelon motherfucker, or base-camp support troop.

repple-depple. Replacement depot, the casual camp where incoming soldiers, replacements, are processed.

re-up. Reenlist.

rifle. An infantryman.

rip cords. Loose threads.

roach wagon. Mobile canteen or snack bar.

rock and roll. (1) To fire an automatic weapon. (2) Automatic weapons fire.

rockers. The lower stripes on an NCO's insignia, which look like the rockers that would be found on a rocking horse. For instance, a master sergeant (or E-8) wears three stripes and three rockers.

Rocket City. Nickname for any base under constant rocket fire.

roll out. To get up.

Rome plow. Bulldozer with a mammoth blade for jungle clearing.

rotate. To return to the United States after a period overseas.

rototilling. Carpet-bombing enemy territory with strategic bombers.

 S

sack. Bed; rack.

S&D. Search and destroy.

sandpaper. Government-issue toilet paper.

sapper. Infiltrator.

sarge. Sergeant.

scope head. Radarman.

scrambled eggs. Gold embellishment on the hat visors of senior officers.

second balloon. A second lieutenant.

seen the elephant. To have been under fire; to have been in combat is to have "seen the elephant." According to *A Dictionary of Soldier Talk* by Col. John R. Elting, Sgt. Maj. Dan Cragg, and Sgt. Ernest Deal, this phrase, which cropped up in Vietnam, dates back to the Mexican War. A longer original version was "I've heard the owl and seen the elephant."

sewer trout. Mess hall fish.

shake-and-bake. Describing any sergeant who has earned rank quickly and without much time in the service, such as a graduate of NCO training school.

shavetail. A new lieutenant. This is an old term dating back to a time when the Army used mules. New mules had their tails shaved so that their handlers could distinguish them from the trained mules.

shithook. The CH-47 Chinook helicopter.

shit on a shingle. Creamed beef on toast.

shoot and scoot. Artillery-firing technique in which the unit is moved quickly after firing to avoid return fire.

short-arm inspection. VD check.

short-timer. Term for one whose

tour of duty or period of enlistment is nearing an end. Such a person is sometimes said to be "short."

short-timer's stick. Defined in Mark Baker's *Nam:* "[When] a soldier had approximately two months remaining of his tour in Vietnam, he might take a long stick and notch it for each of his remaining days in-country. As each day passed, he would cut another notch in the stick until his rotation day, when he was left with only a small stub."

shotgun envelope. For interoffice mail, manila envelope that is punched with holes (so that it is easy to see if anything remains in the envelope).

silk. Parachute.

silo sitters. Those assigned to missile sites.

single-digit fight. Nervous condition of one with less than ten days still at risk in a combat zone.

single-digit midget. One with fewer than ten days remaining in a combat zone.

sitmap. Situation map—that is, one showing the dispositions of friendly and enemy forces.

sitrep. Situation report.

SIW. Self-inflicted wound.

skag. Cigarette.

skate. An easy accomplishment.

sky out. To flee or leave suddenly.

sky pilot. Chaplain.

slick. Helicopter without rockets or other external armament; one used to carry troops and supplies.

SLJO. Shitty little job officer(s).

slop chute. An on-post beer hall for enlisted men not of NCO rank.

slope. A particularly derogatory term for an Asian, especially Vietnamese.

smadge. Term of address for sergeant major.

smart bomb. One that gains remarkable accuracy because it is guided by a laser beam or TV camera.

smokey bear. Drill sergeant.

snake. AH-1G Cobra attack helicopters.

snake eater. U.S. Army Special Forces soldier; Green Beret.

snatch. A capture or a rescue; an operation in which live subjects are brought back. A squad specializing in such operations goes on "snatch patrol."

snowdrops. White-helmeted Air Force Security Police.

snuffy. Recruit or low-ranking individual.

SOL. Shit out of luck.

SOP. Standard (or standing) operating (or operational) procedure.

sorry about that. Ritual response to any bit of ill fortune from the trivial to the tragic.

SOS. Creamed chipped beef on toast, which has long been known as shit on a shingle.

spec. Specialist.

special feces. Special forces.

spit and polish. Attention to outward appearance and show; polished.

squared away. Prepared; ready for action.

stack pencils. To kill time.

stand down. Rest period for a military unit when all operations, except security, cease.

stand tall. (1) To come to attention. (2) Ready.

stateside. The United States.

steel pot. A helmet.

stewburner. Army cook.

straphanger. A useless person; one who has only come along for the ride.

strike. To barhop.

strings. Ropes tossed out of helicopters that soldiers can lash themselves to for a quick evacuation from an area where helicopters can't land. Strings are usually 120 feet long.

swinging dick. Male soldier.

* T

tac air. Tactical air support.

TAD. Temporary active duty.

take down/take out. To destroy.

take fire. To be shot at.

take it in the face. To eat.

tanker/tankerman/tankman. Soldier in a tank unit.

TDY. Temporary duty, an initialism that comes out sounding like "teedee-Y."

tent peg. Stupid or worthless soldier.

thirty-year man. Career Army; a lifer.

Thule coolies. Those on duty in Thule, Greenland.

tiger stripes. Camouflaged tropical uniform.

titi. (Alternative spelling, *tee-tee.*) A little; a small quantity.

T-LAR. That looks about right—applicable in many situations.

toadsticker. Bayonet.

toe-poppers. Small land mines that, despite the cute name, can take one's leg off up to the knee.

top. Top sergeant.

tracer. Round of ammunition treated so that it will glow or smoke, so its flight can be followed.

track/tracks. Armored personnel carrier.

trained killer. Soldier, usually applied facetiously and ironically to boys who seem to be anything but.

treadhead. Soldier whose specialty is armor. A character in Harold Coyle's *Team Yankee* says, "Shit, don't they teach you treadheads anything at Fort Knox?"

tree-eater. Special Forces soldier.

triple A. Air Force slang for antiaircraft artillery, as in, "We gave them a lot of triple A." Triple A was known as ack-ack in World War II.

trip wire. (1) Booby trap. (2) Soldier with a knack for finding traps.

tube steak. Hot dog.

turrethead. An arguer; one who is always spouting off.

turtles. New replacements—so called because they take so long to arrive.

twink. Second lieutenant.

two hots and a Charlie. Combat fare of two hot meals and a C ration.

 U

ultimate weapon, the. Infantryman.

unass. To get up quickly from a sitting position.

Uncle/Uncle Sucker/Uncle Sugar. Uncle Sam; the U.S. government.

use up. To kill.

 V

vampire. American sniper who stalks his prey at night.

 W

wait-a-minute bush. Any bush that had thorns that you could get hung up on.

warm body. Any soldier.

Warthog. Nickname for the airplane formally known as the A-10 or Thunderbolt II.

waste. To kill.

wax. To kill.

wet read. To study a reconnaissance photo while it is still wet from processing.

WETSU. We eat this shit up, an acronym pronounced *wet-soo*.

white sidewalls/whitewalls. Military haircut clipped close to the sides of the head.

whizo. Weapons systems officer.

WIA. Wounded in action.

wild geese. Mercenaries.

willy peter/willie pete. White phosphorus.

willy-peter bag. Bag for white phosphorus, alluded to in this sentence from Philip Caputo's *Rumor of War:* "They did not find enough of him to fill a willy-peter bag, a waterproof sack a little larger than a shopping bag."

wire. Perimeter where trip wires set off booby traps.

wire hangers. Troops who are so far out of the combat zone they can enjoy the luxury of hanging their clothes on hangers at night.

woofing. Talking without saying anything.

woof, woof. Meaningless talk, like barking.

word, the. The latest rumor.

word one. Any word. Someone who cannot get a chance to talk will say that they were unable to say word one.

world, the. As in Vietnam, this

term came into use to mean any-place outside the area where the soldier happened to be.

* X

XO. Executive officer.

* Y

yobo. Lover, from Korean; it is usually applied to a girlfriend.

* Z

zap. Kill.

zebra. Noncommissioned officer in the higher grades (E–6 through E–9), because of their insignia stripes.

ZI. Zone of the interior, a nickname for the United States.

zulu. Casualty report.

SOURCES

Charles D. Poe of Houston, Texas, military-slang expert Frank Hailey, and Joseph C. Goulden helped most with this chapter. It also relies to a significant degree on the research conducted by the author for the book *War Slang*, published by Pocket Books.

28

X'ERS, YUPPIES, DINKS, AND OTHER MODERNS

A Field Guide to the Last Quarter of the Twentieth Century

There is nothing new about slang nicknames for groups of people who are classified by age or lifestyle. We have had our flappers and beatniks, hippies and junkies, lounge lizards and drugstore cowboys. During the 1980s, however, there was a whole new wave of these terms. Some of these were the creations of demographers looking for a handle to put on a group—even groups that had lived most of the century without a snappy name—while others were simply clever neologisms that took off. In any event, they collectively serve to show us a new form of slang that has established itself. For lack of a better description, it is the slang of groups and demographics. It is also unusual in that the British seemed as obsessed with these terms as Americans; in fact, some are imports from the United Kingdom.

Here, then, is a generous sampling of the crop that came on the scene in the last two decades of the twentieth century, many of which were acronyms or derived from them. The fad of creating new ones seems to have lasted a relatively short time, but many of the terms (save for the most convoluted) seem to have stuck. The trick here is to find the right tag. Anne Gowen and Sean Piccoli in the article "A Generation Lost in Time Rebellion? Twentysomethings Find It's Too Much Trouble" in the *Washington Times* of October 15, 1991, pointed out the difficulty of naming the group then in their twenties: "They've been slapped with more stickers than a Dead-head's van: *13ers, baby busters, Generation X, the New Lost Generation, yiffies—yiffies?—young fogies,* and, yes, *twentysomethings.*"

✳ A

afterboomers. Those born after the post–World War II baby boom was over—from about 1965 to 1974. Contrast with BABY BUSTERS and POSTBOOMERS.

✳ B

baby boomers. Those 78 million Americans born between 1946 and 1964. In 1986, when the first baby boomer turned forty, they started to be referred to as "aging baby boomers." They have been cited for many social changes, including this one suggested in a 1985 Knight-Ridder News Service headline: "Baby Boomers Urge Washington State to Make 'Louie Louie' Official Anthem."

baby busters. Consumers born from 1965 to 1974, after the baby boom subsided. This was an era of ecological concern and advocacy of zero population growth, and for the first time in history the birth rate declined for reasons other than war or disaster. Sometimes shortened to *busters.*

biddies. (acronym-derived) Baby boomers in debt.

bimbos. Vacuous, sometimes sexy, females. An old bit of slang given new life in the eighties, with the help of such luminaries as Jessica Hahn (who publicly denied her bimbitude) and Tammy Faye Bakker.

boomerang family. A household where grown children move back in after schooling is completed.

boomerang generation. Name for the working class generation who live in their parents' homes.

boomer babies. Children born between 1965 and 1979, as BABY BOOMERS had babies of their own.

boomers. (1) Short for BABY BOOMERS. A 1996 ad for boomer paraphernalia (T-shirts, caps, etc.) proclaims, "You wore the coonskin cap. You wore the mouse ears. You wore the alligator and pony on your shirt. You are the *Big Chill* generation 70 million strong setting the trend. Now you can wear

the T-shirt and cap that will distinguish you as a charter member of this generation." (2) Those who want to exploit an area's oil, gas, and mineral deposits; who would touch off an economic boom.

breathin'. Room to breathe; space.

buppies. (1) (acronym-derived) British urban professionals. (2) (acronym-derived) Black, upwardly mobile professionals.

BWKs. Boomers with kids.

✳ C

caboose baby. The last child born in a large family.

chuppie. (acronym-derived) Chicano urban professionals.

couch people. Homeless families who live temporarily with friends on their floors or couches. Because they are not on the street, they have also been dubbed "the hidden homeless."

couch potatoes. Those content to spend great amounts of their free time at home watching television. At first a term of derision, it was quickly embraced by those who took pride in their passive ways. The term has been trademarked, and the application for that honor claims that the term was coined on July 15, 1976.

CWASP. Affluent Catholic professional not much concerned with ethnicity. Anne H. Soukhanov in her 1995 book, *Word Watch,* points out that this term was coined by Maureen Dezell of *Boston Business* in 1986. Dezell introduced them thusly: CWASPs are defined by their business or professional status. . . . But they have an added aura. They may lapse into [singing] 'Danny Boy' at private get-togethers on March 17, but they don't venerate that kind of gunk. Basically they'd rather be sailing."

* D

dewks. Dual employed with kids.

diks. Double (or dual) income, kids. Contrast DINKS and SIKS.

dimps. Couples with double (or dual) income, money problems.

dincs. Couples with double (or dual) income, no children. *Dincs* came first but was superseded by DINKS about 1987.

dinkies. Variation on DINKS.

dinks. Couples with double (or dual) income, no kids. The point of this category is that they have more disposable income than the average family. In her "Wordwatch" column in the *Atlantic,* June 1987, Anne H. Soukhanov pointed to the distinguishing characteristics of the dink: "The women usually retain their maiden names, the couples are very career-oriented, the husband is likely to cook the meals, and they usually own property in an upscale location." The term seems to have first popped up in late 1986.

(It was noted by researcher Charles D. Poe that in the 1974 sci-fi film *Planet Earth* there is a female-dominated society in which males are turned into cowering slaves called dinks.)

dissident yuppie or **DY.** Young urban professional who does not fit the mold; nonconforming yuppie, or as one was quoted as saying, "Yeah, I want a BMW, but I don't necessarily like them."

domos. The downwardly mobile, specifically, those in their thirties who downscale their career to find more meaningful work.

droppies. Disillusioned, relatively ordinary professionals preferring independent employment situations.

dumpies. (acronym-derived) Downwardly mobile, middle-aged professionals.

dwems. Dead white European men—the scourge of some multiculturalists.

dwiks. Dual income with kids. This pseudo-acronym is used in place of DIKS, which means the same thing.

* E

echo boomers. Those born after the 1965 baby bust who echoed the post–World War II baby boom.

empty nesters. People whose children have left home, whose homes contain empty bedrooms.

* F

feminazi. Pejorative name for a militant feminist.

flyers. Fun-loving youth en route to success. Identified in 1987 by *USA Today* as a hip group aged thirteen to twenty-five years of age.

folkies. Folk music musicians and their fans.

foodie. Gastronomic faddist.

frumpies. (acronym-derived) Formerly radical upwardly mobile persons.

fruppie. Young upwardly mobile Jew who is religious and observes Jewish customs. It comes from the blend of the Yiddish *fr*omm for "religious" plus y*uppie.*

fundies. Fundamental Christians. Term is likely to be seen as derogatory by those to whom it is applied.

* G

generation X. Those born between the years 1961 and 1971.

GI generation. Those born between 1901 and 1924 and were therefore eligible for service in World War II.

glams. (acronym-derived) The graying, leisured, affluent middle-aged.

golden agers. Old people; senior citizens. The U.S. National Park Service issues passes for discounts in national parks that are called Golden Ager cards.

grampies. Growing, retired, active, monied persons in excellent state.

grumpies. (acronym-derived) Grown-up mature people.

grumps. Grim, ruthless, upwardly mobile professionals.

guppies. (1) (acronym-derived) Gay, upwardly mobile professionals. (2) YUPPIES with ecological concerns; a blend of green and y*uppie.* (3) Grown-up urban professionals.

* H

hackers. Computer zealots who, among other things, have learned to gain entry to other people's computer networks.

hippies. The flower children of the late 1960s and early 1970s who advocated peace, free love, and the use of whatever substance "turned you on." The term is still used in referring to selected groups, such as some of the followers of the Grateful Dead.

hookies. Derived from "Who cares?" Hookies are college students who espouse apathy and noninvolvement. The University of Utah, an apparent hotbed of political apathy, attracted press attention in 1988 because of its large hookie population.

humpies. Horny, upwardly mobile urban professional.

huppie. A blend of *h*ippie and y*uppie,* for a person who is upwardly mobile but spends his or her spare time living unconventionally in the manner of a hippie.

* J

juppies. (acronym-derived) Japanese urban professionals.

✳ L

lampys. Collective term for anyone who has ever worked for the *Harvard Lampoon,* a group that includes such diverse folks as John Updike and Conan O'Brien.

latchkeys/latchkey kids. Children who are left at home alone for at least part of the day—an estimated 5–7 million in 1988—while their parents work.

lips. Couples with low income, parents supporting. Coined in the wake of DINCS/DINKS.

✳ M

maffies. (acronym-derived) Middle-aged, affluent folks.

mallies. Young people who hang around shopping malls.

marpies. Middle-aged rural professionals.

mensans. Members of Mensa, an organization for people who score in the top 2 percent of standardized IQ tests. It is from the Latin word for table and connotes a meeting of minds.

millennial. Member of the millennial generation.

millennial generation. People born after 1981 who come of age at the end of the millennium.

minks. Multiple income, no kids.

moonies. Followers of the Reverend Sun Myung Moon.

moss. Middle-aged, overstressed, semiaffluent suburbanite.

muppies. (acronym-derived) (1) Medical urban professional. (2) Mature yuppie. (3) Mennonite urban professionals. Presented as evidence of how far people have taken the YUPPIE premise. It was spotted in Amish country in 1987 by teacher and writer Robert S. Greenman.

✳ N

never nesters. Families that never have children.

new-collar. Term created for the middle class of the BABY BOOMERS in the workplace. Also called new-collar workers.

notch babies. Describing those born during and after 1917 who get a lesser amount of Social Security income than those born earlier. For this reason they complain, sometimes bitterly, to Congress about the discrepancy.

✳ O

oap. Old-age person. A term that gained some currency in the British Isles in the late 1980s.

oilies. American petroleum workers, but usually used in a foreign context, such as "one of the thousands of American oilies in Indonesia."

oinks. One income, no kids.

opals. Older people with active lifestyles.

P

phonies. People hooked on talking on the telephone.

pink collar. Term for lower-level clerical workers who are almost always women. The term connotes a level of employment that falls just short of white collar.

pink neck. Sophisticated first cousin of the redneck.

postboomers. People born in 1965 and afterward, after the baby boom. Member of generation X and the thirteenth generation.

postie. A postboomer.

postyup. Describing the world of the affluent after the 1987 stock market tumble. It has been described as a less ostentatious world, in which making a living has replaced making a killing.

posy-sniffers. Derogatory term for environmentalists, commonly shortened to SNIFFERS.

preboomers. Those born during or just prior to World War II, from about 1935 through 1945.

preppies. People who go to, or went to, private preparatory (or prep) schools.

puppies. (acronym-derived) Poor urban professionals, or pregnant yuppies, or parent of yuppies.

 R

rubbies. (acronym-derived) Rich urban bikers.

rumpie. (acronym-derived) Rural, upwardly mobile professional. The *Longman Guardian New Words* defines a rumpie as a "relatively affluent and basically conservative young person living in a rural area and engaged in a professional career."

* S

sandwich generation. Those middle-generation couples who find themselves responsible for elderly parents and young children at the same time.

siks. Single income, kids.

Silent Generation, the. Those born between 1925 and 1942 and who came into power during the Watergate era.

sippys. (acronym-derived) *S*enior *i*ndependent *p*ioneers. Financially secure consumers aged fifty-five to eighty having been married once and who are in good health. Sippys have a large segment of the discretionary money in the marketplace.

sised. Excited.

sitcoms. Those with single income, two children, outrageous mortgage.

skippies. (acronym-derived) School kids with income and purchasing power. Coined in the summer of 1987 by marketing people targeting this group.

skoteys. (acronym-derived) Spoiled kids of the eighties.

SLUMPRs Still living under mom and pop's roof—a coinage appearing in Bob Levey's July 18, 1995, *Washington Post* column.

sniffers. Derogatory label for environmentalists, who are often at odds with boomers; it is short for *posy-sniffer.*

snowbirds. Northerners who head south in the winter to escape the ice, cold, and snow.

sofa spuds. Synonym for COUCH POTATOES.

spec taters. Synonym for COUCH POTATOES.

suppies. Senior yuppies.

* T

taffy. (acronym-derived) Technologically advanced family. At a minimum, a taffy owns a computer.

techies/tekky. Technicians, especially those associated with electronics and computers.

thirteener/13er. Member of the thirteenth generation.

thirteenth generation. Those born between 1961 and 1981.

thirtysomethings. YUPPIES, given this name in the late 1980s by a television show of the same name.

ticks. Two-income couple with kids in school (and parents in retirement). Columnist Ellen Goodman termed them the "most-wooed voters of the 1988 election."

toolies. Technical folks (architects, engineers, surveyors, programmers, etc.) who are absorbed with numbers, science, and mechanical pencils (which they pull out in restaurants to make calculations). Given a boost in Stephen Clark's 1987 *Toolies: The Official Handbook of Engineers and Applied Scientists.*

truppie. A truck driver whose family travels in the living space behind the cab of the truck. The quarters are configured like house trailers and ideally suited to husband-and-wife driving teams.

tweener. Those aged eight to fourteen years of age who are in a sociological limbo—too big to be considered little kids but not old or mature enough to be looked upon as true adolescents.

twentysomethings. Name given to those in their twenties in the early nineties, a hand-me-down from the yuppie generation and its now-canceled television show. In the *New York Times* for December 2, 1990, Bret Easton Ellis wrote of this term, "Our style is assimilation, our attitude reaction, even if some visceral rebelliousness remains. While 'thirtysomething' has become high-concept, twentysomething lacks coherence: we are clueless yet wizened, too unopinionated to voice concern, purposefully enigmatic and indecisive."

* U

unyuppies. Term created for those who do not share YUPPIE values, who, for example, are young and professional but don't care much about high-status European cars.

Uppie yuppie. Young urban professional living in Michigan's Upper Peninsula. Anyone from the UP is an *Uppie.*

ustabe. Has-been.

∗ W

whappies. Wealthy, healthy, older people.

whoopies. Well-off older people.

wimps. (1) The weak, meek, and the cowardly. Old slang that was propelled into the new in 1987 when it was applied to George Bush. *Newsweek* ran a cover story entitled "George Bush: Fighting the 'Wimp Factor.'" This so-called W-word picked up a quick set of derivatives, including these cited by the *Los Angeles Daily News: wimpy, wimpish, wimpdom, wimpism, wimplike, wimp out,* and *wimpismo.* (2) (acronym—circa 1985—military use) Weak, incompetent, malingering pussy. (3) (acronym—circa 1995) Whining, insecure male person.

woofies. (acronym-derived) Those who are well-off, over fifty.

woofs. Well-off older folks.

woopies. (acronym-derived) Well-off older people.

∗ X

X condition. Generation X attitude. Quoting *Newsweek* from January 27, 1992: "This is the X condition in a nutshell. We're alienated from our own alienation."

X'er. Member of generation X; baby buster.

X generation. Member of generation X; baby buster.

X-speak. The slang of the X generation, in which *playpen,* in gen-X lingo, stands for apartment.

∗ Y

yaps. Young aspiring professionals.

yavis. Young, attractive, verbal, intelligent, and successful.

yeepies. (acronym-derived) Youthful, energetic elderly people involved in everything.

yiffies. (acronym-derived) Young, individualistic, freedom-minded, and few—a 1991 creation of *Fortune* magazine.

yippies. (1) (acronym-derived) Young, indictable professional person, a name born of the insider stock-trading scandals. Not to be confused with (2) (acronym-derived) members of the Youth International Party, which became known in the late 1960s for civil disobedience and antiwar protests.

yoicks. Young one-income couples with kids.

yorkie. A New York YUPPIE.

Y-people. YUPPIES.

yucas. (acronym-derived) Young, upwardly mobile Cuban-Americans.

yuffie. (acronym-derived) Young urban failure, generally a BABY BOOMER making less than $10,000 a

SAY WHAT?

An article by Anne Gowen and Sean Piccoli, "A Generation Lost in Time Rebellion? Twentysomethings Find It's Too Much Trouble," in the *Washington Times* of October 15, 1991, attempted to pin down examples of the elusive X-speak. Here are some examples from the glossary that was attached to that article:

boinkers. Couples who privately argue all the time yet engage in excessive PDA (public displays of affection).

circular conversationalism. Endless discussion/analysis of would-be relationships and possible career choices. Participants generally female. Usually involves a cheap jug of wine.

eye-spys. Those who pretend to understand *Spy* magazine.

Gap cretins. Do all their shopping you know where.

gradual school. Graduate school.

gradual schoolers. Couples who remain together after college and marry out of fear and to have kids. Also known as wabbits.

Heineken factor. Intense lifestyle pressure exerted by beer ads.

lip-mitment. Stunted relationship characterized by shallow talk, malt liquor, and infrequent (but safe) sex.

paisleyites. 1960s–1990s cross-pollinators who wear tie-dyed shirts, flimsy prints, and leather thongs around wrists or ankles. Affiliation with sixties consciousness ends with clothing.

readers. Those who profess to have given up television in favor of the Sunday *New York Times.* Occurs mostly during Yom Kippur and Lent.

spokes. Bike couriers who aim to combine Lycra fitness with postpunk cool. Handlebar pouch mandatory. Riding gloves and bandanna optional.

units. Parents.

unnatural selection. Tendency to forgo real attraction to find an economically secure mate.

Velvetina. Tall, frail girl with white skin and black clothes.

year. In her book *Too Smart to Be Rich: On Being a Yuffie*, Patty Friedman says, "The yuffie was born with the trappings of success and infinite potential—his daddy's rich and his mama's good-looking and his IQ's over 135. He'd be a yuppie if he weren't so smart. But he ran it all into the ground with the aplomb and finesse of a true genius."

yukkies. Young, upwardly mobile communist—term created in the pages of the *National Review* for Gorbachev's supporters.

yummies. (acronym-derived) Young, upwardly mobile mommies.

yumpies. Young, upwardly mobile professionals—YUPPIES who earn less than $40,000 a year (or did in 1984, when the term came on the scene). Along with *yuppies,* this term was added to the *Oxford English Dictionary* in 1986.

yuppie puppies. Children of yuppies.

yuppies. (acronym-derived) Young, urban professionals with a taste for BMWs, Rolex watches, jogging suits, imported bottled water, and fashionable restaurants.

SAY WHO?

The term *yuppie* was first put in print and popularized by writer Bob Greene in an article in *Esquire* (March 1983) on "networking parties" sponsored by former radical leader Jerry Rubin. Writing in the newspaper *Newsday* (April 7, 1985) Erica Jong pointed out that it was a corruption of *yippie,* which was from Rubin's own Youth International Party.

The publication of *The Yuppie Handbook* in January 1984 gave the term a monumental boost. The concept and the term were said to have lost their relevance with the stock market crash of October 19, 1987.

Derivatives spawned by the term include *yuppification, yuppyesque, yupguilt, yuppieback* (book aimed at the yuppie reader), *yupsters* (yuppie gangsters), *yuppie tax* (such as one put on health-club memberships), *yup-topia, yuppyish, yuppiegate* (for any scandal involving yuppie greed), and *yuplet* (Herb Caen's term for a child yuppie).

The term helped create some nice headlines. On June 7, 1989, an article in the *Baltimore Evening Sun* about the popularity of tropical fish among young urbans was titled "Yuppies Find Guppies Are Ideal Low-Maintenance Pets."

SOURCES

The grackels (generous researcher and contributor of key elements) for this chapter were the late Charles D. Poe, Ross Reader, and Robert Greenman. John and Adele Algeo's "Among the New Words" section in *American Speech* (especially the winter 1992 issue—volume 67, number 4) was most helpful, as was Anne Gowen and Sean Piccoli's "A Generation Lost in Time Rebellion? Twentysomethings Find It's Too Much Trouble" in the *Washington Times* of October 15, 1991.

BIBLIOGRAPHY—SORT OF

———— ✳ ————

One of the ways in which slang differs from conventional English is that one is formal and the other is determinedly informal—and controversial. On one hand, Carl Sandburg called slang "a language that rolls up its sleeves, spits on its hands, and goes to work," while Ambrose Bierce disdained it as "the grunt of the human hog *(Pignoramus intolerabilis)*."

It is, therefore, totally consistent to offer these informal working notes on slang sources:

✳ 1. SLANG DICTIONARIES

A number of good slang dictionaries are on the market today. The best:

The Random House Historical Dictionary of American Slang, the first authoritative historical dictionary of American slang, by J. L. Lighter. The first volume, now in print, is a 1,006-page tome and is seen as the beginning of the definitive work on American slang, comparable to the *Oxford English Dictionary* in importance. Volume I covers entries from *A,* a euphemism for *ass,* to *gytch,* to steal. Volume II of the dictionary, covering *H–R,* and volume III, *S–Z,* will be published later. Among other things, Lighter's opus disproves the commonly held belief that slang is transitory; terms such as *out of sight* and *sweat it out* date back to the 1800s. Use of the word *bad* to mean good isn't new, either, Lighter tells us; he found such references as early as 1877.

The New Dictionary of American Slang, by Robert L. Chapman, is published by HarperCollins. A new book, it builds on an earlier work—Wentworth and Flexner's 1960 book—with a lot of new examples (*greenmail, bean counter, glitterati,* etc.) and some purging of old terms (Gypsy and carnival slang get short shrift). A classic with seventeen thousand terms.

A Dictionary of Slang and Unconventional English, eighth edition, by Eric Partridge and edited by Paul Beale, is published by Routledge. A gigantic book, it contains more than one hundred thousand entries and weighs close to five pounds. It shows us the stunning richness of slang in the English-speaking world. A word like *damper* has no less than ten slang meanings, ranging from a "wet blanket" or "spoilsport" to a "snack." Some words found here are true rarities, such as *degombling.* As used in the Falkland Islands, *degombling* means to shake the snow off one's clothes. If there is a drawback to this immense work, it is that it is much more concerned with Commonwealth and British Isles slang than American slang, especially in areas like baseball and Vietnam-era military slang. One needs an American slang dictionary for terms like *Baltimore chop, frag,* and *tushie.* There are nine meanings of *duffer* but not a single reference to golf, which is its most typical American use.

Slang and Euphemism, by Richard A. Spears, is published in several versions (hardback, quality paper, and mass market paperback) by NTC, a Chicago publisher. It is hard to find a bookstore anywhere that does not stock this one, and for good reasons, since it is excellent. However, to quote from the dust jacket of the edition at my elbow, it is "a dictionary of oaths, curses, insults, sexual slang and metaphor, racial slurs, drug talk, homosexual lingo, and related matters." It is not a general slang dictionary, but a book of the taboo, with nary a page without, at least, an R-rating.

A fascinating and almost impossible-to-find work is Joseph A. Weingarten's *An American Dictionary of Slang,* which was privately published in 1954.

Merriam-Webster has put its *Tenth Collegiate* dictionary and thesaurus on CD-ROM and floppy disk. The CD version has definitions for 160,000 words and is a marvelous engine for seeking topical slang. For example, you can ask for—and get—aviation slang that came into the language in the 1940s. Also published by Merriam-Webster is *Flappers to Rappers* by Tom Dalzell, which looks—topically—at all the youth lingoes of the twentieth century. It is a unique and major contribution.

✳ 2. SLANG THESAURUSES

First, there is the momumental *American Thesaurus of Slang* by Lester V. Berrey and Melvin Van Bark (Thomas Y. Crowell, 1952), which covers everything. A more recent and somewhat more limited effort is the excellent *Thesaurus of Slang* by Esther Lewin and Albert E. Lewin (Facts on File, 1988).

✳ 3. JARGON

Several good jargon dictionaries are on the market, including Joel Homer's *Jargon,* Jonathon Green's *Newspeak,* and Don Ethan Miller's *The Book of Jargon.* One is very British in its orientation, and the two U.S. books are topical and very selective—for instance, both have sections on computer jargon, but neither cover educational jargon. The ultimate limitation of these books is that they cover jargon, not slang (after all, medical jargon is a far cry from medical slang).

✳ 4. NEW WORDS BOOKS

By their nature, books featuring new words are great sources of new slang. I found these two to be most useful: *The Longman Guardian New Words,* edited by Simon Mort and published in London (my copy is not dated), and *The Facts on File Dictionary of New Words* (1989) by Harold LeMay, Sid Lerner, and Marian Taylor.

Atop the pile, however, is Anne H. Soukhanov's 1995 book, *Word Watch: The Stories Behind the Words of Our Lives,* published by Henry Holt and Co.

* 5. ARCHIVES

The greatest single source of help in preparing this book was the Tamony Collection at the University of Missouri, Columbia. It was recently acquired by the university, which wasted no time in making it public. The collection, put together over a long lifetime by the etymologist Peter Tamony, gives America its own archive of native slang. Tamony was considered the leading twentieth-century lay expert on American slang, and his collection is the only thing like it anywhere. It has been a major factor in giving this small book its authority and strength and will fuel other such efforts for many years to come.

* 6. NEW EDITIONS OF THIS BOOK

I am planning to keep this second edition of *Slang* current with contemporary examples with an eye to a new version to appear after the turn of the century. I would like very much to hear from those with suggestions for terms—and topics—that should be included in the monumental third edition. I can be reached at this address:

Paul Dickson
P.O. Box 80
Garrett Park, MD 20896-0080

Thank you in advance.

INDEX

___ ✳ ___